The Independence Party

---

and the Future of Third-Party Politics

William McGaughey ran for U.S. Senate in the 2002 Independence Party primary held in Minnesota. His intention was to differentiate his positions sharply from those of the two major parties. Advancing the twin issues of a 32-hour workweek and dignity for white males, he received 8,482 votes, or 31% of the total, in finishing second to the party-endorsed candidate. McGaughey belongs to a group of landlords which helped oust Minneapolis' top elected officials in the 2001 city elections. He and his wife live just west of the downtown loop.

The Independence Party and the Future of Third-Party Politics

Adventures & Opinions of an IP Senate Candidate

---

by William McGaughey

Thistlerose Publications
Minneapolis, Minnesota, USA

Thistlerose Publications

Printed in Canada

Published by Thistlerose Publications, 1702 Glenwood Avenue, Minneapolis, MN 55405, USA

Library of Congress Control Number 2003091801

Publisher's Cataloging-in-Publication
(Provided by Quality Books, Inc.)

McGaughey, William.
The Independence Party and the future of third-party politics : adventures & opinions of an IP Senate candidate / by William McGaughey.

p. cm.
Includes index.
ISBN 0-9605630-5-9

1. McGaughey, William. 2. Political candidates--Minnesota--Biography. 3. Independence Party (Minn.) 4. Third parties (United States politics) 5. United States. Congress. Senate-Elections, 2002. I. Title.

F610.3.M34A3 2003 324.2776'08
QBI03-200149

Acknowledgment

To my fellow landlords of the Minneapolis Property Rights Action Committee who showed a better way politically and to the dedicated media producers, Jim Jacobsen, Bryan Olson and Ray Whebbe, who spread the message.

Table of Contents

Part I

Part II

Part III

Part IV

Part V

Part VI

Illustrations

Summary of Content by Chapter

Part I

Chapter 1 Me, a Senate Candidate The author decides to run for U.S. Senate in Minnesota's Independence Party primary. He finishes second to Jim Moore, the party-endorsed candidate.

Chapter 2 Developing a Campaign Strategy Frozen out by the party and the state's largest newspaper, he pitches his campaign to newspapers in outstate Minnesota.

Chapter 3 Jumping into the Fray This candidate bombards the media with campaign statements and then embarks upon a tour of cities and towns in various parts of the state. He carries a sign in parades and visits newspaper offices.

Chapter 4 Genesis of Issues What issues can the Independence Party ride to majority-party status? Being "in the center" or running celebrity candidates is not enough. This party needs to stake out positions on fundamental questions differing from those of the Democrats and Republicans. The author chooses (1) a shorter workweek and (2) dignity for white males.

Part II

Chapter 5 Poor-Quality Leaders (a.k.a. My Leftist Critique) By most indications, the economic situation of working Americans has deteriorated. The income gap between our society's most and least wealthy citizens has widened. Soaring executive compensation is not a product of the free market but of corporate conflicts of interest.

Chapter 6 Making the Free Market Work for More People Working people can rig the market for labor by supporting proposals for government to reduce work hours. Americans work longer hours than workers in other industrialized nations. The politics of gender and race create a political climate that prevents challenging bad leadership.

Chapter 7 My Involvement with Labor Issues The author began researching issues of work time in the 1970s. He founded an advocacy group and hooked up with well-known political figures. Eventually these activities led to involvement in the fight against NAFTA and the 1995 UN Social Summit.

Chapter 8 The Economics of Work and Leisure There is a mathematical relationship between work hours, employment, output, and productivity. Increasing levels of productivity bring a displacement of labor with several possible outcomes. The main trade-off has been between shorter work hours and expanding output in the form of economic waste.

Chapter 9 Nuts and Bolts of the Shorter-Workweek Proposal The Fair Labor Standards Act of 1938 established the basic mechanism for reducing the workweek. The requirement to pay overtime wages for hours worked beyond the standard creates an incentive (not a mandate) to cut hours. In the long run, reduced hours do not mean lower wages. On a macroeconomic level, resources might shift back to productive enterprise at the cost of shrinking economic waste.

Chapter 10 A Proposal for Fair Trade The object is to create an international political structure that will accommodate both expanded trade and enforcement of labor and environmental standards. “Free trade” negates that possibility. The author proposes a tariff-based mechanism that would steer global economic development through an orderly process which successively brings greater investment, increased wages, and reduced work hours.

Part III

Chapter 11 Two Events in 2001 The virulent protest that accompanied a small Ku Klux Klan rally at the Minnesota state capitol in August 2001 contrasts oddly with the tolerance of Islamic groups in the aftermath of the September 11th attacks upon the World Trade Center and the Pentagon. This had less to do with the groups' respective propensities to violence than with the liberal temperament.

Chapter 12 About the Ku Klux Klan The Ku Klux Klan went through at least three phases. In its period of greatest influence in the 1920s, this was primarily an anti-Catholic, anti-immigrant organization which ought to restore American values. Klan violence did not significantly exceed the violence of groups which have criticized it on those grounds.

Chapter 13 Demons in the Press The *Star Tribune*, Minnesota's largest newspaper, has abandoned fair-minded journalism to spread social-political propaganda. Its stories have a tendency to demonize certain individuals or groups along the lines of political correctness. The *Star Tribune* is also known for its last-minute hatchet jobs on disfavored political candidates. This chapter offers examples of questionable journalistic practices.

Chapter 14 It Started in the '60s Given to abandoning their supporters, political liberals in the 1960s embarked upon a policy of vilifying white Americans to curry favor with black voters. This led to landmark Civil Rights and Immigration Reform legislation and to policies of affirmative action.

Chapter 15 The Downside to Immigration The bending over backwards to help disadvantaged groups has extended to recent immigrants encouraging the formation of what some have called "a rainbow underclass." The role of Arab immigrants in the September 11th attacks has created conflict between those who would demand greater cooperation from immigrant groups in combating terrorism and those who stress civil liberties.

Chapter 16 About Lawyers and Politicians The vilification of white, nonimmigrant Americans and designation of official victims serves the interests of lawyers and Democratic politicians. Landlords such as the author become lunch meat for enterprising attorneys who can put together a discrimination case. This society is organized to feed the occupational wolf packs which prey upon productive enterprise.

Part IV

Chapter 17 The Gender Chip on my Shoulder Raised in a world of white-male comfort, the author awoke to new realities of hate stirred up by the feminist movement. His arrest for domestic violence in November 1985 sent him on a mission to protest anti-male policies. Laid off from an accounting job at a public-transit agency, he has since gone on to more interesting and rewarding experiences.

Chapter 18 Coming out of the Racial Wilderness The author's advocating "dignity for white males" raises many questions. He has found greater understanding of this position from within the African American community than among whites. The challenge is to discuss such topics without succumbing to hate.

Chapter 19 Roots of White Self-Hatred While a student at Yale, the author questioned the premise that continuous education was the key to personal success. He dropped out of college to seek more basic life experiences. The author believes that educated whites may hate themselves for similar reasons. Our society should rethink the educational process from the standpoint of young peoples' psychological needs.

Chapter 20 Following my Ideas to Somewhere - Inner-City Real Estate and New Women Preoccupied with ideas, the author followed his own path to relevant activities. He connected with labor groups, published books, and then bought real estate. After he purchased a nine-unit apartment building linked to drug dealing, Minneapolis city government condemned this property. As a landlord dealing with crime, the author met and later married an African American woman. Now married to a woman from China, he has written a book on world history and built a close-knit interracial community west of the Minneapolis loop.

Chapter 21 Landlord Politics The author's problems as an inner-city landlord bought him in contact with a group of other landlords who were suing the city of Minneapolis. He helped to build them into a militant political organization to fight City Hall. Through picketing events and a cable-television show, this landlord group succeeded in turning public opinion around on questions of housing and crime. It played a key role in defeating the city's top three elected officials in the 2001 municipal elections.

Part V

Chapter 22 Growing up Politically Raised in a Republican household, the author was an ardent supporter of Michigan Governor George Romney's bid for the Presidency. He later moved in leftist political circles as a result of his interest in the shorter workweek. Burned by Minneapolis Democrats, he now affiliates with the Independence Party of Minnesota.

Chapter 23 Two Campaigns for Mayor After an abortive campaign for Mayor of Minneapolis in 1997, the author again became a candidate for Mayor after the leader of the landlord group dropped out of the race. Carrying a picket sign and distributing literature, he waged an energetic battle against the incumbent administration winning a small number of votes in the primary election held on September 11, 2001.

Chapter 24 Lessons Learned from the Landlord Group The Minneapolis landlords succeeded through action where coercive approaches had failed. Their attitude was internally nonjudgmental. Ignored by the large-circulation newspapers, they created their own media in the form of an alternative newspaper and a cable-television show, thereby acquiring a direct pipeline to public opinion.

Chapter 25 My Campaign for U.S. Senate After attending the Independence Party state convention in St. Cloud, the author jumped into the Senate primary at the last moment. He put together position statements and a campaign web site before driving around the state to visit newspaper offices. The result was a second-place finish on September 10th with 31% of the votes in a three-way contest won by the party-endorsed candidate.

Chapter 26 Paul Wellstone and the Rest of the Campaign The period between the primary and the general election was dominated by Senator Paul Wellstone's tragic death in a plane crash on October 25th. The author had known Wellstone for twenty years. They were in a debate together on October 5th. Though defeated in the primary, the author later campaigned for Independence Party candidates. Norm Coleman was elected to the U.S. Senate.

Part VI

Chapter 27 Building a Third-Party Movement: Part I Because political candidates have a critical need to communicate with voters, the relationship between candidates and the media influences the outcome of elections. Journalists are torn between providing full coverage of campaigns and encouraging candidates to advertise. Third parties, whose candidates receive little free publicity, might consider acquiring their own media capability.

Chapter 28 Building a Third-Party Movement: Part II To build up interest and bring new people into their organization, third parties should let people freely express their opinions, be focused on action as well as winning elections, and keep parliamentary maneuvering to a minimum. The Independence Party has both a legacy of achievement and new opportunities to reach out to a broader constituency.

Chapter 29 Confronting the Demons A fear-based orthodoxy, sometimes called "political correctness", controls public opinions concerning race, gender, and religion. One must confront these demons to gain personal freedom. At the risk of being called "racist" or "anti-Semitic", the author confronts the disproportionately high black crime rate and Hollywood's manipulation of images in entertainment programming to create attitudes favorable to Jews. He offers a belated defense of Trent Lott's statement.

Chapter 30 Is There a Third Way? Social divisiveness and privilege preclude rational solutions to the earth's problems. The author assumes the hated white-male persona as a ploy to break down barriers to a solution. Third-party politics offers the best hope of breaking through the logjam of the current system, producing both social healing and an economic restructuring to benefit ordinary people.

Running

for U.S. Senate

CHAPTER ONE

Me, a Senate Candidate

On primary night, Tuesday, September 10, 2002, I waited impatiently for the results of the U.S. Senate race in the Independence Party primary to be reported. There had been a virtual news blackout concerning this race. I thought it could go either way. Finally, around 10:20 p.m., a brief note flashed across the bottom of the television screen during the Channel Four news program: U.S. Senate Independence Party, Moore 50%, McGaughey 30%. So, with less than half of the precincts reporting, I was finishing second to Jim Moore, the party-endorsed candidate. My heart sank. Still, 30% was a solid showing. I drove over to the Moore headquarters in south Minneapolis to congratulate the winner. The percentages were staying about the same as more precincts reported. A week later, the Minnesota Secretary of State's web site reported the following result:

Jim Moore	13,525 votes	49.44% of total
William McGaughey	8,482 votes	31.00 % of total
Ronald E. Wills	5,351 votes	19.56 % of total

So ended a short but hard-fought campaign. I had driven more than 5,000 miles to all parts of Minnesota during the preceding month. I had visited newspaper offices in more than 100 cities and towns. In the end, I spent about $2,000 on the campaign in addition to the $400 filing fee. People seemed to be accepting the implausible twin planks of my campaign: support for a 32-hour workweek and dignity for white males. I thought, for a time, that I really could win this thing.

But then, in the last week, after a driver with failed brakes struck and wrecked my '92 Ford Escort at the intersection of Cleveland and Roselawn in Roseville, I began to have inklings that the result might be otherwise. Emails from the Independence Party disclosed that volunteers for Jim Moore would be dropping 25,000 pieces of literature in the 5th Congressional District during the week preceding the election. A phone bank would be working on Moore's behalf election eve. Moore's wife, Shari, was responsible for a warm, fuzzy item that appeared in both the St. Paul and Minneapolis papers: she delivered the couple's third child on September 1st. I had a paid ad and article in the *Watchdog*, a small free-circulation newspaper in Minneapolis, but, due to a production glitch, the newspaper came out a week late - on election day. And still the *Star Tribune*, the state's largest newspaper, had failed to print a single word about my or Ronald Wills' candidacy in its reporting of the Senate primary. Under the circumstances, holding Moore to less than half of the vote was not bad.

At the time of the Independence Party state convention, July 13th, I had no plans to become a candidate. It was my first state convention with this party. I had attended its precinct caucuses in north Minneapolis consecutively since 1998 but not any conventions. The caucuses were poorly attended and the participants rather quarrelsome. I also had political interests outside of electoral politics. But then Jesse Ventura's last-minute decision not to seek reelection as Governor, Tim Penny's entrance into the race, and a bizarre personal experience involving Christine Jax, the state's commissioner of Children, Families, and Learning, then a rival candidate for Governor, revived my interest. When the Independence Party's 5th District chair, Peter Tharaldson, offered me a ride to the St. Cloud convention in his van, I accepted. It happened that, in the early morning, we missed connecting. So, I drove to St. Cloud by myself.

Although none of those who had attended the Senate District 58 precinct caucus were at the convention, I did know several other persons. The principal candidates had booths. I talked with Dean Alger and a few others. Jim Moore, the leading contender for the U.S. Senate nomination, had called me before the convention. He was an earnest, personable candidate. However, I do not like political conventions, especially the discussions of rules and procedures. The message which came through during the more interesting part of the program was that the Independence Party was a "centrist" party that avoided the ideological extremes to which the Democrats and Republicans had fallen prey. I tried to pin down some of my lunch companions about what this meant. What were the extremes? What was the center position? There were varying interpretations. Independence Party candidates were just "in the middle".

I listened to the candidates' speeches. The most lively contest was over the endorsement for U.S. Senate. In a contest with Alan Fine, Moore won a substantial majority of votes from the 170 convention delegates. Moore told us how, as a small banker, he had the private-sector experience so sorely missed in government: he could introduce private-sector-like efficiencies to the federal bureaucracy. He believed that schools should be held accountable for results. He was in favor of fiscal responsibility and campaign finance reform. Disapprovingly, he referred to the recent accounting scandals which had shaken the corporate world. He expressed personal admiration for Gandhi and Martin

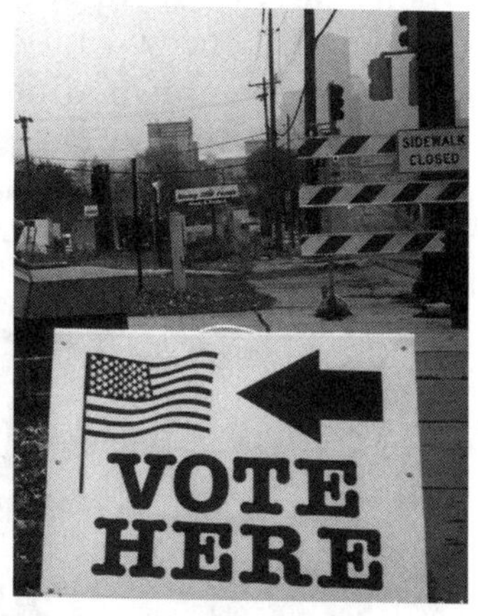

Luther King. As a boy, he had cried when told that Hank Aaron had received death threats.

Listening to all this, I was vaguely troubled. Here was a candidate whom the Independence Party would soon be sending out to do battle with Paul Wellstone and Norm Coleman, each expected to have a $10 million campaign budget. (The U.S. Senate race in Minnesota actually wound up costing a total of $35 million.) With such a bland program, how would Moore get his message across through the glare of better-known candidates from the two major parties? Hadn't I heard most of Moore's talking points before? What made them different from what a Democrat or a Republican might say?

I could do better, I thought. This was no time for calm positions. Independence Party candidates had to mount a frontal attack on both major parties. Polls showed that, while the gubernatorial candidate, Tim Penny, a former Congressman, was running neck-and-neck with the Democratic and Republican candidates for Governor, the party's other candidates for statewide or federal offices were at a severe disadvantage. They needed to distinguish themselves in some way. I thought I knew the type of campaign which had to be run - one with bold positions and raw energy, issuing a visceral appeal for change.

That was, in fact, what I had done less than a year earlier when I ran for Mayor of Minneapolis. Waging a purely negative campaign, I threw caution to the wind. I walked around the streets of downtown Minneapolis with a picket sign and passed out literature. This literature told prospective voters in graphic detail some of the rotten things which the incumbent city administration had done. Its development agency had seized properties by eminent domain, paying the owners pennies on the dollar,

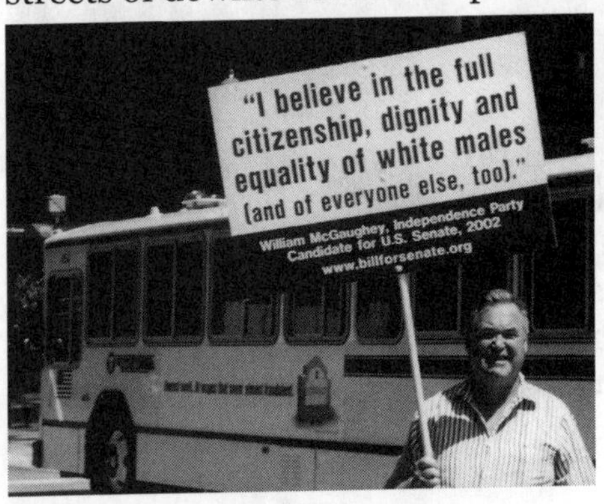
"I believe in the full
citizenship, dignity and
equality of white males
(and of everyone else, too)."
William McGaughey, Independence Party
Candidate for U.S. Senate, 2002
www.billforsenate.org

and then torn the buildings down. Its inspections departments had condemned structurally sound buildings due to political pressures. And now there was a housing shortage. Throw the rascals out! - no subtlety here - was the message. When came the general election on November 5th, Minneapolis voters did vote for sweeping change. The incumbent mayor was defeated. The 13-member city council had seven new members.

While proud to have been part of the process which produced such sweeping change, I was not proud of the results of my own campaign. In a field of 22 mayoral candidates, I finished twelfth, attracting a meager 143 votes city wide. My ballot designation, "Affordable housing - preservation", represented a position which enjoyed overwhelming public support. I had personal credibility on this issue. I had passed out 4,500 pieces of literature. And that was the result? Admittedly, I am not the best campaigner in the world. I'm a 240-pound, middle-aged white guy who wears glasses and occasionally lets his shirt tails hang outside of his trousers. Maybe if I had spent less time pushing my literature on people and more time talking with them, the result might have been different.

Come to think of it, a political candidate who walks around city streets with a picket sign does not project the image of a winner; we think this type of person must be announcing the end of the world. The winning candidates all ride between television studios in chauffeur-driven limousines. In a more charitable spirit, I decided that the voters may not have been paying full attention to me as a candidate because they were distracted by other events. The 2001 Minneapolis primary might not have been conducted under normal conditions because the voting took place on September 11th. I, too, was glued to the television set that day watching the smoke billow out of the upper floors of the World Trade Center towers in New York City prior to their collapse.

At any rate, a decision had to be made in the three days between the Independence Party state convention and the filing deadline on Tuesday, July 16th. With time running out, I drove to the Secretary of State's office in the Minnesota State Office

Building in St. Paul. I filled out a short application form, wrote a check for $400, and officially became a candidate for U.S. Senate.

CHAPTER TWO

Developing a Campaign Strategy

I was running in a third-party primary for what is mainly a policy position. A U.S. Senator is responsible for formulating government policies at the national and international levels. This would give me a platform for advancing proposals in the areas of trade and labor standards, keen interests of mine a decade earlier. I would be appealing to primary voters who were members of the Independence Party, formerly the Reform Party, which Ross Perot founded in 1992. Perot gave this party a heritage of concern with public debt. He also opposed the North American Free Trade Agreement (NAFTA), predicting that there would be a "giant sucking sound" as U.S. jobs went south of the border.

The Minnesota Reform Party scraped and clawed its way to major party status thanks to Dean Barkley's run for the U.S. Senate in 1996. Barkley received six percent of the vote that year as the incumbent Senator, Paul Wellstone, won reelection against his predecessor in the U.S. Senate, Rudy Boschwitz, a Republican. Its moment of glory arrived two years later when Jesse Ventura "shocked the world" by being elected Governor of Minnesota. How dare the voters select a former pro wrestler for such a position! Under Ventura's leadership, the Minnesota Reform

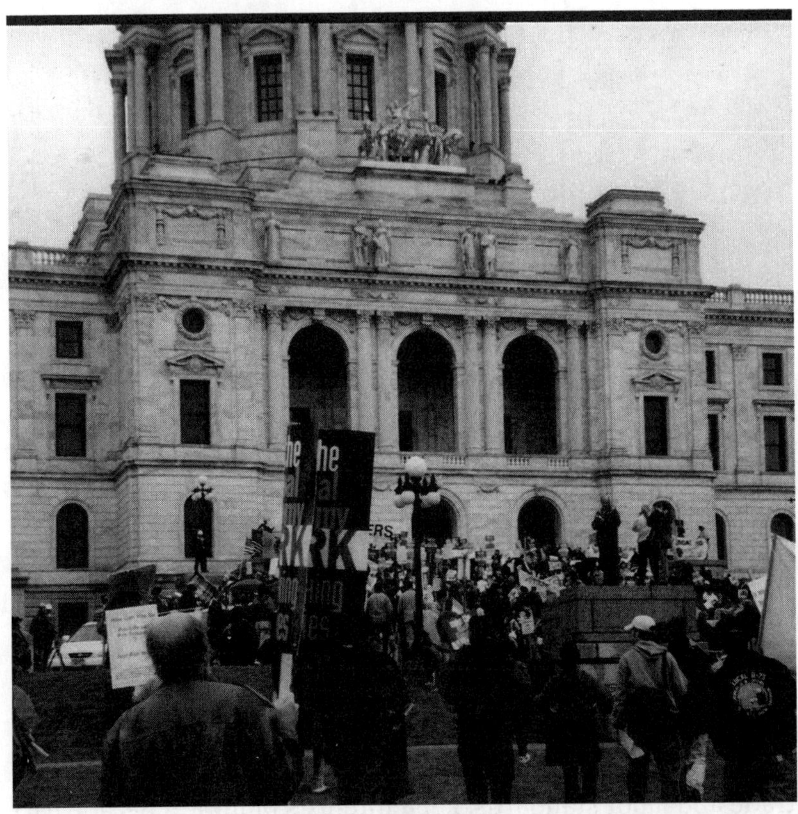

Party broke with the national party when Pat Buchanan took it over. Distancing itself from that effort, the Minnesota party was renamed the Independence Party. I myself was drawn into Reform/Independence Party politics through personal acquaintance with Alan Shilepsky, the Reform Party's candidate for Secretary of State in 1998.

Since I would be appealing to voters in the Independence Party primary, I thought first to write a letter to party members explaining why I had decided to run. To do that I would need the party's membership list. Originally, the Independence Party Constitution called for open inspection of party books. However, a proposed Standing Rule adopted at the 2002 convention tightened access to this information. It stated that where non-endorsed candidates were running in the primary against endorsed candidates, the non-endorsed candidates might gain "access to Party list(s)/ database(s)/information, upon approval by the appropriate governing body of the IP." The endorsed candidates, in contrast, would automatically receive the information.

Wishing to rent the IP membership list, I queried the party chair, Nancy Jorgenson, by email. She informed me that the party's central committee would meet on Saturday, July 27, to consider this and other matters. The committee did meet. It denied my request. Ms. Jorgenson explained that I had had an opportunity to seek endorsement at the convention. Having failed to receive it, I would have to suffer the consequences. That set the tone of my relationship with the Independence Party. I was doing this on my own, running against an officially endorsed candidate. I could only post the letter to Independence Party members on my campaign web site in hopes that a few curious souls would find and read its message.

Lack of party endorsement impacted my candidacy in another way. Candidates for state-wide political office often find it useful to rent booths at county fairs and at the State Fair. Not only is there a high concentration of potential voters near the booths, but these are people seeking novelty and excitement. They do not resent a candidate's intruding in their space. They want to meet political candidates. Because this kind of event is considered an appropriate place for interaction between candidate and constituents, to campaign there favorably colors voters' perceptions of the candidates. For obvious reasons, State Fair officials do not want candidates wandering around the grounds on their own. Candidates must rent a booth or be invited to use a booth rented by a political party.

Jim Moore, the endorsed candidate for U.S. Senate, had full access to facilities belonging to the Independence Party. According to the newspaper, Moore spent the maximum number of hours at the State Fair on each of its ten days. I never set foot inside the State Fairgrounds. I inquired of the party's candidate liaison, Mike Landy, whether I, as a nonendorsed candidate running in the Independence Party primary, might stand in or near the party's booth at the State Fair talking with visitors. His response was in the negative. Still, I did not want to give up on this option. On Sunday, September 1st, an hour or so before my freak automobile accident, I stood at the north entrance to the State Fair grounds displaying my two-foot-by-four-foot campaign sign to persons approaching from the parking lot. After twenty minutes of such happiness, a security guard told me that I was trespassing on State Fair property. I found another spot nearby on Snelling Avenue, less well-traveled but legally not so protected.

For the rest of the campaign, I was a nonperson so far as the Independence Party was concerned. That was to be expected. I did expect that Independence Party officials would want the party's endorsement to mean something. What was unexpected was the attitude of Minnesota's largest newspaper, the *Star Tribune.* This newspaper, dominant in Minneapolis and its suburbs, has an average daily circulation of 415,500 copies on week days (and 674,300 on Sundays), more than twice the volume of the state's next largest, the *St. Paul Pioneer Press.* On Wednesday, July 31st, the *Star Tribune* ran a front-page article on the Independence Party and Green Party primary contests for U.S. Senate. The article, headlined "Major minors: McGaa and Moore could make a dent," spilled over into two full columns on page A8. Disappointing to me was the fact that this newspaper story failed to mention that Moore faced opposition in the primary. There was nothing about me or Ronald E. Wills. One sentence in the article mentioned that Ray Tricomo was opposing Ed McGaa. Here, too, I was a nonperson.

I thought that I might make up at least some of the lost ground by writing a letter to the editor of the *Star Tribune* calling attention to the omission. Once, during the Mayor's race, the newspaper had printed such a letter when a story on a debate between six candidates mentioned four of the candidates, but not me. This time, the tactic did not work. The *Star Tribune* did not print the letter. My next option was to call Lou Gelfand, the Reader Representative. Gelfand informed me, in a message left on my answering machine, that he had no control over publication of letters to the editor. However, he would contact the news department to suggest additional coverage of the Independence Party race for U.S. Senate.

Weeks went by. I paid a visit to the *Star Tribune* office, met briefly in the downstairs lobby with the paper's political team leader, and left samples of my literature. Nothing happened. As expected, the *Star Tribune* did publish information about me and the other candidates in its Voter's Guide, which appeared on Friday, October 6th. Unexpectedly, on the same day, it printed a letter to the editor which I had written to defend the Green Senate candidate, Ed McGaa, against insinuations that he was untrue to his professed interest in environmental protection by having participated in a failed business venture in South Dakota. But that was all. The *Star Tribune* had given Jim Moore a huge publicity advantage over both rival candidates in its news reporting. This newspaper even refused to accept a paid ad from me unless its content was substantially changed.

With respect to news coverage, the huge part of the Minnesota political market which is Minneapolis and its suburbs became like a gaping hole in the doughnut. For the most part, I had to write this off as Moore territory. Not so St. Paul. The *St. Paul Pioneer Press*, to its credit, ran an article on Monday, July 29th, comparable in length to the *Star Tribune* article, giving all Senatorial candidates in the Green and Independence parties at least several paragraphs of coverage plus boxed personal information and a mug shot. My catchy web site domain name, www.billforsenate.org, was also mentioned. So the eastern part of the Twin Cities metro area was adequately covered. Reporter Toni Coleman had done a good job of reporting both the endorsed and nonendorsed candidates' campaigns.

What to do about Minneapolis, my own home town, where I live and own rental property? I thought I had a unique opportunity in belonging to the landlord group, Minneapolis Property

Rights Action Committee. First, I would show up at its monthly meeting in August and become visible either as a guest speaker or a participant from the audience. The meetings are videotaped and shown on the regional cable-television station, Channel 6, in hour-long segments on Fridays starting at 11:00 a.m. and 4:30 p.m. and on the Minneapolis cable-access channel on Saturdays at 6:00 p.m. Many Twin Cities residents watch this show. Second, a free-circulation newspaper, *The Watchdog*, features articles by or about landlords. In response to an inquiry, editor Ray Whebbe proposed that I write a story about my experiences on the campaign trail which he would put in the issue coming out a week before the primary. I placed a paid ad in this newspaper, featuring a picture of me and my wife. With a circulation of 10,000 copies, *The Watchdog* may lack the *Star Tribune's* broad reach, but at least this would be a place where I had an advantage over Jim Moore.

Facing obstacles from my lack of party endorsement, I had to devise an alternative strategy to reach voters. A statewide campaign such as mine had to work through the media. Radio and television coverage would be scarce; I was not a celebrity and did not have the funds to air paid commercials. Forget lawn signs. Forget campaign buttons, telephone lists of eligible voters, and all the other trappings of a modern political campaign. My best shot lay in seeking newspaper coverage. Since the *St. Paul Pioneer Press* had already run a major article and the *Star Tribune* was ignoring my campaign, I would have to go out state. Some coverage would come on its own as the larger outstate newspapers (notably Duluth and Rochester) ran articles about the primary or compiled voters' guides. But most would have to come by pounding the pavement, so to speak.

CHAPTER THREE

Jumping into the Fray

I spent the first weeks of my campaign producing campaign materials. My main piece of literature was a two-sided, 8 1/2" by 11" flier printed on green paper. On one side, the headline read "In your face, Democrats"; on the other, "In your face, Republicans." The flier contained an energetic statement of what I thought was wrong with the two parties, their values, and ideologies. A thousand copies were printed. I fired off a fax to major media in the Twin Cities defending Minnesota Public Safety Commissioner Charlie Weaver's decision to toughen requirements for the Minnesota driver's license in response to the threat of international terrorism. Several groups had filed suit to stop that move. I felt it justified considering the terrorists' abuse of immigration procedures and use of improperly obtained identification documents. To my knowledge, no one picked up on this press release.

As previously stated, I also wrote a letter to members of the Independence Party in hopes of doing a direct mailing. Even if that fell through, the letter and other writings gave me materials for a campaign web site. A friend who was a professional web site designer, Mark Stanley, agreed to host this site for a modest fee. I chose as its domain name http://www.billforsenate.org. How lucky I was that this name was still available - If Bill Clinton ever runs for Senator, he would give his eye teeth to get his hands on such a name!

Since the guts of the campaign would be an outreach to Minnesota newspapers, I needed to work from a list. The best list I could find was a publication titled *Schmidt's Minnesota Media Directory*. The latest edition could be purchased from the publisher for $175. Being on the cheap side, I instead laboriously copied names, addresses, telephone and fax numbers, email addresses, and contact persons into a spiral notebook from a copy of this directory found at the Minneapolis public library. I prepared one-page statements of my candidacy for dissemination in three media.

The first was an announcement of my candidacy. This I faxed to all newspapers on the list during the last week of July. It was a press release divided into several sections which gave personal background, campaign positions, competitive strategy, and so forth. Since my difficult last name might draw a blank, I disclosed to these editors the fact that in 1847 President Zachary Taylor had nominated a certain Edward McGaughey to be Minnesota's first territorial governor. The reason that we haven't heard of him is that his nomination was rejected by the U.S. Senate; I hinted at revenge should I be elected to that body. The fax machine in my bedroom was kept busy for several days.

I next composed a ten-page manifesto, or "position statement" discussing the potentially controversial themes in my campaign plank relating to demographic politics and work hours. I mailed off about seventy copies to rival Senate candidates and to editorial writers at the large-circulation newspapers, making a point to include publications unlikely to agree with my views. There was no response from anyone except for Norm Coleman, whom I encountered by chance on the campaign trail. My third communication was an email to outstate newspaper editors expressing my opinion that I had a chance to win the primary and an interest in visiting their communities. Two or three editors wrote in response that they would be happy to put something in the newspaper if I came to their town in the course of the campaign.

It was time to face the voters. With more than four million residents and only six weeks left before the election, Minnesota had far too many people to approach individually. I had no campaign committee, no organizations that might invite me to speak. An issues-centered campaign such as mine, starved for media exposure, would have to get its message out in unorthodox ways.

I therefore ordered a $168 sign from Budget Signs in St. Paul. The message read on one side, in a black and red color scheme: "I believe that the Federal Government should reduce the standard workweek to 32 hours by 2010." In smaller lettering at the bottom, it read: "William McGaughey, Independence Party candidate for U.S. Senate, 2002, www.billforsenate.org". On the other side, with green lettering on a white background, it read: "I believe in the full citizenship, dignity and equality of white males (and of everyone else, too)." Below this text the same information about me and my web site appeared in white lettering against a blue background. The double-sided sign, two feet tall by four feet wide, was attached to a six-foot plastic pole. I originally thought of ordering a stand, similar to that used for Christmas trees, so that I could set the sign next to me while talking with voters. That idea proved to be impractical.

This sign was an excellent prop for parades. In all, I participated in six parades during the campaign - in New Brighton, Sandstone, Little Falls, Vadnais Heights, Crookston, and Burnsville - carrying the sign as a candidate for U.S. Senate. I also worked as a volunteer for Tim Penny at a parade in Prior Lake. Participating in parades was my way of interacting with

individual voters. I would have to say, in all honesty, that most spectators did not respond to my message one way or the other. They seemed more interested in scooping up candy thrown on the pavement or in cheering acquaintances who rode the floats. As a pedestrian with a sign, I was one of the few non-motorized participants.

The beginnings of the parades, at the staging area, were usually times of pleasant conversation with other participants. Few reacted negatively towards me. Occasionally a spectator would even call out encouraging words. More often we were marching past empty stretches of sidewalk. I do not know how much good these parades did my campaign. I'm sure many people thought I was nuts. The point was, I thought, to get the campaign and its themes before individual voters so that, hopefully, they would remember that someone was supporting those issues and perhaps talk about it with their friends. It was a good supplement to whatever media coverage I might attract.

In carrying a sign in these parades, I might have been facing the same image problem as in my campaigning a year earlier. It signaled that this might be a candidate too poor to afford lawn signs or media advertising. This person running for U.S. Senate without party endorsement and with only a sign must be a kook. My worst experience was at Farm Fest, near Redwood Falls. While the four party-endorsed candidates for U.S. Senate debated in the late morning of August 6th, I stood at the back of the tent holding up my sign. A few furtive glances were thrown my way but mostly people ignored me. It was only slightly better when I walked around the booths. Farmers are a conservative bunch, not much caring for radical ideas or theatrics like mine. It seemed that about the only persons who would shake hands with me at Farm Fest were Norm Coleman and the Elvis impersonator. (In fact, Jim Moore also shook hands. I did not personally run into Wellstone or McGaa on that occasion.)

Leaving Farm Fest, I discovered that a handmade sign attached to the side of my car door in the parking area had been removed. It was on the way home that the campaign came to life. Stopping at newspaper offices in Redwood Falls, Olivia, Willmar, and Litchfield, I met editors and reporters who actually seemed interested in my campaign; one took a photograph of me with the sign and several invited me to come back.

In time, I achieved a happy marriage between use of the sign and outreach to newspaper offices. The trick was converting an immediately kooky event into a colorful spectacle for newspaper readers. For that to happen, I needed to be photographed carrying the sign. The photographs could then be offered to newspapers. I paid a neighbor ten dollars to take pictures of me walking up and down Nicollet Mall with the sign. Jim Swartwood, who was a landlord, took some more pictures at the State Capitol. We wandered through its hallways and into the rotunda, up and down the stair case, in the halls in front of the Governor's office, the Supreme Court chambers, and House of Representatives, on what was otherwise a quiet day, snapping pictures. This activity yielded quite a treasure trove.

I also took photographs during my travels around the state. Once I drove hundreds of miles just to get a certain photograph. It is the one which graces the front cover of this book, me standing with the sign promoting dignity for white males in front of the statues of Paul Bunyan and Babe the Blue Ox. An obliging stranger took this for me in Bemidji. After developing rolls of film at Walgreen's on Broadway in north Minneapolis, I would order reprints of my favorite shots for distribution to newspapers.

In all, I drove 5,557 miles around the state between August 4th and September 5th, visiting newspaper offices. A narrative of those experiences appears in Appendix A. Except for an hour-long interview with Mike Mulcahy and two other candidates on Minnesota Public Radio on September 6th, that was my campaign. If Jim Moore had a lock on the Minneapolis-area vote and the vote of party loyalists, I would take my campaign to greater Minnesota. There, in the small cities and towns, people might appreciate a visit from someone like me. The fact that I had visited them signaled that I cared about their community, was working hard on the campaign, and perhaps could win.

I did not worry about offending people with my controversial issues. People who agreed with them might be motivated to vote for me in the Independence Party primary. People who disagreed would likely be voting for someone else in any case. My strategy for winning was to replicate Jesse Ventura's feat of turning out new voters. That would help the Independence Party more than if I courted current party members. At the same time, I understood that I needed to keep my distance from Tim Penny and other IP candidates who actually stood a chance of winning the election. Let them disavow me and my politics, if they must. I was building for the future.

CHAPTER FOUR

Genesis of Issues

Every American third party wants to think it can be like the Republicans of the 1860s who displaced the Whigs to become a majority party. The Republican Party achieved this by embracing the cause of antislavery. By implication, aspiring third parties today need to find a burning issue to put before the voters. The Reform Party began with Ross Perot's candidacy for President in 1992, building on the fact that Perot was a successful businessman who might bring his managerial expertise to Washington. His business background and concern for MIA's from the Vietnam war gave this new party a conservative flavoring. The issue of reducing federal budget deficits was important. Yet, there was also a left/populist appeal in Perot's opposition to NAFTA. Whether this bundle of issues could translate into a platform for a majority party is anyone's guess. Due to inconsistent campaigning, Perot did not win the election.

Jesse Ventura, elected Governor of Minnesota on the Reform Party ticket, was a celebrity known for his pro wrestling career. Ideologically he exploited the intense partisanship in state politics. He scored points during the gubernatorial debates by making witty remarks about Republican Norm Coleman's and

Democrat Skip Humphrey's partisan positions. Ventura styled himself a fiscal conservative and a social liberal. He believed in balancing budgets and returning excess revenues to the taxpayers, but at the same time was pro-choice and open to the idea of legalizing marijuana. Critics charged that Ventura was merely an entertainer. Although he was the Reform Party's endorsed candidate for Governor, Ventura ran his own campaign operation. Party endorsement gave him a certain claim to participate in the debates and, more importantly, a taxpayer subsidy earned by Dean Barkley's respectable showing in the 1996 Senate race. Once he found a bank willing to lend him money against receipt of the subsidy funds, Ventura could afford to hire Bill Hillsman, Paul Wellstone's original ad man, to produce the cute television commercials which aired on the weekend before the election and pushed him over the top.

Governor Ventura was personally popular but had poor coattails. The Independence Party (as the Minnesota Reform Party was renamed in 2000) failed to elect a single state legislator although one DFL state senator switched allegiance to it. The Minnesota Green Party was meanwhile achieving better electoral results. Ventura kept everyone guessing about his reelection plans until the last moment. Then, in the wake of news reports about his son's wild parties at the Governor's mansion, he withdrew from the Governor's race. Tim Penny, a former Democratic Congressman and advisor to the Ventura administration, received the Governor's blessing to succeed him.

Penny positioned himself in what he called "the sensible center" between the Republicans and Democrats. His record in Congress as a fiscally conservative Democrat - a.k.a., the party of "big spenders" - brought credence to that claim. Suddenly, a half dozen current or past state legislators, many of whom were moderates denied endorsement by their parties, announced that they would switch to the Independence Party. Penny picked one of them, State Senator Martha Robertson, a Republican from the suburbs, to be his running mate.

Most of this switching took place at the time of the Independence Party state convention. Suddenly the party's prospects of thriving in the post-Ventura era seemed bright. However, I had my doubts that a third party could grow to majority status on the basis of not being the other two parties or avoiding their respective extremes. It had to stand for something in its own right. What did the Independence Party stand for? When discussions at the convention failed to provide a clear answer, I thought that I would give this a shot.

It seemed clear to me that a political party which is based primarily on running celebrity candidates or attracting defectors from other parties does not give its rank-and-file members a good reason to participate. Yes, that type of candidate occasionally wins - but what is the point? People join political parties because they want a certain point of view to become public policy. They may have a vision of using government to bring about a better society or they may have something in mind which they wish to eliminate. In any event, a political party, to attract popular support, needs a core of ideas which its members can support. Otherwise, it becomes simply an organization which dispenses policy favors when its candidates are successful - like some other political parties which shall remain nameless.

The Independence Party had a platform, of course. My friend, Alan Shilepsky, chaired the committee which produced it. This platform consisted of twenty-six items ranging from support for developing hydrogen-based fuels to extending the time for the state's ballot access petitioning. Some of the main planks had to do with reforming the process of campaign financing, establishing a unicameral legislature, paying down the national debt, and instituting popular referendums and initiatives. These were all worthy ideas adopted by "no less than sixty percent of convention delegates". In addition, the Independence Party had six "principles": integrity, dignity, justice, responsibility, service, and community - again, worthy ideals.

Something was missing in this approach. There may have been too many planks to leave a clear impression what the party stood for. The party had to take a position on one or two questions of transcending importance to voters, hopefully something which did not duplicate what the Democrats or Republicans were supporting. Where was that new issue, analogous to the abolition of slavery, which the Independence Party might ride to majority status?

In seeking to identify major issues, I thought it useful to review the core values of the Democrats and Republicans. The Republicans seemed to me to have a primarily economic focus. In the power struggle between labor and management, or between rich and poor, or in what is sometimes called "class warfare", the Republicans sided with management and the rich. The Republican Party was a party favoring business interests. It supported minimal regulation and taxation of business, tax breaks for taxpayers in all brackets (but not cuts in the Social Security tax, which are targeted to working people), abolition of the capital-gains tax, the tax on dividend income, and the estate tax, and opposed such proposals as increasing the minimum wage.

The Democrats, on the other hand, were, in my view, no longer a party of organized labor, counterbalancing business interests. This was the politics of a half century ago. Since the 1960s, the Democratic Party had taken on a social and cultural focus. This was a party whose values were forged in the Civil Rights movement. In 1960, when Presidential candidate John F. Kennedy telephoned southern politicians to let Martin Luther King out of jail, King's father and other African Americans went over to the Democrats. The Democrats seeking their political support, in turn, catered to African Americans as a disadvantaged group. Other groups followed - women, gays and lesbians, disabled persons, newly arrived immigrants. All these groups of people faced economic or social discrimination and needed friends in government - i.e., Democrats - to help them.

Therefore, the ideological rift in American politics was not symmetrically balanced. The Republicans, focusing upon the struggle between economic-interest groups, were dominant in that sector. The Democrats, focusing upon social and cultural conflict, were dominant in the other. "Liberal" and "conservative" meant two different things depending on the sector. My idea was to oppose the Democrats' and Republicans' core values in equal measure. On the economic front, the Independence Party might oppose government policies which cater to business at the expense of labor. On the social and cultural front, it might oppose identity politics. While this approach may seem negative, so was opposition to slavery.

The reality is that appealing to business interests would not work as an issue for our party because the Republicans were already there. Neither would appealing for support among all those birth-determined, victimized groups within the post-Civil Rights coalition; the Democrats already had a lock on their votes, even so wooden a candidate as Al Gore. The Independence Party had to stake out another position to claim political space for itself. The party had to provide another option for voters who were not content with the existing politics. This was not negativity for the sake of being negative but a recognition that unopposed positions tend to move toward an abusive extreme.

In reality, the two major parties have moved toward a fusion of the dominant position in both sectors. While the Republicans are the party of business, they are far from being a party opposed to identity politics. Still hoping they can capture the African American vote, they make gestures of sympathy in that direction. While the Democrats are a party that is friendly to socially disadvantaged groups, they are also open to support from big business, especially the so-called "New Democrats". So it is all one big party with nuanced bipartisan differences.

Can the Independence Party enter the partisan fray with yet another nuance, remaining calm and collected, taking pains not to upset anyone? I said to all who would listen: attack both the Democrats and Republicans at their core. Attack them on all fronts as hard as you can. Don't worry about being realistic. Attack, attack, attack, and then attack some more. Then maybe reassess after the smoke clears. A new politics cannot afford to be cautious or approach ends piecemeal. Audacity must be our stock in trade.

In that spirit, I chose for my campaign platform two issues which would be anathema to each of the two major parties. Anathema to the Republicans, the party of business, was the statement: "I believe that the Federal Government should reduce the standard workweek to 32 hours by 2010." Anathema to the Democrats, party of the protected classes, was my statement: "I believe in the full citizenship, dignity, and equality of white males," to which were added the words "and of everyone else, too." In summary, I would make my campaign as obnoxious to the present political establishment as possible. The personal challenge for me would be to see if I had the courage to deliver these messages without evasion or embarrassment. It was not worth my time in becoming a political candidate to seek only minor changes.

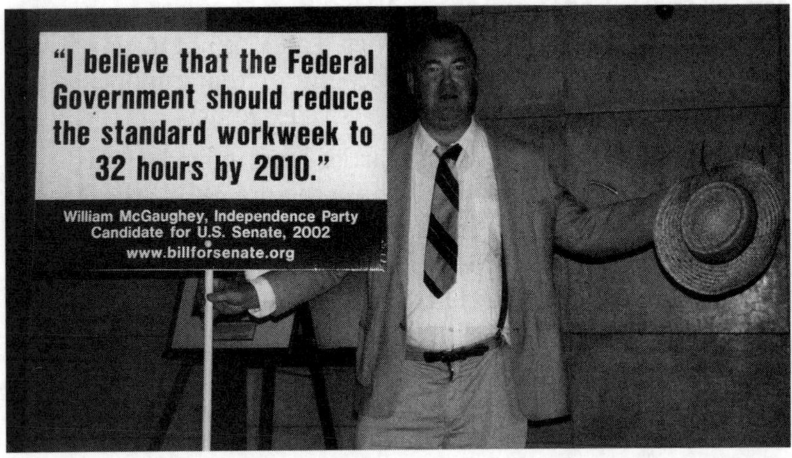
"I believe that the Federal Government should reduce the standard workweek to 32 hours by 2010."
William McGaughey, Independence Party Candidate for U.S. Senate, 2002
www.billforsenate.org

Imagining a Better World

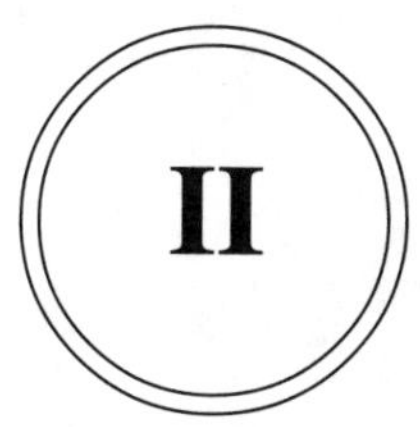

through Shorter Work Hours

CHAPTER FIVE

Poor-Quality Leaders (a.k.a. My Leftist Critique)

Ever since *Time* Magazine ran a cover story in the 1970s pro claiming "the good life in Minnesota", people have had the idea that life was better here in this state. We have a system of good, honest government. We have a Scandinavian heritage that encourages us to be both hard-working and compassionate, tolerant and relaxed. Minnesota was "the state that works." The *Time* cover for its issue of August 13, 1973, had a picture of then Governor Wendell Anderson in plaid shirt holding up a string of fish. The story suggested that, when working Minnesotans have nothing better to do in the summer, they simply take off from work and go fishing. That would never happen in New York City, of course. Garrison Keillor, too, has contributed to this "myth of Minnesota", while betraying a darker and more gender-bending side of the Scandinavian temperament. He calls this place Lake Wobegon, "where all the women are strong, all the men are good-looking, and all the children are above average."

The reality is different from the myth. When a *Time* columnist and reporter, Barbara Ehrenreich, came to Minnesota to find out how the average low-income worker lived, she expected to find a progressive community reasonably congenial to this type of person. The result was a chapter in a book titled "Nickel and Dimed" and subtitled "On (not) getting by in America." In Minnesota, she found the worst situation of any of the three locations where she had lived and worked while writing her book. Ehrenreich worked at a Wal-mart store in an unnamed suburb of Minneapolis. Her starting wage was $7.00 an hour. The book was written to gain insights into the daily experience of low-wage workers, some of whom might have recently been forced off welfare by workfare legislation.

Being a Minneapolis landlord, I am sorry to report that Ehrenreich's chief problem in Minnesota was finding rental housing at a reasonable price. She was forced to live in an $800-a-month motel without screens or deadbolt lock. (My rents for efficiency apartments, which do have functioning screens and deadbolts, are $415 per month.) Rent alone ate up much of her income - and she did not have children to support. She did have a car. Many who did not were forced to endure long bus rides to work each day and long waits at the bus stops. Becoming an employee of Wal-mart subjected one to personally intrusive employment questionnaires, drug testing, and, once hired, a physically demanding routine which might be extended by an hour each day without commensurate pay. In

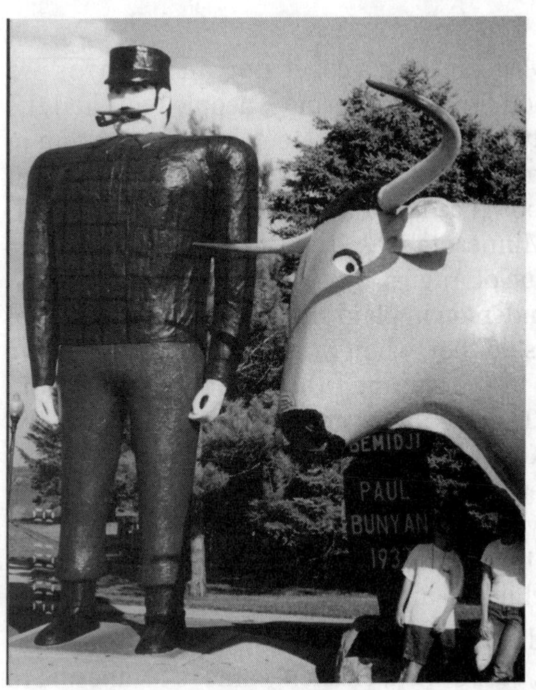

short, even simple, low-paid entry-level jobs are no picnic. Ehrenreich concluded that few persons in these jobs could make ends meet without careful planning and resourceful use of cost-saving techniques. After a few months, she could return from such work to her normal job as a writer for *Time* magazine and *Harper's*. Most of her coworkers were trapped in this type of career.

I think Ehrenreich's book has a message for America's political leaders. Public policy needs to pay much more attention to the millions of honest, hard-working Americans whose wages have not kept pace with expenses in recent years. What political "issue" raised during the last several election campaigns addresses their situation? Neither the Democrats nor Republicans talk of "living standards" any more, perhaps because it would be hard to put a positive spin on their lackluster record.

Statistically, the U.S. economy has shown impressive growth. Its gross national product has risen from $527 billion in 1960 to $9,963 billion in 2000; and, in constant 1996 dollars, from $2,377 billion to $9,319 billion. Total employment in the United States has grown from 54.2 million to 131.8 million workers. The average wage for production or nonsupervisory employees in the private economy has increased from $2.09 per hour to $13.75 per hour while the average workweek has dropped from 38.6 hours to 34.5 hours.

This record of progress is deceiving. Dollar-denominated wages and GNP must be adjusted for inflation. To achieve such striking gains in employment and GNP, it was necessary to lure numerous married women into the work force. The statistical decline in average hours is the result of a massive influx of part-time retail workers into the employment mix. The economic output upon which GNP is based consists increasingly of goods and services - mostly services - which have little connection with human happiness or material well-being. Either the growth feeds unproductive bureaucracies or it goes into functions regarded as "necessary evils." Intuitively, most Americans know that the economy is not delivering long-term improvements in living standards as it did in past generations.

Are people today better off than their parents or grandparents? Some are; many are not. Wal-mart may call their employees "associates" but that does not necessarily mean they are paid a living wage. While the 1980s and 1990s were "boom times" for the U.S. economy, the record shows that, in constant 1999 dollars, the median annual after-tax income for U.S. households rose from $29,456 to $33,676 between 1980 and 1999. Considering that the median annual income of married couples is $66,529 (in 1999 dollars) when the wife works but only $38,626 when she stays at home, it's clear that the increase of married women into the work force was responsible for much of this gain. The unintended result was more latchkey kids and more paid services which pump up GNP with functions that housewives used to handle for free.

A recent study shows that low-income, unskilled workers, especially males over 40, have increasingly turned to Social Security disability as their primary source of income. As the number of recipients grew from 3 million in 1990 to 5.42 million in 2001, outlays for the Social Security disability program have risen to $60 billion a year, making this by far the government's largest income-support program. Evidently, poverty must be medicalized for it to be treated. The share of national income going to the lowest fifth of Americans in terms of income dropped from 5.5% in 1980 to 4.3% in 1999. The share of the 60% in the middle brackets of income distribution also declined during that time. Meanwhile, the share going to the fifth of Americans having the highest incomes, rose from 41.1% to 47.2%; and, of the top 5%, from 14.6% to 20.3% in the years between 1980 and 1999. "The rich are getting richer and the poor poorer," the saying goes. In 1979, Americans in the top 5 % with respect to income earned, on average, ten times more than those in the bottom 20%. By 1999, the income ratio had widened to nineteen-to-one.

Economists look at low wages in terms of their impact on daily living. Some have calculated the income which families would need to get by. In Minnesota, the JOBS NOW coalition proposes that in a two-parent family with two children and one parent employed, the family would need an annual income of

$30,480 to cover life's necessities. This equates to a wage of $14.65 per hour. In 1998-99, 52 % of male workers in Minnesota earned at least $14.65 per hour; 48% did not. Alternatively, a single-parent family with two children would need an annual income of $34,032 to have an adequate standard of living. This equates to a wage of $16.36 per hour. Only 28% of female workers in Minnesota earn that much money.

Each year, the U.S. Census Bureau calculates the number of Americans who live below the "poverty line". This is currently defined as having an annual income of less than $18,104 for a family of four; $14,128 for a family of three; $11,569 for a married couple; and $9,039 for individuals. Between 1993 and 2000, Americans living below the poverty line decreased from 15.1% to 11.3%. During the latest recession, it has risen to 11.7%. The Census Bureau reports that this increase was concentrated "in the suburbs, in the South, and among non-Hispanic whites."

Though I try not to look at these numbers moralistically, I cannot help thinking that they represent much suffering. I am not in favor of large transfers of wealth directed by government or even a revival of the welfare state. Yet, the growing extremes of income distribution indicate a socially unhealthy situation. We are no longer one people but what Americans used to say contemptuously of the socially stratified Central American countries, that they were "Banana Republics".

The prevailing assumption is that the growing disparities of income and wealth reflect "decisions of the free market". Some people earn more because they are worth more to the economy. The usual corollary to this argument is that the employees who are worth more are more highly educated or have sought-after computer skills. By implication, it's the fault of the low-paid workers that they dropped out of school or failed to prepare themselves for work in the computer age. The free market may not be

perfect; but, to paraphrase Churchill, it's the worst system devised except for everything else.

While I agree that specific outcomes should generally be left to the free market, I also think it dishonest to suggest that government does not influence its result. By direct subsidies or tax breaks, government determines that certain industries or business enterprises will be allowed to flourish while others fail. State licensing boards boost incomes by restricting entrance to the professions. George W. Bush became a wealthy man by persuading the Texas legislature to build a new baseball stadium for the Texas Rangers while he was a part owner. Corporate welfare is also a drain on the public purse. Political conservatives want to pretend that the multimillionaires and billionaires became rich by economic "merit". Some who invented new products or built up businesses from scratch may, indeed, have merited their wealth. But that does not explain the upward creep of CEO compensation in recent years.

Back in the '50s, the unions used to scream at company executives who earned, say, $300,000 in a year. Today such a salary, or its inflation-adjusted equivalent, would be an insult to CEOs of large-sized companies. At the 365 largest U.S. corporations, the ratio of CEO pay to the average pay of nonmanagement employees rose from 42-to-1 in 1980 to 691-to-1 in 2000. Was that the result of the free market rewarding them for excellent performance or creating shareholder value?

I will not recite the horror stories of executives at Enron, Tyco, Worldcom, and other businesses in the news today. Instead, look back to the pre-scandal days of 1996 right here in Minnesota. The ten highest-paid corporate executives in our state that year included one retail executive, one computer-firm executive, two airlines executives, and six executives with banks or financial firms. Their total annual compensation ranged from $4.4 million to a whopping $102.4 million. The man in the top position, Lawrence Coss, was CEO of Green Tree Financial Corporation, an offshoot of the old Midwest Federal bank, which went into financing trailer homes, motorcycles, credit-card debt, etc. Mr. Coss was smart enough to merge his firm in time with

Conseco Finance which has recently filed for bankruptcy. Northwest Airlines has also lost money, coping with post September 11th cuts in travel.

Another well-paid executive of that era, Michael Bonsignore of Honeywell, closed down the Minneapolis headquarters when Honeywell merged with Allied Signal and then tried to merge with Jack Welch's General Electric. Booted out after the GE deal fell through, Bonsignore received $9 million in severance pay. He was promised an additional $5 million to $9 million in retirement benefits if he agreed not to work for a competitor within two years or say anything bad about the company.

Does high CEO pay correlate with good job performance and therefore qualify as being the result of an "economic" (as opposed to "political") decision? A 1998 study by United for a Fair Economy and the Institute for Policy Studies found that "CEOs who downsize workers ... who made bad loans in Asia ... (or) who have shifted jobs to Mexico ... are rewarded." Apart from the bad Asian loans, one can perhaps argue that these executives helped to improve earnings per share. Corporate scandals of the last year have revealed, however, that many top executives have manipulated earnings per share for personal gain.

The fact is that the "free market" does not pick corporate executives. They are picked by highly political corporate managers and boards of directors. Corporations, while functioning within free markets, are themselves feudal-like organizations where power is arranged hierarchically along the lines of personal loyalty. Executive pay is largely a political decision, influenced by personal ties as well as by ideas of how far the envelope can be pushed without provoking a reaction. Corporate executives, benefiting from this system, would do well to consider that, in the realm of politics, government remains the top dog. Medtronic's retired CEO, Bill George, has said: "(T)hose of us who are fortunate enough to lead great companies are the stewards of the legacy we inherited from past leaders and the servants of our stake holders ... We do not need celebrities (fetching a big price on the market) to lead our corporations."

CHAPTER SIX

Making the Free Market Work for More People

I have a theory of about free markets: The freer they are, the more quickly producers go out of business. Consumers benefit from systems of free and open competition, but the ones who sell products beat themselves down to the bottom with falling prices. Agriculture is the classic example. Farmers produce much the same commodities as their competitors. When crops are plentiful, supply exceeds demand and the price drops. When crops fail, there is little to sell. Most farmers eke out a living somewhere between those two extremes.

Compare their situation with that of medical doctors. Not everyone can go into medicine. State licensing boards dominated by the medical profession have erected educational barriers in the name of ensuring quality practice. To become a doctor, one has to go to school for many years and then endure several years of residency, working long hours for low pay. Those with sufficient stamina, intelligence, and financial resources to complete the process become doctors. Supply seldom outstrips demand. With respect to demand, doctors enjoy an additional advantage of deciding how much of their service customers purchase. Someone else - an insurance company - pays for it. Doctors can prescribe as many pills or operations as they, in their professional judgment, deem necessary. The patients, who don't have to pay, seldom complain. This system virtually guarantees that doctors will make lots of money.

In other words, to succeed in a free market, you either have to be lucky or else rig the system. How does this situation relate to the average working man or woman? Some workers are lucky - e.g., persons with computer programming skills during the dot-com boom or preparations for the Y2K crisis - but the majority cannot be. This type of worker needs to look to government, the chief rigger of markets. With a little ingenuity, government can pass laws and regulations which drive up wages. The trick is to restrict labor supply.

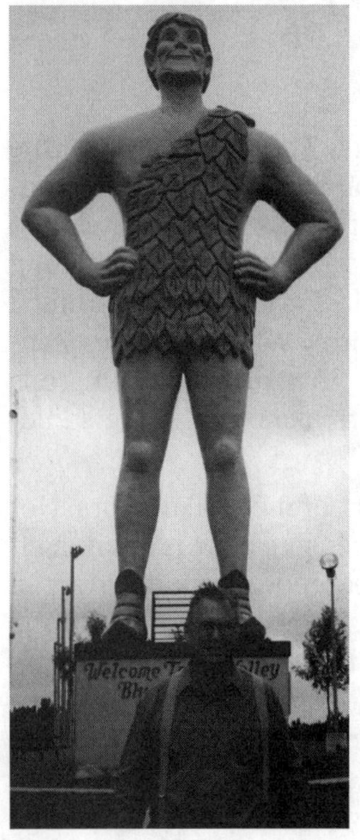

Proponents of increases in the minimum wage do not understand this. They try to force wages up but that only distorts the labor market, causing employers to get rid of some workers. A better way is to pass laws that restrict labor supply and then let the free market do the dirty work. What techniques will accomplish this? The answer was written on my campaign sign: "I believe that the Federal government should reduce the standard workweek to 32 hours by (the year) 2010." Government-imposed reductions in working hours reduce labor supply and, in the long run, drive prices - i.e., wages - up.

The business community (with a few notable exceptions) has been dead set against this approach. Labor unions were once its chief supporter. In fact, the labor movement in the 19th century was primarily a movement for shorter work days. In the 20th century, the eight-hour day was achieved; and, later, the five-day week. The forty-hour workweek became the legal standard through enactment of the Fair Labor Standards Act of 1938. This standard became effective in covered industries and occupations in 1940. Since the 1940s, however, the long-term progress toward shorter work hours has come to a halt in the United States. Census Bureau data show that the average hours of work in the U.S. economy declined from 43.5 hours in 1947 to 38.0 hours in 1982, but have since climbed back up to 39.2 hours in 2001.

Let me suggest several reasons for this reversal of the downward trend. Chief among them is the fact that organized labor has ceased to push for or even support proposals to reduce work time. The business community remains adamantly opposed. Government, too, is opposed since it can't tax leisure; it prefers "economic growth". Before the Fair Labor Standards Act was passed, the president of the American Federation of Labor, Bill Green, expressed reservations because he feared this legislative approach would encroach upon what had long been the unions' prerogative.

The law provided that employers compensate covered workers by paying them at an hourly rate of one-and-one-half times their normal rate of pay when the employers required workers to work more hours in a week than the standard workweek. Unintentionally, the higher pay rate has created a perverse incentive for employees to seek that kind of work. Instead of clamoring for further reductions in the workweek, union workers are individually seeking overtime work. The labor movement reflects its members' priorities. Unions also realize that, because of strong employer opposition, they would risk having production outsourced to another firm, state, or country if they succeeded in getting shorter hours.

While the level of work hours has been stagnant in the United States, the historic reduction of hours has continued in other parts of the world. In February, 2000, the French government introduced a statutory workweek of 35 hours. This law has created or saved an estimated 200,000 jobs. Italy, which earlier had aspired to follow the French lead, instead enacted a law allowing ten months of parental leave. The Dutch, moving to a 36-hour week, work an average of 1,370 hours per year, compared with 1,966 hours in the United States. Many European countries, including the Netherlands, Denmark, Austria, Sweden, Norway, and Switzerland, have significantly shorter work hours than in North America yet enjoy comparable rates of unemployment. In Asia, once known for its long hours, the Chinese government switched to a 40-hour workweek for state and other employees in May 1995. American workers now average more annual hours than the Japanese.

Even so, statistical averages can be deceiving: While the percentage of part-time workers is increasing in the United States, the average workweek of salaried workers who regularly work at least 20 hours a week increased from 43 to 47 hours between 1977 and 1997. Employees putting in at least 50 hours per week increased from 24% to 37% of the work force during this time. Labor won a great victory in June 2002 when the Accreditation Council for Graduate Medical Education decided that medical interns working as many as 120 hours a week could endanger patients' health. From now on, their workweeks will be limited to 80 hours.

In 1970, the International Labor Organization adopted the "Holidays with Pay" convention, calling for employers to grant three or more weeks of paid vacation to employees with at least one year of service. Thirty years later, U.S. workers were still averaging about two weeks of paid vacation per year. Laws enacted in the 1980s gave workers in Austria, Belgium, Denmark, Finland, France, Luxembourg, and Spain a minimum of five weeks' paid vacation per year. French and German workers typically receive six weeks of paid vacation during the summers and sometimes an additional week or two during the rest of the year. American commentators tend to look down upon the Europeans for working shorter hours, suggesting that the "work ethic" might be a key to our economic success. Americans want to work long hours, they suggest. Recent polls show, however, that 49% of

Americans believe that too much emphasis is put upon work and not enough upon leisure.

The responsibility for the long-hours policies clearly rests with U.S. economic and political leaders who ignore international labor standards. By 1996, the U.S. Government had ratified only twelve of 176 labor conventions adopted by the International Labor Organization, the lowest percentage of any industrialized nation. U.S. Labor Secretary Reich indicated, though, that our government that year might soon ratify ILO convention #111, which prohibits employment discrimination based on race, sex, religion, political opinion, and ethnic or social origin. During the 1990s, the International Labor Organization refocused its attention upon a set of "core labor standards", which included the right of association, freedom from forced labor, prohibition of child labor, equal pay for equal work by men and women, and prohibition of racial, religious, or other discrimination. The United States volunteered to be the first nation to be reviewed for compliance with those standards.

It was interesting to me that standards pertaining to wages and working hours are no longer considered to be core labor standards. The ILO's first convention, adopted in 1919 at a conference in Washington, D.C., established the eight-hour work day as an international labor standard. The 8-hour day was the object of the famous "May Day" strikes which took place on May 1, 1886 across the United States and Canada. The May Day holiday, resulting from that action, is celebrated in almost every industrialized country on earth though not in the United States. Obviously, U.S. policy makers want nothing to do with international standards which call for reduced work time. Instead, the "core" standards have to do with such things as gender equity in the work place, the right to form unions, and freedom from racial or religious discrimination, reflecting our core political values today.

All roads lead to the preoccupation which Americans, or the power elite, have with racial, gender, religious, and other discrimination. That is why I chose, as my second issue in the campaign for U.S. Senate, a policy expressed in this statement: "I believe in the full citizenship, dignity, and equality of white males (and of everyone else, too." Dignity for white males is not one of the core values of our current political system. I think this helps to explain why Americans will accept the poor economic and political leadership which they receive.

When we look at this record of poor performance, the question is often phrased: Are women and minorities suffering worse than other people - read, white males? Already, the divisive mentality sets in. If women and minorities are suffering worse, then perhaps we need Affirmative Action or business set-asides for women and minorities. We need more Democrats in office who will promote such policies. If women and minorities are suffering worse, then it might be because of intentional discrimination by white males. Legal action might be required - more work for lawyers. The thought does not arise that everyone - whether it be women, minorities, or white males - may need emancipation from the poor leadership which they have been getting in U.S. society. Is it a surprise that our leaders do not want people to arrive at that conclusion?

MINNESOTA
AFL
CIO
Minnesota AFL-CIO
"I believe in the full citizenship, dignity and equality of white males (and of everyone else, too)."
William McGaughey, Independence Party Candidate for U.S. Senate, 2002
www.billforsenate.org
AFL-CIO

In the 1930s and 1940s, when employers were battling militant labor unions, they sometimes found it useful to hire black strikebreakers. The unions were forced to court the black community as a defensive move. The Communist Party thought that disaffected black Americans might be recruited to its cause. U.S. business and political leaders found it useful to support the nascent Civil Rights movement to quiet black discontent. This gave rise to a socially divisive politics. Elite classes in the United States found that pitting black against white, white against black, diverted attention away from themselves. When the women's movement came along, we now had women fighting men, and men fighting against women, with conflict reaching down into the family.

Since women and minorities were both "victims" of social oppression, the oppressor had to be that part of the population which was left: white males. Affirmative action was instituted to overcome patterns of past discrimination favoring such persons. The new "oppressor" - white males - was also the type of person who had once been stalwarts in the labor movement. Yet, the unions also bought into this concept, thrilled with the prospect of bringing "new blood" into their flagging movement. They were not astute enough to realize that, in accepting this scheme, they were undermining the Solidarity principle upon which the labor movement was based. Union membership dropped from 31.4% of the work force in 1960 to only 14.1% in 1997. The managerial class had won.

What a slick move this was! Affirmative action tells white males, a cantankerous group which had once formed the core of opposition to corporate leadership: You are a privileged class. Women and minorities have suffered at your hands. They are the only authorized victims. You have no right to complain. To women and minorities, it says: Look, we (the bosses) have bent over backwards to help you. You, as you well know, have been hired by other criteria than merit. In any fair and open competition, you might not be here. You, too, have no right to complain. Therefore, neither white males nor women and minorities have any right to complain about the people at the top. Neither side sees what is happening, so bent are they on fighting each other. This is a classic trick of self-perpetuating leaders: Focus attention upon an external threat so that the problems of internal management will be ignored. In this case, stir the pot of racial and gender divisiveness so that we can stay in power, continuing to serve ourselves.

Actually, I think that women and minorities have been dealt a bad hand, though not for the reasons usually suggested. Overt discrimination, while it exists, may be less a factor than poor timing in their bid for economic equality. Before the 1950s, most women stayed home. Blacks were stuck in occupational ghettos. Both groups set their eyes on more ambitious career goals about the time that job opportunities were dwindling. The reason for that was the phenomenon of "automation". With the introduction of labor-saving equipment, labor productivity was rapidly increasing. Greater labor productivity means that a given group of workers can produce more in a given time period; alternatively, a smaller group can handle the same volume of production. In any event, increased output did not create as many new jobs as previously. The number of factory jobs held steady or declined. Workers - mostly white males - who already had jobs held on to them more tightly while newcomers to the work force were frozen out.

A proposed remedy to free up jobs for new people was to shorten the workweek. However, that remedy was rejected. Therefore, the increasing number of black and female job seekers did not find as many opportunities to take high-paying union jobs as previous generations of workers had found. But instead of shortening work time, policymakers hit on the idea of affirmative action, which would ration the new jobs according to racial and gender criteria. It was a solution which appeased political groups but did not solve the underlying problem.

CHAPTER SEVEN

My Involvement with Labor Issues

I first became interested in issues of work time while attend ing a summer camp for high-school students in Deep Springs, California, in the summer of 1957. A fellow camper named Robert Mogielnicki and I were discussing employment questions. At that time, robots were much in the public eye. Automation was threatening to destroy factory jobs. The unions were advocating reduced work time to save those jobs. I remember arguing with my friend about this concept. If robots allowed production to be handled with fewer workers, what would happen if their work hours were cut? Even with the help of robots, these workers would not finish their work in time and the employer would have to hire more people. Then, of course, the employer would install even more robots so that this smaller crew could get the work done. What if the employer automated his plant so completely that the entire process could be handled by machines? Even in that case, my friend replied, it would still be necessary to hire a human employee to push a button to start the process. The employee might do thirty seconds of work and still be paid a full salary. Such an arrangement might save jobs.

I always remembered that conversation when, years later, I began doing informal research on employment questions. While Mogielnicki's argument made sense to me, academics disagreed with the shorter-workweek solution to employment problems. I tried to find out what was wrong with the idea. I wrote economists or questioned them in person. None could give me a straight answer. There was something about a "lump of labor" theory suggesting that shorter-workweek proponents were stupid people who thought there was only a fixed amount of work to be done in an economy. But that was a "straw-man argument". We, of course, recognized that structures of production would change with changing technologies.

When I went to work as a cost accountant at American Hoist & Derrick Company in 1974, my new focus on facts and figures led me to do research relating to work time. I discovered the *Handbook of Labor Statistics* and *Monthly Labor Review* in the library. Studying the methodologies, I compiled my own tables of employment and hours information. Notwithstanding the fact that my father was then a top official of the National Association of Manufacturers, I became a committed supporter of the shorter-workweek proposal. I established my own advocacy organization, "General Committee for a Shorter Workweek", and then an affiliated organization, "Free Time Research Group", which obtained Section 501(c)3 status. However, none of the corporate or other local foundations would give it money to do research into the question of work hours.

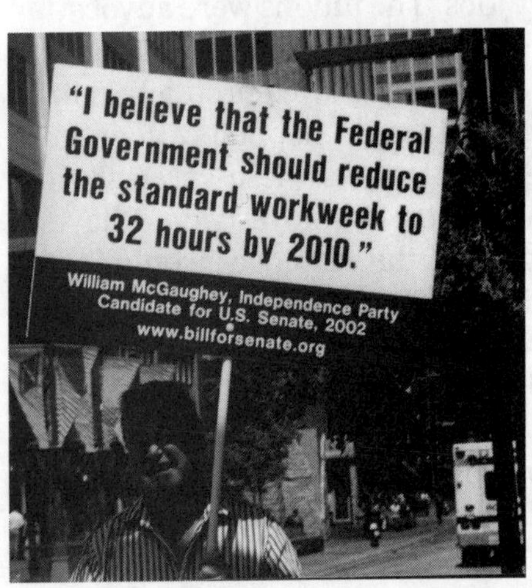
"I believe that the Federal Government should reduce the standard workweek to 32 hours by 2010."
William McGaughey, Independence Party Candidate for U.S. Senate, 2002
www.billforsenate.org

My first break came when a national group called the All Union Committee to Shorten the Work Week was formed to promote this cause. These union activists persuaded

U.S. Congressman John Conyers of Michigan to introduce legislation which would amend the Fair Labor Standards Act to reduce the standard workweek to 35 hours, raise the overtime rate to double time, and prohibit mandatory overtime. I met Conyers and his legislative assistant, Neil Kotler, at a labor gathering in St. Paul.

Since I was able to write cogent articles supporting the shorter workweek, my writings were used to advance the proposed legislation. Congressman Conyers introduced some into the *Congressional Record.* The *New York Times* published one of my articles as an Op-Ed piece. I self-published a paperback book titled *A Shorter Workweek in the 1980s* for which Rep. Conyers contributed a foreword. This book presented a discussion of economic questions pertaining to shorter hours. The Conyers bill received hearings in the House Education and Labor Committee in October 1979 but went no further. The Congressman later enjoyed greater success as chief author of the Martin Luther King holiday bill. My action committee also languished. However, I did meet some interesting people through these activities including a former and a future U.S. Senator.

The former Senator was Eugene McCarthy. In the summer of 1982, he was back in Minnesota campaigning for his old job in the DFL primary. When I contacted the McCarthy campaign, I learned that the Senator wanted to have lunch with me. He had run across my *New York Times* article which identified me as a White Bear Lake, Minnesota resident. I organized a campaign event for Senator McCarthy at the labor center in St. Paul which drew a good-sized crowd. After the election, the Senator and I collaborated on a book project arising from discussions we had about shorter hours in a Washington D.C. restaurant. The result was *Nonfinancial Economics: The Case for Shorter Hours*

of Work, published by Praeger in 1989. This book had a moral focus. We saw leisure as a means of minimizing economic waste.

I met the future Senator, Paul Wellstone, at a labor conference in Minneapolis in the spring of 1983. After his defeat for State Auditor, Wellstone took a job with the state energy agency which had offices in the same building in downtown St. Paul as the one where my employer, the Metropolitan Transit Commission, was then located. We had lunch together once or twice. I attended one of Wellstone's first coffee parties at the home of Tom Laney, a past president of UAW Local 879, in February 1990. I told the candidate about the recently published book which Senator McCarthy and I had coauthored. Wellstone would be the man, I hoped, who would give the shorter-workweek proposal a voice in the U.S. Senate. After he was elected, however, I received a letter from the new Senator noting that *Nonfinancial Economics* had admitted on page such-and-such that the shorter-workweek proposal enjoyed little or no political support. It seemed that he was in no mood for a suicide run.

As a shorter-workweek proponent, I once attended a conference on work time at Adelphi University on Long Island which Israeli social-work professor David Macarov organized. Professor John Neulinger of City College of New York gave me a ride back to New York City. Macarov founded an organization called the International Society for the Reduction of Human Labor. Neulinger became the first editor of its journal. He died after about a year in that position. After John Neulinger's death, Macarov approached me about taking over editorship of the journal. I have never been one to take on journalistic assignments, so I contacted University of Iowa Professor Benjamin K. Hunnicutt whom I knew from conferences in Iowa City. He and I were officially coeditors of the journal of the International Society for the Reduction of Human Labor (ISRHL). Hunnicutt was, in fact, the editor; and I, his assistant.

My most notable enterprise during this period was to call for a meeting of top U.S. business leaders to discuss how the business community might introduce shorter work hours. I wrote a letter to these leaders which announced that the meeting would be held in a certain hotel in New York City on a certain day in June, 1989. Would they please attend or send a representative? A number of prominent executives including Dwayne Andreas, Ted Turner, and Walter Annenberg sent their regrets. More pungent comments were received from other business leaders including the Chicago-area CEO who wrote: "My view of the world ... is diametrically opposite of yours. I cannot imagine a shorter work week. I can imagine a longer one both in school and at work if America is to be competitive in the first half of the next century." This quotation acquired a second life when it was repeated by Juliet Schor, a subscriber to the I.S.R.H.L. journal, in her book, *The Overworked American*, and then in the Wall Street Journal's review of Schor's book. It was clear that the U.S. business community would not be providing leadership on this issue.

Through Tom Laney, I became involved in a set of issues of greater importance to organized labor than reductions in work time: international trade. Rumblings of a North American Free Trade Agreement (NAFTA) began to be heard in the early '90s. Laney belonged to New Directions, a militant group within the United Automobile Workers which had made contact with auto workers at the Cuautitlan Ford plant near Mexico City. A shooting had occurred at this plant the year before when a group of dissident workers challenged the government-run union. Laney and his associates at UAW Local 879 in St. Paul organized a conference on free trade at Macalester College in late January 1991. Three Mexican workers from the Cuautitlan plant, labor activists from Winnipeg (Canada), and local experts including David Morris and Mark Ritchie were among those who made presentations.

I took copious notes and obtained videotapes of the conference. A Mexican-American working at the St. Paul Ford plant, Jose Quintana, had previously filled me in on Mexican political history. From these and other materials came a paperback book, *A U.S.-Mexico-Canada Free Trade Agreement: Do We Just Say No?*, written later in the year. It was self-published in the spring of 1992 being one of the first anti-NAFTA books on the market. This book aspired to present a positive alternative to free trade. It proposed that the international community cooperate to shorten work hours as a developmental tool.

The year 1991 was packed with trade-related activities. Besides the St. Paul conference in January, a group of us took a van down to Chicago in April to testify at hearings on NAFTA held by the U.S. International Trade Commission. Some of the same people took a rented van to Detroit, my old hometown, to attend the *Labor Notes* conference several weeks later. NAFTA was a hot topic at that year's conference. Laney, Quintana, and I filed a formal challenge to Mexico's continued status as a beneficiary under the Generalized System of Preferences, citing violations of worker rights at the Cuautitlan Ford plant and other places. Our petition was rejected.

I was an early program chair of the Minnesota Fair Trade Coalition, before this organization became a federation of labor, environmental, and other groups affiliated with the Citizen Trade Watch in Washington, D.C. On behalf of the Fair Trade Coalition, three of us organized a day-long conference at Hamline University in St. Paul at which notable speakers including the Minnesota Commissioner of Trade and Development debated the pros and cons of free trade. We also met with Minnesota Attorney General Skip Humphrey who was about to visit Mexico for the first time.

In June, an urgent request came from Mexico to send international observers to a union election at the Cuautitlan Ford plant. I was one of two who answered the call. I flew to Mexico City joining up with Mexican human-rights and labor activists. For an exhausting but exhilarating 20-hour period, I waited outside the plant gates with a group of workers aligned with the democratically elected union that was challenging the government union, CTM. Hundreds of shielded Mexican police protected the Ford complex from our small group. My English-speaking guide was a free-lance labor reporter, Matt Witt, who later became communications director of the Teamsters. He fed me tidbits of information which I jotted down in a notebook for my report. I also met a left-leaning deputy in the Mexican Congress, Gilberto Lopez, who told me that he had once been an anthropology instructor at the University of Minnesota. He was later revealed to have spied for the Soviet Union. The results of the election were announced at 4 a.m. The government union had won. Yes, my written report said that the results seemed contrived.

Bill Clinton came to Minneapolis in April 1992 to campaign for the Presidency. While he was shaking hands with people in the crowd, I handed him a copy of my book. The Presidential candidate reacted as if he had been served legal papers, but then sent an aide back to get my name and address. A letter arrived a short time later in which Clinton promised to read my book in the White House. I have sometimes wondered if this book had anything to do with candidate Clinton's speech in North Carolina which pledged to seek "side agreements" relating to labor and environmental protection in connection with any free-trade deal. I do know that Clinton was familiar with the book because, when I attempted to give him another copy two months later, he declined the offer saying that he already had a copy. Like a true politician, he said it was a "good book". The fact of the matter is, however, that the Clinton Administration became a strong supporter of NAFTA, engaging in flagrant pork-barrel deals with members of Congress to gain its approval. The side agreements produced less-than-effective protection.

My level of involvement with trade issues peaked in 1992. In July of that year, Tom Laney, some other labor activists and writers, and I, including reporters from *Labor Notes*, toured the border region between Mexico and Texas to gather information about maquiladoras. I posed as an expert on this subject on Barbara Carlson's morning radio show on KSTP-AM. In February

1993, I was a presenter at a conference on trade sponsored by the Canadian Labor Congress in Welland, Ontario. The U.S. Congress approved NAFTA later that year.

Personally, I was paying more attention to an apartment building which I purchased in August, 1993. My brother Andrew, who had lived in Washington, D.C., came to Minneapolis for a short visit. He was hospitalized from an asthma attack, recuperated, and spent the remaining six years of his life in Minnesota. Crime problems at the apartment building were requiring immediate attention. I formed an alliance, later a relationship, with a woman in the apartment who was addicted to cocaine. She helped me deal with the troublesome tenants and their friends. Several years later, after regaining sobriety, she became my second wife. So it was both a turbulent and interesting period in my life.

Ben Hunnicutt invited Eugene McCarthy and me to make presentations at a conference on issues of leisure and work in Iowa City in late 1993. This became an opportunity to bring elements from my recent experience with trade into the discussion. I continued to champion shorter-workweek legislation at gatherings sponsored by New Directions and *Labor Notes*, along with Barbara Brandt of the Shorter Work-Time Group in Boston. At a New Directions conference in St. Louis, I had an opportunity to meet Victor Reuther, last surviving of the three brothers who had brought the United Automobile Workers to national prominence. He cheered my appeal for shorter work hours from the convention floor.

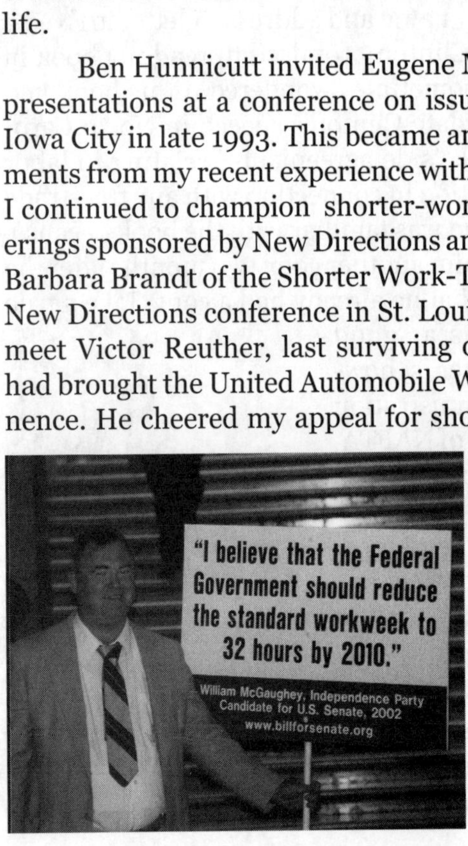

Brandt, Ben Hunnicutt and his son, McCarthy's friend Jeff Platt, and several others decided to create an international umbrella group which would support shorter work hours. We called it North American Network for

Shorter Hours of Work - NANSHOW, for short. Our immediate aim was to present a proposal to the United Nations Social Summit which called for international cooperation in reducing work time. Ben Hunnicutt Jr., Tom Kehoe from St. Paul, and I represented this newly formed organization at the third prepcom held at UN headquarters in New York in January 1995. Eugene McCarthy joined us to put on a workshop in a basement conference room. Despite help from a representative of the Canadian Labor Congress and others, our efforts were "too little too late." To the best of my knowledge, none of our suggestions appeared in the language of the draft document, either at the New York prepcom or the summit itself in Copenhagen.

I was acting globally when I should have been thinking locally. Having left my new wife and family in Minneapolis, I returned to learn that several disturbing events had taken place at the apartment building during the week of my absence. Police had been summoned to look for a gun. There was a growing problem with cockroaches, probably linked to tenants who were in the process of being evicted. This led to problems with the neighborhood group, the city's condemnation of my building, and my association with a group of Minneapolis landlords who became Minneapolis Property Rights Action Committee.

In March 1996, Ben Hunnicutt organized another conference at the University of Iowa called "Our Time Famine." Several well-known persons attended including Eugene McCarthy, Betty Friedan, Jerry Tucker, Juliet Schor, and the Canadian Bruce O'Hara. I proposed, and the group agreed, that the conference issue a formal statement supporting the adoption of a 32-hour workweek by 2000. We called this the "Iowa City Declaration". Back in Minnesota, I did a bulk mailing to 5,000 persons seeking individual endorsements of this statement. Because *Labor Notes* declined to rent me its membership list, I had turned to *Commonweal* subscribers in hopes of injecting religious energy into our movement. But the mailing was expensive and the returns disappointing. Meanwhile, I was becoming more deeply involved in landlord politics. My marriage was breaking up. I lost my job of sixteen years. My rental-property business was under siege. Between 1996 and 2002, my interest in the shorter-workweek issue and in issues related to international trade went onto the back burner.

CHAPTER EIGHT

The Economics of Work and Leisure

The shorter workweek (or greater leisure in other forms) is at the core of my vision of a better society. Why? Leisure is "free" time, and time is the room available for life. If one values the opportunities which life presents, one ought to value one's own leisure time. One can do with this time whatever one wishes within financial and other constraints. (If, as some argue, a workaholic personally enjoys working, he can always choose to do this in his free time.) Therefore, the quest to maximize freedom from the obligation to work is an aspect of freedom itself, so important to Americans. Questions arise over its economic consequences. What would happen to the U.S. economy if the federal government enacted a shorter workweek? If this move brought mass poverty, then, of course, we would not want to do it.

Economic arguments concerning shorter hours of work arise from a formula used to express the relationship between employment, economic output, productivity, and average working hours. This formula is expressed: Output = productivity x employment x average hours. Productivity, expressing output per worker-hour, is the plug figure. Output, expressed in dollar-denominated Gross National Product (GNP), represents the total volume of goods and services produced in an economy. Employment is the number of persons employed, both on a full-time and part-time basis. Average work time is the number of hours that a person works on average in a given time period. Its statistic can be either the time worked in a particular job - which is how the "payroll" series reports it - or the time which a worker works in total. The U.S. Census Bureau collects data for its "household" series according to the second definition. The difference between the two sets of hours statistics becomes clear when a worker holds more than one job. Productivity is output divided by the product of employment and average hours in a given period of time.

Consider the following illustration. Let's suppose that a factory produces cigars. There are five workers employed in this factory (employment). Each worker works forty hours a week (average hours). Each worker can produce three cigars in an hour (productivity). Output is, therefore, five (workers) times forty (hours per week) times three (cigars produced in an hour) for a total of 600 (cigars). Now let us play around with this equation assuming that a change in one variable does not affect the other variables except as the equation requires. Assume first that the market does not support the sale of 600 cigars in a week but only 480 cigars. The cigar manufacturer decides to cut weekly production to 480 units. To accomplish this, he lays off one worker. Now the equation reads: Four (workers) times forty (hours per week) times three (cigars produced in an hour) equals 480 (cigars).

Now assume that the four workers care more about the plight of their laid-off fellow employee than about their own weekly income which we assume is proportionate to their weekly production. They persuade the employer to cut weekly work hours to 32 hours so that the fifth worker can be rehired while output remains the same. The equation now reads: Five (workers) times thirty-two (hours per week) times three (cigars produced in an hour) equals 480 (cigars). The employer has the same cost structure as before. The shorter workweek has saved one job.

This is the classic argument for cutting work hours. Fewer average hours per worker can meet the reduced requirement of labor so that workers' jobs are saved. In the example, we have assumed that the cigar manufacturer needed less labor because he needed less production to satisfy the market for cigars. There is also another way that the employer's need for labor can be reduced. That is through increased productivity. As an illustration, let us assume that the employer buys a machine which allows each worker to produce 3.75 cigars in an hour instead of 3.0. The factory would initially produce 750 cigars in a week: five (workers) times forty (hours per week) times 3.75 (cigars in an hour) equals 750 (cigars). Let's say that the market will support production of only 600 cigars in a week. The employer could lay off one worker. That achieves the intended result: Four (workers) times forty (hours per week) times 3.75 (cigars in an hour) does indeed equal 600 (cigars). The compassionate four workers, wishing to save the fifth worker's job, persuade the employer instead to reduce the workweek to 32 hours. That accomplishes the same result: Five (workers) times thirty-two (hours per week) times 3.75 (cigars produced in an hour) equals 600 (cigars), which is what the employer can sell in the market.

Increased productivity is a driving force for change in labor markets. Increased productivity means more efficient use of human labor. Either a worker can produce more in an hour of work or he can produce the same output in less time, or there is a combination of the two. Worker productivity increases in several ways: When an employer orders a work speedup forcing people to work faster, that is one way to increase productivity. Another, historically more important way is to introduce machines that allow workers to produce more in a given time. For example, a metal fabricator might purchase a larger or more specialized cutting machine. A grocer might introduce electronic scanners to read bar codes on products in a checkout line. In general, the way to improve efficiency is to introduce large-scale production which achieves economies of scale and more refined production techniques. McDonald's has hamburger-making down to a science. General Motors can produce and distribute cars efficiently. Persons employed in modern business firms have both the equipment and methodology to organize work more efficiently and cut costs. That is what makes industrial progress possible.

If productivity increases take place over a long period of time, labor is displaced to other sectors of industry. Agriculture is the classic example. In the 1860s, half of Americans worked on the farm; today, less than 3% of American workers do. Yet, today's farmers produce as much food and other agricultural commodities as our society needs. The surplus farm population must find work in other sectors of industry. As agricultural employment waned, there was first a boom in manufacturing, mining, and other industries which produced goods. In the fifty years between 1951 and 2001, however, employment in U.S. manufacturing industries rose from 16.4 million to 17.7 million workers - an increase of only 8% - while total U.S. employment increased by 2.7 times. The reason for the relatively flat employment is not that the volume of manufactured products stayed flat but that productivity in manufacturing industries rapidly increased. Bureau of Labor Statistics data indicate that manufacturing productivity rose by about 3.5 times between 1950 and 1999.

The productivity figures would suggest that, since there was also a slight increase in employment, the volume of manufactured goods produced in the United States rose between 3.5 and 4 times between 1950 and 1999. This increased output would imply a rising standard of living for Americans. If, however, manufacturing employment had risen proportionate to the increase in total employment, the volume of goods manufactured in our country would have risen by nine to ten times during this time. However, the market would not have borne the increased quantity of goods. It would not have been smart for manufacturers to produce what they could not sell. Instead, they would have cut their payrolls since the productivity increases canceled the need for additional employment. The main reason for the declining employment in manufacturing relative to that in the general economy is, therefore, labor displacement due to increasing productivity. Another reason, of course, has been outsourcing of production to low-wage countries abroad.

So far, our discussion has looked at these relationships in the context of a closed economic system. For purposes of discussion, we have assumed that the U.S. economy was self-contained. However, production has gone global in the new global age. A large share of consumer goods bought by Americans is produced in China, Mexico, Japan, and other countries abroad. That complicates the picture. Indeed, if U.S. workers ever succeeded in gaining a shorter workweek, that in itself would accelerate the flight of production out of the country because employers view shorter work hours so negatively. We, therefore, need to begin thinking about political structures and mechanisms that would shorten work hours around the world. But that gets ahead of the discussion.

First consider an issue raised in *Nonfinancial Economics: the Case for Shorter Hours of Work*. The book started with the traditional argument that, if productivity rose without a reduction in working hours, labor would be displaced and unemployment would rise. That obviously has not happened. In the decades following the Great Depression, U.S. unemployment has remained relatively low, fluctuating within a range of 3% to 7%. What did happen, then? Statistics show that employment rose - faster than the gain in population - and there was a skyrocketing gain in output as represented by GNP. Gross National Product, expressed in constant 1996 dollars, rose from $2.377 trillion in 1960 to $9.318 trillion in 2000 - by almost four times. The U.S. population increased by 1.57 times during the same period. By implication, then, Americans today are 2.5 times more prosperous than they were forty years ago. American workers have thus traded their potential leisure for increased prosperity - or so some would have us believe.

Many people today who remember how their parents and grandparents lived would shake their heads at such an assertion. Conceding that previous generations did not have microwave ovens, VCRs with remotes, DVD movies, personal computers, and other fixtures of contemporary life, today's Americans live in greater insecurity, work at a more frenzied pace, and financially have problems which their forbearers did not have. In a real sense, living standards have not improved or have not improved that much. At least, this is how it seems.

We need to analyze Gross National Product to see what is happening. The three major components of GNP are: goods, services, and government expenditures. In 1960, the distribution between them was: goods, 37.6%; services, 25.8%; government expenditures, 21.5%. In 2000, the distribution was: goods, 28.4%; services, 39.6%; government expenditures, 17.5%. As one might suppose, the percentage of GNP taken up by goods production dropped as manufacturing employment became relatively less important. Government expenditures rose in absolute dollars but declined as a percentage of GNP, especially spending by the federal government. The big story has to do with the increased percentage of GNP going toward "services". What services? Therein lies the rub.

Those services which are needed in life or which make people happy are, in my view, beyond moralistic questioning. We can accept them as legitimate enterprises, even as producing hoola hoops is legitimate if the market demands this kind of product. What is questionable is the growing amount of services which are not wanted but are regarded as a "necessary evil". McCarthy and I called this "economic waste". The government does not publish statistics of activities under this classification. All we can do is cite examples.

A growing enterprise in America is the criminal justice system and its companion, the $35 billion-a-year corrections system. Let's take corrections. In 1950, there were 166,123 persons in state or federal prisons in the United States; the rate of imprisonment was 110.3 persons per thousand. By 1980, the number imprisoned had jumped to 315,974 persons, and the rate to

139.2 persons per thousand. In 1998, the number of federal and state prisoners was 1.3 million. The rate had climbed to 445 persons per thousand. In addition, 592,000 persons sat in local jails. Imprisonment is not cheap - about $35,000 per inmate per year.

Beyond this are costs of the police, prosecutors, and other personnel of the criminal-justice system. A state such as Minnesota makes extensive use of parole and parole officers. Of course, criminals will always be among us; but three times as many per capita as twenty years ago? The main factor affecting the increasing prison population is not increased criminal activity but sentences mandated by state legislatures. And, of course, the "war on drugs" puts many people away for nonviolent crimes. The growth of the corrections industry is important to our economy, especially in rural areas.

Another industry with much growth potential is the lawsuit industry. Money is no object where the courts are concerned. A jury awarded a black woman in Kansas City $1.56 million because security guards at a department store, who may have been racially motivated, stopped and searched her. Maybe the two obese ladies who sued McDonald's for supersizing their meals can win a comparable judgment? Attorneys advising various groups in the Enron bankruptcy, some of whom also gave Enron advice in its questionable business dealings, have already billed the company more than $300 million in legal fees. More than 3,000 of them, typically charging between $300 and $500 per hour, have been trying to untangle the company's complicated structure of deals that went sour. There is yet no plan of reorganization. Enron continues to enjoy massive cash flows but the stockholders will likely receive nothing. Given license to extract large sums of money from productive enterprise, lawyers could rack up huge gains in GNP by exploiting actual or trumped-up disputes that arise in society. Legal activities could expand to virtually any size. Medical malpractice, in particular, has potential.

Nonfinancial Economics attempted to identify the principal types of spending which represented "economic waste". Organized gambling is a $25-billion-a-year industry whose service produces a few big winners and many losers; there may be some entertainment value in that. It costs an average of $18,273 per year for tuition at private colleges; this is money which needs to be spent just to get started in a career. So fierce is the competition for good jobs that young men and women must continue their educations for longer periods. And how about the financial value of consuming mind-altering drugs, drinking alcoholic beverages, or smoking tobacco products? These activities also boost GNP on the medical-services and law-enforcement end. In 2000, the U.S. government spent $377 billion for national defense, or 3.8% of GNP, and that was before the post-September 11th war on terrorism. The pork-barrel aspect of fighting terrorists excites members of Congress and their defense-contracting clients in a number of states.

Medical care, to restore body and mind to a normal condition, accounts for a large and growing share of the "services" component of GNP. Pharmaceutical companies know that they can rack up huge gains in sales of antidepressant drugs by marketing their products directly to the patient. Though these must be prescribed by doctors, insistent patients usually get their way. GlaxoSmithKlein, the maker of Paxil, spent $60 million for advertising during the first six months of 2002 and achieved a 25% gain in sales. Such medications are increasingly given to children and adolescents. The volume of psychiatric drugs prescribed for this age group more than doubled between 1987 and 1996. Some say that is because the insurance companies will pay for medications to treat psychiatric problems but not for other forms of treatment or therapy. Their effect on the children's brain development is unknown.

Christmas gifts, of course, make people happy; but, since retailers count on Christmas sales for half to three fourths of their annual profits, commercials promoting mass guilt must "persuade" customers to buy various kinds of products. **You do love your children** (or your husband or your wife), **don't you?** Christmas is but one of several "commercial holidays" which had a religious beginning. One needs to buy flowers or greeting cards for St. Valentine's Day, a new wardrobe for Easter, or a spooky costume for Halloween. Maybe your wife would like a new diamond ring on her wedding anniversary? If she enters the work force, then you will need to pay a day care center to watch your children; this, too, contributes to GNP.

Likewise, families staved of leisure need to eat out more often. Free glasses of water would not be their beverage of choice; it has to be a branded soft drink. You will need to buy your kid a computer so he or she will not enter school at a disadvantage with respect to the other computer-literate kids. The kid may prefer a toy hawked on television or, perhaps, designer jeans. All products, of course, need to be merchandised aggressively through the media. Promise the potential customer a nonexistent "free vacation" if that's what it takes. Let Ed McMahon persuade some elderly woman that she has (almost) won the Publishers' Clearinghouse Sweepstakes; she doesn't have to, but it might help, if she bought some unwanted magazines.

When I tried to suggest a trade-off between leisure and economic waste at a meeting of a Minneapolis landlord group, a well-to-do woman, whom I consider a friend, suddenly turned hostile. "Why, this is the worst social-engineering scheme I've heard of in a long time," she said. "What if I want to drive my Volvo or Mercedes? Who are you to try to take it away?" I told this woman that my proposal had nothing to do with her choice of cars. It was about eliminating waste in forms which, hopefully, everyone might agree would not be missed.

What if there were no crime? Would we miss the nonexistent punishment? If there were no illness or war, would the subsequent medical treatment or bustling war production be missed? Admittedly, individual businesses whose business it is to supply corrections services, medical treatment, or arms would miss supplying those products if the need for them no longer existed; and so might government, which depends on tax revenues from their enterprise. However, the general public would be better off if people did not have to work to pay for more products of this kind.

In economic terms, increasing GNP does not go towards producing food, clothing, shelter, and other of life's necessities. As consumer products, such products are relatively inelastic in an expanding economy. The rapidly growing parts of GNP lie in the more "wasteful" types of output. That's why people today do not experience rising standards of living though statistical data suggest that they should.

CHAPTER NINE

Nuts and Bolts of the Shorter-Workweek Proposal

What is the shorter-workweek proposal? How might it af fect the economy? The principal mechanism to reduce work hours is the Fair Labor Standards Act passed by the U.S. Congress in 1938 and signed into law by President Franklin D. Roosevelt. This law prescribed a "standard" workweek of forty hours that would go into effect in October 1940. The law applied mainly to hourly workers in offices and factories; those who were managerial or professional employees or who worked on the farm or in certain other occupations were exempt from its provisions.

The significance of the forty-hour standard was that employers were required to pay covered employees one-and-one-half times their normal hourly rate of pay for each hour which these people were required to work in a week beyond the standard. The Fair Labor Standards Act did not prohibit scheduling more than forty hours a week but made it financially less attractive for employers to do so. Overtime hours would cost 50% more than hours worked within the standard schedule. If employers needed extra work, they would be motivated to hire an additional worker, who would work up to forty hours a week and be paid straight-time wages, instead of scheduling overtime work for their current work force.

The 1930s were an unusual time for the U.S. economy. Most Depression-era workers were already working less than forty hours a week. With U.S. involvement in World War II, government deficits financed war production. Young men went into military service while some women became factory workers. Consumer goods were rationed. Unspent wartime wages and lack of consumer products created a pent-up demand for these products after the war.

It is difficult to say how the Fair Labor Standards Act affected employment under those circumstances. Compared with the years following World War I, there was a smooth transition to a peacetime economy. Conditions of low unemployment and a boom in production and spending carried through most of the 1950s. One might say that the standard week and overtime penalties enacted in 1938 prevented the workweek from rising to a higher level than forty hours after the war. That, in turn, brought a strong demand for new workers which kept unemployment from rising in response to productivity gains. This historical experience provides negative evidence to suggest that shorter workweeks do strengthen employment though other factors are, of course, involved.

Karl Marx noted in his writings that after the 10-hour day was adopted in England in the late 1840s, a great prosperity ensued. The expected drop in production and decline in living standards never took place. When the British government adopted an emergency 3-day workweek during the 1973 coal miners' strike, economists were surprised to learn that industrial production declined by only 6%. Improved productivity and reduced

absenteeism took up most of the slack. There were, again, enormous gains in productivity as Japanese employers reduced working hours in the late 1960s.

Forced to generalize, I would cite a French study which determined that "a 1 per cent cut in weekly hours of work would lead to an average fall in production by 0.6 per cent." That means that, typically, 60% of the production-shrinking effect of shorter work hours will be made up by increased employment and 40% by improved productivity. Cuts in work hours tend to stimulate both productivity and employment, in a 40%-to-60% ratio. Basically the trade unionists' argument that shorter workweeks relieve unemployment is correct, though part of the job-creation potential is offset by higher productivity.

There is another factor in this equation: consumer spending. If shorter work hours reduce unemployment, then more people are employed and have money to spend on consumer products. Consumer confidence rises if workers no longer fear for their jobs. That means that the demand for consumer products will increase and, with it, employers' need to employ people to make those products.

Henry Ford, the automobile manufacturer, cited another advantage of shorter hours. He argued that, as working people have more leisure, they will perceive a greater need for various consumer products since it is mainly in one's spare time that one uses these products. He pointed out, for instance, that if workers had to be in the shops from dawn to dusk, they would have little use for automobiles. Most people would be too tired to do anything but work. With time off on weekends or at certain times of the year, Americans will want to purchase cars to drive around town in shopping errands or for leisurely visits or to travel to more distant places during their vacations. There is a direct economic benefit to businesses engaged in providing goods or services related to those purposes.

Although the U.S. business community has steadfastly opposed proposals for reduced work hours, this change would, in fact, stimulate business by creating a stronger market for consumer products. Obviously, it would not be in a single employer's interest to hire more workers for the purpose of strengthening the general market; but this would be to the advantage of the business community. A creative business leader such as Henry

Ford let his vision of a better society guide personal business decisions. With respect to shorter hours, he was willing to back this up with action.

Today's business leaders who are engaged in siphoning off wealth for themselves from corporate entities have a more short-term perspective. They feel little responsibility for nurturing the consumer market. If, however, we want to revive an anemic economy, it would be well to listen to what its creators had to say. Henry Ford observed that "it the influence of leisure on consumption which makes the short day and the short week so necessary. The people who consume the bulk of goods are the same people who make them. That is a fact we must never forget - that is the secret of our prosperity."

A question often asked in response to such proposals is what impact shorter work hours might have upon wages. Would workers have to take pay cuts? The answer is that it varies according to the situation. During economic recessions, companies sometimes introduce work-sharing arrangements. Employees work shorter hours and take corresponding cuts in pay. This is an unwanted, albeit altruistic, short-term move by the workers on reduced work schedules. It does save a few jobs. In the long run, however, reduced workweeks do not reduce income, because they create more favorable market for labor. Work hours are a component of labor supply. If the government causes average work hours to decline, labor supply therefore drops and the price of labor tends to rise.

A French economist, F.S. Simiand, found, contrary to expectations, a " negative correlation between wages per hour and the number of hours worked" in the 19th Century French coal-mining industry. Paul Douglas, an economist who became a U.S. Senator from Illinois, studied the relationship between hours and wages in seventeen U.S. industries in three periods of time: 1890, 1914, and 1926. He wrote: "The industries with relatively high hourly earnings tend to be those with a relatively shorter week than the average, while the industries characterized by a relatively low hourly wage scale tend to be those with a longer than average working week." Douglas' and Simiand's work has been updated and substantially confirmed by more recent studies in the 20th Century.

Now we come to the big question: What would happen to the U.S. economy if the federal government cut the standard workweek to 32 hours? Legally, employers would be required to pay overtime wages to covered employees who worked more than 32 hours a week. Does this mean that average hours would actually be reduced? Not necessarily. Several evasions are possible.

First, because the fixed-cost component of employment (in the form of pensions, vacations, training costs, etc.) has risen in comparison with the direct hourly cost of labor, some employers might continue to schedule workweeks beyond 32 hours and pay the extra money. The 32-hour workweek law would then become a vehicle for a disguised pay hike. The workers would like that, of course. The employer might try to make it up by offering a lower rate of straight-time pay, which the workers would not like but still might accept. Because of this possibility, I support increasing the rate of overtime pay from time-and-one-half to double-time; and, lest chronic overtime become a substitute for higher straight-time pay, I favor taxing away the additional premium which the employer has to pay. The disincentive to the employer should be increased without creating a positive incentive to the employee to work long hours.

A second type of evasion has to do with classification of workers covered or not covered under the law. If a shorter workweek is imposed on employers, some might try to reclassify previously covered employees to be exempt from the law, calling them managers or professionals. Employees who aspire to be promoted into management positions might find the reclassification hard to resist. To combat this type of evasion, federal enforcement agencies should adopt clear criteria for coverage. It is reasonable to say, for instance, that an employee who does not supervise another employee is not a manager or a management employee. The employee is probably not a professional if his or her salary is less than the firm's median. Finally, some employers might simply ignore the law as many already do. Tougher, more consistent enforcement is needed to stop that. Government leaders also need to communicate the importance of reduced work hours in their scheme of community improvement.

Assume that these obstacles have been overcome. Employers face higher payroll costs if they continue the existing work schedules. Most employers would try to arrange for the work to be completed within 32 hours each week. Firms which are overstaffed or which have tolerated loose work behavior might still be able to get the work done in a shorter time without hiring new employees. They would tighten up or restructure operations for greater efficiency. Some employers, facing higher labor costs, would invest in labor-saving equipment. Others would crack down on the abuse of sick leave or unexcused absences.

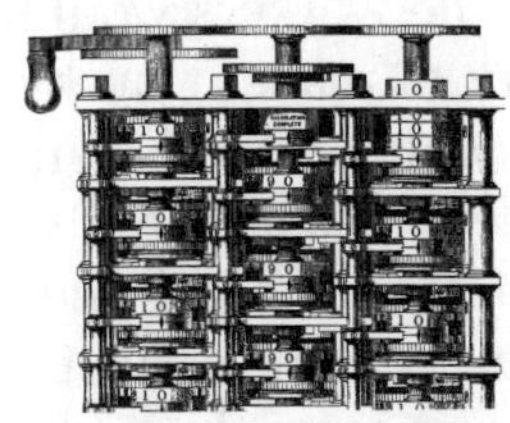

While these productivity-enhancing moves would be the employers' first reaction, the plan is that eventually they would be forced to hire new people to satisfy their production requirements. Employers would be seeking employees wherever they might be found. The pool of unemployed workers would be an obvious source of labor. Those "not in the work force" - retired persons, housewives, students - who had the time and needed extra money, might be offered special incentives to work. Some workers might be lured to better-paying jobs from positions with other employers. As the labor market tightened, employers might be forced to hire people with lower job qualifications or to improve pay.

How might a shorter workweek affect GNP and the mix of industries and occupations comprising the economy? We do not know. Parkinson's Law states that work expands to fill the time available for it. I think that is what has happened in the macro economy. Productivity increases have increased the "time" available for work and the economy has filled up with wasteful enterprise. How would Parkinson's Law look in reverse? What would happen if "time" shrinks? One would hope that the economic functions would prevail over the political.

People need to eat food, wear clothing, live in houses, drink clean water, and so on. They do not need to go to war to defend their political or religious values, sue each other over racial or gender discrimination, or advertise commercial products to the hilt. If there is a shrinkage of time available for work, I would imagine that a massive restructuring of industries might take place in the direction of what people need for their daily lives. All the unneeded, unwanted things produced by our bloated economy would tend to fall by the wayside or, at least, be reduced in scale. I am imagining, in other words, that patterns of growth over the past half century will be reversed and our economy of waste will revert to an economy of sensible, needed production.

Concretely, how might this economy look? Maybe some people would go back into agriculture, mining, and manufacturing as shorter workweeks depleted the time which existing work crews had to handle their production. Because people had only to work 32 hours a week, they could work harder, with less illness and stress, and still produce all the things which human beings need for a healthy and happy life. The shorter hours would be purchased at the cost of giving up many wasteful things currently being produced.

I am not so naive as to think that defenders of the status quo would give up without a fight. What about the two million persons in U.S. jails or prisons? If society cannot afford to keep them there any more, we may just have to find a way to release these people regardless of what the courts have decided. Maybe if this nation offered reasonably good jobs to members of the underclass, fewer young people would be attracted to a life of crime. Maybe the big payoffs from gambling will seem less attractive if a better life is available right now from honest work.

Maybe it won't be necessary for the U.S. military to "protect American interests" in the Middle East and elsewhere if Americans learned to enjoy the simple things in life and required less oil brought from afar. If we had more free time, we could cook our own meals, mend our clothing, repair broken-down products instead of buying new ones, and live in the real world instead of consuming Hollywood-produced fantasies in the short snatches of time that we have between one frenzied activity and another. A shorter workweek offers a way to have full employment and fuller lives without expanding material production and depleting the earth's limited resources. Why on earth would we not seize that opportunity?

The reason is, of course, that there are powerful interest groups which prefer the present system. An enormous economic, political, and social structure is supported by the existing financial arrangements. Leisure, while humanly beneficial, has one great drawback: there is no money attached to it. No one stands to make money if you sit on a park bench watching the squirrels instead of renting videos or if you read library books instead of enrolling in school. Thief like, you are getting some of the best things in life for free. Sadly, our society discourages this behavior because, to "make progress", its economy must grow in dollar-denominated GNP.

The monetized value of the society's goods and services must continue to grow to keep financial commitments already made. Various persons and groups have loaned out money at interest and need to be repaid. Repayment of money loaned out at compound interest requires a continually "growing" economy. Government, too, needs economic growth to meet its tax requirements. Since so many powerful groups all have their hooks in the system, we peons must work to earn and spend money. A business which defaults on its loans or a government whose currency is debased loses face. Since that often leads to a loss of power and position, these groups are insistent that mere human happiness does not justify a lack of interest in money and working long hours. The financial bubble must continue to grow. It would take a revolution of sorts for individuals to choose the alternative, the pressures are so great.

If such a revolution is to occur, it will need political support from certain groups. One would think that organized labor would comprise one such bulwark of support. Today, labor is ambivalent about reduced work hours. There remains, however, a core of idealists within the labor movement who would support such proposals. A second possibility, more remote, is support from the business community. Perhaps some modern-day Henry Ford will emerge to champion this approach?

We must also look to the religious community for possible allies. The Jewish Sabbath is a model for a "day of rest". Because this Sabbath falls on a Saturday, religious Jews were an important base of support for the 5-day week in the 1920s when Saturdays were added to the weekend. Because the Moslem day of rest falls on a Friday, some have suggested that American Moslems might now support a 4-day workweek and a 3-day weekend including Fridays. Some Christian groups - not so much the mainstream churches as the evangelicals - might also welcome more leisure as a statement of spiritual priorities, giving parents more time to spend with their children.

Finally, we come to government and to organized efforts within the larger community to promote reduced work hours. A group known as the Simplicity Forum plans to stage a nationwide demonstration in support of more free time on October 24, 2003. It's called "Take Back Your Time day". My own campaign for U.S. Senate, which expressed support for legislation bringing about a 32-hour workweek, was an example of solutions sought through electoral politics.

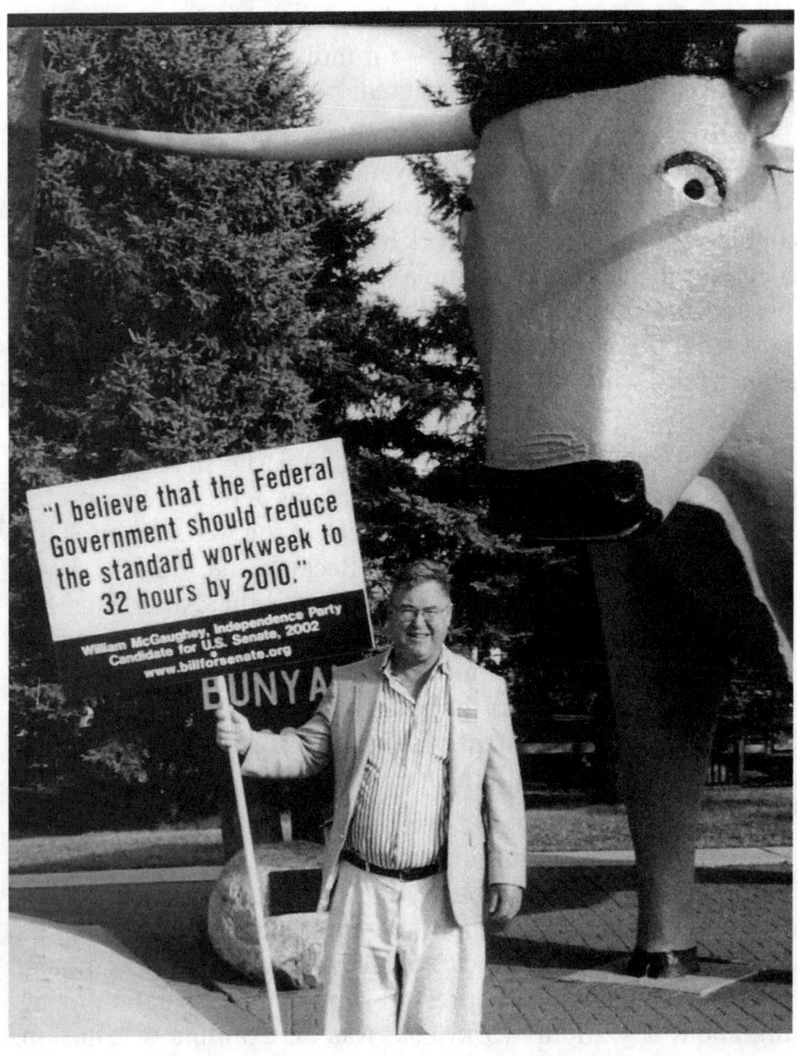
"I believe that the Federal Government should reduce the standard workweek to 32 hours by 2010."
William McGaughey, Independence Party Candidate for U.S. Senate, 2002
www.billforsenate.org
BUNYA

CHAPTER TEN

A Proposal for Fair Trade

I must backtrack to an earlier point about employers' expected reaction to government-imposed reductions in hours. The U.S. economy is not a self-contained system. In the event of shorter-workweek legislation, it's likely that some employers in manufacturing and other sectors of industry would accelerate plans to move production to other countries. With a liberalized trading order, multinational corporations can move production freely to foreign countries with assurance that they can sell those products back in the United States. There is strong bipartisan support for free trade in the U.S. Congress and in the White House. However, this book is not about political realities; it is about dreaming of a better world.

That better world, in my view, includes both a robust system of trade and maintenance of social standards. The solution is not isolationism but a trading system which promotes, rather than retards, the advancement of labor and environmental standards. We need not accept the idea that the current model of "free trade", pushed through by the large corporations, is the only system possible.

The world political order needs to develop to the point that it can regulate international production and trade much as national governments regulate economic activities within their own domains. Clearly, shorter-workweek legislation enacted within a single country will be counterproductive if it serves only to drive business abroad. (And then opponents will seize upon this piece of evidence to argue that shorter workweeks don't work.) Such regulation, to be effective, needs to be adopted at an international level. While the world community is still many years away from having a strong central government, it does have specialized organizations which function quite well within their areas of concern.

The two which would pertain here are the International Labor Organization (ILO) and the World Trade Organization (WTO). The ILO, conducting tripartite discussions between employers, employees, and governments, sets global standards relating to labor. However, it lacks an enforcement mechanism. The WTO, representing trade officials of many countries, establishes and enforces the rules of international trade. The enforcement lies in its authority to sanction retaliation against a country judged to have engaged in "unfair" trade practices. Other countries are allowed to slap tariffs on the offending country's products. There is a tribunal which decides trade disputes.

Currently, the aim of WTO regulations is to remove impediments to world trade both in the form of protective tariffs and non-tariff trade barriers. Whatever restricts trade is considered a problem. From our standpoint, it is unfortunate that WTO rules consider it a trade barrier if importation is restricted because a product was made in violation of fair labor standards. Manufacturing process is not supposed to be a factor in evaluating products. That is the present rule; it could be changed. The rules of international trade could just as easily include incentives, built into its enforcement mechanism, for em-

ployers to observe fair labor standards. In practice, those incentives would consist of penalties for noncompliance with the standards. The Secretaries of Labor in the Carter and Clinton administrations, Ray Marshall and Robert Reich, were both in favor of linking ILO-set labor standards to the rules of world trade. However, they did not propose to include shorter work hours in the package of standards.

The gap in industrial development between rich and poor nations has been a major stumbling block to adoption of such a system. Representatives of the poor countries fear that if labor standards become a trade criterion, they will be used against countries which cannot afford to meet the standards. Even a $1-per-hour wage might be too costly in a nation such as Sri Lanka. On the other hand, data from the United Nations Conference on Trade and Development (UNCTAD) show that the world's 48 poorest countries, many in Africa, "are not benefiting from free trade and globalization and instead face worsening poverty." The poor countries want their products to receive preferential treatment in world markets. The Foreign Minister of the Philippines, Domingo Siazon, has suggested that the rules of world trade might resemble the handicap system in golf, where the less able players receive equalizing points. U.S. Labor Secretary Reich agreed that certain labor standards, called "developmental standards", should be gauged according to a nation's stage of development rather than be applied in absolute terms.

The world community considers adequate leisure, wages, and standards of living to be a fundamental human right. Article 24 of the *Universal Declaration of Human Rights* states: "Everyone has the right to rest and leisure, including reasonable limitation of working hours and periodic holidays with pay." Article 25 states: "Everyone has the right to a standard of living adequate for the health and well-being of himself and of his family.." Such "rights" assume, of course, that society, or certain persons within the society, will take the necessary steps to provide resources to support them. What is considered adequate depends upon a society's economic base and, in turn, its stage of development. For such things as wages and hours, there cannot be a single standard for workers throughout the world. I would accept the argument that an industrially advanced nation such as the United States should be required to meet a higher standard than that set for Third World countries. It should also be required to show long-term progress toward improved conditions for workers.

With respect to the level of work hours, the U.S. economy has failed to show progress. It might already be considered substandard in several respects. A report issued recently by the International Labor Organization has revealed that, while annual working hours continued to fall in most industrialized nations, they have risen in the United States. The average American worker worked 1,979 hours per year in 2000, compared with 1,943 hours in 1990. The 1,979 annual hours are 137 more hours than required of the average Japanese worker, 260 hours more than for the average British worker, and 499 hours more than for the average German worker, all of whose work hours continue to decline while ours rise.

The U.S. example is a drag on further progress toward shorter hours in Europe. In the 1980s, a Frenchman named Victor Scherrer published a book, *La France Peresseuse*, which argued that the French economy could not afford to shorten its workweek while facing stiff competition from the overtime-hungry Americans. He was an executive with the Pillsbury Company who was impressed by his hard-working colleagues at the Pillsbury headquarters in Minneapolis. Ironically, Pillsbury was taken over by a British food conglomerate, Grand Metropolitan P.L.C., after Scherrer's book was published.

If the long hours worked by Americans were, as some suggest, a matter of personal choice, they would be of less concern to policymakers. But the fact is that only a few workers (such as elite computer programmers with specialized skills) can dictate or even effectively negotiate their own work schedules. Most workers must accept what the employer offers. The so-called "work ethic", translated into a willingness to work long hours, is a compulsory attitude expected of workers who want to remain fully employed at their firms. Since the labor unions have largely given up on the goal of winning shorter work hours, workers cannot expect to control their hours collectively. To change work schedules, one must put pressure on employers through government regulation and, ultimately, upon government itself.

Such pressure can come in the form of adverse publicity. For instance, the Japanese government decided to adopt shorter hours in order to combat its "sweatshop" image. The U.S. government seems less susceptible to external criticism. It might, however, begin to pay more attention if, accused of tolerating substandard work conditions, the WTO allowed other nations to impose sanctions upon U.S.-made products. Even as a candidate for U.S. Senate, I would not hesitate to encourage such a move against "the United States" by foreign governments if I felt it might improve working conditions here.

I seek not to be unpatriotic but to question whether current policies of the U.S. government are being directed, as they ought to be, towards improving the average person's situation in life. I also ask this in the context of improving people's lives around the world. So involved are we Americans in trade, immigration, and global affairs that we can no longer afford to isolate ourselves from the rest of the world. We cannot aspire to enjoy advantages of natural bounty and a developed economy while others in the world are suffering. We must envision a better global society as well as one in the United States.

The process of "globalization" is said to produce "many winners and a few losers". Political conservatives think the losers should tough it out or go back to school until better times arrive.

Political liberals are more into helping displaced workers with welfare-like benefits while also proposing to send them back to school. Neither wants to consider whether a realistic alternative exists to free trade and, if so, what its shape would be. Perhaps that is because such an alternative implies central planning on a global scale. The degree of industrial development within a nation would be a critical element in this planning.

I believe that national industrial development occurs or can occur in three stages:

First, we have the flow of foreign investment into an underdeveloped country. Manufacturers build factories to take advantage of cheap labor. They reap profits from this enterprise. One might say that this is where we now are in most cases. The escape of investment capital to less developed countries is not necessarily bad from the standpoint of U.S. workers because it creates the possibility of rising living standards in those countries and reduces the need for emigration to the United States. In the long run, it creates export opportunities for American-made products.

In the second stage, workers in the poor countries become dissatisfied with their low wages. They form unions to agitate for wage increases. If successful in that struggle, wages rise and workers enjoy higher standards of living. A prosperous middle class emerges. Because of organized labor's role in that process, international political bodies have consistently supported workers' "right of assembly" - i.e., the right to form and join labor unions. Even with strong support in theory, this right is often violated. Union organizers and their supporters are prone to layoffs, firings, or even worse.

There is also a third stage. It's possible that working people have succeeded in forming unions and obtaining wage increases. As productivity continues to rise, the condition of being employed and receiving high wages becomes associated with a shrinking group of workers who are currently employed. Union members horde the high-paying jobs for themselves as would-be newcomers are frozen out. In this situation, we need shorter work hours to spread the employment opportunities to a broader group of

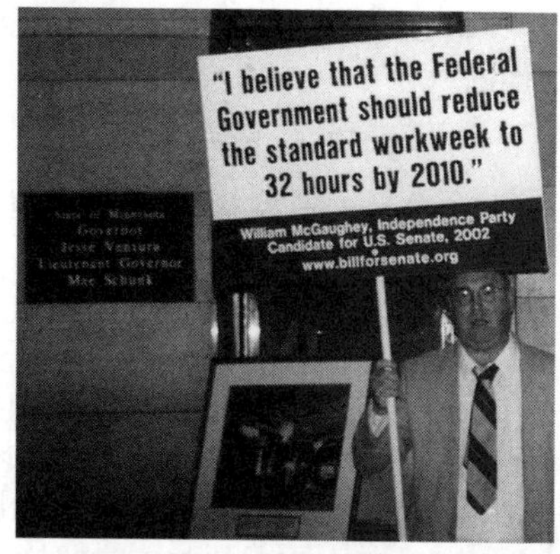
"I believe that the Federal Government should reduce the standard workweek to 32 hours by 2010."
William McGaughey, Independence Party Candidate for U.S. Senate, 2002
www.billforsenate.org

people. I would say that the U.S. economy has failed to clear this last hurdle while those of western Europe have succeeded.

Using this model, it's possible to track a nation's progress toward greater economic development. Wages and hours, though developmentally graded, can be measured objectively. It may be that a certain level of wages or hours, acceptable in a poor country, would be substandard in a country such as ours. Standards are relative to the nation's stage of development. The penalty for substandard performance would be for the WTO to sanction tariffs on products exported to other countries which were produced in this way. Now, of course, we are talking about a system which does not yet exist. The WTO wants to do away with tariffs altogether, not use them to advance developmental agendas. The current trade rules prohibit evaluations of process.

In the "better world" which I imagine, the WTO and its "free trade" rules would be replaced by a trading system linked to labor and environmental objectives. Tariffs would be an important tool of enforcement. I would, however, suggest one additional feature. Evaluations of compliance with labor and environmental standards might take place at the level of the business firm rather than at the level of a national economy. The tariffs would be applied, for instance, to General Electric products made in Mexico rather than to all Mexican products, or even to the particular GE product made in a certain factory. We need to target penalties for noncompliance with standards as closely as possible to the actual offender.

Any system which evaluates traded products from the standpoint of compliance with labor and environmental standards will include the following three elements:

1. It would set standards of desirable business and trade practice.

2. It would inspect for compliance with the standards.

3. It would enforce compliance by assessing penalties for noncompliance.

The standard-setting function would be left to economists and accountants who gather data on wages and hours in particular countries. The standards would apply only to products exported to other countries, not those produced for domestic consumption. I would propose that the standards be set high. It might be expected, for instance, that the manufacturer of exported products would pay the highest hourly wages and schedule the shortest workweeks of any business firm (or perhaps the highest quintile of firms) found in the particular industry in the country where the goods were produced. We would want foreign-owned exporters of products to set an example of improved wages and benefits, not precipitate a race to the bottom. The standards for wages and hours would be related to a country's actual stage of development. Businesses would not be required to meet the standards but be financially pressured to do so. After gathering data about the actual wages and hours worked, the number-crunching bureaucrats would work this information into a standard. I cannot say how these calculations should be done. International bureaucrats following principles and procedures accepted by the national governments would do the math.

The inspection function would be left to professional auditors. As certified public accountants review business documents to make sure that a firm's financial statements comply with generally accepted accounting principles, so labor- or environmental-standards auditors might review wages, hours, and environmental practices at a company's production facilities around the world. There is a precedent for auditing the nonfinancial aspects of business performance in the ISO-9000 certification of quality-control practices and the ISO-14000 certification of environmental practices. Some companies such as Levi Strauss already employ international auditors to monitor compliance with labor standards. Alternatively, the U.S. Department of Labor employs its own teams of inspectors to see if businesses have complied with the wages-and-hours law.

The enforcement function would occur at national borders as goods produced in one country enter another. Each imported product would be assigned a tariff based upon an index number which was calculated by the trade bureaucrats using information certified by the standards auditors. This number would be compiled from several weighted factors representing the relative compliance with labor and environmental standards in the facility where the goods were produced. The higher the degree of compliance with the standards, the lower the tariff. The lower the degree of compliance, the higher the tariff. No tariff would be applied when the standard was fully met. Such tariffs would be designed to offset the cost advantage which a firm might derive from "social or environmental dumping". Such a system would not bring a burdensome increase in paperwork. In this day and age, computers can easily and quickly process computations to grade products exchanged in international trade. Barcode technology adds convenience to product handling. This may well be a regulatory process whose time has come.

Americans today, especially the young, are concerned about goods produced with sweatshop labor. However, the usual remedy is hit-or-miss. Fact-finding is anecdotal. Enforcement consists of turning the spotlight of adverse publicity upon businesses which produce or sell sweatshop products. In some cases, attorneys may become involved. This is an overly adversarial and expensive approach to enforcing social standards. The accounting model is comparatively benign from a business standpoint. The purpose is not to embarrass or punish business firms but give

them an incentive to improve performance. We want to create a more level playing field between socially responsible and irresponsible competitors. This system of trade would discourage U.S. businesses from moving production out of the country to gain a cost advantage from cheap labor or lax environmental regulation. It would provide incentives for wages to rise, work hours to drop, and living conditions to improve for workers in foreign countries.

The economic and social objective is to hasten the day that peoples in underdeveloped countries can acquire a thriving middle class and engage in balanced trade with us in the United States. It is to ensure that their economic "growth", unlike ours in the past, does minimal damage to the environment. It is to bring all the world's people into an orderly process of development which results in generally increased standards of living. The move to universally short working hours would be an important part of this process.

I confess that we are talking here of an internationally planned economy, involving UN bureaucrats and other types unpopular in our culture. Yet, the mechanisms of the free market, including supply and demand, would continue to function. We are talking of a plan to combat world poverty not through forced charitable donations from the rich countries but through controlled development which gives more people an opportunity to work productively. This is also an economic system which would tread lightly on the natural environment. It is one which would give the world's masses of people both a reasonable level of income and the chance to enjoy it.

Therefore, whatever your political philosophy might be, don't pretend that there is no plausible alternative to free trade. A fair-trade model does exist. And, no, even in my short-hours utopia, you and a few others can still drive a Mercedes Benz.

Dealing with

PC Phobias & Complaints

CHAPTER ELEVEN

Two Events in 2001

On Saturday, August 22, 2001, members of the Ku Klux Klan and a neo-Nazi organization held a public rally on the steps of the Minnesota state capitol in St. Paul. A newspaper article reports that "46 bigoted men and women (and, tragically, a few children)" stood up there "in robes, jack boots and Nazi skinhead regalia, sporting confederate flags, and red swastika arm bands paying homage to Hitler with raised arm salutes." On the other side of a barricade manned by 100 state troopers, with an additional 200 St. Paul police officers in full riot gear standing nearby, were approximately 1,200 anti-Klan protesters. The two sides carried on their respective demonstrations for about an hour. Both the DFL and Republican state parties held anti-Klan rallies at other locations on the same afternoon. An organization called "Can the Klan" rallied on the State Capitol steps an hour before the Klan demonstration. The Minneapolis YWCA had a similar event the night before. In total, an estimated 3,000 persons turned out at these separate events to protest a rally staged by fewer than 50 Klan members.

What the Klansmen said at this rally was not reported. The newspaper described the event as follows: "The spectacle of the sick and buffoonish Klan in the new millennium is enough to make any sane human seethe. It was sadly ironic to observe many (among the anti-Klan protesters) filling with the very anger and hatred they had gathered to affront ... For some this boiling energy teemed over into physical action. A handful of Klan backers were taunted and spit upon before being escorted into the Capitol as the flock behind them became increasingly menacing. A group of six alleged KKK supporters (two men, two women, and two young girls), dressed in strip mall normalcy, were escorted onto a side street by a ranting swarm of protesters - intimidating and threatening them. Anti-Klan protesters hurled golf ball-sized chunks of concrete at the group." A photograph accompanying the newspaper article showed a sign with the message: "Pray to heal the haters' brokenness."

This event paralleled one that took place in April, 1998, when an out-of-town group called the National Socialist Movement tried to meet in a Minneapolis suburban motel. Attorney General Hubert (Skip) Humphrey III and others belonging to "Minnesota's Compact against Hate" denounced the meeting. The manager of Golden Valley Inn where the meeting was scheduled to be held canceled the Nazi group's reservation and refunded their deposit. Eleven members of this group instead rallied in front of the federal court house in St. Paul. Twice as many persons gathered to confront them. A newspaper story reported that when the neo-Nazis gave the fascist salute and yelled "Sieg heil", "they were drowned out by the protesters, many of whom threw

rocks at the neo-Nazis. Others spit on them, still others grabbed the Nazi flags."

This was too much for David Gross, a Jewish man from Golden Valley, who wrote a commentary piece for the *Star Tribune* complaining of the "intolerant" attitudes of the Nazi haters. "I saw him (Skip Humphrey) lash out with hate-filled language, all the while blaming the other guy who hadn't said anything yet, for what he might possibly say. This is crazy, oxymoronic double-speak: 'I hate hate-mongers; I have zero tolerance of intolerance.' ... Can you say, 'prior restraint'?" It would have been better, Gross suggested, if tolerance-loving Minnesotans had simply ignored the neo-Nazis.

There was a curious sequel to the August 22nd rally. Two young men from Inver Grove Heights, Jarod L. Sparks and Michael J. Pigg, were among the 46 persons who joined the Klan demonstrators - by Sparks' account, for ten minutes or so. It was their first involvement with this group. After they returned home, an observer saw Pigg push a racially mixed 4-year-old boy off his bicycle and heard him use a racial slur. Sparks was accused of doing similar things. Pigg spent three months in jail after the witness complained and Inver Grove Heights police arrested him. He was then sentenced to an additional three months of home monitoring, ordered to watch a film, *To Kill a Mockingbird*, and then discuss it with a member of the Red Wing Human Rights Commission. Sparks was sentenced to one and a half years in prison. Instead of that, the judge allowed him to serve five months in jail, followed by five years of probation. He also had to do thirty days of community service, take chemical-dependency treatment, and read five books including *Roots*, *Black Like Me*, and *To Kill a Mockingbird*.

The interesting thing about Sparks is that he had been engaged to the victim's mother, Carrie Summitt, for more than a year. She told the judge "that her son misses Sparks and asks about him daily. 'He loves Jarod and misses him,' she said. 'Jarod has done more for him than his own father. He has been a good influence on Nick. I think what happened that day was because of alcohol.'"

The *Star Tribune* followed the saga of these youthful "racists" with keen interest. Pigg's mug shot, expressing bewilderment and confusion, revealed a blue-eyed teenager with shaven head and one eye slightly out of focus. The story's "hook" was the enlightened sentence that the Dakota County judge handed down to redirect his mind from racial hate to redemption. David Harris, a retired surgeon of the Jewish faith, was the man from the Human Rights Commission court-ordered to have discussions with Pigg on socially sensitive topics.

The newspaper article declared: "Harris and Pigg's lives could hardly be more different. Harris, 67, lives in historic Red Wing in an old brick house filled with books and music ... An upright piano holds sheet music by Chopin; Harris' wife of 45 years, Nancy, played beautiful classical piano until afflicted with arthritis. Their library contains an extensive collection of books about race, prejudice, and social justice... Pigg, who declined to participate in this story, was 20 and living in South St. Paul when he met Harris. He worked at the stockyards, where he made about $6.50 an hour. Pigg's musical tastes leaned toward heavy metal bands. He didn't like books, because his reading skills were weak. He didn't have many friends." Nevertheless, because of Harris' patience, Pigg was beginning to open up his hate-filled heart and accept racial healing.

Less than three weeks after the Ku Klux Klan rally at the Minnesota state capitol, the nation experienced another hateful incident on that dark day known as "September 11th." At 8:46 a.m. a Boeing 767 jetliner, which had departed from Boston's Logan airport bound for Los Angeles as American Airlines Flight 11, crashed into the north tower of the World Trade Center in New York City, killing all persons aboard. Seventeen minutes later, at 9:03 a.m., a second commercial airplane from Boston, associated with United Airlines Flight 175, crashed into the World Trade Center's south tower, with similar loss of life. The north tower stood for 102 minutes, and the south tower for 56 minutes, before crumpling from the weight of collapsed upper floors and crashing to the ground.

If that were not enough, terrorists hijacked a third jetliner associated with American Airlines Flight 77, which had taken off from Dulles International Airport in Washington D.C., bound for Los Angeles. They redirected the plane back to Washington, where it crashed into the Pentagon killing 190 persons in that building. A fourth aircraft, associated with United Airlines Flight 93, which had left Newark at 8:01 a.m., was hijacked over Ohio and redirected toward Washington and, possibly, the White House. Due to courageous intervention by passengers and crew, the hijacked plane never reached that destination but crashed in a field near Shanksville, Pennsylvania. The combined death toll from the four hijackings was initially estimated to be 5,000. The latest estimate of casualties in the World Trade Center attacks is 2,792.

Intelligence and police officials learned that these four hijackings were the work of Islamic terrorists associated with the Al-Qaeda network headed by Osama bin Laden. Bin Laden was the son of a wealthy businessman from Saudi Arabia who had turned against the U.S. Government when it used Saudi air fields as bases during the Persian Gulf war. Nineteen persons, mainly young men from Saudi Arabia, took part in the hijackings. They commandeered the aircraft wielding knives and box cutters brought through airport security.

Mohamed Atta, an Egyptian who had spent the previous night in a motel in Portland, Maine, was one of the ringleaders. Atta's luggage, which did not make it onto the flight, included handwritten documents in Arabic that included both spiritual encouragement and practical advice for carrying out terrorist attacks. Before embarking upon their perilous mission, the terrorists "should ask God for guidance ... Continue to pray through this night. Continue to recite the *Koran* ... Keep a very open heart of what you are to face. You will be entering paradise." Most of these men had entered the United States legally for the purpose of taking commercial-flight courses. Another man, Zacarias Moussaoui, suspected of intending to be the 20th hijacker, was arrested on August 16, 2002, at the Pan-Am flight school in Eagan, Minnesota, when he expressed interest in piloting a large commercial airplane without learning how to take off or land.

The reaction to these events was curious. People were, of course, worried about terroristic attacks taking place on our soil. They generally supported President Bush's strong military response. At the same time, political and opinion leaders in Minnesota and elsewhere went to great lengths to disassociate these attacks from persons of Middle Eastern descent, the Islamic community, or the religion of Islam. Numerous public events took place to discourage anti-Muslim prejudice.

For example, a forum sponsored by Twin Cities public television and the *Star Tribune* focused on the dangers of racially profiling persons from the Middle East. Minneapolis city officials and civic leaders, together with representatives of the Christian, Jewish, and Islamic faiths, held a two-hour discussion of "the economic, security and spiritual effects of the Sept. 11th terrorist attacks." An email campaign, which began in Washington, D.C., urged non-Islamic women to cover their heads with scarves on Monday, October 8th, to show solidarity with their Islamic sisters who might be distressed by an anti-Muslim backlash. Even this gesture proposed by the "Scarves for Solidarity" campaign brought criticisms that for non-Muslim women to wear scarves might be interpreted as being disrespectful to the Islamic community.

While observing this reaction, I thought of the Ku Klux Klan rally that had taken place three weeks earlier in St. Paul and of the fierce response this had aroused. Why was it that 46 individuals standing peacefully on the steps of the state capitol to express their social and political views could inspire thousands of Twin Cities residents to demonstrate in sometimes violent opposition while the same types of people showed only understanding and compassion for religious beliefs that inspired extremist elements to kill thousands of innocent persons in the September 11th hijackings? Why was the Ku Klux Klan so offensive to Minnesotans? This was, after all, a movement which peaked in the 1920s, never had much influence in Minnesota, and is today so reviled that it could hardly represent a threat to the American way of life.

True, its members express hateful views about some groups but so do Muslim fanatics from which the hijackers sprang. The latter groups, embodied in the Al-Qaeda network and other terrorist organizations, have both the will and present-day capacity to harm large numbers of people. They are an imminent threat to public safety. Is the Ku Klux Klan, though presently peaceful, reviled because of its violent past? Islamic terrorists in one day - September 11, 2001 - may well have killed more innocent people than Klan members did in their entire history.

I have some theories about why the Klan is more hated. First, the Ku Klux Klan is a group exhibiting selective animosity against certain groups of people. In its early 20th Century reincarnation, it was primarily an anti-Catholic organization. In the popular folklore, however, it has become an organization bent on lynching black people and expressing anti-Semitic views. Jews and blacks have, therefore, an intense desire to make sure that the Ku Klux Klan is repudiated by non-Jewish white Americans. To this observation, I would add that the Ku Klux Klan has a problem associated with its visual appearance. The burning-cross image evokes both antagonism from non-Christian groups and the primal fear of fire. For Klan members to hide their personal identities at public rallies by covering their faces with a hood suggests that these people are cowards who are ashamed of what they are doing. In the hands of Hollywood, this combination of attributes adds up to evil incarnate.

A second reason for the monolithic anti-Klan sentiment is that the Klan and its sympathizers represent a minuscule portion of the population. They represent a demographic element which is shrinking in relative importance. In contrast, the Islamic faith is one of the fastest growing religions in America.

Persons of this faith comprise an increasing part of the U.S. population. The disparate reactions to Ku Klux Klan and Al-Qaeda violence may have less to do with the violence itself than with the nature of liberal politics: Liberals do not want to get on the wrong side of groups whose numbers are growing. It may be that Islamic immigrants, in coalition with other minority groups, may become our future majority population.

On the other hand, the Ku Klux Klan, though potentially violent, represents such a small group of people that it can be attacked with impunity. It's always fun to kick someone with a reputation of being menacing and powerful who is, in fact, is quite weak. You're guaranteed to be a winner. In this context, Islamic violence is not really such a problem. Let's face it: Liberals are titillated by violence. They were when African Americans rioted in the '60s and they are today. So long as the Islamic religion has a good side, a peaceful and compassionate side, that part can be overlooked.

CHAPTER TWELVE

About the Ku Klux Klan

Both my parents came from central Indiana. They grew up during the 1920s when the Ku Klux Klan had a membership of more than a million persons nationwide. Indiana was a center of Klan influence. This organization controlled the Indiana legislature at one time. My maternal grandfather was then a state senator. However, I doubt that the Klan controlled him because he was a Democrat in a Republican-controlled legislature. I doubt that the Klan had much influence on my father's side either. His family was Roman Catholic and the Klan was an anti-Catholic organization. Even so, a top Klan leader named D.C. Stephenson lived in the same part of Indianapolis where my father's family lived. Stephenson took an attractive young woman on a train ride to Chicago where he murdered her. Put on trial, he was convicted. The sensational publicity which this trial generated sealed the Ku Klux Klan's doom. By the end of the 1920s, it had rapidly lost members and ceased to be a political force.

If you want to know what the Klan was like in its heyday, a good source of information would be Robert S. and Helen Merrell Lynd's sociological study, *Middletown*, which is based on conditions in Muncie, Indiana. "Coming upon Middletown like a tornado," the Lynds wrote, "the Ku Klux Klan has emphasized ... potential factors of disintegration. Brought to town originally, it is said, by a few of the city's leading business men as a vigilance committee to hold an invisible whip over the corrupt Democratic political administration and generally 'to clean up the town,' its ranks were quickly thrown open under a professional organizer, and by 1923 some 3,500 of the local citizens are said to have joined. As the organization developed, the business men withdrew, and the Klan became largely a working class movement. Thus relieved of the issue that prompted its original entry into Middletown, the Klan, lacking a local issue, took over from the larger national organization a militant Protestantism with which it set about dividing the city; the racial issue, though secondary, was hardly less ardently proclaimed. So high did the local tide of Klan feeling run that in 1924 a rival group in Middletown set up a rival and 'purer' national body to supersede the old Klan. Tales against the Catholics ran like wildfire through the city."

What did the Ku Klux Klan have against Roman Catholics? Heavy immigration from Catholic Europe was an issue. The Lynds quoted Protestant sermons suggesting that the Pope intended to take over the United States: "They say the Catholics are building a great cathedral in our national capital at Washington which is to become his (the Pope's) home." Another Klan argument was that Catholics held certain women, called "nuns", prisoners in the convents. The "confessions" of Helen Jackson, "an escaped nun", enjoyed brisk sales at Klan rallies. Because the Catholics considered it sinful to wear jewelry, one poor woman allegedly had her bejeweled fingers cut off when she entered a nunnery.

"I believe in the full
citizenship, dignity and
equality of white males
(and of everyone else, too)."
William McGaughey, Independence Party
Candidate for U.S. Senate, 2002
www.billforsenate.org

"To this Catholic hatred," the Lynds wrote, "was added Negro and Jewish hatred fed by stories that the Negroes have a powder which they put on their arms which turns their bodies white, and that the Jews have all the money, but when the Klan gets into power, it will make a new kind of money, so that the Jews' money will be no good." The Ku Klux Klan was against the Jews for traditional reasons: they had rejected Christ. They were against the Negro because of miscegenation. The Bible said it was wrong to mix blood. That is how Rome fell and, as Lincoln said, "a house divided against itself cannot stand."

Ultimately, the moralistic fervor could not be sustained. The Lynds observed that "Klan feeling was fanned to white heat by constant insistence in season and out that 'every method known to man has been used and is being used by the alien-minded and foreign influence to halt our growth.' Social clubs were broken up and church groups rocked to their foundations by the tense feelings all this engendered. The secret of this eruption of strife within the group probably lies in the fact that it blew off the cylinder head of the humdrum. It afforded an outlet for many of the constant frustrations of life ... by providing a wealth of scape-goats ... and two of the most powerful latent emotional storm-centers of Middletown, religion and patriotism, were adroitly maneuvered out of their habitual uneventful status into a wild enthusiasm of utter devotion to a persecuted but noble cause. The high tide of bitterness was reached in 1923, and by 1925 the energy was mainly spent and the Klan disappeared as a local power, leaving in its wake wide areas of local bitterness."

There is no indication in the Lynds' book that members of the Middletown Klan engaged in violence against any group. That does not mean that the Klan did not have a violent history. What we have been describing pertains to its reincarnation as a national organization at the time of World War I. The original Ku Klux Klan was founded in 1866 in Pulaski, Tennessee, during the Reconstruction era. After the former Confederate general Nathan Bedford Forrest gained control of this organization, it became a "secret army" to fight Republican rule in the South. A principal objective was to terrorize the northern Carpetbaggers and blacks and, by destroying their morale, keep them from voting. The hooded Klansmen would ride ghost-like through the night, kidnapping people from their homes, whipping, assault-

ing, or lynching them. The tactic worked. Because the Klan enjoyed popular support, southern law-enforcement offered little resistance to its activities. White Republican militias and, ultimately, federal troops destroyed the Klan in 1871 and 1872. Its legacy was ninety years of white-supremacist rule in the South where the Democrats exercised firm political control.

There was also a third period of Klan activity beginning in the late 1940s. In this case, the Civil Rights movement and fear of communism provided the impetus to its counter organizing effort. This movement was based among poor, relatively uneducated southern whites. Its membership peaked at 17,000 in the 1960s. Today, Klan-related groups have an estimated 4,000 members nationwide. The Klan's attempt in the 1960s to derail the Civil Rights movement, as its forbearers had done a century earlier with Yankee-imposed Reconstruction, backfired badly. Individual and mob violence brought a police response, much adverse publicity, and major federal legislation including the Civil Rights Act of 1964 and the Voting Rights Act of 1965.

Behind those events stood a fundamental political change that began with John F. Kennedy's election as President of the United States in 1960. Kennedy was the first (and only) Roman Catholic to be elected President. His maternal grandfather was Mayor of Boston during the 1920s when Klan-inspired sentiments against Catholics ran high. Kennedy was elected President, in part, by appealing to Protestants to rise above anti-Catholic prejudice and by arranging for Martin Luther King to be released from jail. After he was assassinated three years later, the new President, Lyndon B. Johnson, pushed through legislation favorable to blacks. Southern whites, starting with Senator Strom Thurmond, bolted to the Republicans during the 1968 national elections. The Democratic party thus turned its back on its previous base of support in white-supremacist politicians who had comprised the "solid South" while the Republicans lost support of the black people whom they had so actively assisted during the Reconstruction era. They gained, however, a new base of support among the southern white population. The Ku Klux Klan became universal pariahs.

Where does this leave us with respect to racial violence? First we need to know how many people the Ku Klux Klan killed. This particular statistic may be unavailable. According to the *Encyclopedia Americana*, 4,763 persons were lynched in the United States between 1882 and 1968, which included 3,446 blacks and 1,297 whites. Lynching was most prevalent during the last decade of the 19th Century, when an average of 154 such incidents took place annually, and in the American south. Before the Civil War, the overwhelming majority of lynching victims were white. This does not indicate black violence against whites but, more typically, the efforts of southern whites to maintain the slave system by punishing abolitionists and persons assisting runaway slaves. In the north, lynching took the life of the Illinois abolitionist editor, Elijah P. Lovejoy. Cattle rustlers in the west also received this treatment.

Thomas Dixon's 1905 novel, *The Clansman*, inflamed white-racist fervor. D.W. Griffith's 1915 film, *The Birth of a Nation*, glorified Klan activity during the Reconstruction period, prompting the group's revival on a national scale. Some lynchings occurred during this time. The black victims of lynching were usually males accused of raping white women or of murdering or assaulting whites. Sometimes this was the result of "lynch mobs" randomly selecting blacks or of race riots such as the one which occurred in Atlanta. The image of individual black males being hanged from a tree branch, surrounded by a crowd of white onlookers, is etched in public consciousness as a result of photographs that were widely circulated, sometimes in the form of postcards. In the 20th Century, the number of lynchings gradually diminished as southern whites imposed segregationist rule. According to the *Encyclopedia Americana*, the last reported lynching in this country took place in 1981.

The public image of Klan violence is, therefore, part fact and part fiction. Certainly there were a large number of blacks killed by white-racist individuals or groups. Members of the Klan were involved in many of those activities. Yet, as we have seen, the Klan movement had other interests, especially in the period of its greatest influence. Many people at the time saw it as a heavy handed and divisive, though often well meaning, attempt to reassert "American values". The low-born, uneducated whites drawn to this cause embraced kooky ideas such as the idea of a powder which black people put on their arms to turn white. In the end, however, most white Americans rejected the Ku Klux Klan. It was an example of a philosophy being rejected in the free competition of ideas. Then came the process of demonizing the Klan in Hollywood films and the communications media. Here the image of the Klan morphed with that of the Nazis to present a totally menacing and sinister picture of an organization bent on violence. It is that political agenda which I wish now to challenge.

The murderous activities of the Ku Klux Klan and its members are certainly to be condemned. This ought to be the common denominator of all such discussions: how many people did they kill? If one accepts that premise, however, then one is obliged also to ask how many people others have killed. Let us consider black-on-white violence. In many large American cities, blacks account for significantly higher numbers of violent crimes per capita than whites. Much of this is black-on-black crime, which is equally deplorable, yet some is interracial violence. White people, Asians, and other nonblacks are today victims of the disproportionately large number of violent crimes for which blacks are responsible. Having 12% of the population nationally, African Americans accounted for 56% of all arrests for murder between 1992 and 1996; 40% of arrests for rape; 57% of arrests for robbery; and 37% of arrests for aggravated assault.

Yes, Ku Klux Klan members did a horrible thing in the 1963 bombing of a church in Birmingham, Alabama, which killed four

children, or in the murder of the three Civil Rights workers. But the cold-blooded killing of four young white people in Wichita, Kansas, on the night of December 14, 2000, by Jonathan and Reginald Carr, two young blacks, which involved torture and rape as well as murder, was also reprehensible. Closer to home, a gang of young black thugs shot and killed a 70-year-old white man named Robert Fernlund while he and his wife were returning home to their home in south Minneapolis around midnight on the night of October 28, 1998. On April 15th of that year, a Minneapolis landlord found the stinking body of Ann Prazniak, a 77-year-old white woman, stuffed in a cardboard box in the closet of her apartment. Wrapped in plastic and a blanket, she had been dead for about two weeks. A group of young drug users, all black, had taken over her apartment. One was convicted of the murder.

While the last reported lynching in the United States took place in 1981, these and many other acts of black-on-white violence have happened recently in my own city. Our perceptions of racial violence may be determined less by how often these incidents occurred than by how persistently they were memorialized. Were the Klan killings worse because a sinister-looking organization was associated with them while the latter were the work of undisciplined, high-spirited youth? Murder is murder. Were they worse because blacks and not whites were the victims? That needs to be discussed.

It's not just ghetto blacks and low-class white Klan members who kill people. While we're at it, let's discuss the murderous record of other rather more sacrosanct groups. The second chapter of *Exodus* reports that Moses murdered an Egyptian foreman who was working the Hebrews too hard; yet this man later found favor with God. In the twentieth chapter of *Deuteronomy*, this God is quoted as telling the Hebrew invaders of Palestine first to make an offer of peace to the cities located there and then, if the cities surrendered, enslave all the inhabitants. If they refused, God issued this command: "You shall put all its males to the sword, but you may take the women, the dependents, and the cattle for yourselves, and plunder everything else in the city."

That was the mild treatment, reserved for "cities at a great distance". "In the cities of these nations whose land the Lord your God is giving you as a patrimony, you shall not leave any creature alive. You shall annihilate them - Hittites, Amorites, Canaanites, Perizzites, Hivites, Jebusites - as the Lord your God commanded you, so that they may not teach you to imitate all the abominable things that they have done for their gods .."

Present-day adherents of Judaism and its daughter religions need to be asked whether those words from the *Bible* are still operative policy. Evidently, Ben-Gurion thought so when he spoke to the 1938 Jewish World Council in Tel Aviv: "After we become a strong force as the result of the creation of the State, we will abolish this partition and expand to the whole of Palestine ... The State will preserve order, not by preaching, but with machine guns." The Arab population of Palestine dropped from 950,000 to 138,000 persons in the six months after the state of Israel was created. Most, I assume, went to live in refugee camps rather than to rest in cemeteries.

With respect to Christianity, Jesus was a comparatively peaceful person who, like a lamb, submitted to his own execution. Yet, there are elements of violence in Jesus' driving money changers out of the Temple and in quotations attributed to him about not bringing peace but a sword. The Christian crusaders practiced unprovoked violence against the Moslem occupants of the Holy Land. With respect to the religion of Islam, the Prophet Mohammed was a political and military ruler as well as a messenger of God's word. Islam was spread by the sword. In our own day, Islamic fundamentalists have carried out terroristic bombings, assassinations, and, of course, the September 11th attacks on the World Trade Center and Pentagon.

Were the September 11th attacks the work of misguided religious zealots or did they result from Islamic teachings? Osama

bin Laden claimed justification for his bloody acts in the *Koran*: "But when the forbidden months are past, then fight and slay the pagans wherever you find them, seize them, beleaguer them, and lie in wait for them in every stratagem (of war)." It seems clear that the Islamic idea of holy war, or jihad, is traceable to sacred texts, though religious scholars may debate its application to particular events. I raise this point to cast aspersions upon those "good people of Minnesota" who, while abhorring a peaceful demonstration by 46 persons supporting the Ku Klux Klan, went to great lengths to separate the September 11th terrorists from the Islamic religion.

One might argue that, although the Klan demonstrators were not themselves violent, their ideas represented violence. Therefore, anyone associated with the Klan was implicitly expressing approval of those practices and should be rebuked. On the other hand, Osama bin Laden could plausibly argue that his bloody deeds were given sanction in the *Koran*. Therefore, by the same logic, anyone associated with the religion of Islam was condoning violent practices and should be rebuked. Or do we have a double standard here? The burden of proof is upon the Islamic community to reconcile interpretations of sacred text that have been used for terroristic purposes with the present-day need for a peaceful world. Either the Al-Qaeda terrorists were acting outside the scope and sanction of this religion, or the world community has a major problem on its hands.

I could go on to mention the self-righteous killings carried out by U.S. military personnel on orders from President Bush. The point is that our attitude toward violence depends on who is the perpetrator and who the victim. It also depends on whether or not the perpetrator is too big and strong or too prestigious to criticize.

If Klan "racism" is the issue, then take another look at the Bible where Moses tells the Hebrews that "the Lord will make you the head and not the tail: you shall be always at the top and never at the bottom." (*Deuteronomy* 28: 13) Consider Joseph's dreams about other people's sheaves of wheat bowing down to his. Judaism teaches that the Hebrews' tribal god Jehovah is the most powerful god in the world - indeed, the only God - and that the Hebrews are this God's "chosen people." Is that not saying to other people, in so many words: We're better than you? Who are they, the followers of this kind of religion, to talk about racism?

Some of Judaism's successor religions have taken up this idea of group superiority, suggesting that God's particular favor has passed to them in a new revelation or new covenant. Is it any wonder, then, that religions of this type, as opposed to native American or east Indian religions, have been quarreling and warring with each other for millennia? Before the well-mannered, god-fearing people raised in the Judeo-Christian tradition go off criticizing the Ku Klux Klan for its crudely expressed and uncouth racist ways, I suggest they go look in the mirror.

A disturbing aspect of this situation is that those who target "hate groups" most vehemently seem less concerned with actions than the fact that these people have expressed their opinions. While violent crimes are downplayed, all is directed at controlling what is thought and said. The idea seems to be that some opinions are so repugnant that they must be nipped in the bud whenever anyone starts to say them. I maintain, to the contrary, that "hate speech" is permitted under Constitutional guarantees of free speech.

The harmful thing is not opinions in themselves, not even hateful and demeaning ones, but opinions imposed on others by force. In my view, a free society can afford to have an Adolf Hitler ranting on the street corner, but it cannot afford a Hitler who has become Chancellor of Germany. In other words, it can not afford laws or legal interpretations which prescribe acceptable modes of thinking. It cannot afford political or social values which stigmatize some groups of people while extolling others, especially when these values are enforced by state power or given exclusive expression in the press. Such values would constitute, in a broad sense, a state religion; and, in a free society, state religions are constitutionally prohibited.

CHAPTER THIRTEEN

Demons in the Press

I have a love-hate relationship with the *Star Tribune*, which calls itself the "newspaper of the Twin Cities", and, to a lesser extent, with other publications staffed by writers of the liberal political persuasion. I love these newspapers because I read them avidly and believe that they still offer the best opportunity to become informed about community affairs. I hate them because, in my view, they have abandoned evenhanded and objective reporting to foist a moralistic, hateful point of view on readers. Instead of reporting hard facts, they personalize the news by telling how selected individuals have reacted emotionally to a given event. In regards to political and social issues, they cheerlead the public on how they ought to feel. In the process, they have become agents of political demonization.

Michael Barone, author of *The Almanac of American Politics* and editor of *U.S. News & World Report*, once told a gathering in Minneapolis that "feminist thought police patrol every news room" in America. John Leo of *U.S. News*, who has made a career of debunking political correctness, quoted Peter Brown of the *Orlando Sentinel* to the effect that "journalists are far more likely than other Americans to approve of abortion, to express disdainful attitudes toward suburbs and rural areas, and to identify strongly with people who see themselves as victims. Reporters tend to be part of a broadly defined social and cultural elite, so their work tends to reflect the conventional values of this elite. The astonishing distrust of the news media isn't rooted in inaccuracy or poor reportorial skills but in the daily clash of world views between reporters and their readers."

The perceived media bias has to do with choice of stories. Columnist Michael Kelly of the *Washington Post* observed that "most journalists learn to see the world through a set of standard templates into which they plug each day's events." Michael Janeway, former chief editor of the *Boston Globe*, has described how "the politics of the street came into the newsroom ... Suddenly newsrooms had de facto caucuses organized by gender, race, and ethnicity. Suddenly coverage of controversial stories had to be negotiated within the newsroom as well as outside."

The editorial department is the least of our concerns. Those of us who disagree with editorial positions recognize that the newspapers at least label it as opinion. At the *Star Tribune*, editorials tend to exude schoolmarmish pride in the accomplishments of women (and other certifiably good people) or high-minded concern when someone oversteps the bounds of community good taste as the editorial writers see it.

That bull in the China shop, Jesse Ventura, was a real problem for the editorial writers. A *Star Tribune* editorial right before he was elected Governor was headlined: "It's been fun, but the election's near." While it might be a lark to tell people you're voting for this outlandish candidate, the editorial opined, it's harder to come up with a rational explanation of why Ventura would make a good governor. "Many will conclude that with all due respect to Ventura ... the time has come to elect a governor who has shown he can do the job." Hillary Clinton, in town the same weekend, called Ventura a

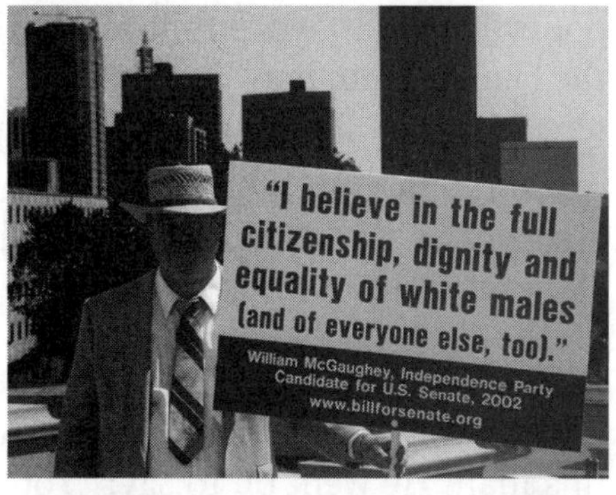
"I believe in the full citizenship, dignity and equality of white males (and of everyone else, too)."
William McGaughey, Independence Party Candidate for U.S. Senate, 2002
www.billforsenate.org

"sideshow", suggesting that people get serious about picking a Governor.

After Ventura's surprising victory (which might reflect the fact that people don't like to be told how to vote), a politically soul-searching editorial in the *Star Tribune* was headlined "This Odd Election - What will it mean for Minnesota?" It was fun to watch the editorial writers and news reporters deal with the fact that Jesse Ventura would be our Governor for the next four years and try to find the right tone of respect for his office while maintaining the proper values.

I begin to have more serious problems with this newspaper when its moral cheerleading leads to demonization of individuals. The *Star Tribune* has a tendency to pick trivial events and, because they represent a negative element in its lexicon of political correctness, run a major story or perhaps a series of stories on them, replete with photographs and often on the front page. The stories about Jarod L. Sparks and Michael J. Pigg, two young men who had the misfortune to attend a Ku Klux Klan rally before getting into trouble with the law, are an example.

Even though this did not rise quite to the level of demonization, I also thought it in poor taste for the *Star Tribune* to run a commentary piece debunking Queen Elizabeth's mother, the "Queen Mum", in the week following her death. A disaffected Brit wrote how the English people "saw through" the Queen Mum's act. In private, she had "extreme right-wing views". She was a spendthrift with the taxpayer's money, insisting on all her royal prerogatives. This writer even ridiculed the Queen Mum's and her late husband's visits to bombed-out neighborhoods during World War II "which she claimed put her on the same level as the people of East London." In polite society, people usually cheer persons who have lived to be more than 100 years and do not criticize too harshly those having a ceremonial rather than policymaking role in public affairs. For the *Star Tribune* editors, the Queen Mum may have had the wrong personal stats.

In February 2000, a Republican state legislator named Arlon Lindner underwent a long process of demonization initiated not by the *Star Tribune* but his fellow legislators. A DFL state representative from St. Paul, who is Jewish, was arguing on the floor of the House against a proposal that would allow House sessions to begin with denominational prayers. "Don't impose your irreligious left views on me," Lindner snapped at this man. He went on to say: "You know, we're told there's one God and one mediator between God and man. The man is Jesus Christ. And most of us here are Christians. And we shouldn't be left not able to pray in the name of our God ... And if you don't like it, you may have to like it. Or just don't come." It is reported that there was an audible gasp in the House chambers following those remarks. Four DFL legislators brought charges of anti-Semitism against Lindner in the House Ethics Committee.

I thought Lindner's remarks, however ill considered, to be well within the limits of permissible free speech. In fact, for Lindner's critics to use a government agency to attempt to silence or censor him for expressing his religious views was itself a violation of the doctrine separating church and state. I said so in a letter to the editor published in the *Star Tribune*, pointing out that, while I was not personally a Christian, "neither do I have a chip on my shoulder with respect to people who are." Since Republicans controlled the House and its Ethics committee, Lindner was not punished.

Even so, Arlon Lindner was a tainted man. The next time he let his fundamentalist Christian views show in public the *Star Tribune* weighed in with a series of reproachful, front-page articles. The occasion was the Dalai Lama's visit to the Twin Cities in May 2001. The Dalai Lama, a Tibetan Buddhist, was invited to address the Minnesota legislature. Lindner let it be known that he would boycott the Dalai Lama's speech. He would sit it out in his office. Since this decision smacked of religious intolerance, Lindner was again severely criticized. The same tone of moral outrage was heard. Interestingly, the Dalai Lama himself was asked about Lindner's statement. He simply replied, "He's entitled to his opinion. There are many different views in this world." I thought that was the way this incident should have been handled from the beginning.

Several months earlier, a locally infamous man named Elroy Stock was in the news again when he sued Augsburg College for breach of contract. Stock was an accountant who had retired from West Publishing Company. Having made lots of money from his West Publishing stock, he wanted to make a gift to Augsburg, his alma mater. In 1987, Stock agreed to give this college $500,000 to construct a new building. Part of the building would be named the "Elroy M. Stock Communications Wing." All went well until WCCO-TV's investigative journalists reported that Mr. Stock had sent letters to hundreds of interracial couples or persons who had adopted children of different races. Stock was a devout Christian who believed that the Bible forbade interracial marriages and mixing of blood. Augsburg was pressured to return the money to this unworthy donor.

The original scandal was that the college declined to do so. It decided to keep Stock's money while also weaseling out of its commitment to give Stock a conspicuous honor. Stock's money was used to build a wing on the building where a small plaque in the hallway disclosed "Major Funding by Elroy Stock". But Stock had a commitment in writing that the wing would officially be named after him. When he repeated his request for satisfaction of the contract in 1999, the college refused. The building was built, and that was all there was to it. So Elroy Stock sued the college.

I do not remember whether Stock prevailed in his lawsuit. I do remember an article about him in *City Pages*. The graphics were remarkable. A caricature on the front cover depicts Stock as a hunchback handing out money. His face is green-colored. He has droopy eyelids, a cross on his belt buckle, and

dark horn-rimmed glasses. His two arms are thin as a snake's body. A photograph of Stock accompanying the article manages to make him even more sinister-looking. Stock's right eye bulges out in an unfocused way as his left eye, lurking in the shadow of his face, looks straight at the camera. This photograph occupies a full page. I do not know how the photographer managed to get this, it is so monstrous-looking.

Stock's vital statistics also fit the part. He was a 78-year old "virgin bachelor" who lived by himself in Woodbury and seldom traveled outside the state. He cooked his own meals from canned food. He apparently spent most of his days scouring the newspapers in search of information about couples in interracial or interfaith marriages. He then would mail these persons copies of religious texts which he had reproduced on a photocopying machine in his home. The *City Pages* story reported that, after the WCCO expose broke, "both the *Star Tribune* and the *St. Paul Pioneer Press* weighed in with editorials supporting the college's decision to keep the cash, while excoriating Stock as 'pathetic' and 'vile'." There were, of course, the usual quotations from recipients of his letters who felt violated.

I, too, received one of Elroy Stock's letters. It was shortly after I had published an opinion piece in the *Star Tribune* about "hate crimes" legislation. The envelope, which bore Stock's name and return address, contained photocopied sheets of religious literature in which certain passages were underlined. That was all. There was no cover letter to explain the point of this communication or what Stock wanted me to do. I could not make sense of the underlined passages. Stock's mailing could be described as "creepy", but nothing more. If he had known that I had recently been married to an African-American woman, it might have changed his message to me but would not affected my attitude toward him. Elroy Stock was a character in the Twin Cities subculture of notorious racists or religious nuts, a celebrity in his own way. To receive one of his letters was rather intriguing.

Besides, his views on interracial marriages were not that unusual. I once heard a college student, my Yale classmate Tommy from Baltimore, ask Dr. Martin Luther King if the end of segregation might not mean more interracial dating and births of mixed-race children whom neither race would accept. King's response was not to condone this practice but to state that, in his opinion, desegregation would not necessarily lead to more racially mixed marriages.

Another example of *Star Tribune* demonization is based on events in the fall of 2002. For years, as I drove down Lake Street in Minneapolis, I would pass the River Lake Gospel Tabernacle, a large brick building with a sign proclaiming "Jesus Light of the World." A father-son team of evangelists, Luke and Paul Rader, used to preach there. I remember reading once abut a young man nationally prominent in the New Left with the colorful name of Dotson Rader. He might have been Paul Rader's son. Anyhow, this empty building gave testimony to a religious culture which had once flourished in the Twin Cities. Billy Graham began his preaching career here in the 1940s. There was a kind of poor-white Protestantism that fed the souls and bodies of Depression-era Minnesotans. Bereft of worldly hope, hundreds of society's down-and-out would gather at the Gospel Tabernacle for meals and spiritual uplift from singing Gospel songs at the Sunday revival meetings. The Raders also conducted one of the first radio ministries in the country. Even though I never affiliated with this type of religion or set foot in the Raders' church, the place had a romance about it that kindled my imagination as I drove past this building.

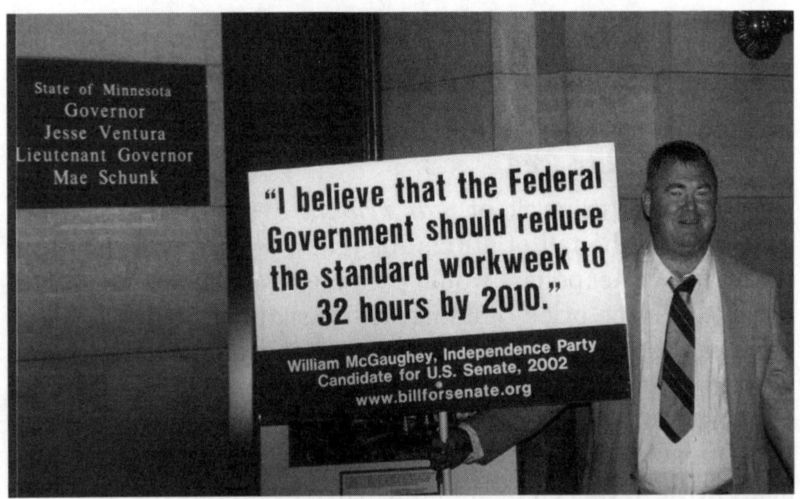
State of Minnesota
Governor
Jesse Ventura
Lieutenant Governor
Mae Schunk
"I believe that the Federal Government should reduce the standard workweek to 32 hours by 2010."
William McGaughey, Independence Party
Candidate for U.S. Senate, 2002
www.billforsenate.org

After being abandoned for decades, a developer purchased the site and made preparations to raze the building to make room for an apartment-and-retail complex. He sought approval of this plan from the Heritage Preservation Commission. The commission's staff proposed to designate the site as a historic site and recommended that a plaque marking the tabernacle be placed in the building to be constructed. These plans came to the attention of Stephen Silberfarb, executive director of the Jewish Community Relations Council of Minnesota and the Dakotas. Silberfarb and his colleagues objected to the anti-Semitic content of Luke and Paul Rader's sermons.

The demonization machine at the *Star Tribune* swung into high gear. Three lengthy articles about this controversy followed. A rabbi prominent in interfaith affairs published a commentary piece. Under pressure, the Commission staff decided not to recommend commemorating the tabernacle and its broadcast facilities. The Commission itself voted to overturn the staff recommendation. The project next went to the Zoning and Planning committee of the Minneapolis City Council, which voted unanimously not to allow the plaque. The final step was a vote by the full City Council which was scheduled for November 12th but was, instead, settled by an administrative decision. The hate-spewing Raders would not be recognized in any way.

What did these preachers actually do? According to an unpublished doctoral thesis written by a man now on the staff of the Jewish Community Relations Council in Cincinnati, they "preached that Jews were cheating, blasphemous and unfit to live." Luther Rader said that "Satan's synagogue" controlled international finance. He called the New Deal the "Jew deal". Also, the Raders preached that Anglo-Saxons were the "true Israelites." Someone remembered that Paul Rader had remarked in a 1946 sermon that "the Jews aren't fit to live." This was juicy enough, but who remembered it and when was it said? What exactly did Paul Rader say? All this loose talk dredged up from unavailable texts that were compiled by highly partisan individuals, it seemed to me, amounted to a kind of McCarthyism of the cultural left, a smear campaign against "defamation", to which only a sleazy, religiously and politically opinionated newspaper would devote coverage.

The *Star Tribune* articles quoted Hy Berman, a history professor at the University of Minnesota, to the effect that in 1946 Minneapolis was the most anti-Semitic city in the United States. "It (the River Lake Gospel Tabernacle)," said Berman, "was the worst place, barring none in the Twin Cities, as far as anti-Semitic vitriol (was concerned.)" So notorious was this place that "Jews were afraid to walk past Lake and River Road." (Characteristically, the *Star Tribune* is here reporting personal feelings as a substitute for fact.) The idea of rampaging Christians assaulting Jews on the street after listening to one of Rev. Rader's anti-Semitic sermons seemed quite ludicrous to me. During the same period there were, in fact, violent Jewish gangs in Minneapolis that assaulted people who said or wrote the wrong things. Isadore Blumenfeld, a.k.a. "Kid Cann", was the leader of one such gang. His organization is believed to have murdered a crusading newspaper editor named Walter Liggett.

I thought it my duty to make at least a feeble attempt to present the truth in this politically charged environment. I contacted my City Council representative about an opportunity to make a public statement before the full Council took a vote. Her assistant called back to report that the matter was "a done deal". There would be no further opportunities for comment.

During this time, the *Star Tribune* also devoted much coverage to allegations of anti-Semitism at St. Cloud State University. Three Jewish faculty members had sued the state university system because they were not promoted or given tenure. Anti-Semitic "ethnic slurs" proved that the reason was that the professors were Jewish. One of the plaintiffs said that "History Department colleagues tried to discourage him from talking about the Holocaust and talked about having to fumigate his office." Under the $1.1 million settlement, the plaintiffs received $265,000 (and their lawyer an equal amount), the college agreed to create and fund a Jewish Studies and Resources Center, and all students and faculty members were required to take diversity-training courses that included a section on anti-Semitism.

I thought that lawsuit settlements were a poor way to set college curricula. My problem with the *Star Tribune* was that it was essentially cheerleading the public to reach negative conclusions about St. Cloud State. Again, juicy details such as the remark about fumigating the professor's office were given without context. Essential facts such as the percentage of Jewish faculty were omitted. This ongoing story appeared often on the front page of the newspaper or in editorials. A front-page story in the *Star Tribune's* Sunday paper was headlined "St. Cloud State still finds prejudice" because a recent poll had found that 20% of the professors believed that there were too many Jews on the faculty and they had undue influence over university policy compared with 57% who disagreed with that statement. Zero tolerance of dissenting opinions on such questions seems to be the policy of this newspaper.

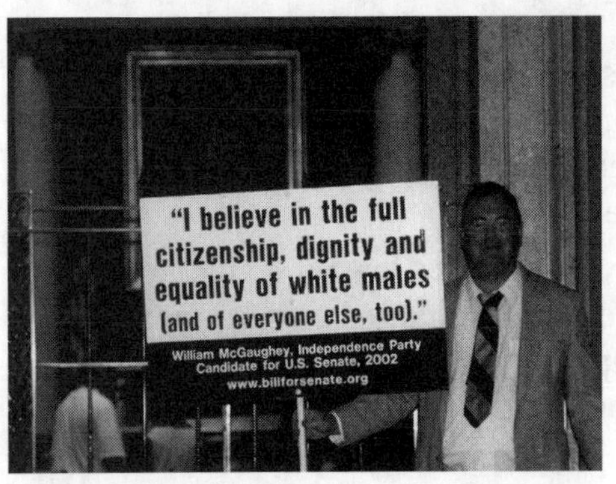
"I believe in the full
citizenship, dignity and
equality of white males
(and of everyone else, too)."
William McGaughey, Independence Party
Candidate for U.S. Senate, 2002
www.billforsenate.org

The worst kind of reporting by the *Star*

Tribune involves last-minute attacks on political candidates whose philosophy its editors and reporters dislike. What long-time resident of Minnesota can forget the 1990 election campaign which produced not only the first election of Paul Wellstone but Arne Carlson's improbable election as governor through a write-in campaign. The endorsed Republican candidate was Jon Grunseth, a conservative with backing from Christian fundamentalists. Two weeks before the election, the *Star Tribune* ran a lengthy, front-page story telling how Grunseth had hosted a July 4th party at which Grunseth and teenage girls swam nude in his backyard swimming pool. Grunseth promptly abandoned his candidacy, setting up the opportunity for Carlson.

In 1998, the *Star Tribune* again intervened in an election for state senator in district 58. John Derus, for whose campaign I had distributed literature, was running against Linda Higgins. Derus, a former Hennepin County Commissioner, represented old-style, labor-oriented Democrats while Higgins was a feminist candidate. On election day, the *Star Tribune* ran a picture of Derus with a caption identifying him as having been involved in a charity swindle. Derus had nothing to do with any swindle. The *Star Tribune* later claimed that it had mislabeled the photograph because of a "computer glitch". Some, remembering that this newspaper had similarly maligned Derus once before, were not so sure.

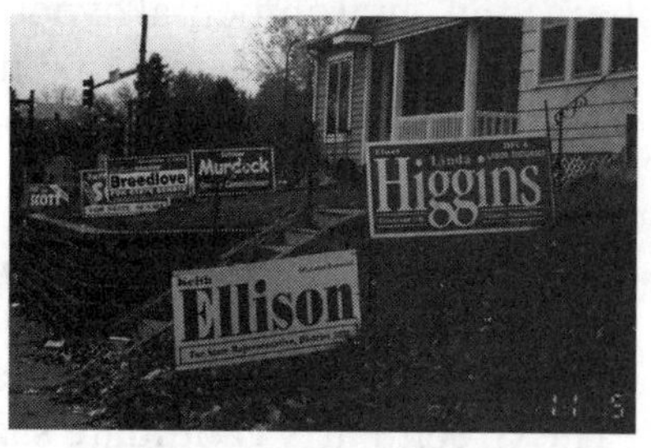

The 2002 race for U.S. Senate, in which I was a candidate, provides another example of *Star Tribune* intervention in political campaigns. In this case, the demographically unlikely victim was Ed McGaa, a native American who was the Green Party's endorsed candidate for Senator. It is thought that some liberals disliked McGaa because his candidacy might take votes away from Paul Wellstone. Possibly he was disliked because of his expressed pride in being a veteran.

In any event, the *Star Tribune* ran a front-page article about Ed McGaa on September 3, 2001 - one week before the primary election - which pointed out that in 1986 McGaa had written a letter to South Dakota state officials supporting a business venture that called for shipping sewage ash from Minnesota to the Pine Ridge Indian Reservation, extracting gold and other metals from the ash, and then redepositing the treated ash in the soil. Evidently, the company involved in this operation was unable to deliver on its promises and the contaminated ash sat in warehouses for a long time. McGaa was an employee of that company. The *Star Tribune* story implied that he was an environmental hypocrite who, perhaps knowingly, had participated in a scheme to dump toxic waste in South Dakota. Was this the type of person who should be representing the Green Party in its race for U.S. Senate?

I read the article carefully, looking for the meat of the case against McGaa. Sure, he was involved in a failed business venture, but did that show evil intent? A subtitle to the story stated: "The Green Party candidate said he had no regrets about being involved in the project." I found no information substantiating that statement. What I did find were quotations from some of the project's South Dakota critics attaching adverse labels to McGaa. It was a prime example of Star Tribune-style emotional journalism in which the way people feel takes the place of facts. For example, a critic named Deb Rogers was quoted: "How the Greens got messed up with him (McGaa) I'll never know." She added: "If ten years ago someone had predicted this to me, I would have laughed them out of the room ... I mean, you can't even imagine a person who is less compatible with their (the Green Party's) philosophy." And again: "My bottom line is that this guy caused a lot of damage in South Dakota."

The *Star Tribune* article did acknowledge that others, including officials of the Metropolitan Waste Control Commission, were also taken in by the business firm's proposition. Its newsletter had described the process as "the ultimate in recycling" and claimed that adequate environmental safeguards had been taken. Pointing out that he was simply an employee of the firm, McGaa asked "Why do you want to turn around and blame Mr. Indian here?"

I was on the campaign trail, sitting in the lobby of a newspaper office in Mankato, when I read in the (Mankato) *Free Press*: "Green's McGaa losing party support". The opening sentence said: "Some Green Party members, including gubernatorial endorsee Ken Pentel, are distancing themselves from their endorsed Senate candidate, Ed McGaa, after learning that he was part of a 1980s business deal involving sewage ash shipped from Minnesota to South Dakota." So, McGaa was being left hanging in the wind. I saw McGaa as a victim of one of the *Star Tribune's* patented last-minute political attacks. The facts of the case did not seem to me to justify the treatment he was receiving.

When I returned home, I telephoned McGaa and, as a U.S. Senate candidate from a rival party, proposed that we jointly picket the offices of the *Star Tribune.* McGaa declined, saying that he had several other opportunities to tell his side of the story. But he did appreciate the call. I also wrote a letter to the editor of the *Star Tribune* defending McGaa against his critics. To my surprise, the *Star Tribune* published this letter on September 6th - four days before the primary election. I was appeased.

The result of this incident, however, is that Ed McGaa lost the primary to his Green Party rival, Ray Tricomo, by a margin of 3,438 to 2,567. I also lost in the Independence Party, but, as a second-place finisher, received 2,000 votes more than McGaa's and Tricomo's vote total combined. As the Greens had deserted McGaa, it appeared that Minnesota voters were now deserting the Greens.

CHAPTER FOURTEEN

It Started in the '60s

If I may generalize, liberals and conservatives have a different attitude toward their constituencies. The conservative attitude is straightforward: If we are a privileged class, then hang on to that privilege as tightly as possible. Punish your enemies and reward your friends. Be remorseless in squeezing every ounce of advantage from a given situation. And don't worry about it. We deserve to be on top because we are superior. The liberal attitude is morally more complicated. Liberals want to hang onto power just as much as conservatives do, but they also want to be seen as being virtuous. They are sensitive to criticisms about associating with unsavory characters for the sake of power. These liberals have "principles". The solution often lies in jettisoning loyal supporters, especially individuals who are personally unattractive or unpopular, to save their own skins.

These liberal tendencies came out during the Kennedy administration. President Kennedy was a Democrat. His party's base of support lay in labor unions, the "solid South", and big-city "bosses". So what did John and Robert Kennedy do? They went after corruption in the labor unions. They withdrew support from Carmine de Sapio, the Tammany boss of New York

City. They supported Civil Rights protesters against the southern political establishment which had always been loyal to the Democrats. They cracked down on organized crime - yet another doublecrossing if reports that ballot-stuffing crime bosses helped John Kennedy win Illinois are true.

This attitude carried over into foreign policy. When South Vietnam's president Ngo Dinh Diem seemed unable to restore order in his country, the Kennedy administration secretly gave its blessing to a military coup against Diem, a U.S. ally. The coup resulted in the deaths of Diem and his brother, Ngo Dinh Nhu, the country's security chief. (Remember Nhu's wife, dubbed the "Dragon Lady"? She was a bad woman if you can believe U.S. newspapers.) The point man for this policy was a State Department official, Roger Hillsman, who saw a parallel between protesting Buddhists in South Vietnam and Civil Rights protesters in the American south. Interestingly, it was reported that Ho Chi Minh and Mao Tse-tung, talking over the situation following Diem's assassination, both felt that Diem was not such a bad leader.

It was not just the Kennedys. Senator George McGovern, the Democrats' Presidential candidate in 1972, called a certain South Vietnamese government official, perhaps Nuygen Cao Ky, a "little tin-horned dictator". When his announced running mate, Thomas Eagleton, was discovered to have been treated for mental illness, McGovern first said he supported Eagleton "one thousand percent", then dropped him from the ticket. Jimmy Carter withdrew support from a longtime U.S. ally, the Shah of Iran, paving the way for the Ayatollah Khomeini's takeover of Iran. And, of course, I saw the same pattern in the Minnesota Green Party's treatment of its endorsed Senatorial candidate, Ed McGaa. For political liberals, "principle" trumps personal loyalty. We must always be seen as morally superior people who will have nothing to do with wrongdoers. From another perspective, however, this posture has given

the U.S. Government the reputation of doublecrossing its allies while being self-righteous about it. Our friends know instinctively that they must watch their backs.

I say this as a prelude to discussing race relations. The U.S. population has long been dominated by persons of European ancestry. A minority - perhaps 10% of the population - consisted of blacks who were descended from African slaves. Other relatively small groups such as native Americans or immigrants from Asia and Latin America also entered into the racial mix. A century ago, there was indeed a feeling among America's majority population that white people were superior to other races. After all, European nations had colonized much of the world. In this country, an Anglo-Saxon aristocracy concentrated in New York, Boston, Philadelphia, and other large cities was positioned at the top of society. Their offspring attended the best colleges and became top-level corporate managers or partners in professional firms. The upper-middle classes from the Midwest and other provincial areas aspired to join their ranks. In the American south, the white gentry dominated a largely rural society which kept black people subservient under Jim Crow policies.

All this started to change in the 1950s and especially the 1960s. We had the murder of Emmett Till and the resulting outcry. We had the Montgomery, Alabama, bus boycott led by the Rev. Martin Luther King, Jr. in defense of Rosa Parks. We had "Freedom Riders" from the North traveling down to southern communities to aid in desegregation efforts. Jews, who had long suffered from social disadvantage, were entering prestigious colleges in greater numbers. Dominating the entertainment industry, they were also making inroads into journalism, law, medicine, and other professions. Other ethnic groups were also enjoying new prosperity as managers, professionals, and members of labor unions. The Anglo-Saxon hegemony was being challenged.

A major fault line lay across the college campuses. During this period, U.S. colleges were opening up to other kinds of students than those from traditionally privileged groups. Jews and even a few blacks were being admitted to the Ivy League colleges. The professors held left-leaning political, social, and religious views which William F. Buckley and others believed were at variance with the views of mainstream America. Educated young people began to engage in behavior that shocked their parents. They engaged in promiscuous sex, took drugs, listened to rock 'n roll music, supported black people's bid for civil rights, flirted with communism, and opposed the Johnson Administration's conduct of the war in Vietnam.

With respect to race relations, young white Americans were feeling the influence of black culture, especially in music and sports. College campuses were hotbeds of support for the Civil Rights movement. The assassinations of President John Kennedy, Senator Robert Kennedy, and Dr. Martin Luther King, set against the backdrop of the Vietnam war, created an atmosphere of violence and social unrest. Then came the race riots following Martin Luther King's death. Detroit and other U.S. cities burned. The Black Muslims, "Black Panthers" and other armed groups gave the impression that, despite Martin Luther King's nonviolent stance, black Americans might soon use violence to overthrow the social order. White conservatives were suitably alarmed. Mayor Richard Daley gave Chicago police the order, "shoot to kill", when rioting blacks tried to set fire to buildings in his city. White liberals had another reaction. There were reports of "limousine liberals" in New York City hosting parties for Black Panther luminaries.

Why was this? One should keep in mind that the college-educated segment of the U.S. population was developing attitudes and tastes at variance with those of small-town America, blue-collar workers, and other residual elements of the white society. The picture of southern segregation was before its eyes. Maybe other parts of the country were also "racist"? The Civil Rights Act of 1964 and the Voting Rights Act of 1965 had empowered southern blacks politically while northern blacks,

through their numbers, were beginning to take over big-city governments.

Hoping to capitalize on these trends, the Democratic Party began catering to blacks. The nation's political leaders used flattering rhetoric about them. (Politicians always get excited about groups waxing in power. They want to get in on the ground floor of any trend that might carry them along to future election victories.) Blacks had a higher birth rate than whites. They were becoming more assertive and cohesive as a group in demanding their rights. Black violence was not such a problem. Violence, especially when accompanied by the morally superior, "good cop" posture of Martin Luther King's nonviolent Civil Rights movement, had much appeal for these '60s liberals. Such was the social and cultural environment in which political liberals, predisposed to doublecross their supporters, prepared for the future. The odd man out was white America.

After President Kennedy's death, the new President, Lyndon B. Johnson, became a champion of legislation to advance black people's interests. The Civil Rights Act of 1964 banned discrimination in public accommodations and in the work place, creating the Equal Employment Opportunity Commission to enforce the measures. A sponsor, Senator Hubert H. Humphrey, dismissed fears that this law would create racial quotas. He promised to eat the pages of the civil-rights bill "one after another" if that ever happened. Yet, before long, the federal bureaucracy was beginning to pressure employers to adopt racial quotas in the guise of goals and timetables. Affirmative action replaced colorblind treatment. In 1968, the Small Business Administration began to award grants and low-income loans targeted to "socially disadvantaged" - i.e., black - persons.

An agency at the U.S. Department of Labor devised the "Philadelphia Plan" to ensure that federal contractors hired minorities according to their share of the population. While this plan was abandoned under public pressure, Richard Nixon revived it a year later when his Labor Department issued Order

Number Four requiring federal contractors to submit goals and timetables for minority hiring. Soon, the EEOC was requiring all private businesses to do this. Evidently, Nixon thought he could win support from black voters by adopting such measures. Thus, racial preferences favoring blacks and disfavoring whites became law through administrative action. This system of "double treatment under the law" has survived a number of court challenges.

In 1965, the U.S. Congress also passed the "Immigration and Naturalization Act" which replaced quotas based on national origin (mirroring the current population) with a system giving preference to would-be immigrants on the basis of occupation or family connections. Senator Edward Kennedy was its chief sponsor. The immigration reformers, concerned that the old quotas were "racist", nevertheless assured the public that the change in the law would not result in greatly increased numbers of new immigrants or change their composition by country of origin. They were wrong on both scores. The 1965 law capped annual immigration at 290,000 but, in 1985, 570,000 immigrants legally entered the country. The new immigrants were disproportionately from the Third World.

What had happened was that, once new people entered the country as professionals or politically persecuted refugees and acquired permanent-residency status, they were able to obtain visas for their spouses, children, brothers and sisters to enter the country. Numerous others found that they could enter the United States illegally and stay on for an indefinite period due to lax enforcement of immigration policies. There was then increasing political pressure to legalize their status. The Immigration and Refugee Control Act of 1986 (a.k.a. "Simpson-Mazzoli act") tried to deal with this problem by creating a "temporary" guest worker program, offering amnesty for illegals who had lived here since 1982, and providing sanctions against employers who knowingly hired illegals. Yet, Congress also created a new office within the Justice Department to prosecute and fine employers who discriminated against 'foreign-looking" workers. Employers had to accept any two of thirty possible documents as proof of legal residency, all easily forged.

CHAPTER FIFTEEN

The Downside to Immigration

Immigration has become a major, if understated, public-policy issue. Most Americans do not want their communities to be overrun by relatively impoverished newcomers eligible for welfare, free schooling, and other expensive services. This country is blessed with a large land mass, many natural resources, much open space and natural beauty, as well as a well-developed economy, which we Americans, deservedly or not, are able to enjoy. This advantage would disappear if our nation's population soared through unrestricted immigration. On the other hand, most immigrants are honest and hard-working people who often take jobs that American natives shun. Eight million immigrants, both legal and illegal, entered the U.S. work force between 1990 and 2001 out of a total of thirteen million who entered the country.

Most Americans are themselves descendants of immigrants who ought to appreciate the plight of others now in that situation. (As a point of personal disclosure, I have myself recently brought a new wife and stepdaughter into this country, taking advantage of our nation's immigration policies.) I would feel embarrassed to look a newly arrived immigrant in the eye and tell him that he has no right to be here. We are all human beings. It is certainly not the immigrant's fault if he took advantage of laws which others have enacted to better his personal situation. It is, however, a legitimate question of policy to review a system which seems to be out of control. The high volume of illegal immigration gives cause for concern if only because it shows disrespect for our laws and our community.

Someone told me that Lutheran Social Services was sponsoring more than one hundred AIDS-infected immigrants from a Third World country to come to the United States and receive treatment at the Hennepin County Medical Center at an average cost of perhaps $150,000. As a Twin Cities resident who has lived and worked here for a long time, I resented the fact that newcomers who had not previously paid taxes could receive expensive medical services courtesy of Hennepin County taxpayers while those of us locals who lost our jobs could not afford this. How can someone make such a decision sticking someone else with the cost? Where was the justice in such policies?

A newspaper story in October, 2002, reported that, when the Mayor of Lewiston, Maine, wrote an open letter to the Somali community asking its members to tell relatives and friends not to move to that community because the swelling immigrant population was putting a burden on the city's limited resources, hundreds of people, mostly non-immigrants, marched to protest the mayor's insensitive request. A sign in a photograph accompanying the story says: "Love thy neighbor." It might more honestly have said: "Let someone else pay." Someone else, usually the general taxpayer, does often pay for decisions made by another. The federal government sets immigration policy. Once an immigrant enters the country, he or she is free to move to any locality and utilize the public services there.

For me, immigration becomes a problem mainly in the context of "rights" for socially disadvantaged groups. This is a legacy of the Civil Rights movement. In earlier times, new groups of people entering this country started on the bottom rung of the social ladder. These newly arrived persons worked in low-wage

jobs, were verbally abused, and taken advantage of in various ways. One after another, the Irish, Germans, Italians, Poles, Russian Jews, and other immigrant groups worked their way up into the middle class. In contrast, today's immigrants soon pick up on the fact that their situation translates into politically recognized and encouraged victimhood. They have rights which can be played to their advantage. As recognized victims, they enjoy special legal protections. Just as some blacks use "racial discrimination" as an excuse for personal bad behavior, so some immigrants use the moral and legal options available to them to demand special treatment.

When federal law-enforcement officials arrested former St. Paul resident Abel Ilah Elmardoudi and three others in Detroit for allegedly operating an Al-Qaeda cell, this action "prompted vocal protests from leaders of Detroit's Middle Eastern community," according to a news report. The imam of a mosque in Dearborn Heights, Mich., said: "There is a feeling in our community of being a victim, which is a painful experience after September 11." He knew what political buttons to push.

Mortimer B. Zuckerman, editor-in-chief of *U.S. News & World Report*, published an editorial, "Our Rainbow Underclass", which noted differences in the experience of immigrants between this and earlier times. "What is disturbing," he wrote, "is that the longer these new immigrants stay in the country the worse they do, reversing the history of upward mobility in previous waves of immigration. Why? Traditionally, there were well-paid manufacturing jobs for immigrants ... Those days are gone ... The original European newcomers could also send their children to high-quality urban schools. Assimilation was swift ... There was no linguistic minority to dominate any large city the way Spanish speakers now dominate Miami and Los Angeles."

In contrast, he wrote, the children of today's immigrants "form a rainbow underclass, caught in a cycle of downward assimilation, poverty combined with racial segregation. Often separated for long periods from their parents, especially their fathers, during the immigration process, they stop doing homework, reject their parents' values, and succumb to the dangers of an overcrowded inner-city culture. They face overwhelmed teachers, limited social service resources, and a decaying infrastructure, and they often adopt the negative behavior pattern of their peer groups, such as academic indifference and substance abuse, leading to dropout rates three times as high as for native-born Americans. Even the stellar performance of Asian children declines - studies show that by the third generation, Chinese students no longer exceed whites in educational success."

On the morning of Tuesday, September 11, 2001, Mohammed Atta and four companions arrived at Boston's Logan airport and paid cash for one-way tickets for a flight to Los Angeles. They carried knives and box cutters. Airport security raised no objections. Both in 1999 and 2000, Arab-Americans who had been kept off flights had sued the airlines for "racial profiling". Some believe that legal fears may have prompted security personnel at Logan to overlook such an obvious risk.

Three weeks earlier, Zacarias Moussaoui was arrested for suspicious behavior at a flight school in Eagan, Minnesota. French intelligence had told U.S. officials that this French-Algerian immigrant was a suspected terrorist. Yet, when the Minneapolis FBI requested permission to search Moussaoui's computer, lawyers at FBI headquarters repeatedly refused, fearing to breach intelligence guidelines imposed by the Clinton Administration. The political question arising from the terrorist attacks is whether concerns about group profiling trump the need for security, as they normally do in domestic politics, or the September 11th attacks elevate security requirements above them.

One of my first acts as a candidate for U.S. Senate in the Independence Party primary was to send a faxed memo to Twin Cities media in which I expressed support for Minnesota Public Safety Commissioner Charlie Weaver's new rules for issuing drivers licenses. These rules required that first-time applicants present two forms of identification (including a passport or U.S. birth certificate), that licenses of temporary foreign visitors indicate the expiration date of their visas, and that the licenses bear a full-face photograph of the applicant without exception.

The Minnesota Civil Liberties Union, Arab Anti-Defamation League, Jewish Community Relation Council, and thirty individuals petitioned the Minnesota Court of Appeals to overturn those rules. These groups argued that requiring full-faced photographs would violate the privacy and religious freedoms of Somali women and that putting visa expiration dates on drivers licenses would stigmatize certain immigrant groups. Weaver argued that drivers licenses are used for general identification purposes and criminals often obtain them fraudulently. The measures which he proposed were needed to strengthen internal security, he said. Since I was considered a minor candidate, the media ignored my statement. Interestingly, the Republican candidate for Governor, now Governor, Tim Pawlenty, supported the rules changes in a late October blitz of television commercials. He started rising in the polls about that time.

So it does seem, at least among the general public, that some of the old political phobias are losing their punch. For sure, no one wants to go back to the bad old days of World War I, when German-Americans were openly persecuted, or of World War II when Japanese-Americans were relocated to internment camps (except for one young man of Japanese descent whom my parents took in as a lodger in our Detroit home). On the other hand, more should be expected from today's immigrants than complaints of prejudice.

John Leo of *U.S. News & World Report* has observed that "there is a downside in the nation's overwhelmingly positive treatment of Muslim Americans. Perhaps out of guilt over treatment of Japanese-Americans during World War II, the

United States and its media have framed attitudes toward our Muslim citizens almost wholly in terms of hypertolerance and bias, rarely in terms of what allegiance a minority owes the rest of the nation in time of peril. The press relentlessly churned out articles about the alleged backlash against Muslim Americans and has continued that effort long after it was obvious no such backlash existed." Marc Fisher of the *Washington Post* wrote that an eighth grader at the Muslim Community School in Potomac, Maryland, had told him: "Being an American means nothing to me. I'm not even proud of telling my cousins in Pakistan that I'm American."

We (nonimmigrant Americans) are not patsies. Others may think that we are when immigration policies are so loose or when our political leaders and media people are continually blaming nonimmigrant white Americans for their hateful ways. Do we think so badly of ourselves that we will put up with that kind of talk without objection?

Jewish groups who focus on the horrors of the holocaust in Europe and on anti-Semitism everywhere in the western world should show a bit more gratitude for the predominantly non-Jewish soldiers who stormed the beaches of Normandy and liberated their coreligionists from Nazi concentration camps, albeit not soon enough. Some now have the gall to join a lawsuit trying to overturn reasonable security measures intended to protect Americans against Islamic terrorists who blame America primarily for supporting Israel (due to domestic political pressure from Jewish interest groups). Have they no shame?

And black Americans, even though their ancestors were brought to this continent unwillingly as slaves, should have some sense of gratitude that predominantly white abolitionists pointed out the moral shortcomings of the race-based slave system and that hundreds of thousands of mainly white Union soldiers lost their lives so that their enslaved ancestors might go free. A bit more sympathy from them for persons of other races might not be such a bad thing. And those of us who are left could perhaps show a little more backbone when faced with that type of relentless, ungenerous complaint.

CHAPTER SIXTEEN

About Lawyers and Politicians

I may be accused of hating black people and immigrants if I continue to express this kind of opinion. Let me say in defense that, for the most part, nonimmigrant white professionals are my problem. The presumably downtrodden immigrants and blacks are pawns in a game played for profit by these professionals; for it's an American tradition to use others as a front while seeking to advance one's personal interest. To whom do I refer? First we have the Democratic party, working hard to capture votes from these groups by expressing grievances on their behalf. Second we have lawyers, also interested in grievances, but, in this case, focusing on complaints that can be brought to court.

I am the type of person against whom grievances are brought. It is not that I am personally predisposed to cause injury to another; rather, the grievances stem from the nature I received at birth and the nature of my occupation. Politicians will be interested in the fact that I am a white male who can be lambasted for failings of his group and then outvoted. Lawyers will find profit in the fact that I am an inner-city landlord. Deep-pockets justice puts their dinner on the table.

With respect to African Americans, Bill Clinton has shown that a friendly nod and a wink can win their votes, regardless of policies. All you have to do is play the game of racial victimhood. An oppressed class, however, requires an oppressor; and that's where my type fits in. In theory, we know that people should be treated on the basis of the content of their character and not their skin color. Individuals, not groups, are judged under the law. But if there are good and bad people in any group, only certain types of people can be called "racist" according to the prevalent interpretation of that word. Black people with the same attitudes and behaviors as racist whites are not "racist" because, by definition, they cannot be. The politically correct definition of racism is "prejudice plus power", not prejudice alone. The argument is made that, because whites are the majority population and hold most leadership positions, only whites can have power. Therefore, only whites can be racist.

A problem with this argument is that the most "racist" elements within white society tend to be people without power. The Civil Rights movement was directed mainly against poor rural populations in the nation's poorest section, the South. The rich educated classes favored racial integration to a much greater degree. Indeed, "racism" became such a pejorative term precisely because it contained the idea of being lower class. One-sided definitions of racism are self-serving and specious as political talk generally tends to be.

Immigrant populations have always been grist for the political grinders who sometimes do them favors but always want votes. The life of immigrants has traditionally been tough. They are vulnerable to economic exploitation. If it were not so, the business class would not actively support loose immigration. In past generations, immigrant groups have applied themselves to their new situation, worked hard, and thrived. They expected and received few excuses for failure. The problem today is that politicians of the Democratic persuasion have added immigrants to the list of officially victimized groups. There is welfare available for indigent persons among them where, in previous generations, there was not. Certain ones among the immigrants quickly pick up on the fact that they have political leverage which others may not have.

As the discipline of a hard life is relaxed, attitudes become cocky, even cynical. (A friend sent me a scurrilous poem from the Internet which captures a sense of this mood. It is reprinted in Appendix G.) America seems to be a place where anything goes. Bad behavior is treated almost the same way as good behavior. In that environment, group morals tend to degenerate. It would be easy, in that case, to point the finger at the immigrants and their children when they are associated with criminal acts or delinquencies. I would argue that the fault, instead, lies with the politicians and lawyers. They are the ones who created the situation.

The most difficult case is Islamic terrorism. Immigrants admitted legally into the United States committed the worst acts of violence in our history when they carried out those September 11th attacks. What should be the community's response to the attacks? A renewed commitment to maintaining the civil liberties of Arab-Americans? I don't think so. Profuse statements about the glories of the Islamic religion? I am suspicious of the fact that it took the terrorist attacks for people to discover the many good things about Islam. Like any self-respecting nation, we Americans must take the necessary steps to protect ourselves from further violence. That is government's first priority. When violent attacks are made upon our people, we should expect all citizens and residents of the United States to condemn the attacks with a clear voice.

Immigrants owe a certain amount of loyalty to a nation which gave them shelter. Some reports indicate that the response from the Arab-American and Islamic communities has fallen short of that mark. A retired CIA official told the *New Yorker* magazine that members of the U.S. intelligence community believe that these groups have sheltered terrorists instead of reporting them to authorities. Our national leaders need to use their political capital to put effective security measures in place even if this means transgressing political norms that have prevailed since the Civil Rights era.

Having said that, I also believe that incompetence on the part of U.S. intelligence, immigration, and security officials was largely responsible for the success of the September 11th attacks. When the INS sends Mohamed Atta and Marwan Al-Shehhi final approval of their student visas six months *after* they piloted aircraft into the World Trade Center, one suspects that there's more to security problems than meets the eye. Before our government makes sweeping changes in the name of fighting terrorism, it needs to assure the public that the fundamentals of sound national security have been met. Otherwise, all this governmental sound and fury could be a smoke screen to cover their own failings.

It may well be that many individuals of Middle Eastern descent have been improperly arrested and detained. The case of prisoners held in legal limbo, without access to lawyers or specific charges brought against them, seems obviously to reflect questionable policies. I also doubt the justice of seeking the death penalty for Zacarias Moussaoui when his crime was *wanting* to commit terroristic acts. It makes little sense to put student visas

from China on hold for an indefinite period in order to fight terrorism. Instead, we need such things as government computers that can talk with each other, intelligence agents and police who talk with immigration officials, and an end to the "visa express" system in Saudi Arabia.

Perhaps the most egregious "security measure" is the Bush Administration's proposal to go to war with Iraq. Wars, even if effective, kill many innocent people. International terrorism is a problem for the international political community rather than for a single national government, albeit a military superpower.

As a landlord, I have employed Mexican roofers who did quality work. I have had Mexican, Somali, Hmong, and other immigrant tenants who have paid their rent on time and not caused damage to the property. Day in and day out, hard-working business people of Middle Eastern descent operate small shops in my neighborhood. I have made a reasonably good living from renting apartments to a predominantly African-American clientele. The African-American caretaker has done a good job of making needed repairs and keeping the place clean. Without help from people of different races and nationalities, I would not still be in business.

So why am I making an issue of immigrants or the African American community? It is because the politics of immigration and race are amiss. There is a disconnect between race relations as I personally know them and what I read in the newspaper. My inner-city neighborhood is not seething with racial animosities, not to my knowledge at least. Enter lawyers and the picture changes dramatically. There must be discrimination in our community because that gives lawyers an opportunity to ply their trade. There must be social injustice for the politicians to fix. Society must be structured to give these people a role.

As a landlord, I sometimes feel that I am surrounded by sharks waiting for me to make a wrong move. On KMOJ, the local African-American radio station, I heard several public-service announcements which let people know that there are almost a dozen ways that landlords can illegally discriminate against tenants. The Urban League has a hot line for tenants to report problems and learn possible legal remedies. Vanessa Williams, too, has a recorded message about this. I have heard of social-service agencies that conduct sting operations against landlords who might be engaging in racial discrimination. If you have an apartment vacancy, they will send two teams of persons posing as prospective applicants, one white and the other black, to see if you treat them differently. If you make the wrong choice, you wind up in court. A landlord friend tells the story of an applicant with an arrest on his record whom he sent downtown for a document relating to its disposition in court. An employee at City Hall told this man he had a discrimination case against my friend - presumably, discrimination against persons who had served their sentence for a crime. Fortunately, the applicant did not pursue the complaint.

In 1997, however, a Minneapolis jury awarded an African American tenant $490,181 because the white landlord had exhibited four different types of discrimination - race, gender, disability, and public-assistance status - against her and her children. Allegedly, he had used the "n-word". The landlord, whom I interviewed, denied saying this word. The tenant had claimed that the furnace was not working but would not let anyone into her unit to fix it. When, after knocking, the landlord entered this apartment to check the thermostat at the furnace repairman's request, the tenant claimed that he was peeking at her in the bathroom. She shopped around for an attorney until she found someone willing to work that angle. Financially put threw the wringer, this landlord is now dead. The tenant used the proceeds of her settlement to buy a house and new furniture. The plaintiff's attorney used her court victory as a springboard to run for the state legislature as a DFL-endorsed candidate.

There is an industry of legal-aid and other attorneys who specialize in housing discrimination cases. While this is considered bottom-feeding for the large law firms in town, they do sometimes assign their new employees to such cases to gain trial experience. (Even if the work is done pro bono, these firms can collect fees if they win.) The legal-aid attorneys are entrepreneurs of the law, seeking to develop new angles to prove discrimination.

I once attended a legal workshop to learn how these people operate. The presenter was discussing cases of discrimination against Somali tenants. I always assumed that if a landlord had fewer Somali tenants than their share of the population, he might be vulnerable to discrimination lawsuits. At this workshop, I learned that the landlord could also be vulnerable if the percentage of Somali tenants exceeded their share of the population, the theory being that Somali immigrants are persons who may not know their legal rights and landlords would naturally want to rent to them to take advantage of their ignorance. The problem was proving such a case. The presenter had devised an esoteric set of arguments to pursue discrimination cases under such circumstances involving a concept called “disparate treatment”. I asked the presenter if Somalis actually did face this type of discrimination in Minneapolis. His response showed that he considered it more a professional challenge than anything else.

Another insight into emerging legal strategies came at a conference held at the William Mitchell School of Law in March 2001. A physically attractive young woman with spiked blonde hair, horned-rim glasses, and a black leather miniskirt, who headed a project for Hennepin County Legal Aid, lectured conference participants on how to sue landlords for sexual harassment. She prefaced her remarks by observing that the typical landlord was a white-male entrepreneur out to rape his tenants, especially minority women. At first, I thought that this was the type of sexual harassment which she proposed to combat. More important than landlord-tenant harassment, though, were cases of one tenant harassing another. As employers are held liable when employees harass each other at the work place, so landlords might be held legally responsible for allowing an environment to develop in their buildings in which tenants felt sexually pressured or embarrassed. I could feel interest building up in the room when she went on to mention the $250,000 jury awards which attorneys in Ohio had recently won pursuing this type of case. Afterwards, a swarm of young lawyers crowded around the presenter seeking further details.

Lawyers and neighborhood groups persuaded Minnesota state legislators to pass a law which allows neighborhood organizations to petition courts to take over management of buildings whose owners have neglected maintenance, thereby gaining access to the owner's checkbook to the extent of his equity in the property. The Statute is numbered Section 504. A young white-male attorney named Greg Luce teamed up with a female social worker who worked in the Somali community to form "Project 504", a legal machine to apply the state statute to Minneapolis rental properties with special attention to Somali immigrants. Luce recruited law students to work for free while gaining work experience from his projects. The landlords, of course, had to match those efforts by hiring other attorneys unless they had personal expertise in the law.

The landlord from whom I bought my apartment building had bought another building on Park Avenue, the site of Ann Prazniak's murder, which now housed primarily Somali tenants. This landlord believed that attorney Luce was leafleting this building to suggest that he could get tenants several months of free or reduced rent if they had maintenance problems. At another nearby building to which the 504 law had already been applied, Luce reportedly entered the building with a male infant strapped to his chest. Angry work crews at the site believed he was interfering with their work, interpreting the strapped-in baby as a human shield. The *Star Tribune* did a story on Greg Luce and his partner, depicting them as gritty idealists. In October, 2001, Project 504 received a "nonprofit innovation award" from the Minnesota Council of Nonprofits for its many contributions to the cause.

I view this situation in ecological terms. Lawyers individually serve a useful function. Theirs is not, however, a productive function. Like wolves, they are predators on other occupations. Public policy should be concerned with the balance of population between the wolf packs and herds of prey. Minnesota has a population of 22,000 attorneys, twice as many as in 1980. Even so, the University of St. Thomas has established a new law school, located in downtown Minneapolis, which plans to stress "service to the poor" - read, suing people like me. In the meanwhile, the city of Minneapolis has lost thousands of rental-housing units. A thickening pack of lawyers thus seeks to make a living off a dwindling stock of landlords, especially those at the low end of the rent scale.

The irony is that federal Fair Housing laws are probably unconstitutional. Congress wrote this legislation on the basis of its power to "regulate foreign and interstate commerce". If there is one commodity which seldom crosses state or national borders, it would be housing. But constitutional foundations are endlessly elastic in today's legal environment. I would question

whether the productive economy should be turned into lunch meat to feed litigious attorneys or society itself be reconfigured to become more congenial to the interests of the Democratic party. I would also question whether employment in our community should be conditioned upon undergoing political indoctrination in the form of diversity-training workshops. In Minnesota, the supreme court now requires that attorneys take such courses as a prerequisite for practicing law in the state.

As a landlord, I see cases of tenants, behind on their rent, who make promises of payment when certain monies are received. More than a few refer to lawsuits won or expected to be won. It seems to me that young African Americans, in particular, have the idea that their path to prosperity lies in filing and winning lawsuits rather than working in a career. Is this helpful? From their personal standpoint, perhaps it is. From the community's standpoint, however, this is an extension of the casino mentality of getting something for nothing. I believe that, if the economy will not otherwise provide enough good-paying jobs for honest work, a policy of shorter work hours could bring those jobs to African Americans and others currently excluded.

As for the lawsuit mentality, this could be stopped quite simply by putting caps on permissible jury awards and attorney fees for certain types of cases. How about asking the Minnesota legislature to set an absolute dollar limit of, say, $25,000 per person (including attorney fees) on all court settlements of cases relating to discrimination or sexual harassment? Without costing the taxpayers anything, such legislation would immediately improve Minnesota's business climate and attract many new businesses with jobs that might divert our lawsuit-hungry population. I'm afraid, however, that because it would affect the number of lawyers doing business in the state and because the Democrats depend on financial support from trial lawyers, my suggestion is politically impractical.

Making of

a Political Heretic

CHAPTER SEVENTEEN

The Gender Chip on my Shoulder

As a boy growing up in Detroit, I was aware of gender and racial issues but they hardly affected me. My family lived in a white enclave on the east side of Detroit called "Indian Village". It was surrounded by less prosperous neighborhoods where the blacks lived. After attending public school in my Detroit neighborhood, my parents arranged in 1951 to send my brother Andy and me to a private school in Grosse Pointe. It was an all-boys school until my last year. Then my family moved to the northern suburb of Bloomfield Hills, again largely white. I spent 10th grade in the public high school and finished the last two years at Cranbrook, a boy's prep school. My schoolmates and companions during these years were mostly white although some blacks attended the neighborhood elementary school and, on a token basis, Cranbrook. Some conservative friends expressed concern that my family might sell the house on Seminole Avenue to blacks when we moved from Detroit. They did not, although the house was later bought by a black family. I also re-

member doing a writing assignment in my 10th grade social studies class about "prejudice". My mother took me and some friends downtown to hear a talk by Jackie Robinson on race relations, which was starting to be an important political issue. We were more interested in Robinson's baseball career.

In the fall of 1958, I entered college at Yale University in New Haven, Connecticut, then an all-male college. Here and at the Telluride House at Cornell, which I almost attended, I became exposed to Civil Rights fervor. I listened to the East Coast students, many of them Jewish, talk passionately about race relations. The Yale chaplain, William Sloane Coffin, was one of the northern "Freedom Riders" who lent their name and support to southern desegregation efforts. Martin Luther King, Malcolm X, and other Civil Rights luminaries visited the Yale campus. While trying out for the *Yale Daily News*, I remember covering an incident at the Yale Law School. A pair of young men from New York City who claimed to be white racists were surrounded by angry law students who were shouting at them. I tried to take notes to record what the racists were saying. One of them complimented me for being willing to listen. On the whole, I was suspicious of the desegregation agenda, though not with any conviction, because of the blanket accusations against white people. I thought this might be a problem for me somewhere down the line. But still I had no firm opinions about race. I had little contact with the South.

After graduating from Yale and attending Rutgers business school in Newark, New Jersey, for two semesters, I moved to the Twin Cities in January, 1965. I wished to live in the Midwest but not necessarily in Detroit, which would be following too much in my parents' footsteps. Minnesota had a relatively low minority population and a liberal political culture centering in Senator Hubert Humphrey. I visited my old Detroit neighborhood after the 1968 race riots. Parts of the east side had burned. A friend of my father expressed anti-black sentiments and some sympathy for George Wallace. When I raised a few mild objections, he called me naive, suggesting that white Minnesotans had little idea of what was happening racially. While parts of Minneapolis had also burned the year before, I lived in another area of the Twin Cities. I was indeed inexperienced with respect to race relations. I was also unsure of myself around women. I was pretty much a loner, pursuing ideas and a writing career which at that point led nowhere. But it was also a life of reasonable contentment.

I married for the first time in the summer of 1973 and stayed married for ten years. The '70s were a time when feminist ideologies were building up steam. The White Bear Unitarian Church, where I served as president of the congregation for one year, had an active feminist contingent which put on programs that ruffled male sensibilities including mine. As congregation president, I also had to deal with conflicts arising from our gay minister's theatrical use of his position to promote personal causes. When I lost my job of six years, my wife grew antagonistic, accusing me of not trying hard enough. This was partially true; I did have other interests.

Our divorce, stretched out over four years, was an eye opener for me. The feminist revolution of the past decade had had its effect on legal and police bureaucracies. When my wife locked the door as I was trying to remove my personal belongings from our home, the Ramsey County Sheriff's deputy summoned to the house told me that my wife could make me "eat off paper plates" if she chose to do so. The judge in our divorce case, the Hon. Roland Faricy, was a total jerk. He was openly sarcastic towards me in the courtroom and assigned my wife the bulk of our marital assets while assigning me the debts. I successfully appealed to the Minnesota Court of Appeals which remanded the case back to Judge Faricy. After dithering for six months, Faricy issued another ruling which ignored the appellate court's instructions. My wife and I came to terms after I filed in the appellate court for the second time.

In little ways, too, I saw bureaucrats empathizing with women while "throwing the book" at men. When our last joint income-tax return was audited by the IRS, for instance, I remember the female agent excusing my wife's complete lack of documentation for her deductions and then glaring at me and saying, "I want to see this, and this, and this", for a deduction that I took. Or maybe I was being overly sensitive about gender-equity issues at that point.

I connected with Rich Doyle of the Men's Rights Association, which helps men with divorce, and wrote a few articles for his newsletter. Doyle and I attended one of the public meetings of the Minnesota Supreme Court's "Task Force on Gender Fairness in the Courts." It was obvious that this committee was following a preconceived agenda hostile to men. I pointed this out in an opinion article published by the *St. Paul Pioneer Press*. The task force, I concluded, "seemed to have a gender fairness problem of its own." I dated sporadically. But mostly I tended to my new day job as cost accountant at the Metropolitan Transit Commission while pursuing writing projects in the evenings and on weekends.

I am rather conservative both in employment and dating. Even long after it became clear that my MTC job was going nowhere, I clung to employment there. I am uncomfortable in bars, never having mastered the arts of small talk. Maybe that is because, having buried myself for a long time in narrow personal interests, I feel I lack the common experiences that other people have. Occasionally, though not often, I have placed a personals ad in the newspaper hoping to meet that special person. Those encounters never worked out for me. I remember having coffee and pastries with a rather attractive professional woman who asked me to say a little about myself. I told her about my accounting job and about my

real interest which lay in writing. After a few minutes of this, she interrupted me to say, "In fifteen years, I think you will be a retired accountant."

While living on the east side of St. Paul after the divorce, I took the bus to my job. The bus company was also my employer. A smiling young black woman boarded the bus at the same stop. We talked several times, both on and off the bus. Summoning my courage, I knocked on her door around the block from mine to ask if she would go to the Minnesota State Fair with me. She declined because of an impending trip to San Francisco. A month later, there was a knock on my door. It seemed that she and her girl friend were being evicted for nonpayment of rent. Could she stay with me for a short time? I agreed. I had a spare room in my living quarters on the second floor of a house rented from my friend, Harvey Hyatt. This young woman, named Linda, said she was a lesbian. Linda had come to the Twin Cities from St. Louis because she wanted to be part of the music scene centering on Prince and because her mother lived here.

Linda and I had many interesting discussions. She told me all about gay life from a lesbian's point of view. She introduced me to the music of the day including singers like Whitney Houston and the Pointer Sisters. She herself aspired to be a singer, having won an amateur talent contest at First Avenue. I accompanied her to a "job interview" where a cocaine-snorting manager offered her a job if she would sleep with him. One evening, Linda took me on a tour of the gay and lesbian bars. I posed as a gay man. Linda dressed me up in suitable clothing and put a special wave in my hair which homosexuals would recognize. As an attractive young black woman, she was lionized at such places where I, the shy man, was happy to be tagging along. The best night was when Linda decided that she was no longer entirely a lesbian. She wanted me. We lived for the next several weeks as a satisfied couple. But winter was approaching, and Linda could not stand the cold apartment. Harvey heated the house with a wood-burning stove.

During the afternoon before Thanksgiving, Linda and I discussed the meal that we would have together. She would prepare it. I would purchase the ingredients. There was tension involving Linda's lesbian friend. We had an argument. She slapped my face. I slapped her back. She was indignant that I would do this, telling me that I should "be a man" like John Wayne, who had taken a woman's on-screen slap in the face. We argued some more. Linda grabbed a kitchen knife and chased me around the room. Just when I thought I had her calmed down, she called the police to report domestic abuse. The St. Paul police officer arrived. When he asked what had happened, I referred the question to Linda. There were no signs of bodily injury or even a scuffle. The officer seemed disinclined to believe anything had happened. I maintained silence the entire time.

Then Linda accused the officer of ignoring an assault victim. The officer thought it over for a moment and slapped the handcuffs on me. He drove me to the St. Paul police headquarters which had jail cells on the second floor. I spent the next thirty hours - Thanksgiving Day, 1985 - locked up in that jail, staring out the window at the red "Taystee" bakery neon sign across the freeway. I was released on bail thanks to a cell mate whose family had contacted a bondsman. Linda was not at home when I returned. She reappeared several days later. We packed her bags and she moved back to St. Louis.

I should have had the sense to take my licking in silence. Instead, I interpreted this event in terms of men's rights. That is because I had read in the newspaper that a national police institute had reported a study which found that rates of domestic abuse dropped significantly if police had a policy of automatically arresting the man when a woman complained of domestic abuse. Minneapolis police chief Tony Bouza was a champion of this policy. That, evidently, was what had happened to me. Was this fair? Was it even legal? Of course not. I called the St. Paul human-rights department to complain of discrimination against men. The representative referred me to the state human-rights department, saying that his agency was prevented from pursuing a complaint against the city. The state agency did take my complaint but then sent me a letter with the argument that two conflicting state laws precluded its acting in this matter. Meanwhile, the city attorney declined to prosecute the case against me because the "victim" was unavailable to testify.

Despite what had happened, I remained on friendly terms with Linda. In St. Louis and later in Denver, Colorado, she gained some attention as an actress. She became a sexual superstar, snagging a championship golfer, a former Presidential candidate, and several NFL head coaches. A Republican, she also became a casual acquaintance of the Bush family. Before Monica Lewinsky, she was a White House intern; but when she complained of sexual harassment, she was quietly transferred to the office of Colorado's Republican Senator. I was on the phone with Linda when the news about Clarence Thomas broke. She had just met him.

Linda has since graduated from college and from grad school, married, and started a computer business. I have seen her one time since her departure and, as a result of attending a party at Paisley Park as her guest, met Prince. She also signed a letter recanting her accusations on the police report. But I remember Linda mostly for her spunk. Once, after she broke up with a white guy in Colorado, she told me that she called the local chapter of the Ku Klux Klan to pass along information that this man had been dating a black.

I continued to have a chip on my shoulder about anti-male bias. I wrote a letter to the director of the First Bank System foundation complaining of a feminist conference that it had funded. When his response did not satisfy, I bought First Bank System stock intending to make a statement at the next stockholder's meeting. The foundation director meanwhile was let go. Because I bought low, I made a good profit on the stock purchase. It helped to fund expenses related to my apartment.

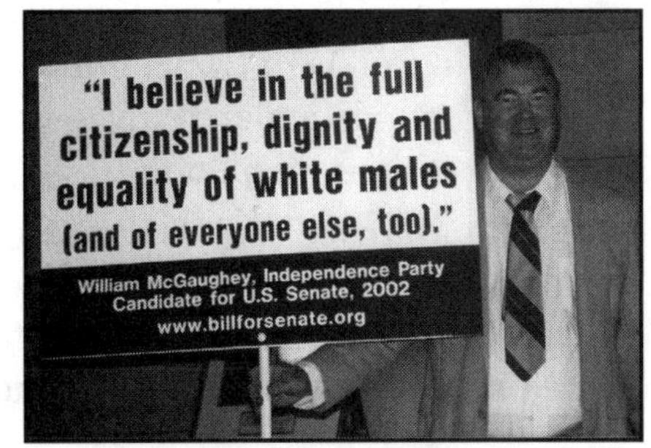
"I believe in the full citizenship, dignity and equality of white males (and of everyone else, too)."
William McGaughey, Independence Party Candidate for U.S. Senate, 2002
www.billforsenate.org

Rich Doyle asked me to talk to a reporter from the *Star Tribune* who was doing a story on groups supporting men. I was quoted in a single sentence. Because the quotation was inaccurate, I wrote a short letter to the editor calling attention to that fact. Lou Gelfand, the newspaper's Reader Representative, intercepted the letter. He suggested that I run my complaint through his department, promising me some say in stating my position. When he reneged on the promise, I took the *Star Tribune* to the Minnesota News Council. Learning that two other persons who were quoted in the article also believed they were misrepresented, I told the News Council I would present our complaints together. On the day of the hearing, the others' cases were dismissed because they were not present. My own typed statement was not photocopied beyond the first page. The committee unanimously rejected my complaint. I could tell from the discussion that political correctness was a strong influence within the journalistic community.

This experience opened my eyes to bias in the news media. Since the *Star Tribune* had made it an issue of my word against the reporter's (who, of course, had proof), I requested that the News Council compel production of the reporter's notes. That request went nowhere. I pointed out at the hearing that the reporter had used a journalistic trick to discredit the men's rights advocates. Several times it had stated that these advocates (leading with their emotions) "believed" or "felt" something when, in the next clause, it would cite a study that supported the opposite position. I knew that one of my co-plaintiffs had sent the reporter a study to document his statement that almost as many men were battered by women as women by men. Why did you not mention that study in your article, I asked? The managing editor said in response that the study was so obviously false that his newspaper would be "laughed out of town" if it gave credibility to such nonsense. I had the satisfaction several months later of reading an article in the *New York Times* on the same subject which did mention that particular study. I sent a copy to the *Star Tribune* editor. He did not respond.

The Metropolitan Transit Commission, like most corporate employers, aggressively pursued affirmative-action policies and promoted stereotypes unflattering to men in posters for United Way or Women's History month. Whispered news about my arrest for domestic violence spread around the agency. The first and only time that I have appeared on a program on commercial television, the interviewer, referring to my arrest, began by asking me to tell about how I had beaten up my wife. I became a gender complainer. I filed a complaint against my employer for sexual harassment under the alternative definition that the anti-male posters created a "hostile work environment". It was rejected, of course. Many of my male coworkers privately agreed with me but dared not take my side.

These gripes plus the fact that I was taking part in a union drive (hoping thereby to acquire some power to fight back against my increasing marginalization at the agency) doomed my accounting career. For three or four years, I was under the continual threat of being fired for poor work performance. Finally, in 1996, I was laid off, or maybe retired, when the Commission was merged with the Metropolitan Council. This was three weeks before I would have become eligible under the agency's severance package to have my health-insurance coverage extended until age 65.

For the last five or more years, my attention has turned away from issues of gender fairness. I joined a singing group organized by Robert Bly, thinking that he might champion the men's rights cause. However, Bly and his associates are into personal issues rather than injustices against men. For the past ten years, the group has met weekly to chant songs and recite poetry, recreating the Sufi experience. I also remarried twice - both times to minority women. I married an African American woman with five young children in January 1995. We were divorced a year and a half later. In January 2000, I went to China to marry my current wife who has a college-age daughter. Lian has given me a stable marriage. Race relations were a submerged element in my dealings with Minneapolis city government and neighborhood groups as I grappled with problems of being an inner-city landlord. But mostly this set of concerns was put

on the back burner. I revived them when I became a candidate for U.S. Senate.

CHAPTER EIGHTEEN

Coming out of the Racial Wilderness

Not long ago, David Letterman interviewed NBC news anchor, Tom Brokaw, on the Late Night Show. Brokaw told of his experiences as a white boy growing up in South Dakota. By coincidence, he had graduated from high school in 1958 and from college in 1962. I also graduated from high school in that year and would have graduated from college in 1962 had I not dropped out for two years. So my ears perked up to hear what my contemporary had to say. Brokaw described the period of his youth as "idyllic" for a white male such as himself. He had made a few mistakes as a young man, but the community took him under its wing and gave him a second chance. Having dropped out of college, a professor agreed to take him back after he got the wildness out of his system. Brokaw acknowledged that for women and minorities, of course, this period might not have been so supportive.

I related to this because, like Brokaw, I came from a personally nurturing environment. This earlier part of my life is compartmentalized from what my life has become since I moved to Minnesota. It's almost a past-life experience. I came from a life of privilege in Detroit and at Yale, where great things were ex-

"I believe in the full
citizenship, dignity and
equality of white males
(and of everyone else, too)."
William McGaughey, Independence Party
Candidate for U.S. Senate, 2002
www.billforsenate.org

pected of me, and by my own choice moved to a place where I was a stranger. A few kindly souls are to be found here, of course, but, by and large, it is a place of interpersonal coldness, political correctness, and submerged rage. We call this "Minnesota nice".

While I was holding up my sign near the State Fairgrounds that called for "full citizenship, dignity, and equality for white males", a woman who was passing by remarked disapprovingly: "White males are doing OK." I would agree with that assessment. It would be ludicrous to portray white males as a victimized class in the conventional sense. White males do hold most of the top economic and political positions in our society. Was I advocating a reverse quota system to try to make the concentration of them even greater? I am not quite that much an ideological fool. It was difficult to get across the point of my campaign in a few simple words.

White males do, I believe, suffer from a certain social and cultural disadvantage. There is a stigma attached to them as a group. There is an undercurrent of resentment and hate. These hostile currents in our culture do not affect the powerful white males as much as persons in subservient, marginal positions. This leads to another point: The hate and suppression directed against white males could not be effectively expressed unless condoned, and perhaps even promoted, by those few white males at the top. The anti-white male attitude in our society becomes, in a sense, an expression of self-hatred. In my campaign for U.S. Senate, I argued that it was also something more.

My perception of this situation starts with the observation that every corporate or bureaucratic environment where I have ever worked was dominated by white males. Invariably, the top managers of those institutions were also staunch supporters of affirmative action. Were the white-male leaders taking that position out of heightened social concern? Were they socially conscious saints "bending over backwards" to be fair? I don't think so. Many of these people struck me as self-seekers. Lyndon B. Johnson and Bill Clinton, who embraced the cause of compensatory "racial justice" the most, were not the most savory individuals to become President of the United States. The assumption is that white-male leaders feel a sense of solidarity with other white males and that other white males are, therefore, openly or secretly favored. Have you heard of self-hatred? Have you heard of treachery? These words describe the situation better than simple assumptions of group solidarity. No, I take little personal comfort in the fact that the society's power elite is demographically like me.

I tried to relate this theme to the economic issues that were also the focus of my campaign, especially the need for shorter work hours. During the last forty years, when the values of the Civil Rights movement have been in the ascendancy, the situation of the average American worker has worsened. Real wages have been stagnant, average working hours have risen, and health and pension benefits are being eroded. The income gap between the richest and poorest segments of our society has widened. Private-sector unions are in decline. Money controls the political process even more than before.

Politics could bring a solution to those problems - if people were able to unite behind a particular program of reform. But the fact is that people can't unite. We are so divided as a people that we just let the incompetent, corrupt leadership slide along without a serious challenge. I think that the existing leadership benefits from that situation. They want to keep people divided by policies that tell white people that the reason they were not promoted is because some less worthy black person was slated to fill that spot. Let black and white people, men and women, fight each other over their shrinking piece of the pie while the leaders' share grows larger.

Corporate America would have us believe that leftist political and social pressures are forcing them to accept gender and racial preferences, but, the fact is, they want to keep it that way. Even when President Bush provided political cover to oppose affirmative action in the lawsuit against the University of Michigan's admission policies, a group of Fortune 500 corporations including 3M, Coca-Cola, Dow Chemical, Pfizer, Microsoft, and General Motors filed a friend-of-the-court brief in favor of continued racial preferences in higher education. It's interesting that, in addition to such words as "pipe bombs", "job offer", or "resume", many company-owned computers are programmed to trigger an alarm when an employee types in "David Duke".

During my campaign for U.S. Senate, I deliberately expressed my opinions about white-male dignity in front of black audiences. I did this, for instance, at a meeting of Minneapolis Property Rights Action Committee on Wednesday, August 14, 2002. Hennepin County Commissioner Mark Stenglein and two African American men, Shane Price and Gary Cunningham, were the featured speakers, talking about the African American Men's project. I also made a point of raising this issue and displaying my sign at a debate at Augsburg College sponsored by the Twin Cities black journalists and two other groups among the Senate candidates.

I found a surprisingly mild reaction to my message from African Americans. Newscaster Angela Davis, moderator of the debate, smiled when she first saw the sign and politely asked my name. Shane Price gave me a hug after the Property Rights meeting. Duane Reed, an African American man running for the state legislature, told me that he could understand what I was doing.

It may be that this was the African American version of "Minnesota nice" or these people were doing their Christian duty of "loving your enemies" and "turning the other cheek". But I don't think so. Maybe, as African Americans, they were free of pressures to conform to political correctness. They might have appreciated my candor. I prefer to regard it as a new, more mature model of race relations where people can say what they think and, despite their differences, deal with each other in an environment of mutual respect.

In my everyday life, I am continually dealing with many kinds of people, including African Americans. My apartment building on Glenwood Avenue has always had a predominantly African American base of tenants. We are not engaging in an avant-garde social experiment; we have a business relationship and personal relationships arising from that. We do not think of ourselves as being people of different races, not openly at least, but of individuals who are doing something together. After Linda, African Americans are no longer a novelty to me. I am not curious about what black people do or how they think.

My Chinese wife was puzzled when she heard about my campaign plank defending the "dignity of white males". After hearing of my political plans, another Chinese woman who had been involved in politics for a long time told my wife, in Chinese, that I was an odd ball and a horrible racist. My wife figured out her own response. She would sometimes say, if we disagreed about something, "But, of course, you are right; you are a white male". Then a little smirk would appear on her face. Once, during a conversation whose content I have forgotten, she called me "a white male with a red face."

In my opinion, people of all kinds can work out their differences without help from the experts. It is not necessary for elite commentators to be guiding us along in a certain direction. I'm tired of these virtuous virgins of race relations telling me what I ought to be doing or thinking about race. I live in the city, in one of its most racially diverse neighborhoods; many of them, no doubt, live in communities to which white people have escaped. They work in corporate environments not overcrowded by racial minorities. The same goes for the churches which play on white suburban guilt to extract donations. I'm sure that, because I make a living from renting apartment units to low- or middle-income blacks, I must be a predatory businessman in their eyes.

In my own neighborhood, which has had a relatively high crime rate, I see the politics of putting a white face on black crime. I see civic-minded homeowners, black and white, uniting to condemn me, the white landlord, for being too lenient with his black tenants who may or may not be committing crimes. I must be ruthless in rooting out the criminal element, even at the risk of violating people's rights. Then the police and community groups can take the credit for "cleaning up the neighborhood". Of course, no one else wants to assume the legal risk. All these nice Minnesota people, with their enlightened views on racial and gender relations, focus their righteous judgment on me and my kind.

My theory is that it is mostly white people who enforce the values of political correctness. Many blacks recognize that years of supposedly favorable treatment haven't done that much for their community. Fifty years ago, there were thriving communities of black business and professional people, even if they were segregated from their white counterparts. Today too many African Americans have become clients of social-service agencies providing high-paying jobs for educated whites. These are the people mainly who defend the legacy of black disadvantage: the whites whose jobs depend on it. There are also, of course, the black "community representatives" who are plugged into the liberal political machine and receive government or foundation money for "advancing" race relations.

As for the journalists, educators, and others who cherish the Civil Rights movement, I think this reflects a generational experience. These people feel good about themselves for having done so much for black people back in the '60s. Such values are the cultural glue that binds people together in today's news rooms. As China's political elite holds power through the ideological heritage of Marxism, so those educated persons who occupy privileged positions in management and the professions in America exhibit certain values on gender and race as a badge of their legitimacy. Such persons are easily irked by someone like me.

Forty years ago, white America bought into the idea that racial prejudice directed against black people was wrong. They could hardly have imagined that "doing the right thing" then would result in a more virulent form of prejudice and discrimination directed against themselves now. If prejudice against blacks was wrong, so is prejudice directed against whites. The idea of a legally "protected class" is incompatible with the concept of "equal justice under the law". Such double standards cannot withstand a legal challenge unless the judges are totally dishonest. If that is so, then U.S. society is rotten at its core. No one can trust our leaders to acknowledge even simple truths, so intensely partisan are they. Hate which masquerades as love, "tolerance" being implacably intolerant of intolerance, and all the other Orwellian formulations of the dominant politics are a political luxury which we can no longer afford. Someone has to stand up and do the "Emperor's New Clothes" routine. That is why I carried my obnoxious sign in the campaign.

You can call me a race hater or a woman hater or both. I will speak my mind. Unlike some other people whose job depends on exhibiting the right opinions, I can't be fired from my job of being a landlord (though the neighborhood group has tried). I realize it's hard to sympathize with a big, rich country like ours and the easy life it affords certain people. We like to think of ourselves as underdogs. But let's be honest: This "identity politics" that we have today is not a legitimate politics. It does not depend on processing honest differences of opinion but

on exploiting differences in the way people were born. It is an underhanded, rancorous, dirty kind of politics, bringing in old ancestral grudges. Go back into your hate-filled hell holes, you who are promoting this politics. Once a small measure of truth seeps back into political discussions, you will cease to intimidate. Previously unspeakable subjects will be discussed. However, we need to establish some ground rules.

First, let me say that selfishness and hate are fundamental ethical problems. They are problems, however, to be addressed within one's own heart, not in someone else's heart. Government is not the proper instrument for eliminating hate because government deals in coercion. No worldly power can force a hating heart to change. Individuals must want to do that themselves. If anything, religion would be the proper instrument to bring about a change in personal values. Religions teach people to control their selfishness. Racism is selfishness defined in terms of racial groups. Selfishness is, however, a normal human condition. All people are selfish to some degree. Just because someone exhibits group selfishness does not mean that he wants to lynch someone or man the gas chambers at a concentration camp. There is no need to stigmatize one's political opponents to that extent.

Second, it is not proper to hate or despise someone because of the way he was born. The person had no control over that situation. Identity politics throws up a smokescreen: We think we are dealing with a group of people when all that is happening is that we are dealing with their often self-appointed representatives. "Jews" as a group do not do or say anything. Representatives of the Jewish community say things. But who are those representatives? For the most part, individual Jews are born into that religious community, as blacks, whites and others are born into their respective racial communities. They do not join it as one would join a conventional organization. While the Jewish representatives may reflect the views of many Jews, they do not represent all Jews. Some Jews may simply want to be left alone. They may not want to have to carry the baggage of their religious heritage.

It is always legitimate to respond to a public statement which a group spokesman makes. It is always proper to criticize statements which one sincerely believes are wrong. It is not, however, proper to hold individuals belonging to those groups personally responsible for the words or deeds of their "spokesmen" unless those individuals authorize such persons to represent them.

The fight for white-male dignity is not, as I see it, a fight to advance group interests as the NAACP or a similar group would do. It is not a vehicle to express group selfishness along the lines of a labor union. Rather, it is a struggle against selfishness. The goal is to overcome political demonization. Demonization of the Ku Klux Klan, Nazis, communists, Jews, WASPs, fundamentalist Christians, atheists, or "perverts" is relegating one's political opponent to a subhuman status. Doing that sometimes makes small people feel good about themselves, but let's try to be bigger than that. My dream is to be on reasonably friendly terms with everyone from the extreme left to the extreme right. Personally, it is to be able to purge hate from my own heart. One can take stands against that with which one disagrees without hating anyone. Gandhi once said that, if you point your finger at someone else in anger and reproach, you unwittingly point three fingers back at yourself.

CHAPTER NINETEEN

Roots of White Self-Hatred

When I was a young boy growing up in Detroit, I attended public school and played with my friends in the alleys and streets. We kids wrestled and punched each other, dug tunnels in the ground, climbed trees, flipped pen knives, and played a stupid game in the alley called "duck on rocks" with crushed beer cans. Under those relatively unsupervised conditions, I built up emotional energy and a sense of masculine self-esteem. Then my parents sent me to private school in Grosse Pointe. My rough-housing personality continued for a year or so. Then I learned how to study and became a good student, placing at the top of my grade-school class for several years. Others considered me a bookworm. My time was taken up reading class assignments and preparing for tests. This went on through high school and then into college. I was on a track to success.

Some time around my third year of college, I began to regret what I had become. College students write papers on sublime concepts of philosophy or art and on important issues facing society. While I was immersing myself in those concerns one afternoon, I thought to myself that I really did not have the base

of experience to write intelligently about them. Here my father was paying thousands of dollars a year to me to have valuable intellectual experiences. I could not relate them to what I had personally experienced and knew to be true. I needed more basic life experience. Then I had a brainstorm: Why not drop out of college for a year or two, gain that needed experience, and then return to college, better equipped to understand what I was studying?

Actually, I would not be missing a beat. Young men were then under an obligation to do military service. Why not join the army and get that obligation out of the way, and then return to Yale as a more knowledgeable, experienced adult? I had a plan. My plan was to enlist in the army under a program called the Six Months program - six months of active service followed by several years in the army reserve and then return to college. After being examined by doctors at an enlistment center, however, I learned to my surprise that the army had rejected me. Either it was because I wore glasses or had failed several of the psych questions, depending on whom I asked.

I had dropped out of Yale without any immediate plans. Back in Bloomfield Hills, Michigan, I lived for a time with my parents. I was a "college dropout" - not a flattering term in those days. I spent my time memorizing poetry, writing artsy prose, and attending debutante parties including Anne Ford's until my parents and I reached an agreement that I should go to Germany. That I did in the fall of 1961. I lived in West Germany - Bavaria and Berlin - until Christmas, 1962, except for short visits to France and to Greece. Although some of my time was spent in such "basic life experience" activities as crating oranges in a Munich train yard and working in a Berlin factory which built engines for oceangoing vessels, I mainly attended German language school, read aimlessly, and wrote about subjects far away.

It was a reasonably stimulating experience, though not particularly adventurous. I then returned to Yale in January, 1963, and completed my remaining year and a half of college. I can't say that my experiences as an itinerant college dropout improved subsequent comprehension of the course materials.

My career goal was to become an accountant. Accountants like Robert McNamara were then filling important positions in business and government. This was a skill which might take me to high places. After graduation from Yale, I enrolled in a one-year program at the Rutgers School of Business in Newark, New Jersey, which offered accounting and business courses. This was my first exposure to double-entry bookkeeping. It had certain charms. But I again grew restless, especially when prospective employers presented an escalator-like path of career advancement with their firms which would occupy much of my life. It was deja vu all over again, just like school.

I recognized that I knew nothing about the practical side of accounting. Why not take an accounting job somewhere utilizing my present knowledge, learn the craft through practice, and work my way up through the ranks? Browsing through business magazines in the Rutgers library, I came across several articles about companies in Minnesota - 3M, Honeywell, Control Data - where opportunity seemed to lie. Minnesota was a land of corporate opportunity combined with open spaces and many clean, beautiful lakes. Alternatively, I imagined it was somewhere out on the Great Plains. I picked up brochures about Minnesota at the New York World's Fair. That was where I would live. Cutting short my studies at Rutgers, I boarded the Greyhound bus two days after New Years Day, 1965, and began the next part of my life.

The job interviews in Minnesota did not go well. Employers were not lining up to hire this particular Yale graduate. I remember one corporate interviewer asking me who was my psychiatrist. Eventually, I found an accounting job in the Department of Public Welfare, State of Minnesota. It was fun to go to work and have coffee with the other employees but the job itself was routine. I quit after a year to take up writing full time. For the next several years, I bounced along in several unrewarding projects and then returned to school at the University of Minnesota to take more accounting and business courses in preparation for the CPA exam. I passed the exam. This was more how successful accounting careers are launched. Even so, I managed to botch a job with a public-accounting firm. I then went back to writing, got married, and finally took a job with American Hoist & Derrick Company, a St. Paul manufacturer of cranes, which lasted for five and a half years.

My idea of starting at the bottom, seeing how the business worked, and then being promoted to high places was not how the career system worked, at least not in my case. I had the notion that computers would take me somewhere. I would find a new way to use computer technology to gather and interpret information about a firm's operation and that would make me an expert. Cost accounting would put me in touch with the nuts-and-bolts side of the business. That was the idea I had at American Hoist and also at the Metropolitan Council Transit Operations, at the end of my accounting career.

Computers were becoming an increasingly important part of accounting work. Personal computers put this tool at one's own finger tips. My crowning achievement at the bus company (next to being assigned to the transit-redesign team) was to develop a cost-accounting method to assign costs to individual bus routes, tying directly into the scheduling data base. Calculating those costs on a quarterly basis became part of my regular job assignment. The agency used my subsidy-per-passenger numbers to decide which routes to eliminate in the next restructuring of service. I sometimes referred to myself as the Dr. Kervorkian of the transit agency. Sixteen years later, I was still in the job position for which I had been hired.

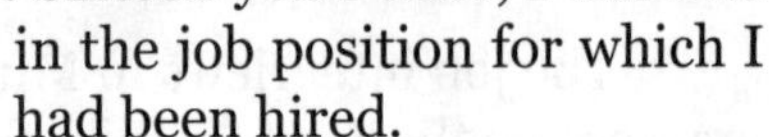

I learned from my real-life business experience that people count more than operational knowledge. To get promoted within a bureaucracy, you probably need a mentor. I was older than the average entry-level employee and my Yale background might have put off several of my superiors - no mentors for me. My one solid job in management, as controller of a small paper-goods manufacturer in western Wisconsin, lasted for only six months. I might have cut my own throat in calculating the firm's breakeven point, which told upper management that it had to cut staff. In more than twenty years of accounting work, I was promoted once while being fired or laid off several times. It was a lackluster career, peaking at an annual income of $35,000. Mine may have been an extreme case of conflict between expectations arising from my own emotional needs and the way the world works.

I tell this humiliating story as an attempt to explain why white people in America may succumb to racial self-hatred. Historically, middle-class whites have been caught up in the promise of education and later success in corporate or professional careers. One's life experiences are controlled as one "rides the escalator" to economic and social success. The idea of going to college, from the perspective of upper-middle-class Midwestern families such as mine, was that this package of life experiences would perpetuate the upward mobility of one's forbearers. The children of prospering middle-class families would attend schools where the children of the aristocrats were. At Yale or Harvard, these young people would learn the finer points of culture so that they would know how to fit in with the cream of society. Going to a prep school or an elite college meant that one was on a "success track".

The downside was that, as a young person who identified with and cooperated with this type of upbringing, one was making a statement of claiming to be better than other people. One was better because one knew all about the society's rich culture. However, this type of success did not measure up against other types based upon heroic or courageous struggles. True success is the fruit of an uncertain life.

I suspect that many young people, predominantly white, feel, as I felt years ago, that their lives are being built on false pretenses. I could not claim to be superior to others because I

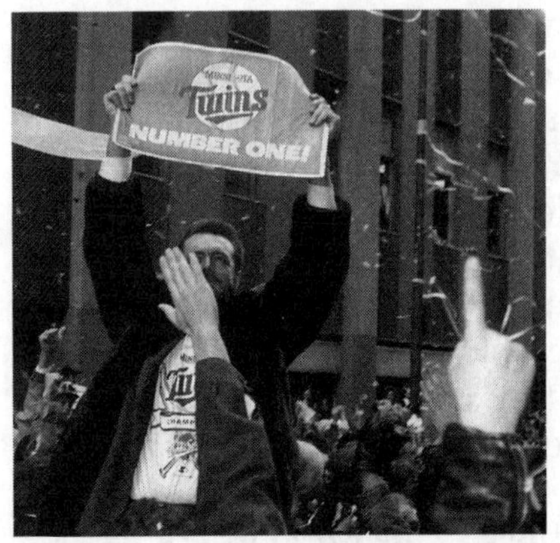

knew that I had not really lived. "Really living" for me meant to be that boy knocking around the Detroit alleys with his friends, living out his fantasies, making his own mistakes, gaining unstructured experiences that made authentic connections with life. It did not mean slavishly following a path which well-intentioned adults had laid out for me. The path to true success lies in overcoming personal difficulties. The bigger the challenge, the greater the achievement. Such success does not lie in expectations of wealth and respectability if one gets good grades in school. The roots of white self-hatred might lie in the false promises of education and the fact that we fell for them. Could we, pretending to be superior by virtue of having graduated from college, look someone in the eye whom life itself had revealed to be a superior person? We knew we were living a lie.

Black Americans did not face that situation. One of the benefits of being socially downtrodden is that life's raw experiences press in upon oneself every day. Boys and girls brought up in that environment learn to cope with adult-sized issues at an early age. Through street smarts or luck, some do prosper and rise into a higher socioeconomic class. Back in the '50s, my generation of white American was exposed to elements of black culture which we found emotionally appealing. We knew Jackie Robinson's story of how, as a black man, he had to be better than the other ball players to break into the Major Leagues. We knew about Jesse Owens and Joe Lewis and Harry Belafonte. We knew about the black blues singers whose music expressed agonies of the soul. We inexperienced youth knew about the easy sexuality which many black men and women seemed to possess. Rock 'n roll music, originating in the musical subculture of black America, took white America by storm. Here was Elvis Presley, a poor white man from Mississippi who imitated black singers, exhibiting raw sexual power. There were also young blacks courageously desegregating lunch counters in the South, risking their very lives.

Such images from black America proved appealing to young whites pretending to be on a success track in school. The blandness of our actual daily experience compared unfavorably with the black experience. Having to prove that you're better than someone else - making this the basis of your personal pride - would be hard for anyone. (Jews, with their supremacist heritage, have solved this psychological problem by positioning themselves as the world's chief victim.) It is doubly hard for a young person still trying to know who he is. Can't we all just be left alone to find purpose in what comes our way? Why all this social pretending? That was our parents' idea, not ours. Moreover, the promise that one would join a social aristocracy by going to college was undermined by the fact that nowadays everyone goes to college. We could obviously not all become aristocrats. It seemed that white Americans were on a treadmill moving faster and faster toward nowhere. To the extent that we acquiesced in this false dream, we set ourselves up for self-hatred. Many of our more adventurous peers became rebels against the system.

The current President of the United States, George W. Bush, graduated from Yale four years after I graduated from there. Vice President Dick Cheney - like me, a Yale dropout - might have been there at the same time. I must admit that, having been a college student in the early '60s, I have sympathies for them that others may not have (although I do not agree with the Bush-Cheney approach to the impending war with Iraq or their idea of an "axis of evil"). I have heard persons who came from a different background ridicule George W. Bush for being stupid. A decade earlier, they ridiculed Dan Quayle for the same reason. They said that George W. was born with a silver spoon in his mouth and had an easy upbringing; it was only because of help from his father's friends that this unremarkable white boy ever succeeded. What these people really meant to say was: Why can't a high-IQ, self-aware individual like me become President if he could? Life isn't fair.

Let me say that I think both Dan Quayle and George W. Bush succeeded through personal merit. I have seen Quayle in action; as a political schmoozer, he's one of the best. Put him down as a genius under the theory of "multiple intelligences". With respect to the younger Bush, I once read in the newspaper of an incident involving the Yale chaplain, William Sloane Coffin, while Bush was a Yale. Coffin, the original "Freedom Rider" and pianist Artur Rubinstein's son-in-law, was a likable though arrogantly brash practitioner of "afflicting the comfortable" and bringing about social change. After George Bush the elder lost the 1968 Senate race in Texas to Lloyd Bentsen, Rev. Coffin told the younger Bush to his face that the better man had won. They say that George W. partied his way through Yale, consumed too much alcohol, and was at loose ends for several years following his college graduation. Then he met his wife, Laura, stopped drinking, and pulled out of his personal funk. And, yes, with the help of his father and his father's friends, he later became a career success. Even if George W. Bush did not grow up dirt poor, I call this overcoming adversity.

We need perhaps to rethink our approach to education if it deprives young men and women of an authentic life. Let's not just assume that the time which they have to themselves is "wasted time". What is happening during the time spent in the classroom? Is this truly quality time? Are the courses interesting? Do they excite young people's creative imaginations? Do they arouse positive hopes for the future? Or does a leaden, self-serving educational bureaucracy produce an experience which deadens that part of the soul?

Of course, society has made the decision, not to raise basic questions such as this, but expand the educational process to wider circles. If white kids are stifled in school, then why not stifle black kids on an equal-opportunity basis? Why not take away their opportunities to experience life in the raw? Let's develop social-studies courses that tell white kids how badly their forbearers have treated blacks and hang pictures of Martin Luther King on the wall. Let's tell boys that they must control their male chauvinistic tendencies and look up to girls as models of behavior. Let's scare everyone into staying in school for longer and longer periods; let's make them study harder and jump through more hoops. You should take Advanced Placement courses. You should earn good grades. You should participate in extracurricular activities to show admissions officers that you are personally well rounded. If you falter in school, that will end your chances to be a success in this society. Stay in school whether you like it or not or whether it does you any good.

Consider for a moment the young white male who comes from an undistinguished social background, let's say in the suburbs. What is our society offering that type of person in terms of education? All this racialized, genderized culture is telling him that he is a bad person. While previous generations of Americans had George Washington to admire, we have the Civil Rights heroes who, though displaying many admirable qualities, were basically presenting a complaint against white America. Why should the average white kid be expected to identify with this? Who are his people? Who are his role models? The fact is that today increasing numbers of young men are choosing not to go on to college. Given a choice, they may not wish to subject themselves to further psychological abuse.

Schools are not panaceas. Educators are not judges of young people but persons hired to give them high-quality experiences. We need to resell young men and women on the joys of the intellectual life. We need to bring back the kind of tolerant,

offbeat environment which produced the personable, individualistic scholar. I think of academics like Kenneth Boulding or Milton Friedman, who, even if they disagreed with you (as they did with me on my proposals for a shorter workweek), were at least willing to engage in personal dialogue. Politically correct education, deconstructionism, and the rest have banished that type of scholar. In the end, it's about money.

I do not want to leave the impression that I do not appreciate my prep-school or Yale education. I was the beneficiary of many outstanding teachers. There is one thing about Yale that outsiders may not know. By and large, it is not a place of grim self-hating competitors. The atmosphere there is one of sociability. In the freshman dining hall, I remember how often someone would stick out his hand and introduce himself if you sat down at the same table. I have gone back to class reunions rather reluctantly, fearing to expose a painful contrast between my own lack of career achievement and what my classmates have accomplished. The experience has almost always been a positive one. Even though most of my time at Yale was not spent with the Class of 1964 (my graduating class) and I knew few in attendance, that did not seem to matter. People again introduced themselves and did not brag.

At the last reunion, there was a panel of classmates who had changed careers late in life. I remember a Jewish guy who had been CEO of a billion-dollar-a-year pharmaceutical company telling us how, feeling personally unfulfilled, he had abruptly resigned. (There was nothing to bringing out new drugs, he told us. It was a completely routine procedure.) He had spent much of the next year staring at a television screen. Then he had found a young wife. They had had a baby and moved to Israel. This, too, was an acceptable model of the Yale man. We each need the freedom to lead our own lives in our own way. That can be antidote to what ails white society: We each become our own underdog.

CHAPTER TWENTY

Following my Ideas to Somewhere - Inner-City Real Estate and New Women

I made the choice. No one coerced me into it. I became a man not entirely of this world. Starting even while I was in high school and certainly in college, I cultivated ideas for certain projects. I put their descriptions in an "idea notebook". The first idea was for a perpetual-motion machine. A physics professor later explained to me why that scheme was impractical. Many of the earlier ideas in the notebook pertained to inventions that might make me rich. In time, they gravitated toward ideas related to philosophy or another intellectual pursuit. For I was a philosophy major in my junior year of college. This remained an even stronger interest than my interest in English literature, my eventual major.

I numbered these scattered ideas in the sequence that they were typed. I still have copies of most; there have been many series of typed notes over the years. The next step, then, was to try to make something of those ideas. That meant gathering related themes and creating a coherent written structure. So I became a writer. I pursued this secret life while I was employed in an accounting job, being a husband, or whatever. My attention and memory were focused on ideas for the latest project.

A consequence of this type of life is that one neglects other interests. I was interested in my career, in entertainment, in sports activities, in dating, and in other aspects of life; but my attention was also focused on those ideas. As I result, I did not try as hard as I might have done to advance myself in a career or find a wife. Because my narrow, idea-centered interests could not be shared with other people, I tended to withdraw into myself. I never took the time to develop a social facade that would allow me to meet people easily. I felt uncomfortable in settings that called for mere socializing. Therefore, I never came across "the woman of my dreams". It was easier for me to engage in deep personal conversation than idle chit chat. If I could get over the hurdle of making a good first impression, I usually did all right. The fact was, however, that I had little to say to other people, unless there was business to conduct, because I did not share the experiences that others had. I was, as my first wife said, "retarded" in certain ways. I lacked the knowledge to say intelligent things. And that did not help me with respect to career advancement. I became a rather marginal person.

Being a Yale graduate, I found that people had certain expectations of me which were not correct. I lacked social sophistication. I was a poor dresser. I'm sure that many people tagged me as a loser who had had all the advantages yet failed to capitalize on them. I found it painful for others to refer to my Yale education. This had happened so long ago and was not formative in the way that people expected. My Yale education just created another barrier between me and other people. I seldom attended meetings of the local Yale club because at such an event in 1966, I felt like such a freak when I tried to explain what I was doing as a

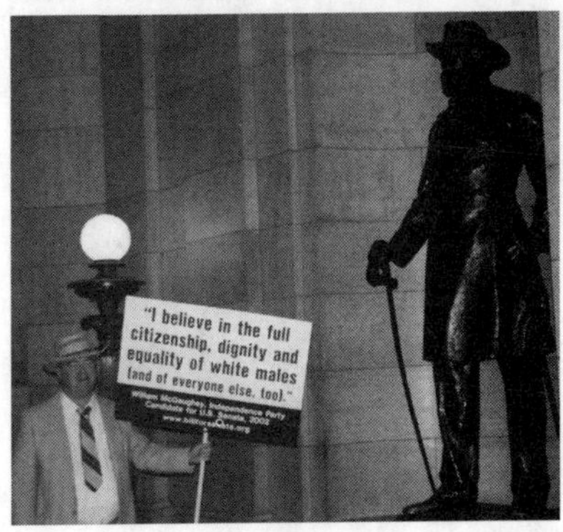
"I believe in the full
citizenship, dignity and
equality of white males
(and of everyone else, too)."

man without a job trying to write books. That conclusion was perhaps unfair to my conversation partners. I might have given up too easily.

MINNESOTA
AFL
CIO
Minnesota AFL-CIO
"I believe that the Federal Government should reduce the standard workweek to 32 hours by 2010."
William McGaughey, Independence Party Candidate for U.S. Senate, 2002
www.billforsenate.org

In the late 1970s, I tasted my first fruits of success as an ideas man. In June 1974, I had begun gathering information related to proposals for a shorter workweek. Beginning my accounting career in earnest about the same time, I was drawn to statistical compilations developed by the Bureau of Labor Statistics. I picked out pertinent statistics, typed my own schedules, and wrote short theoretical articles incorporating this material. After meeting Congressman John Conyers in late 1978, I was drawn into efforts to support the shorter-workweek legislation which he had introduced in Congress. My first wife and I drove to Washington, D.C., to attend hearings of the Conyers bill in the House Education and Labor committee a year later. I was gratified to learn that my writings were useful in that context. This interest climaxed in publication of a book published in 1981. Its title (or, I should say, mistitle) was *A Shorter Workweek in the 1980s*. A photograph of Luciano Pavarotti enjoying himself in a swimming pool graced the front cover. It was my first book.

I was meanwhile trying to organize a grassroots organization in the Twin Cities to support proposals for shorter hours. Being a nonunion accountant, I faced problems in that regard. Another difficulty was that my father was then Senior Vice President of the National Association of Manufacturers in Washington, D.C., an organization traditionally hostile toward shorter-workweek proposals. But we were able to compartmentalize. I had my life and he had his. Through much effort, I was able to whip up enough interest for perhaps a dozen persons to attend a meeting once. My introverted personality and focus on writing

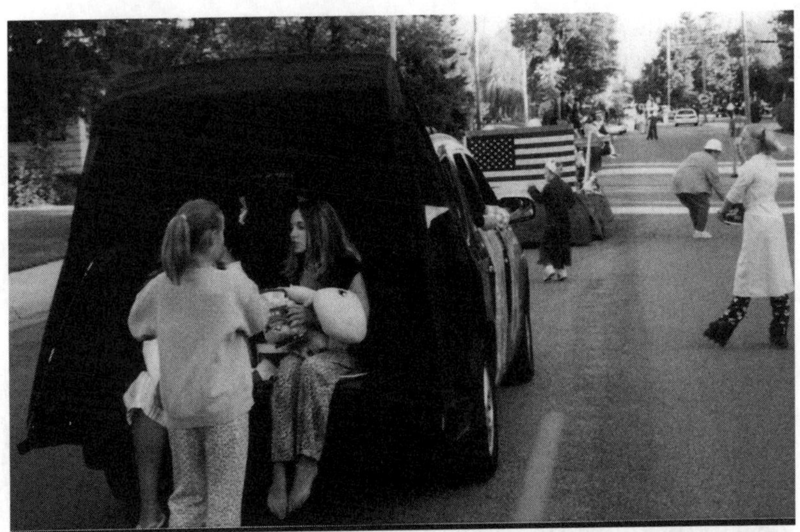

would not allow the group to go further. My own politics were shifting to the left. I was persuaded to become active in seeking union representation for office workers at the Metropolitan Transit Commission. Tom Laney, former president of a UAW local, encouraged those efforts. He led me into my next set of issues which were related to international trade.

During the same days in 1991 that Saddam Hussein's Iraqi armies invaded Kuwait, I was doing research on trade issues at the Minneapolis public library. I wrote a short paper which related the idea of reduced work time to laws concerning international trade. The Institute of Agriculture and Trade Policy put it on their list of publications. Then came a series of conferences, hearings, protest demonstrations, and other events related to trade. From those experiences came a book, *A U.S.-Mexico-Canada Free Trade Agreement: Do We Just Say No?*. As a self-published work, it enjoyed modest commercial success.

My Minnesota labor friends and I were ahead of the curve. NAFTA-related developments were then becoming big political news. I thought I had found just the right twist to reintroduce the proposal for a shorter workweek, that "dead horse" I had long been beating, into contemporary political discussions. The Minnesota Fair Trade Coalition was established. While I was one of its early leaders, another person with a more solid labor-left background took over the organization and managed it as a coalition of labor and environmental groups during the 1993 campaign to defeat "fast-track" authority in Congress. I became a bit player, which was fine with me.

Meanwhile, the shorter-workweek movement itself was showing signs of revival thanks to the efforts of Juliet Schor, Ben Hunnicutt, Barbara Brandt, and others. As author of a pioneering book on this issue in its post-labor phase, I had a respected place in the movement. Hunnicutt put on conferences in Iowa City and Brandt's group agitated in Boston. Eugene McCarthy was often available to lend a helping hand. We created an organization called NANSHOW (North American Network for Shorter Hours of Work) to join with our Canadian and, hopefully, Mexican brothers and sisters to submit shorter-hours proposals to the UN Social Summit whose third prepcom was held in New York City in January 1995. As I said earlier, my career as an international labor activist came to an abrupt halt when I returned home from the UN conference to find neighborhood critics and Minneapolis city officials threatening my livelihood.

Back up for a moment. In the spring of 1992, I received the shipment of the NAFTA-related books. I was then living in a one-bedroom apartment in Minneapolis not far from work. Space was limited. One day I noticed a large boarded-up building across the street. This turned out to be a HUD house. It would give me needed space to store the book cartons. I put in a successful bid of $20,100 to purchase the house. It had no plumbing because thieves had removed the copper pipes. I spent tens of thousands of dollars on plumbing and other contracted work to fix up the house. Then I rented out the two downstairs units, keeping the upstairs apartments for myself. Within months, the police SWAT team conducted a drug raid on one of the units.

Even so, I was foolish enough, in August 1993, to purchase a nine-unit apartment building next door after a real estate agent approached me on the street about buying it. One unit was condemned. The eventual purchase price was $72,000. Being a relatively thrifty accountant who had made some good stock-mar-

ket investments, I was able to make a sizable down payment and finance the rest on a contract for deed. I did not know the full extent of the problems.

There was active drug dealing in the apartment. Only one of the nine tenants had paid the last month's rent. Within days, I had visited all the apartment units and held discussions with tenants about what to do to put the building back in shape. On Saturday, August 13, 1993 - less than two weeks after I closed on the property - the Harrison Neighborhood Association's housing and crime committee held a meeting to discuss "problem properties" in the neighborhood, including mine. Our ward's City Council representative, Jackie Cherryhomes, was there. Members of the neighborhood committee berated me for having purchased the building. I "should have known better" than to do that, they said. When I expressed my desire to improve the building with the tenants' cooperation, Cherryhomes called me an unfit person to manage a building. Everyone demanded that I evict all the tenants immediately and start over with a new tenant base. Being the stubborn, self-righteous individual that I am, I refused. As an alternative, I agreed to evict only those tenants who had a criminal record. Three tenants fell into that category.

The same afternoon, I wrote a memo to the building's tenants explaining what I had to do. I knocked on doors to serve the eviction notices. Apartment number 1 was occupied by a tenant named "Jimmy", an African American man who seemed to be involved in drug dealing. When I opened the door to explain my mission, the man started yelling at me. He threatened to sue me because my memo had identified him and the other intended evictees as persons with a criminal record. It seemed that he had a point. I just stood there dumbfounded listening to the tirade. Suddenly, a beautiful young African American woman appeared in the doorway from the back of the room. "Don't be so hard on him, Jimmy," she said. "He's only doing his job." That's how I met my second wife. However, it took another month or so for us to become acquainted. She was then a cocaine addict.

The rest of 1993 was a difficult time for me. I pressured and negotiated with the three tenants to vacate the premises, and, in some cases, to facilitate the move, purchased their furniture and other belongings. I accepted other tenants to fill the vacancies. As often as not, they turned out to be drug dealers or persons with a habit. Each evening, until the evictions took effect, apartment number one was a den of drug activity filled with guests who smoked cocaine and talked through the night. Someone stole the keys to my house. My living quarters next door were burglarized. I was hemorrhaging money. A rookie landlord, I trusted several persons in the building who gave me information about persons involved in the drug activity or help with maintenance problems. More often than not, this trust was misplaced. The city police called to my building to handle disturbances were hostile; I was the proprietor of a "crack house". It was like Fort Apache - me, a solitary white man, facing a group of black tenants some of whom used drugs.

One of those users, my future wife, became my confidante. She would tell me what was going on and, if she was to be believed, protect me from some of dire plots being hatched against me in the building. I managed to restore relative order to the building through 1994. My future wife, Sheila Foresta, went into treatment, relapsed once, and then, with the Lord's help, achieved permanent sobriety. We were married on January 2, 1995, the New Years Day holiday, in the juvenile detention center in downtown Minneapolis in the chambers of a judge who filled in at the last moment for another judge who stood us up.

Meanwhile, I had other family obligations. My brother Andrew, who suffered from schizophrenia, visited me in June 1993. Within three days, he was hospitalized with a severe asthma attack, followed by appendicitis. Placed in a nursing facility to recover from this operation, he may have pestered the head nurse too hard for his daily cigarette ration. She accused him of sexual harassment. This resulted in court proceedings and in his involuntary commitment to the Anoka Regional Treatment Facility. I attended the trial in district court. The other attorney slipped the judge a slip of paper which said that, because I was under "criminal investigation" by the Minneapolis police for activities related to my building, "under no circumstances - repeat, no circumstances" - should my brother be allowed to live with me as a less restrictive alternative to commitment. I had to take the stand to deny the allegations of criminal misconduct. Later, when I demanded that the police give me information about their alleged "investigation", no one remembered anything.

The female judge decided to commit my brother to Anoka. The Court of Appeals upheld the commitment. The Minnesota Supreme Court, however, overturned the commitment and my brother was a free man. I almost wish he had stayed in the facility. My brother moved to a halfway house, met a woman there, and got married. They moved to my fourplex in a unit next to mine. It did not have air conditioning. During an especially hot night, between July 23 and 24, 1999, my brother, who took psychotropic medication, was having severe problems dealing with the heat. In the following morning, I found his dead body lying face down on the floor.

My mother in Pennsylvania was frantic about my life as a Minneapolis landlord. Please, please, sell your building and move to a better neighborhood, she pleaded. My parents also did not approve of my marriage to Sheila. Neither did my brother. I shrugged off these appeals. I liked Sheila and her five young children. Besides, I was starting to settle into a groove as a landlord. Despite the difficulties, it was a strangely satisfying role. For the first time in my life, I was in charge of something. I made the final decisions. So long as I had the money, I did not have to answer to anyone else. I could tell the neighborhood group and City Council representative "no", even if I might later pay a price.

Remember, for much of my life I had been part of the proletariat of college-educated persons who thought they were influential but actually were not. Minneapolis is full of these unpaid policy wonks, self-trained experts in housing, transportation, crime, or whatever. They write newspaper articles and sit on committees advising important government officials. But I, owner of a small apartment building, was better grounded in my power. People came to me for everyday decisions. So long as things stayed reasonably on course, I was boss of my own little kingdom.

Marrying Sheila was a problem for many people. I had met her in difficult circumstances. She had five young children and two others who were grown. She was black. I have never been one to use my head in situations like this. Yet, Sheila and I could talk and laugh about many things. I trusted her judgment in matters about which I knew little. She was personally attractive and engaging. The downside was mainly financial. I did not know at the time that she opened up three joint credit cards, forged my signature and charged the cards to the limit thinking that she could handle the minimum payments. Without my permission, she wrote checks to herself on my blank checks and altered the amounts on checks I had written. I was tolerant of these practices when they came to light, opening myself up to further abuse.

I knowingly paid more than $10,000 in attorney fees to engage legal counsel for Sheila's teenage son, Tony, who was put on trial for murder in February, 1996. A gang member living with friends, he had killed a young woman when a bullet which he fired at a member of rival gang who he thought was reaching for a gun under the front seat of a car ricocheted off the car and struck this woman who was standing nearby. The County Attorney's office put him on trial for first-degree murder charging him as an adult. Thanks to attorney Demetrius Clemons' efforts, Tony was not convicted of this charge. He was instead convicted of involuntary second-degree murder and sentenced to fifteen years in the state penitentiary.

My marriage with Sheila was doomed. While we were married, we were reasonably happy except that Sheila tended to accuse me of things that I never did - like having an affair with a tenant who had told Sheila that she and I "had an understanding" about paying the back rent. My mother, perhaps wanting to get rid of Sheila, offered to pay for my trip to China as an escort for my brother. When I returned from the trip, Sheila and the children had moved out. We were divorced in November, 1996.

I am currently married to a Chinese woman named Lian (Yang Lianlian) partly as a result of that trip. Aware of my increasing problems with Sheila, I talked about my marriage and about the possibility of meeting Chinese women with the tour guide, who had an unmarried younger sister. This tour guide later came to the United States to attend college at the University of Tennessee in Chattanooga. There she met Lian's sister at a local Chinese-American function. They talked about me. The sister put me in touch with Lian. We corresponded for a time and then drew closer together through emails. I married Lian on January 28, 2000 during a visit to Beijing. It took eighteen months to get a visa for Lian and Celia, my new stepdaughter.

Despite our language differences, Lian and I could communicate quite well. She hired an interpreter to accompany us while I was in Beijing but, actually, could get by in English on her own. She knew how to tell amusing stories. Lian was no destitute economic or political refugee but someone who gave up much to marry me. Daughter of a high-ranking Chinese military officer from the revolutionary period, she had had a successful career as general manager of several hotels. She was then manager of the hotel-management department of the China Everbright Corporation. Lian put the opportunity to have a family above her career. She won my heart by explaining, in her broken English, Chinese women's attitude toward marriage: "If marry a chicken - is a chicken. If marry a dog - is a dog." In other

words, the woman adapts to her husband's situation. This was unlike what I imagined were the priorities of American women.

I am, however, a bit uncomfortable about my history of interracial marriages. Robert Bly once suggested that my goal in life was to marry someone from each of the three races. I am obviously not a hyperliberal wanting to make that kind of statement. It may have something to do with racial self-hatred. I pick up in the attitude of many white women, especially in Minnesota, a contempt for men like me. Maybe we are all college-educated mama's boys. Maybe we aren't successful enough in a career. At any rate, I never met the white woman of my dreams; it seems I was always rejected when I attempted to broach the subject of romance with these women. Black women came more easily. I was boss of my own apartment building and, therefore, someone of substance in their eyes. Lian and I met with the understanding that we might become maritally involved.

I know that at least 50% of my problem with white women was my fault. There probably was someone out there for me if I had tried hard enough, but I was too lazy, fearful, and self-absorbed. As I grew older and increasingly aware of my unimpressive career, weight gain, and other impediments to finding the right woman, I seized my opportunities as they came. I let the hateful atmosphere of gender relations in our society color my perceptions. I formed a conclusion that white females were predisposed to put me down or, in most situations, "make the man pay". There may be, I realize, a white woman somewhere who is loving and sincere and not wanting to compete with me careerwise. There are also, of course, plenty of white men and women in happy relationships. With Lian, I at last have a sense of belonging to an ethnic and racial community which respects itself. I married a woman from China so the Chinese are now also my people. Though self-hatred may also affect Chinese society, I have myself escaped from that trap.

In January 2000, I published a book on world history titled *Five Epochs of Civilization: World History as Emerging in Five Civilizations.* If I may say so myself, it is a pretty good book. Not a single U.S. newspaper would publish a review. On the other hand, when I mailed literature about the book to editors of English-language newspapers in other countries around the world, it resulted in reviews in five newspapers - in India, Nigeria, and Pakistan - all favorable. Additionally, a review has appeared in the Chinese news agency's Xin Hua Book Studies, thanks to my wife's efforts. My book has also been translated into Chinese and will soon be sold in China. I have also found that the book's web site, www.worldhistorysite.com, which contains parallel pages in six languages, is attracting steadily more visitors speaking a language other than English. Spanish-speaking visitors are now almost as numerous as those speaking English. My world-history book does have a worldwide reach.

With limited success, I have tried to sell this book and its concepts to both the general and academic markets in the United States. A modest number of books have been sold to history teachers in the United States thanks to direct-mail campaigns. Still, academic historians in this country want to view world history through the lens of trade contacts and migrations popularized by William McNeill rather than taking a broader view. The impact of imperialism upon the role of women is what excites them rather than what my book proposes as a central focus, the impact of communication technologies upon emerging civilizations.

Together with a retired history professor from the University of Minnesota and several others, I recently tried to start a charter school in St. Paul centering upon a curriculum in world history but was unsuccessful in obtaining grant money from the Gates Foundation. Five other schools with better political connections won the competition administered by the Center for School Change. Our group was trying to put together a curriculum in world history which would be a creation story of human societies. We were also open to the idea of "big history" which would tell the story of the natural world from the Big Bang forward. Ultimately we wanted to establish a charter school centered in this curriculum which would use students' interest in history to draw out reading, writing, and speaking skills and, perhaps, hook up with schools in foreign countries. I discussed this possibility with one of my wife's friends in China who was a school official. I imagined that we were in the vanguard of a new world culture.

Intellectuals are often more comfortable in a land other than their own, viewing the greener pastures on the other side of the fence. I have some of those tendencies within myself. I also feel that a person such as me has a calling which is less appreciated today than it might have been a century ago. Persons devoted to cultivating ideas are largely an anachronism. Our society vibrates according to the electronic culture. I continue to write and self-publish books such as *Five Epochs of Civilization* and *Rhythm and Self-Consciousness*, which went into sports psychology and music theory, hoping to find at least a small group of interested readers. *Rhythm and Self-Consciousness* was a philosophical study of values brought out in the age of electronic communication. I tried to look at the concept of rhythm in much the same way that the Greek philosophers had looked at such concepts as goodness and beauty in their static, writing-based culture. Self-consciousness was a negative force in this culture ensnaring intellectuals. It was the culmination of my own theoretical speculations, begun in my college years.

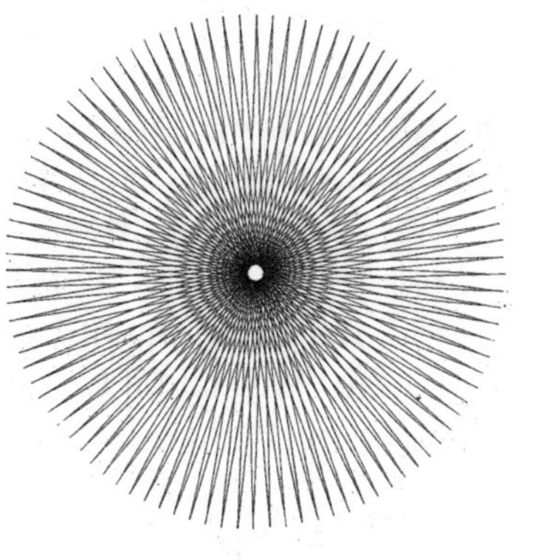

Financially, all has worked out well for me, at least for the time being. I have two buildings in Minneapolis without mortgages, now worth perhaps $500,000. I have bought a third building, a condemned house across the street, which I am incurring some debt to renovate. The banks are reluctant to lend me money because of my second wife's bankruptcy pertaining to a fraudulently obtained joint credit card. Also, because of the money poured into the building renovation, my ratio of debt to last year's income they say is too high. Not to worry. I bought a vacant lot across the street for $300 seven years ago and recently sold it for $43,000. My stock-market investments are also doing well. To pay my current bills, I am an owner of rental property. There's another house in Pennsylvania, also without a mortgage.

My second wife's brother, Alan Morrison, has been a tenant in my apartment building for six years. An independent contractor, he is helping to fix up the condemned house. The caretaker, Keith Baker, wants to marry a Chinese woman, who is a friend of Lian's, if he can get a passport to visit Beijing. He couldn't get the passport because he has $3,500 in unpaid child support. The banks won't lend him the money to pay this off, even with my cosigning, because there is a judgment for his child support. He had his fifteen seconds of fame recently when the local television station found a copy of his loan application with a large bank in an open dumpster near the bank's processing center. The bank said it was sorry. I guess I'll have to become the banker for his $3,500 loan when my money from the land sale is received.

My wife Lian has taken a job at Target. I am writing this book. Our daughter Celia is a freshman at St. Olaf College. Lounging around the house somewhere is my faithful companion of the past twelve years, Toni the cat. So we have our own little community here in Minneapolis. Thanks to the landlord group, it seems reasonably secure against political attack.

CHAPTER TWENTY-ONE

Landlord Politics

When I returned to Minneapolis from the prepcom for the 1995 UN Social Summit, I found my second wife trying to hold down the fort in a deteriorating situation at the apartment building. An eviction process was underway. Relatives of the evicted tenants were living there without authorization. Though the building was being treated regularly by a licensed pest-control firm, there were cockroach problems. The police had been summoned to look for a gun. A Rental Property Owners' committee of the neighborhood group wanted to meet with me and my wife. At the meeting, I started to explain how I was evicting three related tenants in response to allegations of drug dealing. The staff person interrupted me to say that she did not want excuses but action. Specifically, she wanted me to set a date to turn over management of the building to someone else. I refused.

Two days later, a condemnation placard of the Minneapolis health department was posted on the front door of my apartment building. All tenants would have to leave within three weeks. Several days later, a letter arrived informing me that the city would do a complete "rental-license inspection" on the building while it was vacant. In other words, while I was not collecting rents for the apartments, the city would impose heavy maintenance costs upon the property. (The work orders included changing the placement of windows to meet current city code and resurfacing the parking lot. In all, it cost me more than $40,000 to put the building back in service.) If I did not have sufficient financial resources to complete the work orders, I might have to dispose of the building. The city would decide when, if ever, to lift the condemnation.

The neighborhood "Red Guards" had another treat for me. They leafleted the neighborhood to announce a special community meeting at which my property would be discussed. Could I talk over the situation with the Neighborhood Association board, I asked? No, it was too late. I had had my chance to be cooperative. There were approximately forty persons at the meeting on Saturday, April 1, 1995. Jackie Cherryhomes, now President of the Minneapolis City Council, was among those on hand to denounce me. Like a leper, I sat by myself in the middle of the front row of chairs, surrounded by empty seats on both sides. The "neighbors" had two principal demands: (1) that the apartment building sit vacant for at least six months to give the community "a breather" from the nefarious activities occurring at my building, and (2) that I relinquish management of the property. I later learned that, had I agreed to the six months' vacancy, that would have put my building into the "nuisance property" category and allowed the city to have it demolished at my expense.

The meeting did not go as my enemies had expected. First, I embarrassed Council member Cherryhomes before her constituents by catching her in a lie. Second, I rebutted my chief accuser among the landlord contingent by pointing out that, while she was accusing me of tolerating crime, gang graffiti spray-painted in huge red lettering had not yet been removed from her own building across the street. Third, I gave the entire group a tongue lashing for its hypocrisy in dealing with crime. I told these people that I had sent out press releases calling attention to their cowardly event. I invited any interested person to come to my home immediately after the meeting to review the facts of the case. The air went out of the room. The would-be jackals left in small, orderly groups.

I later learned that Marcia Glancy, the staff person who had orchestrated this event, was not hired as the Association's permanent executive director. I was told she had hoped to run for political office after taking my scalp. Several weeks later, Jerry Finkelstein, the owner of the apartment building across the street whose manager had denounced me at the meeting, called me to offer to buy my apartment building for $50,000 cash. I told him I was not interested in selling. I learned there had also been other discussions in the neighborhood about who might buy me out or who might manage it under the new ownership.

Such was my introduction to being a landlord in one of Minneapolis' poorer neighborhoods. I soon learned that the city police had little interest in helping me as a tax-paying citizen deal with criminal activities in or near my building. Under the label of "community policing", it instead formed alliances with "crime and safety committees" of neighborhood associations such as Harrison's ostensibly for the purpose of controlling neighborhood crime. In practice, these groups framed the discussion of crime in terms of "problem properties" whose uncaring owners did not properly screen applicants for their apartments. A common remedy was to use inspections to find code violations at police-targeted buildings which would allow the city to close them down. Then, presumably, the crime problems would go away.

From my point of view, Minneapolis city officials were making landlords a scapegoat for their own inability to control crime as waves of experienced drug dealers from Chicago, Los Angeles, or Detroit exploited the lucrative drug market in the Twin Cities. Contrary to popular opinion, the "community police" were not officers who patrolled neighborhoods on foot getting to know local residents but persons who sat around the table with neighborhood activists drinking coffee and deciding that a third party, the "absentee landlord" (a.k.a. "slumlord"), was responsible for crime rather than the criminals themselves.

I once asked if the police would write me a letter telling me who was dealing the drugs, promising to evict them if they were tenants. The system did not work that way, I was told. Instead, if I encouraged tenants to call 911 whenever they spotted drug activity in my building, the police would keep count of the number of calls coming from the building and, if it exceeded a certain number, use this as evidence that my building was out of control. I would be considered a negligent landlord who had required excessive police resources and deserved to be punished.

The idea that landlords "profited from" drug dealing in their buildings was, of course, ludicrous. Our rents were not graded by ability to pay and we would be fools to invite gun-toting thugs into our buildings. As a novice landlord, I had little idea what a drug dealer looked like. I was hoping that the police would shed some light on such questions. They were more into blame-shifting. With an annual budget of $3 to $4 million, the Minneapolis SAFE (community police) unit had the resources to win the public-relations battle against the city's landlords both by hiring "crime-prevention specialists" to peddle police propaganda full time in the course of their work and by doling out money to obliging community groups. I as the solitary proprietor of an apartment building in a crime-ridden neighborhood was fair game to be vilified and have my property taken. It was a turkey shoot.

When a northside landlord called for a tenant reference, he told me about a group of landlords in south Minneapolis, headed by Charlie Disney, who were suing the city. One of this group, Bob Anderson, called me when he read my opinion piece on "Community Policing" in the *Star Tribune*. There would be a meeting of the Minneapolis City Council at a southside community center to discuss a proposed ordinance holding landlords responsible for tenant misconduct. Disney and friends would be there. So I hooked up with the group of landlords which would later become Minneapolis Property Rights Action Committee.

Charlie Disney was a nine-time state table-tennis champion who had operated Disney's Table Tennis Center on Lake Street until it closed because of neighborhood crime. In the mid 1970s he was president of the U.S. Table Tennis Association. He was present at the historic tournament in Nagano, Japan, where the U.S. team was invited to tour China in an event that became known as "ping-pong diplomacy". In any event, Charlie Disney was a man who knew how to build an organization. Through force of personality, he presided over a biweekly gathering of disgruntled landlords who met in a real-estate office on Blaisdel Avenue. They shared "war stories" and chipped in for a class-action lawsuit filed against the city alleging improper training and supervision of city inspectors and inconsistent inspections enforcement.

I became a regular at those meetings. Disney asked the landlords each to take several pages of a print-out listing the city's rental-property owners and write letters to those people. With self-publishing experience, I convinced the group instead to do a bulk mailing. Soon memberships and money to support the lawsuit started pouring in. However, a judge dismissed our case in federal court. We continued to meet regularly to decide what to do next. I thought we should try public protests. Our first protest demonstration took place in January, 1996, in front of the Minneapolis City Hall. A reporter from the public-radio station was among those covering the event. He interviewed me on the front steps of my apartment building.

The *Twin Cities Reader*, an alternative weekly newspaper, did an article on Charlie Disney and Kirk Hill, head of the Minnesota Tenants Union, calling them "the odd couple". Despite their different interests, the two were in agreement on the folly of fighting crime by targeting rental properties. Disney and others, including me, expressed our views on talk radio. We wrote letters to the editor of the *Star Tribune* and tried to get opinion pieces published. Disney dubbed me the group's "chief writer".

Members of Disney's group attended community meetings that were concerned with housing and crime issues. When the Minneapolis City Council sponsored a "town hall" meeting to air community concerns on September 19, 1996, the first five persons signed up to speak were landlords. This prompted an angry column by the editor of the *Reader*, personally attacking Disney and me. We threatened to sue the newspaper when an unsigned letter in the same vein appeared, which we suspected might have been written by the editor. An apology appeared in one of the *Reader's* last issues. We met with the new Minneapolis police chief and his staff to discuss landlord concerns. We met with a representative of the *Star Tribune* editorial board. Like gangbusters, we hit the annual meeting of the Hennepin County Board. We picketed the Fourth Precinct police station when city officials demolished an apartment building whose owner was said to be a notorious "slumlord". Since most of that building's "crimes" had occurred on the street, we thought that the police should accept some ownership of those problems considering that its headquarters were less than two blocks away.

A young African American woman, Helen Hughes, had been killed by gun fire as she was buying ice cream cones for her three children in front of that building at 1030 Morgan Avenue North. I knew her. I had recently given her a ride to the Dollar Store on Lowry and Penn. She and her children had stayed in my apartment building just a few months earlier. Unfortunately, she was related to the people whom the neighborhood group had accused of drug dealing. While the Mayor's picture was on the front page of the *Star Tribune* compassionately hugging this woman's mother, the city had closed down my building because I had not evicted her (the mother) and her relatives fast enough.

At the urging of group members, I filed a lawsuit against the city of Minneapolis, the two city inspectors, and the City Council member alleging that abuse of process had taken place when my building was condemned. The city had used its power to inspect buildings, presumably for health and safety purposes, for unrelated purposes such as crime control. Unfortunately, the facade of official secrecy surrounding the incident prevented gathering of hard evidence. Andy Ellis, a retired housing inspector belonging to the group, assured me that to condemn a building for cockroach infestation when it was under the care of a licensed pest-control firm was not standard practice. Even so, the courts give cities broad discretion in regulatory matters. I abandoned the case when I learned that it would cost me more than $20,000 in attorney fees to take it to court. Being now without a job, I could not afford to jeopardize my future to finance a test case.

On Labor Day weekend, 1996, our landlord group set up a card table on the corner of 19th and Portland, said to be the site of the worst drug dealing in town, and held a news conference. We pointed out the obvious fact that, while city officials were punishing landlords for failure to control drug dealing in their buildings, a flourishing "open air drug market" was taking place out on the street as police squad cars whizzed by. This was our first big event. Camera crews from three television stations and the *Star Tribune's* ace City Hall reporter, Kevin Diaz, covered it. (Diaz was a fearless reporter who at this event knocked on the front door of a suspected drug dealer's house in pursuit of an interview.) Adding to the excitement, Diaz's article reported that "just before 2 p.m., what sounded like a gunshot rang out ... from the direction of Portland and Franklin Avenues. It was widely assumed to be a sign of the neighborhood's illegal drug trade."

The crime problem in Minneapolis - a.k.a. "Murderapolis" - had gotten to be so bad that the Governor of Minnesota ordered National Guard helicopters to fly over parts of the city and shine spotlights down on the streets. While many liberals scoffed, we publicly applauded the Governor's action. In response, I received a let-

ter from Governor Arne Carlson, dated September 20, 1996, which read in part: "I commend the Minneapolis Property Rights Action Committee and its proposed agenda for addressing criminal behavior within the City of Minneapolis. It is concern and commitment such as that which is being demonstrated by your organization that is important in confronting criminal and anti-social behavior."

Charlie Disney regularly accused the Minneapolis police of ignoring street crime in the Phillips neighborhood, which he called "a crime containment zone." Several of us testified before the Hennepin County Commission in favor of building the new jail. Our agitation seemed to have little effect on city officials. To turn up the heat a few notches, Disney and Mel Gregerson, owner of an apartment building on Park Avenue, began conducting what were called "Minneapolis crack tours". A block club in Phillips had actually printed a brochure for these "tours". Charlie and Mel drove a large van through Phillips streets, the scene of intense drug dealing, posing as suburban drug customers while important government officials sat in the back seat. Mel and Charlie would arrange to buy cocaine for their mysterious guests, but, of course, the deal would fall through at the last moment. More than twenty of these "tours" took place; it's lucky no one got shot. We even offered to conduct crack tours for members of the Democratic National Committee who were considering Minneapolis as a site for its 2000 convention.

Needless to say, the city's political establishment hated us. A human-rights attorney posted a notice on the city-issues email discussion group that the crack tours showed the "racist" nature of our organization. We were making fun of the mostly black drug dealers. In response, I argued that the crack tours were intended mainly to put pressure on the police. But, I wrote, "if you are determined to find racism, I'm sure you will succeed." For that comment, I received a warning from the discussion-group host not to post personal attacks in the future.

This went on for the better part of five years. To say the least, Minneapolis Property Rights Action Committee was not a "team player" on the local political scene. Through our actions

we did, however, manage gradually to persuade the community that buildings do not cause crime; people do. The city police, not landlords, are the community's main crime fighters. Particular neighborhoods such as Phillips should not be used as "jail substitutes". Police should arrest criminals and judges should issue meaningful sentences.

Against our own economic interest as landlords, we also argued that the city should not demolish structurally sound buildings. We picketed two sites of such buildings scheduled to be demolished. A triplex at 3330 Chicago Avenue South, owned by the Minneapolis Community Development Agency, was bulldozed even as our protest was taking place. We made sure that members of the Minnesota legislature learned how state tax dollars for Minneapolis community development were being spent. We also held a rally in front of a building at 2727 Portland Avenue South near the Honeywell headquarters. By then, our group was equipped with bull horns and satirical sheet music. We were regularly able to turn out a crowd of twenty to thirty activists to put the spotlight on bad city practices. When the "affordable housing" crisis became a cause celebre in 2000 and 2001, the landlords could honestly say: We told you so.

The city of Minneapolis was tearing down buildings to appease neighborhood groups that wanted the land for public gardens and side yards. Sometimes individuals sitting on their housing committees arranged to acquire these properties, fix-up grants, or other government benefits for themselves. When David Sundberg, a landlord, told me how a committee of the Central Neighborhood Improvement Association was arranging sweetheart deals for its members, I went to the next meeting under cover. There I learned that the committee was recommending to the city that it demolish three buildings in the neighborhood because an appraiser had estimated that the cost of repairing the buildings was more than their worth. Furthermore, the owners could not be located.

I managed to locate the owner of one building who said she had arranged with a contractor to renovate the building for a price much less than what the appraiser had estimated would be needed. We staged a demonstration at this building with the owner and her son. Reporter Lou Harvin covered it for the public-television station, KTCA. This incident illustrated how city-approved appraisers justified building demolitions by the use of questionable cost formulae. We also upset the housing committee members when our cable-television show producer, Bryan Olson, set up his camera equipment at one of their meetings and, despite objections, recorded the proceedings.

When Ann Prazniak's decomposing body was found stuffed inside a cardboard box in an apartment building, the city blamed the owner of the building for the tragedy. At a public gathering, City Council member Jim Niland vowed that the city would "descend like a ton of bricks" on the property owner if he did not fix the problem soon. Television news programs reported that inspectors had spotted rats near the building - a sure sign of impending problems with the city. Minneapolis Property Rights Action Committee swung into action. Over the weekend, Charlie Disney and several others interrogated the man who until two weeks earlier had owned the building. Were the locks functioning? Was maintenance being kept up? Did he carefully screen applicants for the apartments?

Satisfied that the landlord was not at fault, the Property Rights group sent out a press release that it would hold a public meeting on the Prazniak murder in the Minneapolis mayor's office. The release stated that this group had five-hundred members. Some media reported that five-hundred landlords would be gathering in the mayor's office. About fifty of us were there. The mayor graciously let us use her anteroom for the meeting. Charlie Disney led the building's previous

owner through a set of questions that were intended to show his innocence. A battery of television cameras recorded the event.

It soon became apparent that the mayor, Council member Niland, and other city officials, as well as the media people, did not much care for the process that we had devised. Niland read a statement from a community-police officer to the effect that the apartment owner was a bad landlord. The mayor asked for permission to speak. Eyeing a good sound bite, she gave a five-minute pep talk about how we all ought to work together to solve crime problems, how the city was ready to work with landlords to deal with problem tenants, etc. I stood up to reply. The Prazniak murder, I said, was not caused by negligent landlords or misbehaving tenants but by drug-addicted thugs who had broken into the building from the street. Turning around to Jim Niland, I said, "Don't ask landlords to solve the city's crime problem, Mr. Niland. That's the responsibility of the police."

There was thunderous applause. Then, one after another, the mostly minority tenants of the troubled apartment building who were in the audience came up to the front table to denounce city officials for wanting to toss innocent people out on the street. The mayor and Council member beat a hasty retreat. The mayor's assistant, listening to this angry talk, promised that the mayor would visit the apartment building at 1818 Park on the following day to listen to tenants' concerns and propose solutions to their housing needs. This event made all the local news programs and was the subject of a front-page story in the *Star Tribune* written by Kevin Diaz.

The other high (or low) point in the group's activist history was an incident that took place on the Friday before the general election in November 1998. The city was proposing the revoke the rental license of a five-unit apartment building owned by a man named Russ Erkkila who had just put $100,000 of his own money into renovations. The community police (CCP-SAFE) had orchestrated this move. Erkkila had received his third warning letter in a year which, according to city ordinance, triggered a license review by the City Council. I interviewed Erkkila. None of the incidents associated with the three letters seemed to me to be a legitimate cause of revoking his license. Either Erkkila had dealt promptly with the situation, he did not receive the letter, or he had done nothing which met the statutory definition of landlord neglect.

Nevertheless, a City Council committee headed by Joe Biernat, the Council's vice president, had approved the revocation. Biernat remarked at the hearing that he seldom went against the recommendation of a SAFE officer, adding infamously that, in this case, the officer was a "goddess". I wrote up a summary of Erkkila's case and sent copies to each of the City Council members. Then we sent a letter to the goddess-like police officer, Hillary Freeman, telling her to be in her office on Friday morning at 9 o'clock sharp since we wanted to talk with her about the Erkkila situation.

Equipped with placards, a bull horn, American flag, and other protest paraphernalia, thirty people gathered outside the SAFE headquarters downtown. Besides members of our group and my brother and his wife, the protesters included candidates for state-wide office from several minor parties. Hillary Freeman was, of course, on vacation. We talked instead with a Lieutenant Diaz. Upon hearing that the City Council had already voted to revoke Erkkila's license, our group headed over to the Council chambers a block away. A meeting was in progress.

We first sat obediently in the benches. Then Charlie Disney rose to get things started. We began circling the spectator area of the Council chambers carrying our picket signs. The City Council members sat stone-faced conducting their business. Then, one of our group, Keith Reitman, shouted, "Hey, there's a demonstration going on here." Jackie Cherryhomes, the Council President, banged her gavel. "This is our meeting, sit down," she said. "No it isn't," replied Bob Anderson, an ex-cop; "It's our meeting."

All hell broke loose as members of our group began shouting at the Council members. We had a camcorder to record the event. "Legalized extortion! You people ought to be put in prison!," yelled a former landlord who had lost his triplex to the city's development agency. The City Council members huddled

in small groups to decide what action to take next. Evidently because a mass arrest might affect the state election next week, the Council leadership decided to ride out the storm. Joe Biernat made a brief statement. His insulting remarks only brought more shouts from our side. We left after half an hour. The article in next morning's *Star Tribune* called it the worst disturbance at City Hall in over twenty years. The City Council purchased additional security equipment.

We also took on the poverty group ACORN and the Legal Aid society when they tried to harass landlords. On November 18, 2000, ACORN conducted a "slumlord tour" for the media, taking a bus to three sites. Our people also climbed aboard. The first "slumlord" was one of our own members, a man with a reputation for keeping his place in good repair. A tenant who had put a pizza box in the oven was claiming that the landlord had ignored calls for maintenance on this appliance. Unfortunately for ACORN, another tenant told the television crew that this apartment was the best one where he had ever lived. The second site also did not seem to be in "slum" condition. It was the third one, however, which really caught our attention.

A tenant had accused the landlord, a pregnant Hmong woman, of neglecting maintenance on the roof. She also said the building had no heat. When we arrived at the apartment, the hallway seemed well heated. The tenant claimed there was no heat in her apartment unit but would not let anyone enter to verify that fact. In an empty unit, work was being done on the ceiling. We later learned that the landlady had repeatedly tried to get the roofing contractor to come back to repair a defective installation. There was ice buildup. Water would trickle through the ceilings when the ice thawed. During one such incident, while she was set to deliver her baby and in no condition to respond, a legal paraprofessional was at the building gathering evidence of the landlady's negligence. My caretaker and I went over to repair a ruptured ceiling in the complainant's apartment so that the evidence of negligence would be removed. Infuriated, the legal note taker tried to find out my name from my caretaker but he wouldn't tell.

The Legal Aid Society of Hennepin County did learn all our names a bit later when several of us landlords went to the County Commission to testify in favor of cutting its budget. I wrote a letter to the Commissioners pointing out that the Legal Aid Society was threatening to break the Hmong landlady financially by imposing heavy legal costs if she did not settle on their terms. As a condition of settlement, she was required to lie to prospective landlords who might later be interviewing her former tenants for an apartment. The landlady had been told that some of those tenants were using drugs. And here Legal Aid was trying to keep the tenants in her building while extorting several months of free rent. During my own testimony to the Commission, I turned to the head of Legal Aid, seated next to me, and blasted him for the stipulation about lying. Maybe that's how you do it in the courtroom, I said, but not around me. Others from our group also denounced Legal Aid and its tactics. We later received letters from a Commissioner saying how glad she was that we had showed up to testify. Usually it was those on the other side who appeared at Commission hearings.

Oddly enough, our group's main activity was not public testimony or protest demonstrations but producing a cable-television show. Back in December 1996, a member named Mike Wisniewski persuaded Disney that it might be worthwhile to videotape our meetings and show them on public-access television. With our expanding membership, we moved the meetings to a community room at a Minneapolis city park. The two-hour meetings were divided into two one-hour segments to fit into available television time slots. Eventually, a freelance video cameraman and producer active in Reform Party politics, Bryan Olson, took over production of the show. It aired on the regional cable-television station, Channel 6, and on MTN, the Minneapolis cable-access station.

The once freewheeling landlord "gripe sessions" turned into a staged discussion. Charlie Disney was the moderator. The program featured experts on housing and crime issues, along with politicians. At the same time, it was an audience-participation show at which members of the audience were free to speak out or ask questions. I used to describe our event as "a cross between a public-policy discussion and the Jerry Springer show." If audience members did not throw chairs or expose themselves, they certainly used politically incorrect language. Even so, we found that the show could attract serious guests. It attracted a growing audience and was watched at City Hall.

Minneapolis Mayor Sharon Sayles Belton was the guest of honor at our June 2000 meeting. We tried to treat the mayor respectfully without giving her such an easy time as to create a publicity windfall. At the meeting, the mayor agreed to begin a serious dialogue with our group; hopefully, this would usher in a new era of cooperation between landlords and city government. Part of the process was to develop lists of issues that were of mutual concern. I was the group's point man in that endeavor. We held meetings to refine our issues. I met with the mayor's representative to review each point. The idea was that the mayor's office would formulate a response. Out of this might come some proposals for change, we hoped.

After the one face-to-face meeting, I checked in periodically to see what progress was being made. There was no progress. Inconclusive discussions were still being held within the city bureaucracy. After several months of this, we began to play a little game on our television show. I would pretend to be the eternal optimist still waiting for the mayor's office to come through with a good proposal. Another man, Jim Swartwood, would call me a "Neville Chamberlain" who favored appeasing the mayor. Long after it was clear that our "dialogue" was a political charade, we kept up this game. Finally, in the spring of 2001, when the mayor announced her plans to run for reelection, we learned that her main housing proposal consisted of expunging Unlawful Detainer records - making it more difficult for landlords to learn if an applicant for an apartment had previously been evicted! Yes, we had indeed been had. We began discussing the possibility of Charlie Disney's running for mayor.

Our group had been active in the previous city election. The election of 1997 pitted the incumbent mayor, Sharon Sayles Belton, the first woman and first African American to hold that position, against Barbara Carlson, hostess of a radio talk show (and also the Governor's ex-wife). I announced that I would run for mayor that year but bowed out to support Carlson. The landlord group formed what we called our "political committee" to support favored candidates. Members of this committee tended to be landlords not active in our group. We in the regular group were dismayed to learn that the political committee was positioning itself as a committee of "responsible landlords" (as opposed to the irresponsible ones in our group) and developing criteria for membership. Since the committee had been formed with our money and membership lists, that stance seemed ungrateful. Another problem was that the committee, meeting once a week, spent all its time debating policy statements. By the late summer, little or nothing had yet been done to help candidates.

Meanwhile, Charlie Disney and friends were out in the campaign trenches. Our hand-lettered signs, exhibited at a mayoral debate at Lucille's Kitchen, nearly precipitated a race riot. One sign read: "A vote for Sharon is a vote for crime." A white woman carrying that sign was physically assaulted by a black woman. When the first woman's husband pulled up in a car trying to rescue her, the mayor's personal bodyguard fired a shot at his car as it sped away. This could have been a major political embarrassment for Sayles Belton had Carlson not taken the "high road" and joined in the mayor's plea for racial harmony. I was not in town at the time. Neither was our "political committee" involved in any of this. While it had endorsed several candidates (most of whom lost), this group was still debating resolutions and policy statements two months before the election.

The main landlord group offered its membership list so that the political committee could telephone landlords to ask for lawnsign locations. Instead, it voted to wait another month before taking action. At this point, I took it upon myself to gather up all the copies of our membership list and tell the committee to fend for itself. That caused hard feelings. After the umbilical cord with its parent had been severed, the political committee became defunct.

This experience caused me to think about what kind of a group Minneapolis Property Rights Action Committee was. It was not democratic. It did not pass resolutions or take votes. The group's leadership was unelected. Yet, more than most groups involved in politics, it got things done. It was not like our own "political committee" or most neighborhood groups whose members just sat around talking and taking votes. This was an action committee. We all looked to Charlie Disney for leadership in organizing the action. While Charlie had his critics, he was by far the group's most hard-working member. He was its communication center, on

the telephone for hours on end. He was the one who knew all the people both inside our organization and out. We trusted Charlie's judgment in deciding group affairs.

Democracy, I thought, is not all it's cracked up to be. Sometimes, the best kind of organization is one which acts by consensus and takes direction from a recognized leader, even someone who was never elected to that position. When Charlie Disney resigned from the leadership of our organization in the summer of 2001, his departure put that theory to the test.

Taking

Action

CHAPTER TWENTY-TWO

Growing Up Politically

My full name is William Howard Taft McGaughey, Jr. My father, after whom I was named, was born in 1912. President William Howard Taft was seeking reelection that year. My paternal grandfather, a medical doctor from Indianapolis who died in 1931, was an ardent Republican. Democrat Woodrow Wilson won the 1912 Presidential election because Taft and Theodore Roosevelt, the "Bull Moose" candidate, split the Republican vote.

My maternal grandfather, on the other hand, was a Democrat. He represented Greencastle, Indiana, and surrounding area in the Indiana Senate. In the late 1920s, he was minority leader of the Senate. His main claim to fame was that, when the Republicans tried to gerrymander the Indiana legislature, my grandfather and his Democratic colleagues disappeared for a time so that a quorum could not be reached. Senator Andrew Durham and friends holed up in a hotel somewhere in Ohio beyond reach of the law and negotiated with the Republican majority about the redistricting plan until it was acceptable to them. This grandfather died in 1954. The last time I saw him he was telling my mother about how he had the Putnam County Sheriff impound equipment belonging to a power company when it tried to erect a power line across his farm land without his permission. He and Paul Wellstone (also a power-line protester) might have had some interesting conversations.

In other words, both my parents came from political families. Both were pages in the Indiana legislature although they were not acquainted then. My parents first met when my father approached my mother, president of Kappa Alpha Theta at Depauw University, about admitting his sister into that sorority. Years later, both journalists, they ran into each other again on the streets of New York City. In the late 1930s, my father was a reporter for the *Wall Street Journal*, then a relatively small trade paper. He belonged that group of Depauw graduates, headed by Bernard Kilgore, who built the *Wall Street Journal* into a large-circulation newspaper. A corporate history of the Journal describes my father as "a talented rewrite man".

My mother, too, enjoyed a successful career in the newspaper business. She worked her way up from community papers to become a columnist for the Associated Press. In 1939, she was invited to attend a public demonstration of a new gadget at Rockefeller Center: television. My mother then wrote a column about how audience members should behave in a television studio. Lou Gehrig's wife invited my mother to visit the couple's New York-area home to see how they were coping with Gehrig's illness. Her AP story pointed out that the "iron man" of baseball also had an "iron wife". This story was bylined "John Durham" because the editors evidently did not think that a reporter named Joan would be writing a baseball story. My grandfather, reading his daily newspaper in Greencastle, was amused.

My parents were married in New York City on November 18,1939. Walter Winchell mentioned their marriage in his news dispatch. Within a month, my parents moved to Detroit where my father took a new job as public-relations director of the Automobile Manufacturers Association. This was an exciting time to be working in the automobile industry. The industry would soon be converting to war production to fight the Germans and Japanese. Detroit factories became "the Arsenal of Democracy", and my father was in the thick of it. My father's boss was George Romney, later CEO of American Motors and Governor of Michigan.

I was born in Detroit on February 21, 1941. My brother Andrew was also born there in June 1942; another brother, David, in June 1944; and a sister, Margaret, in May 1948. By then, my parents had both become Republicans. Even though they had voted for Franklin Roosevelt in 1936, they worked as volunteers in the 1940 Presidential campaign of Wendell Willkie. He, like them, was an Indiana native who had made good in New York City. In his public-relations position, my father became a fixture in the Detroit business community. He was the publicity director of the 1946 Automobile Golden Jubilee, a civic celebration marking the 75th anniversary of the first automobile, which brought old-timers such as Barney Oldfield, William S. Knudsen, and Henry Ford together for the last time.

Upward mobility was always difficult for me because, at each point in my life, my father had done better in his career at the same age. A newspaperman in the 1930s, he was a trade-association executive in the 1940s, vice president of an automobile company (American Motors) in the 1950s, a senior vice president of another trade association (National Association of Manufacturers) in the 1960s and 1970s, and, in his retirement years, a fund raiser for Business-Industry Political Action Committee (BIPAC). As a social helpmate for my father, my mother was there at each step of the way.

Together, they were sent to Great Britain in 1948 to try to persuade Winston Churchill to come to the United States to take part in celebrations of the 100 millionth automobile. Churchill could not arrange the visit but he did take time to talk with my parents about American politics. (He thought Eisenhower had bungled his chances for the Presidency in 1948.) In 1953, George Romney brought my father to Nash-Kelvinator to be his assistant. After a merger with Hudson Motors, the firm was renamed American Motors. It was the fourth largest automobile manufacturer in the country. After its chief executive, George Mason, died, Romney took over both as president and board chairman.

My father became vice president of American Motors for Communications in the mid 1950s. Having responsibility for the company's advertising budget, he reviewed a list of potential television shows that American Motors might sponsor. The show which he and my mother picked out was one called "Disneyland". He flew to California for business discussions with Walt Disney. Disney gave my father four autographed cartoon celluloids, one for each of us children. We were photographed in Detroit with Fess Parker who played Davy Crockett in the Disneyland television series. My parents were present at ceremonies opening the original Disneyland park in Anaheim. American Motors had an exhibit called "Circarama" there; my dad gave Frank Sinatra and Sammy Davis Jr. a sneak preview.

The popularity of the Disneyland television show, with George Romney as product pitch man, propelled the "compact-car revolution" of the late 1950s. In television commercials, Romney held up a clay model of a dinosaur symbolizing the "gas-

guzzling" automobiles of that era. Sales of Ramblers soared, sparking the compact-car revolution. My father became general chairman of the 1956 National Automobile Show in New York City. Because this was an industry revival, he had to persuade General Motors' chairman, Harlow Curtis, not to put on a separate automobile show. That summer, Romney's son Scott and I took classes in welding and housewiring at Cass Technical High School in Detroit. The Mormons believed that each young man should have a useful trade to fall back on in hard times.

My political inclinations followed my parents' in the early years. We were Republicans who rooted for Robert A. Taft at the 1952 convention both because of the name and the fact that an Indian Village neighbor was an ardent Taft supporter. The United Automobile Workers, headed by Walter Reuther, were a negative force for person of that persuasion. I myself was a bit more open minded when, as a senior at Cranbrook School, I was head of a student organization which invited a UAW representative to speak on campus. Civil Rights were not such an issue in Detroit. Political controversy was instead centered on domestic and international communism. When I went to Yale, I felt a certain alienation from values of the Eastern social and political establishment. In my heart, I was a Detroit chauvinist who believed that the truly great things happening in America were related to the automobile industry, industrial labor, and so forth, rather than to the political and cultural concerns of academics. Thomas Edison and Henry Ford were my heroes, not James Joyce.

George Romney was elected Governor of Michigan in 1962. There was talk of his running for President of the United States. I was excited at the prospect of such a man, my father's mentor and friend, entering the realm of big-time politics. In Landshut, Bavaria, during my period as a college dropout, I produced a book-length manuscript postulating a new conservatism with Romney as its champion. (The genesis of this was the idea that it was illegitimate for government to redistribute wealth through taxation and spending. If that happened, I argued, the voting system should be changed to give people the same number of votes as the money they paid in taxes.) This project, focused on faraway events, helped to hone my writing skills. My father had several copies mimeographed and bound. I presented them to Romney's associates and to the Governor himself at a "Michigan Day" luncheon in 1963.

In fact, my scheme was delusional. While George Romney did have his eye on the White House, he became a liberal stalwart within the Republican party. That political positioning went against the conservative tide which brought Barry Goldwater's Presidential nomination in 1964 and Richard Nixon's election in 1968 and 1972, followed by the Reagan revolution of the 1980s. As a new resident of Minnesota, I joined the Young Republican League, hoping to assist Romney in his presidential efforts. Shaking hands with me in a reception line in St. Paul, the Governor asked "What are you doing here?", before turning to the next person.

In 1968, my dreams of George Romney being elected President were dashed. In February, he withdrew from the race for the Republican nomination before the first primary after polls in New Hampshire showed him badly trailing Richard Nixon. Romney was done in by a careless remark about having been "brainwashed" by the Johnson administration during a visit to Vietnam. It was an early example of the "gaffe politics" practiced by journalists: Romney was tagged as an intellectual lightweight. In fact, the Michigan governor was plenty smart. His undoing was the fact that he was an outsider to the Eastern political-cultural establishment, not to mention being a liberal Republican. But the damage was done and I moved on to other interests.

Years later, in the summer of 1994, while traveling through Michigan, my brother Andy and I stopped by the Romney home unannounced and had a short, but cordial visit with Lenore Romney, the governor's wife who was herself a former Republican candidate for U.S. Senate. Her husband was then in Massachusetts helping their younger son, Mitt, campaign for Senate against Ted Kennedy. They had recently been guests of the Bushes at their home in Kennebunkport, Maine, she proudly told us. George Romney later sent a note to my father saying that his wife had enjoyed our brief visit. He died two years later. Mitt Romney, fresh from a stint with the 2002 Salt Lake Olympic Committee, is today Governor of Massachusetts.

Romney's withdrawal from the 1968 Presidential race was the first of many shocks that year, ranging from President Johnson's decision not to seek reelection to street violence at the Chicago convention and two assassinations. My political allegiance shifted to Richard Nixon, who was more conservative than Rockefeller and yet, despite his "loser" image, surprisingly in tune with current developments. I attended a Minnesota organizational meeting for Nixon where I met persons who would innocently figure in the Watergate scandal - Kenneth Dahlberg, the Midwest Nixon treasurer who deposited a check traced to the Watergate burglars' account, and Clark MacGregor, who succeeded John Mitchell at the President's reelection committee. I was an usher at a Nixon rally in Minneapolis and, on election day, an election judge.

Still, my contributions were minimal. I was then a person without a job whose thoughts centered on Walt Whitman - at one time, in the mid 1960s, I could recite from memory almost a third of Whitman's poem "Song of Myself" - schemes to organize relay marathons, and other pie-in-the-sky ideas. Too much the loose cannon to fit into any Republican organization, I was mostly a bystander to the turbulent events of those times.

My feelings about the Vietnam war were mixed. On one hand, I felt that the Johnson administration spent young American lives as freely as it spent tax dollars; on the other, I resented the anti-war protesters' cavalier attitude toward their fellow countrymen who were fighting in that war. Being passively conservative, I did not partake of my generation's political experience. Instead, I pursued my own loosely focused writing projects. For three months during 1970, I lived in an empty house in Milford, Pennsylvania, which my parents owned. In December of

that year, I attended the 75th anniversary "Congress of Industry" put on by the National Association of Manufacturers. My father was the staff person charged with overseeing that event. The featured speaker in 1970 was President Nixon.

I had the grandiose idea of approaching one of Nixon's cabinet members, Robert Finch, to propose that the President's re-election campaign stage a gigantic marathon run across the country to whip up excitement for the campaign. The Levander for Governor campaign in Minnesota had given its blessing to a similar project of mine in 1966, but I was unable to generate enough support to carry it out successfully. Finch canceled his appearance at the NAM gathering so that my proposal never had a hearing. In retrospect, anything would have been better for the Republicans than the dirty-tricks operation that led to Watergate.

My political views shifted to the left because of my interest in the shorter-workweek issue. Actually, I began researching the shorter workweek issue when the Young Republican League called for its members do policy research in areas of personal interest. The local Republicans were not hostile to the idea of shorter working hours; it's just that the project fell through. When, in 1974, I resumed the research and founded a shorter-workweek organization, I naturally gravitated toward people who might support this approach, namely labor activists and socialists. Carter's election as President softened my heart toward liberals. I liked Jimmy Carter and his wife, Rosalyn, small-town people from Georgia. I conducted a public-opinion survey on work hours in 1976 and, a year later, founded General Committee for a Shorter Workweek. A companion organization with Section 501(c)3 status, Free Time Research Group, came later. But these were mostly organizations representing my own dreams.

It would serve no purpose here to repeat my acquaintance with persons or groups interested in work-time issues and in international trade. Getting to know Eugene McCarthy on a personal basis was rather ironic in view of my earlier enthusiasm for Romney's Presidential prospects. In 1968, George Romney's political career went into the tank as Eugene McCarthy's Presidential campaign was blazing across the political landscape like a comet. Also, McCarthy had a hand in the fallout from Romney's remark about having been "brainwashed" by the Johnson Administration. McCarthy had told the press that, in Romney's case, brainwashing was unnecessary: a "light rinse would do it." Yet, Romney apparently bore no ill will toward McCarthy. I once published an article in the *Star Tribune* which identified me as a McCarthy partisan. My father sent a copy to George Romney who sent him a kind note in return.

I was meanwhile caucusing with the Democrats both on the east side of St. Paul, where I lived from 1984 to 1989, and in north Minneapolis, my present home. Being the ideological misfit, I can't say that I was more comfortable with the people who attended those caucuses than I was with their Republican counterparts. The DFL party in District 58 has a caucus system at their conventions which allows delegates to caucus by interest according to self-chosen categories. When I tried to caucus as "pro-Wellstone, pro life" at the 1992 convention, I was told there was no such animal. Caucusing by preference for Presidential candidates, I followed the lead of a delegate who supported Eugene McCarthy. He received only a few votes in the first round of balloting and was dropped.

My ward's representative on the City Council, Jackie Cherryhomes, approached me in a cheerful mood, inviting me to "join the party" for Bill Clinton. She said her political career had begun years ago when she worked in McCarthy's campaign. With some reluctance, I joined the Clinton caucus. I later contacted Cherryhomes to ask if she would sign a petition to support a shorter workweek. She said she would check with her husband who was an official with a city-employee union. Evidently, the husband turned thumbs down. Cherryhomes called me to say she would not sign the petition. I argued with her. Next year, after I became a landlord, Cherryhomes turned on me. I have sometimes thought that my advocacy of a shorter workweek marked me in her eyes as a naive idealist or, at least, someone who could safely be kicked.

Politically, I am not a socialist. I believe in the free-enterprise system because ownership of a business creates an incentive for its managers to make decisions that are in the organization's best long-term interest. Managers with clear authority to make decisions can do so quickly, with minimal red tape, according to the situation. I as owner of an apartment building can be foolish or wise with my own money. I must seek to be wise lest I go out of business. The problem with publicly owned enterprises is that the managers' interests may not be aligned with the long-term needs of the enterprise or the constituency to be served. They manage their organizations with "other people's money". Appearing to belong to nobody, one is tempted to try to get one's hands on this. Public-sector managers are often in conflict with their constituencies and, generationally, with their successors in a position. Since perceptions are everything, they have inadequate incentives to be faithful stewards of the public trust.

I believe in representative (rather than direct) democracy. The system of direct, participatory democracy practiced in Minneapolis neighborhoods calls forth some of the neighborhood's least savory characters; these are persons who apparently have nothing better to do with their lives than to attend an endless series of meetings. More often than not, the purpose is to snag some of the "other people's money" floating through the system. Elected officials, engaged in close political relationships with these community activists, sometimes excuse their own bad de-

cisions by saying they were heeding their constituents' wishes. Where this kind of politics turns hostile, it brings out the wolf-pack instinct. The Red Guard model of revitalizing community affairs doesn't work.

My particular passion is for greater openness and transparency in politics. Having seen my apartment building be condemned through secretive processes, I loathe decision makers who do ill to others concealed behind an institutional facade. Some said the Minneapolis police had city inspectors condemn my building. Others said the neighborhood group did it, or the head of a nonprofit community group who wanted me to sell or donate my building to her organization. Inspections would not reveal the process by which my building was closed except to say that it wasn't a tenant who had complained. The law required that such information be kept confidential.

As a member of Minneapolis Property Rights Action Committee, I approached the Minnesota legislature about changing this law. A DFL member of the House introduced a bill which would have made communications between government officials pertaining to local inspections a matter of public record; however, a Republican house member who chaired the pertinent committee would not schedule a committee hearing. The rot behind the woodwork of city government must stay concealed!

I think it important that public officials be willing to put their names on their actions. It's also important in public life to put one's own name behind one's opinions. I am myself a regular contributor of letters to the editor of my local newspaper, always signing my name. I wish those on the newspaper editorial staff would likewise disclose theirs. Occasionally, some individuals have wanted the Property Rights group to front for their personal agendas. A political candidate suggested that we exhibit posters of repeat criminals whose black faces would signal the racial dimension of neighborhood crime. Another person created a web site for the group, slipping in a few pages that blamed low-intelligence blacks for the failings of the Minneapolis school system. At my urging, Charlie Disney rejected the web site that contained these pages. We said it was OK to put any kind of opinion in a web site so long as the person puts his own name to it. Just don't use our name.

So, where does this leave me politically? Clinton Democrats (and their sympathizers in Minneapolis city government) are political "realists" who use gender and race to advance their political careers but are mainly interested in money - lots of other people's money. After what they did to me as a landlord, I could never again join them. Republicans are an extension of the corporate culture. I fit into neither two-party camp. The Greens are

idealists - which is good - but they have some unhelpful ideas about gender and about business. As a small businessman, I would like to be pro-business but not if it means letting people who support themselves through honest work sink farther into economic despair. I am a nationalist but also an internationalist: Cannot we not be on friendly terms with all peoples? The cult of the imperial Presidency leaves me cold.

If only because of their enemies, Jesse Ventura and the Independence Party are for me the most positive example. However, they need an infusion of new ideas. My experience with landlord politics has put certain ideas in my head. But it is the old ideas, related to labor and political correctness, that I think are most applicable to the political situation. That's where I now stand.

CHAPTER TWENTY-THREE

Two Campaigns for Mayor

Minneapolis Property Rights Action Committee gave me a situation that I had never had before. I had friends who shared common experiences. I had something to talk about knowledgeably and persons willing to listen. The fact that we were a despised group in the city made us landlords feel emotionally close. At our monthly meetings, I could stand up before the group to speak my piece without having to worry about my performance or even prepare for it. This experience improved my self-confidence as a speaker. I felt better about myself at public gatherings. Not being the group's leader, I also enjoyed the luxury of not having to do everything myself. Others also pitched in to advance the cause. On the level of city politics, it was possible to make things happen. I could personally meet the principal players in city government. It was not like tilting at windmills to affect change on a national or international level. We were showing that, united, individuals could fight City Hall.

The Property Rights group was more a political-pressure than an economic-interest group. Outsiders did not realize this. Many of us, including me, did not own enough property to make it worthwhile to invest great amounts of our personal time and energy in the landlord cause if the goal was merely economic improvement. We would then be giving free labor to the big landlords who did little to help us. They would be the principal beneficiaries of our efforts. No, we were doing this work for the same reason that any political activist does: to improve the community. Secondarily, our members derived memorable personal experiences from working with others towards a worthy end. What more can one expect from life than this? It boils down to people. The landlord group brought me together with interesting, admirable persons who shared my life. I had few regrets about spending five or six years in the "landlord struggle" with a benefit such as this.

Minneapolis Property Rights Action Committee was like a union for landlords. Its motto could easily have been: "An injury to one is an injury to all." In this case, however, we were not organizing against tenants but against neighborhood groups and city government. Inevitably, we were drawn into electoral politics, which is both a score card for political activity and a special opportunity to be heard in community affairs. I knew that I was not a gifted political candidate. That did not matter if I was modestly well organized and had a good cause.

My first venture into electoral politics was to enter the race for Mayor of Minneapolis in 1997. Up until May, no one else stepped forward to challenge Sharon Sayles Belton's bid for re-election. John Derus, her opponent in the 1993 general election, had not expressed interest in running again. Charlie Disney approached radio-talk-show hostess, Barbara Carlson, and received word that she would not run. So I decided to step into the ring. I sent out announcements of my candidacy and was rewarded by reporter Kevin Diaz's generous article about my campaign in the *Star Tribune* which ran eight paragraphs.

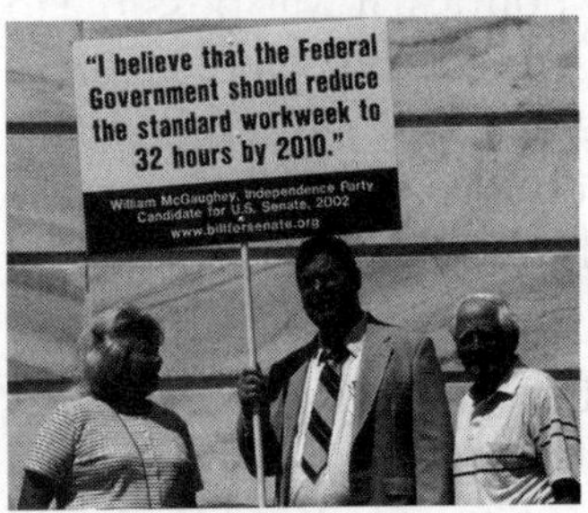
"I believe that the Federal Government should reduce the standard workweek to 32 hours by 2010."
William McGaughey, Independence Party Candidate for U.S. Senate, 2002
www.billforsenate.org

For most of one Saturday, I stood in front of Sy Melby Hall at Augsburg College, where the DFL party was holding its city convention, with a picket sign announcing that I was an independent candidate for Mayor of Minneapolis. This activity produced several interesting discussions. Later that afternoon, I sought the Republican endorsement for Mayor. The group decided not to endorse, perhaps because I had revealed that I was neither a Republican nor a Christian. On Sunday, I marched in the May Day parade to Powderhorn Park. In the following week, Barbara Carlson attended our landlord group's meeting. Soon afterwards, she made a public announcement that she was considering a run for mayor. I immediately suspended my campaign saying that I would support Carlson if she ran. She did run. That was the end of my political candidacy the first time. Carlson received 45% of the vote in the general election. I would have done worse.

Minneapolis city officials were up for reelection again in 2001. I urged Charlie Disney to run for Mayor this time. He was fairly well known in the city as a result of hosting our cable-television show. He would be supported by most persons in our organization. Unlike me, he was personally outgoing and down-to-earth. In our discussions, it was clear that no one, not even Charlie himself, expected Charlie Disney actually to win the election. He would be running for the purpose of raising issues. Being a candidate for Mayor gave him a soap box to discuss city problems from a landlord's perspective. Charlie was evasive until the last moment. At an executive committee meeting of the group held at his house, Charlie went around the room asking people if they thought he should run. Nearly everyone encouraged him to do so. Charlie decided to do it. He would seek the DFL endorsement for Mayor.

The DFL city convention was again held on a Saturday in early May in Sy Melby Hall. This time, we were on the program and had a literature table downstairs. As Charlie's unofficial campaign manager, I wore a college-style mortarboard hat with large mouse ears - I'm for Disney, get it? Some people thought this hat was to protest the mickey mouse spending on education. We put our literature on all the seats. We had a delegate who was willing to put Charlie's name in nomination for Mayor and someone to second it. I gave the nominating speech. Charlie then gave his candidate's speech. As representatives of a group which had bedeviled city officials for so many years, I thought the DFL delegates treated us quite respectfully.

R.T. Rybak, a newcomer aligned with progressive causes, edged out the incumbent mayor, Sharon Sayles Belton, to gain the most votes at the convention. A member of the City Council friendly to our cause, Lisa McDonald, finished third. Charlie received six votes at the convention, for a fourth-place finish. I had met Rybak when he came to our group for support in January. We did not expect him to do that well. Our money was on Lisa McDonald.

Charlie Disney held a campaign strategy meeting. A man who had once run for state legislature gave a presentation on what it took to run a proper campaign. He said that we needed to raise lots of money. We needed to appoint people to certain campaign positions: a press secretary, a volunteer coordinator, a campaign-office manager, a legal advisor, etc. He and another man at the meeting urged Charlie to raise immigration-reform issues. After listening to this talk for awhile, I finally said that I thought these suggestions were ridiculous. Charlie was not a major candidate for a state or federal office. The press would not be beating on his door for interviews. He had to stick to landlord issues where he had credibility. Realistically, Charlie could expect to do most of the campaign work himself. He would have to be out there meeting people at public gatherings, discussing issues, and passing out literature. Perhaps, a few people would help him. Then, if he got lucky, the press might start to take an interest in his campaign.

I did not realize at the time that my analysis depressed Charlie. This discussion laid the foundation for his subsequent withdrawal as a candidate. I may also have contributed to the campaign's demise when, with Charlie's consent, I sent out a memo to the other candidates and to the press stating that Charlie's campaign goal was to receive at least 3% of the vote in the DFL primary. I also said good things about each of the other candidates. This was later interpreted as being defeatist. My purpose was to set low expectations which would be exceeded and so enhance our prestige after the primary.

The most damaging event, however, was Eve White's open support for Hennepin County Commissioner Mark Stenglein's mayoral candidacy. Eve White, a former stripper who had bought several large apartment buildings in south Minneapolis, was a female landlord who through her courage and wit had become an increasingly influential member of our group. She was politically close to Stenglein. At one of our meetings, Eve had taken a dislike to Lisa McDonald for what I thought might be rivalry between two strong-willed, attractive women. McDonald was trying to block Mark Stenglein's candidacy because she and Stenglein would split the conservative vote. Charlie Disney was close to Lisa McDonald.

At a party in Charlie's backyard after our monthly meeting, Eve White solicited a lawnsign location for Stenglein from a group member. Charlie was furious. This act he considered to be disloyal to him as the group's candidate. He said we had all promised him that we would support his candidacy. That was not quite how I remembered it. I thought we should try to be on good terms with all the mayoral candidates excepting perhaps Sayles Belton. I defended Eve's right to support whomever she wished.

Returning home to Minneapolis from a trip to Tennessee, I learned that Charlie Disney was no longer a candidate for Mayor. He was bitter at having been betrayed by the group. He thought I had stabbed him in the back. I regarded that accusation as unfair since I had spent the most time of anyone working on Charlie's campaign. It had not been my decision to abandon the campaign. An unstated problem, I believe, was that Charlie could not bear the thought of entering a contest which he could not win. He was used to winning athletic tournaments. Anything less than victory was personally humiliating. Then Charlie suffered two major heart attacks. The doctor had said that he was suffering from a broken heart.

Charlie withdrew not only from the race for Mayor but from the Minneapolis Property Rights Action Committee. He was no longer its executive director. He and his fiancee, Cheryl, were buying a house in Roseville. He would soon move from Minneapolis. The Property Rights group was in crisis. The Executive Committee selected Eve White as Charlie's replacement.

When Charlie's withdrawal became known, I filed as a candidate for Mayor. I would run the type of campaign that I had urged for Charlie. There would be lots of personal contact with voters. Unfortunately, I had to be out of town for two long stretches of time, once to attend my mother's funeral in Pennsylvania and then to greet my new wife and stepdaughter arriving from China at the Newark airport and once to visit my wife's sister in Chattanooga, Tennessee. I would have to use the remaining time efficiently.

For my party or issues affiliation appearing on the ballot, I chose the title "Affordable Housing - Preservation." I prepared a green-colored sheet of campaign literature, 8 1/2" by 11", double-sided. The front side gave biographical information and a general statement of issues. The back side presented landlord "horror stories" involving city abuse. I also had a picket sign left over from my 1997 mayoral campaign. My standard mode of campaigning consisted of distributing literature as I walked about town or stood with my sign. My favorite places for campaigning were the Minneapolis Farmer's Market, the Uptown area near Hennepin and Lake, and the downtown Minneapolis loop. In all, I gave out about 4,500 pieces of literature.

Public attention centered upon the four major candidates: Mayor Sharon Sayles Belton, R.T. Rybak, Lisa McDonald, and Mark Stenglein. Many of the debates included only those candidates. Because of an out-of-town trip, it was too late for me to participate in the Elliot Park debate on crime which included all the candidates. Like other minor candidates, I had two minutes to make my case at the MICAH-sponsored debate on affordable housing. My only real opportunity was the candidate debate on the Neighborhood Revitalization Program (NPR) which I had not originally planned to attend. I leafleted this event outside and then sat down to listen to the candidates for City Council. As I was about to leave, Mark Stenglein intercepted me at the door. He said that the four major mayoral candidates had agreed to allow the two minor candidates who were still at the meeting, Leslie Davis and me, to participate in this debate with them. So I sat at the front table between Lisa McDonald and R.T. Rybak, trying to answer the questions without much knowledge.

My strategy, to differentiate myself from the other candidates, was to tell the audience of NRP activists that I thought the NRP program was mostly a waste of the taxpayer's money. The city could not afford to continue to fund this "experiment" until its budget situation improved. (In fact, Minneapolis city government, facing a budget crunch, has recently come to the same conclusion.) At one point, I offered Rybak the first twenty seconds of my response time so he could finish an amusing story. This brash, lighthearted approach seemed to work. One or two people told me I had made some good points. Even the Mayor greeted me with a warm smile and hand shake after the meeting. However, the *Star Tribune* article about this event in next day's newspaper neglected to mention that Leslie Davis and I had participated in the debate. I wrote a letter to the editor pointing out that admission. It was printed.

Media coverage was always a problem. I wrote an opinion piece for the *Star Tribune* about the bribery scandal involving a City Council member. It was not accepted. I also wrote an article about the religious coalition for affordable housing, suggesting that housing was a business rather than a charity. The community newspaper, *Pulse*, first said it would print this as a letter to the editor but then decided that to do so would favor a particular candidate. Such policies, by no means confined to the *Pulse*, actually gave political candidates less opportunity to present their views than if they had not been candidates. My best shot at publicity was to participate in a 10-minute candidate interview by Kathy Wurzer on Minnesota Public Radio. Station KFAI-AM also gave mayoral candidates two minutes of air time to make statements. The *Minnesota Daily*, the University of Minnesota newspaper, published an article about my candidacy which included quoted comments from one of my tenants.

The biggest coup was to persuade three of the Twin Cities commercial television stations, public radio, the *Pioneer Press*, and other media to cover a last-minute event at Peavey Plaza involving all the "minor" mayoral candidates. My press release began, with a slightly bitter edge, "You may not have been interested in our ideas but perhaps you'd like to hear us sing." Five of the candidates present at the NPR debate had said they would participate in such an event. Only two, Leslie Davis and myself, actually appeared. As the journalists stood by, I tried feverishly to round up a few extra voices from persons on the street. Two men agreed to join us. So it was that a pair of minor mayoral candidates and two others, holding pages of sheet music, serenaded Twin Cities television audiences with our personal rendition of patriotic songs on local news programs of Monday, September 10th, the evening before the primary election.

None of this mattered when, on the following morning, terrorists hijacked four airplanes and crashed them into the twin towers of the World Trade Center, the Pentagon, and a Pennsylvania farm field. I, like the rest of the world, was stunned. When the vote totals were tabulated that night, R.T. Rybak and Sharon Sayles Belton were the two winners. The votes tapered off sharply after the four major candidates. I finished twelfth of twenty-two candidates, winning just 143 votes city wide. Frankly, I had expected to do better.

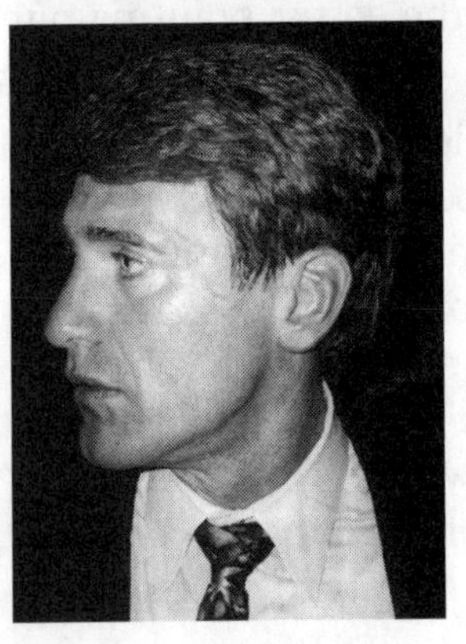

Rybak and Sayles Belton slugged it out for another two months. The eventual winner of the 2001 mayoral election by a landslide was R.T. Rybak. I had distributed literature with him in the Bryn Mawr neighborhood on the Saturday before the November 6th election and then did my own precinct for him. Rybak had made two post-primary appearances at televised meetings of our landlord group. He had met with us again at his campaign headquarters to go over a list of issues.

We could not have imagined how sweet the general election would be for our group. All year long we had set a large poster sign at the front of our meeting place. This poster gave the names of four incumbent City Council members whom we supported and four whom we proposed to defeat. On election night, the four Council members whom we supported all easily won reelection. Three of the four whom we opposed were either defeated or, in one case, did not seek reelection. The fourth person on our hit list, Joe Biernat, who was reelected, resigned from office a year later after being convicted of a felony. As for the replacements, Dean Zimmermann, Natalie Johnson Lee, and Robert Lilligren, who were nonincumbent candidates winning City Council seats in the general election, had appeared as guests at our meetings.

Natalie Johnson Lee's dramatic upset of City Council President, Jackie Cherryhomes, was especially satisfying. We landlords had played an active role in her campaign. I was a poll watcher for Johnson Lee's campaign on election day. Other landlords held up her campaign signs on street corners, drove voters to the polls, or circulated through the northside neighborhoods in a black limousine promoting her candidacy by loud speaker. ACORN, a group previously unfriendly to us, distributed literature throughout the 5th ward written by a member of our group. It asked Cherryhomes twenty-one pointed questions. That night, we landlords and our friends whooped it up. Our political efforts had succeeded beyond our wildest dreams.

CHAPTER TWENTY-FOUR

Lessons Learned from the Landlord Group

Coming to the unexpectedly fruitful end of a chapter in the annals of the landlord group, I had time to reflect upon the lessons of this experience. It seemed that Minneapolis Property Rights Action Committee constituted a new model of political activity. Few recognized our achievement, for landlords as a group came under the radar screen of self-respecting political types. City liberals continued to view us as "exploiters of the poor" - translation: we provided housing for poor people in exchange for rents, we made money off this function. Suburban conservatives may have considered us a part of the urban mess, unworthy of their attention. The *Star Tribune*, *Pioneer Press*, *City Pages*, and other newspapers never said a thing about our role in knocking off the city's most powerful political leader, Jackie Cherryhomes, or even mentioned the group in their post-election coverage. Ironically, Cherryhomes herself gave us grudging credit when, in an interview with WCCO-TV following her defeat, she referred to that horrible group of landlords who had picketed her home the previous summer.

Even if the newspapers did not, we knew who we were and what we had accomplished. Thinking it over, I concluded that we had followed the right strategy in getting politically involved with limited hopes of success. Our goal was total change, and that was what had happened. While we may not have been among the mainstream groups supporting Rybak's victory, we had played a significant part in producing the victory. We were a feared player on the political scene. We had teeth.

The Property Rights group had begun with a class-action lawsuit against city government. It had tried its hand at lobbying the state legislature. It had formed a political committee to promote candidates for elective office. All these ventures had failed. The lawsuit was thrown out of federal court. Our bills introduced in the state legislature stalled. The committee formed to promote candidates was ineffective. Judged by conventional political standards, our group had failed. In fact, it was a big success. Representatives of a reviled occupation within the city, we had turned city politics around. We had stumbled upon an alternative model of politics which worked quite well.

The old model was based on solutions of force: Force the city to do something by court order. Pass laws which force people to comply. Elect candidates to offices with coercive powers of decision. The new model was based on changing public opinion. We had stood up for ourselves against forces that had tried exploit us. We had testified to our own experiences of city government. We had shown those who would intimidate and divide us that we could endure. We did not try to curry favor with our tormentors: we hit them over the head with a 2-by-4, we beat them into submission. The fact that many of the winning candidates in the 2001 city election sought our support indicated progress toward a more substantial end than gaining power: introducing new values into the city's political culture. We had demonstrated that action can be as powerful as passing laws.

One of the sweet ironies of this election was that we inner-city landlords, often called "racists" by our liberal critics, had provided critical support to the only African American elected to the City Council, Natalie Johnson Lee. Johnson Lee was given no chance to win. The black establishment of the 5th ward, heavily in debt to Cherryhomes for political and economic favors, was supporting her opponent. I was the only white person present at Johnson Lee's campaign-strategy session several weeks before the election. It was a grim situation. Yet, when Johnson Lee called for a protest demonstration at the scandal-plagued site of "Heritage Park" along Olson highway, at least half of the protesters were members of our group. We provided help on election day. Travis Lee, Natalie's husband, told me that had his wife not won the election, they probably would have "had to move to Missouri". (Cherryhomes had a reputation for personal vindictiveness.) I could relate to this. We were all comrades in arms, black and white, down there at Lucille's Kitchen, the same place where a race riot provoked by our signs almost took place during the city election campaign four years earlier.

I began to savor the ironies. A year earlier, we landlords had a major falling out with the people from ACORN when they conducted their "slumlord tour" for the media. I wrote in a flier which we passed out this statement: "When you need a place to stay, you go to landlords, not politicians or poverty pimps." ACORN's leader, a candidate for the Minneapolis City Council, objected strenuously to that statement. I agreed to apologize for the "poverty pimp" comment if they would stop referring to us as "slumlords". We never did resolve the argument. A year later, ACORN activists were distributing the anti-Cherryhomes literature that our people wrote. So we were comrades with them as well. Politics is a strange business. If it can occasionally reconcile antagonistic extremes, there may be spiritual value in it as well. My wife, whose family suffered persecution during the Cultural Revolution, has sometimes quoted her father's opinion that politics is "dangerous". She personally disliked political events though, as a good trooper, she would support me. I, however, found politics personally exhilarating.

Another thing that I learned from the landlord group is not to be judgmental. We were frequently being told that, because the public viewed us as slumlords, we had to work extra hard to clean up our image. We needed to position ourselves as a "responsible" landlords' group. We needed to set ethical standards for our members. That's how the smart professional groups work, we were told. I always rejected that advice because it was playing into the "divide and conquer" strategy of our enemies.

Occasionally, in discussions with hostile groups, someone would say to soften me up: "I'm not talking about you personally, of course. I'm sure you're a good landlord. I'm talking about those other, bad landlords." To that, I would respond, "I'm a certifiably bad landlord who has been denounced by my neighborhood association for coddling criminals." That would always shut the other person up. Dividing and conquering the landlord community would not work in my case. We did not try to tell our fellow landlords how they should run their businesses. We were more like a labor union. I will always remember a conversation with Sean Rice, a former judge who had been disciplined by a judicial ethics committee, while I stood with my sign outside the 1997 DFL city convention. He said that, from his experience, those who serve on ethics committees were the least ethical people.

This attitude extended to our videotaped meetings. We might have tried to control and polish our image so that people would see us as "the good guys". Instead, we hosted a free-speech forum. Anyone could come to the meeting. Anyone could stand up before the microphone and say anything that he or she wanted to say. Some individuals, especially when they had been drinking, would make statements that came off as racist. It did not matter. The public, used to slick public-affairs shows, began to recognize that our meetings were authentic. Real people were up there speaking their minds. Our reputation for tolerating free speech became a source of strength. Black people, tenants, and others of diverse background started coming to our meetings. Political candidates, wanting free air time, were not ashamed to be seen on our show.

We could survive being called "slumlords". We could survive all the slanders attached to our name, even the free-circulation *Property Owner* newspaper which contained lots of typos and printed off-color jokes. After Natalie Johnson Lee was elected to the City Council, I was horrified to hear that one of our members, dead drunk, had ridden around with her in the limo on election day telling stories about picking up underage boys in Brazil. Natalie took it in stride. At our next meeting, she wryly referred to "Mr. Brazil" when he stepped up to the mike to ask a question. Where she could have been huffy, I was grateful that she instead showed restraint.

Freed of the need to defend our respectability, I felt that the group was strong. We had a cohesive group of individuals with diverse talents who worked unselfishly together. We did not have ideological quarrels because we were an action group. Unlike some, we were also a group whose members had resources. Our annual "dues" of $55.00, supplemented by emergency contributions from the group's heavy hitters, covered the cost of retaining the hour-long time slot on Channel 6 and what we paid Bryan Olson to produce it. This show appeared twice on Fridays and several times more on the Minneapolis cable-access station during the weekend.

In truth, the Property Rights group had become a media operation. Our "meetings" were staged cable-television events. In addition, the "Property Owner" newspaper, published by Jim Jacobsen, gave us a monthly presence in the print media. Another member, John Penterman, set up a web site for the group at www.propertyrights-mn.com. In the name of the group, I submitted an application for a license for a low-watt radio station. However, our license never came through. Congress imposed restrictions on use of adjacent frequencies which crippled the FCC initiative in large cities such as Minneapolis. But that was enough: a cable-television show, a web site, and a free-circulation newspaper, plus whatever publicity we could generate in the large commercial media. As a political operation, we were firing on all cylinders.

After its City Hall reporter Kevin Diaz moved to Washington, D.C., the *Star Tribune* stopped reporting our activities except once, in a story on Rybak's housing policies, when it referred to us as a "rump group of landlords organized around the banner of property rights", and once again after our 2002 demonstration at City Hall against Joe Biernat's remaining in office. The same was true of *City Pages*. We had numerous protest activities which sometimes attracted commercial television crews and reporters from other newspapers, but never from *City Pages* or the *Star Tribune*.

I suspected that this might be because Charlie Disney and I had threatened to sue the *Twin Cities Reader* while a man named Claude Peck was its editor. Peck may have first taken a dislike to me when I bugged him for permission to reprint an article. Perhaps I was too pushy: I had called him back several times one afternoon while I was racing to finish certain business

before leaving town. When we finally made contact, Peck shouted insults at me over the phone.

Peck, as editor of the *Reader*, then wrote a derogatory column about Disney and me after we and other landlords spoke out at the Minneapolis "Town Meeting" in September, 1996. "A number of these apartment-owning malcontents, woe-is-me City Hall haters, these politicking whiners, hogged a lot of mike time at last week's Town Meeting," Peck wrote. "After hearing their pain, it's clear that you can put half-glasses and a sport coat on a problem landlord, you can give him a clipboard and perch a peak cap on his noggin, but you just cannot get the dunderhead to shut his pie-hole."

For me, worse than the rhetoric was that Peck's article included a false statistic - that my apartment building had attracted 290 police calls - after the *Twin Cities Reader* was informed of its falsity. (A malicious staff person from Harrison Neighborhood Association had fed that statistic to *Reader* reporter David Schimke. I pointed out the error in a letter to the editor which the *Reader* published a week or so before Peck's column appeared.) Then, in a later issue, his newspaper published an anonymous letter to the editor continuing the attack on us which, after an investigation, we strongly suspected was written in house. Our threatened lawsuit against the *Reader* forced a public apology for that stunt. After the *Twin Cities Reader* was merged into *City Pages*, Peck went over to the *Star Tribune*. He became the features team leader in the paper's Metro section.

In that position, I imagine that Peck by himself might have been able to block proposed stories about our Minneapolis landlord group, but more likely he needed help. Peck had an additional capability in that he was an out-of-the-closet gay man. I know this because a subsequent column in the *Reader* written by Peck referred to that fact. The *Star Tribune*, like most other U.S. newspapers, has demographic lobbies in the newsroom, presumably including one for gays and lesbians, which influence news coverage. Such lobbies give members "instant friends" throughout the organization. Sharing each other's political values, they may act in concert, enlisting support not only from members of their own group but from other demographic groups comprising the cultural left. All this is, of course, opaque to readers of the newspaper; we see only the result of the reporting. I can therefore only speculate as to whether what seems to me to be chilly treatment of our landlord group and, perhaps, of me personally by the *Star Tribune* is due to Claude Peck's influence, alone or reinforced by cultural lobbies in the newsroom.

Kevin Diaz once described the Minneapolis DFL party as a coalition embracing three principal groups: feminists, members of public-sector unions, and gay/lesbian/bisexual/transgendered (GLBT) individuals. Was the Property Rights group burdened by animosity from Peck or others in the gay community directed at me? Were gay men reacting negatively to something in my personality? My paranoid suspicions increased when a newly elected, openly gay member of the Minneapolis City Council, Gary Schiff, refused to shake Eve White's hand at a public meeting, commenting that, now that he was elected, he "did not have to be nice to landlords any more". We asked a City Hall insider about this. The response was that Schiff did not like Bill McGaughey because "he (McGaughey) does not speak the King's English". In my plain-speaking, perhaps too aggressively male way, I had pressed police officials to justify their policies at a public meeting which this Council Member-elect had also attended.

It would serve no useful purpose for me to pick a quarrel with the gay community even if a connection could be established between a "gay mafia" in the *Star Tribune* newsroom and the paper's treatment of me or the landlord group. Gays and lesbians do face real discrimination in society. I may be entirely off base in my suspicions of Claude Peck. The issue here is the influence of individual journalists with an ax to grind and of hidden groups in the newsroom. No one knows what personal agendas its editors and reporters may have in covering a story or in deciding whether or not to run a story. If the media are consistently biased in a certain respect, that poisons the atmosphere for the entire community. At a meeting of the Property Rights group, I once likened advocacy journalism to a basketball team which was also allowed to record the game's official score; if the team found itself a point or two behind, it could erase several of the other team's baskets to win the game.

The news media, setting the agenda of public discussion, is like a fourth branch of government. As such, it is the only branch in private hands. That means that media employees are shielded from public criticism to a great extent. You cannot fire a reporter or editorial writer with whose policies you disagree as you can vote a government official out of office. Hostile journalists at the *Star Tribune* could be "in office" for decades. When such a dominant newspaper exhibits consistently biased reporting, this becomes a political problem for the community. The problem is compounded when the newspaper's articles and editorials are published anonymously, without a byline, or when unseen editors behind the scene control point of view. I would respect these journalists more if they came forth as individuals and said, "I hate you," or "This is my opinion." But to practice attack journalism while hiding behind an institutional facade is like scribbling obscene messages on a bathroom wall. Greater public disclosure is required.

The principal lesson that I have learned from my experiences with the Minneapolis Property Rights Action Committee is that a political organization, or indeed the political community as a whole, cannot function effectively without media support. Especially in cities with newspapers like the *Star Tribune*, you cannot depend on the large commercial media to do the job. The trick is to bypass these people. As political actors, you need your own media. You need to amplify the image of what you are doing and thinking to reach the larger community. Otherwise, the realm of politics will be too large for individuals to affect events. You will not be able to "fight City Hall".

We did fight City Hall successfully because we had our own pipeline to community opinion. However small the pipeline was, its content was within our control. Hundreds, perhaps thousands, of people regularly watched our cable-television show, and thousands more read the newspaper. This may not seem like much competition for the *Star Tribune*, but its authenticity made up for size especially when the public was fed up with bias in the mainstream media. We were on to something important. It may be that media coverage, or lack thereof, will be a critical battleground of politics in the future.

I must report that the year following the 2001 city elections has been difficult for the Minneapolis Property Rights Action Committee. Membership has dwindled. We have had barely enough money to continue the cable-television show through the year. As Charlie Disney carped from the sidelines, Eve White valiantly tried to hold the group together. We have made some mistakes. Personal rifts have appeared within the group - between Charlie and Eve, between me and Keith Reitman, between Eve and Jim Swartwood. The last was especially serious because it signified a rift between the group's cable-television operation and the new *Watchdog* newspaper founded by Swartwood and Frank Trisko. A small group of people associated with a reviled occupation cannot afford rifts.

Another mistake was to let politicians and political candidates take up too much time on our cable-television show. Besides winners such as Attorney General Mike Hatch and State Auditor Pat Awada, there have been Green Party candidates for assorted positions, unelectable Republicans running in heavily DFL districts, and, yes, a nonendorsed Independence Party candidate for U.S. Senate (me) taking up precious air time. We need to return to our core themes of housing and crime. Why should landlords underwrite free media exposure for political candidates unless they benefit from it?

Our reputation for political potency took a drubbing when, running for Greg Gray's vacated House seat in district 58B, attorney Keith Ellison was elected with 67% of the votes, running against four other candidates. The candidate whom we supported, Duane Reed, finished third in the voting. The DFL party ran an ad in *Insight News* during the last week of the campaign attacking Reed for his association with us, called "an anti-community group". Disk jockeys on radio station KMOJ spread rumors on election day that voters were being turned away at the polls because they had UDs (unlawful detainers) on their rental-

history records. Those evil landlords were at it again! Ellison and Reed were both African American men with substantial community support. It was a shame to see Reed, the superior candidate, lose the election due to hateful messages directed at us.

Early in the year, I recognized that the Property Rights group faced two new problems. First, since the 2001 city elections had gone our way, we no longer had the bogeymen in city government (Cherryhomes and Sayles Belton) to hold up before the landlord community when we sought financial contributions. We did twice protest the fact that Joe Biernat remained in office after federal prosecutors went after him for crimes related to free plumbing work on his house; but that was a less compelling event than our protests the year before. Even though Biernat qualified as a certifiable villain from our point of view, this was too much like kicking a man when he is down. Some who accompanied us to City Hall shouted insults at our friends in city government. We were at risk of coming off as a pack of mad dogs.

Second, our membership was declining, in part, because property values were rising in the city. Landlords who were trapped in sour real-estate investments once desperately joined our group. But now we were receiving notes from former landlords who had cashed in their Minneapolis real estate. Good luck, the notes would say, but I have moved on to other pursuits. I thought it might be time for me to move on as well. Seven long years of intense, unpaid work on behalf of the city's landlord community was enough. I would continue to support the group but channel my main energies in another direction.

The new direction led to a rather nutty venture called "Orange Party". The Orange Party, sounding like a rival to the Green Party or some such organization, was not meant to be a political party at all but an instrument for political action. This "Orange Party" was, in fact, a generic version of Minneapolis Property

Rights Action Committee. What we had accomplished in the city of Minneapolis for owners of rental property might be accomplished for any political interest group that followed the same methods. The key was to have a media capability. The Orange Party, as I saw it, would be a coalition of interest groups, ranging across the political spectrum, which would have its own cable-television show and free-circulation newspaper. The constituent groups would, of course, have to work out the financial arrangements to support that enterprise. They would have to work out the details of organization. But it could be done. We Minneapolis landlords had shown that a successful political organization could be built upon those principles.

I produced literature for the Orange Party, which was printed in two sides on bright orange paper, and also created a web site at www.orangeparty.org. The next step was to take the idea to persons of known political interest. One could find such people at political parties' state conventions. Since I planned to be in China during the DFL state convention in early May, I asked two of my landlord colleagues, Bob Anderson and Frank Trisko, to pass out Orange Party literature at this convention held at the Minneapolis Convention Center. They distributed one thousand pieces. It was my turn, then, to hit the Republican state convention held at the Xcel Center in St. Paul. I spent the better part of a day there on June 14th, passing out several hundred pieces of literature.

While running into old acquaintances and having some interesting conversations, I also realized that the concept of an "Orange Party" was too subtle to gain acceptance. It sounded too much like an ordinary political party; and what was I doing soliciting people who were committed Republicans? I was tilting at windmills again. I was again being that isolated writer with ideas to save the world who came off as a bit of a kook. No one responded to the web site. I received just one telephone call expressing interest in the project. The Orange Party would have to be put on the shelf.

CHAPTER TWENTY-FIVE

My Campaign for U.S. Senate

I have caucused with the Independence Party in each biennium since 1998. My wife and I contributed our $100 political donation to the party early in 2002. Even so, I had never until that year attended an IP state convention. My experiences at the caucus in Senate District 58 had left an unpleasant taste. One year, when I submitted a resolution opposing free trade, several caucus attendees attacked the idea. I accepted "friendly amendments" only to have the amended proposal voted down by the same people who had offered them. With only a handful of persons in the room, the caucus conveners were using heavy-handed parliamentary procedures to control the discussion. I thought, this enterprise is going nowhere. I had a better outlet for my political energies, Minneapolis Property Rights Action Committee.

Governor Ventura's sudden decision not to seek reelection sparked a surge of new interest in the Independence Party. People were urging a Ventura adviser, former Congressman Tim Penny, to seek the Independence Party nomination for Governor. Christine Jax, Ventura's Commissioner of the Department of Children, Families and Learning, also threw her hat into the ring. A *Star*

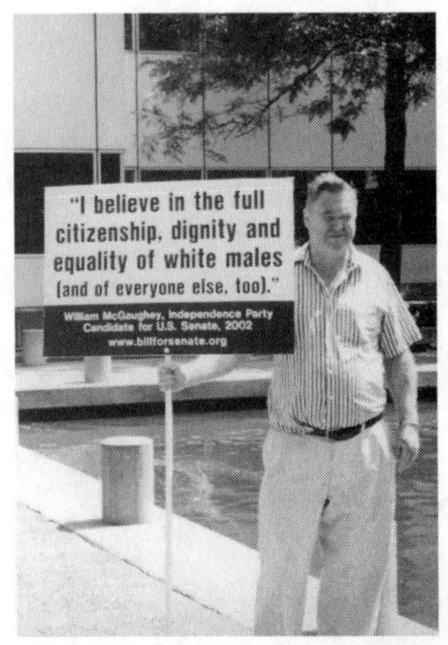
"I believe in the full
citizenship, dignity and
equality of white males
(and of everyone else, too)."
William McGaughey, Independence Party
Candidate for U.S. Senate, 2002
www.billforsenate.org

Tribune article about Jax reported that she had said "she offers two qualities that Penny cannot. 'I'm not a politician and I'm not a white male. I know there are a lot of people interested in someone like that.'" Red flags went up within me. This was standard DFL practice. It was straight out of the editorial pages of the *Star Tribune*. When DFLers Judi Dutcher and Becky Lourey were passed over for Governor in favor of Roger Moe, that newspaper was full of comments from unhappy individuals that one of those meritorious female candidates was not nominated. Women are good, men are bad - that's the bottom line of *Star Tribune* editorial wisdom.

To amuse myself, I wrote a satirical argument for Jax's candidacy in the form of a campaign flier. This "flier" was titled "Two Reasons Why You Should Support Christine Jax for Governor". The text read: "1. 'I am not a politician.' OK, she's married to a veteran DFL legislator and her brother-in-law was Vice President of the Minneapolis City Council ... but, of course, these political connections had nothing to do with her being appointed Commissioner of the CFL ... and, as the clincher, she has never run for public office before. 2. 'I am not a white male.' White males are the scum of the earth. These are the kinds of people who enslaved the ancestors of African Americans and stole the American Indians' land. They've raped and pillaged wherever they've gone and foisted their pretentious culture and patriarchal religion on other people. And, males have been oppressing women for thousands of years ... With their high testosterone levels, they are drawn to violent activities like war. Putting the two together, we see that white males are really bad people and Minnesota voters would probably not want to elect them to public office. You shouldn't nominate one either."

I put this mean-spirited piece "promoting" Christine Jax's gubernatorial campaign into a drawer. Then, one day, I received a letter from Jax soliciting my support at the Independence Party convention. Since she had written me, I would write her. I sent her a copy of my satirical flier along with a cover letter stating that I did not think much of her campaign selling points. Jax's response was startling. She began in boldfaced type: "**If you ever show this to anyone, I will sue you.**" She went on to call my piece of writing "the meanest thing I have seen since I was in the 8th grade" and make other such remarks, evidently believing that I was planning to pass off my work as Jax campaign literature.

I felt like a terrorist caught in the act. The only useful thing to come of this was Jax's disclosure that the *Star Tribune* article had given the wrong impression of what she actually said. Asked how she was different from the other candidates, she had responded that she was not a white male. She was not intending to use this as a selling point. I could understand how newspaper reporters twist things to fit their story line. Pointing out that my "flier" was a spoof, I wrote Jax what was intended to be a conciliatory letter. I proposed that we meet at the Independence Party state convention and discuss the matter further. However, Jax withdrew as a candidate. She was not at the convention.

This incident was fresh in my mind when I received a telephone call from the 5th Congressional District chair, Peter Tharaldson, asking me if I was planning to attend the IP state convention in St. Cloud. He offered me a ride in a rented van along with several other persons. I accepted his offer conditioned on my being able to bring a friend. The friend could not be reached. I was set to go with Tharaldson but, due to an early-morning misunderstanding, wound up driving to St. Cloud by myself. I do not want to repeat the story here of how I decided to become a candidate for U.S. Senate. Suffice it to say that I thought my running might help the Independence Party find itself in terms of issues or, at least, raise useful questions. The "white male" bugaboo, hitting a raw nerve with Jax, showed that something needed to be done in this area. After several days of indecision, I filed on July 16th.

Since issues were my focus, I spent the first several weeks writing campaign literature and position papers. I put together a campaign web site, www.billforsenate.org. Many of those writings appear in an appendix at the back of this book. In a green-cover spiral notebook I copied the names and addresses, telephone and fax numbers, key contact persons, and email addresses of general-circulation newspapers in Minnesota. Behind this was the same information for many radio and television stations and special-interest newspapers. I carried the notebook around with me on the campaign trail as a reference material.

Having filed as a candidate, I began receiving letters from political-pressure groups. Most wanted me to declare my position on questions of interest to their members. My first inclination was to send these groups polite letters stating that I had no developed position on their questions. My campaign was about two issues only and I would stick to them. That stance might offend some but it was not as bad as pretending to be what I was not. As a minor candidate, I was unlikely to receive their endorsement anyhow.

On the whole, I thought it would be to my advantage to make forthright, specific statements of my positions. The election was not mine to lose by statements antagonizing constituencies; it was mine to win, or at least do well, by attracting support from individuals who agreed with me. There were also good-government groups sternly requesting a written promise from me not to engage in negative advertising. There were teachers who wanted me, as a political candidate, to appear in their class. There were persons wanting samples of my campaign buttons or bumper stickers, preferably mailed in damage-proof containers.

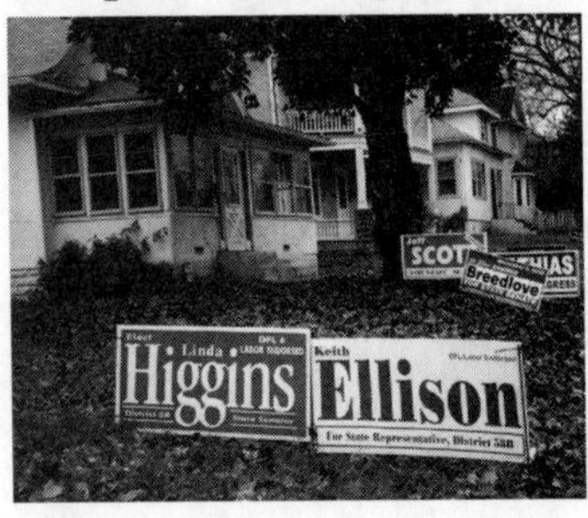

To research issues, I went to the Wilson library at the University of Minnesota to review back issues of *Monthly Labor Review* which contained recent information about work hours. I went through a large stack of back copies of *U.S. News & World Report*

in my office. These I reviewed in search of answers for the League of Women Voters questionnaire. I looked for articles that concerned each type of question in search of pertinent information. It was surely to my advantage to respond to questionnaires from organizations such as the League of Women Voters or from newspapers such as the *Star Tribune*, *Pioneer Press*, or *Duluth News-Tribune*, which published voters guides. That might be my main way to communicate with voters in the large population centers. Attractive personal photos were also important.

I devoted special attention to the issues statements. In addition, most newspapers presented personal information about the candidates. They invited candidates to answer a standard set of questions. The *St. Paul Pioneer Press* ran a full-length story about the U.S. Senate primary written by reporter Toni Coleman. Reporter Scott Thistle handled that function for the *Duluth News-Tribune*. The Rochester newspaper, the *Post-Bulletin*, covered the U.S. Senate race from its Washington, D.C. office. Coincidentally, I received a call from Angela Greiling Keane, a reporter there, on the day after I had visited the *Post-Bulletin's* Rochester newsroom in person.

As in the previous year's race for mayor, I tended to take a contrarian position on some of the peripheral issues. Most Senate candidates favored a strong prescription-drugs benefit for seniors. I argued that the country could not afford this new program which might cost tens of billions of dollars annually. Besides, U.S. doctors were over medicating their patients. No one cared because someone else, an insurance company, was paying for it. I thought the federal government might more usefully fund studies to show the effect of drugs on particular patients utilizing information from the human-genome project. If we wanted a new medical entitlement, the government might give everyone a voucher for annual physicals up to a certain dollar amount.

I tried to straddle questions which pitted the environment against economic development. I was in favor of privatizing part of Social Security pointing out the "sweetheart" deal that the U.S. Treasury had with the trust funds. I answered "strongly disagree" to the question posed in the *Star Tribune* Voter's Guide as to whether the United States should go to war against Iraq. Wellstone had "mixed feelings" and both my Independence Party opponents were mildly in favor. Norm Coleman did not respond to the questionnaire.

Faced with the need to respond to questions off the top of my head, I generally favor the technological quick fix. Instead of going to war against Iraq, I think the U.S. Government should pour money into developing technologies for automobiles powered by hydrogen-based fuels or electric batteries. It should promote wind-generated electricity and solar cells. The problem of big-city traffic jams might be addressed by two proposals with which I have some acquaintance. An entrepreneur in Oregon, Bob Behnke, has been promoting a concept called "smart jitneys" which would use wireless technology to form instant car pools. A Minnesotan with whom I have recently served on the World Federalist Association state board, Ed Anderson, has developed the technology for Personal Rapid Transit (PRT) which would move people through congested areas along elevated guideways. Both projects have languished for years for lack of funds to do a demonstration project.

The relatively small number of dollars needed for this development might bring a cheap solution to transit problems. But I have a theory about how government operates: The cheap solutions will never be funded because they lack a constituency. The more expensive alternatives associated with the status quo are all promoted by lobbyists riding a wave of money.

My core issues, however, were the shorter workweek and opposition to political correctness. I knew that I was raising ideologically sensitive issues. Media outreach was the name of the game. That called for a campaign manifesto. I wrote a ten-page statement explaining my two issues. These I mailed to the editorial departments of major newspapers, to publications or civic groups representing organized labor and minority communities, and to the other Senate candidates. While he was lining up for the parade in Little Falls, Norm Coleman told me that he had received a copy of my statement. Otherwise, there was no reaction.

To a few publications, I faxed a press release which defended Public Safety Commissioner Charlie Weaver's decisions concerning drivers licenses. I faxed the entire group of Minnesota newspapers an announcement of my candidacy. Then, to those newspapers which had email addresses, I sent another announcement telling how and why I thought I had a shot at winning the IP primary. After a few days on the campaign trail, I did a mailing to major newspapers giving "news" of the campaign and enclosing a few photos. It would be a real attention grabber if the newspapers ran photographs of me and the sign. Toward the end of the campaign, I sent an email message to some Minnesota radio stations hoping that they would pick up on my argument that "political correctness" was like a state religion. None did. Many of these statements, representing the distance-bombardment phase of my campaign, appear in Appendix B.

The guts of the campaign - the ground war, so to speak - was a month-long series of trips around the state. There is no need to recount those experiences here. A travelogue-type narrative is included at the end of this book as Appendix A. I originally wrote this narrative at the request of *Watchdog* editor, Ray Whebbe, who promised to publish them in an issue of *The Watchdog* appearing just before the primary. In fact, my travelogue was truncated, and the newspaper itself came out on election day. This was a disappointment. On the other hand, Whebbe's request to describe the campaign from the standpoint of a personal experience rather than a presentation of issues inspired the approach taken in this

book. The photographs which I took to illustrate the *Watchdog* article have been used as illustrations here.

I thought I would enjoy an advantage in the metro area in belonging to the Minneapolis Property Rights Action Committee. Those expectations were misplaced. Not only did the *Watchdog* publicity fall through but also much that might have been gained through the cable-television show. My hour as a guest was shared with a (nonpolitical) representative of Peace House and Dave Berger, the Green Party candidate for state auditor. Both went on for about twenty-five minutes, leaving me ten minutes at the end. Then, two members of the landlord group attacked me for bringing up issues like the shorter workweek and international trade. Their statements came too late to be included in the taped version of the show which went on the air.

Eve White was upset to learn that I would be at the meeting intending to speak my mind on race issues, when Hennepin County Commissioner Mark Stenglein and two representatives of the African-American Men's Project would be making a presentation. She did not want me to sit at the front table with them. Another member told Eve that I had every right to go on the show and talk about "the White Man's party". That was not quite what I had in mind. Still, there might not be enough time to go into the subtleties of the situation. Standing at the floor mike, I tried to press my case as hard as I could without creating a racial incident.

There was a lull in my touring schedule on Thursday and Friday, September 5th and 6th, the week before the primary. The *Star Tribune* Voters Guide came out on September 6th. On September 5th, I read in the newspaper that candidates for U.S. Senate would be debating that evening at Augsburg College. In attack mode, I faxed Twin Cities media lamenting the fact that I had been excluded from the debate. Then, as an afterthought, I called Augsburg College. Soon I received a telephone call from a man at the Urban League. I was welcome to participate. I faxed all the media another statement headlined "Oops, Egg on my Face", which apologized for the previous fax.

The evening event, sponsored by Augsburg College, Unity VOTE, and the Twin Cities chapter of the Society of Black Journalists, called for a debate among the candidates for state auditor in the first hour and then among the Senate candidates in the second hour. I sat in the audience to hear the state-auditor candidates debate. Dave Hutcheson, the Independence Party candidate for that office, told me that he owned rental property in Minneapolis and had attended one of our landlord meetings. The Senate debaters, besides me, included the Independence Party's endorsed candidate Jim Moore, the endorsed Green Party candidate Ed McGaa, and Paul Wellstone, the DFL incumbent. The Republican endorsee and eventual winner, Norm Coleman, did not participate. I told Paul Wellstone, an old acquaintance, that I was running for his Senate seat. "A worthy opponent!," he replied in a jovial mood, shaking my hand.

My single most important campaign opportunity was to participate in a radio interview on Minnesota Public Radio on Friday, September 6th. Not only was this interview timed well to influence the September 10th primary election; it lasted for a full hour and was shared by only two other candidates, DFLer Alve Erickson and Independence Party candidate, Ronald E. Wills. I was the only candidate present in the St. Paul studio with host Mike Mulcahy. Erickson was participating from MPR studios in Duluth, and Wills from an airport telephone booth in Michigan. After requesting brief opening statements, Mulcahy questioned Erickson and me on such subjects as terrorism, civil liberties, and Social Security financing. Wills unexpectedly joined us and discussed the entire range of issues. (He had a substantial business and public-affairs background and had helped prepare Reagan for the Presidential debates.) At the end, it was Erickson and me again.

I told Mulcahy during the break that I had other issues I wanted to discuss: the shorter workweek and political correctness. He obliged. Mulcahy asked about and challenged my views on affirmative action. He wanted me to explain why I thought shorter-workweek legislation would help the economy. Though time did not do justice to these topics, it was at least getting our feet wet. I know that many people listened to the Mid-Morning show since I later met three or four persons who had heard me on the show and also received an email message from a former work colleague. I am grateful to MPR for the opportunities it has extended to us lesser known candidates for political office.

Mostly, then, I ran a media campaign, trying to pack as much voter exposure as I could into the available time. The core of my campaign consisted of seeking newspaper coverage in the small- and mid-sized newspapers out state. I carried my two-sided sign in six parades. It was a different kind of campaign than a year earlier. My mayoral campaign had consisted of distributing literature and carrying a sign. In the 2002 Senate campaign, the literature and sign were used more for newspaper stories. During the final days of the campaign, when it was too late to expect published articles, I again resorted to personal campaigning. On Monday, September 9th, I spent several hours walking down Nicollet Mall talking with people and handing out literature. People gave me feedback on my issues, some negative, of course, but also positive.

It is a paradox that, in campaigning for Mayor of Minneapolis on an issue that enjoyed overwhelming voter support (preservation of affordable housing), I received only 143 votes and finished twelfth. A year later, I received 8,482 votes and finished second in a statewide race stressing two issues that were anathema to the political establishment. (See Appendix H for an analysis of the election results.) I had spent less than $2,000 altogether on the campaign excluding the $400 filing fee. Who says that politics is not full of surprises or that democracy is dead? Only in America - actually, in Minnesota - do such things happen.

CHAPTER TWENTY-SIX

Paul Wellstone and the Rest of the Campaign

After my primary defeat on September 10th, I tried to be a good soldier for the Independence Party. I went to Jim Moore's campaign headquarters on election night and pledged my support. While waiting for a call for help from the Moore campaign, I began writing this book. On October 25th, Minnesotans and Americans were shocked to learn of a plane crash near Eveleth, Minnesota, which killed Senator Paul Wellstone, his wife and daughter, and five other persons. For me, it was this year's violence - equivalent to the September 11th terrorist attacks - which overshadowed the election.

With hundreds of others, I stood outside Williams Arena in the evening of Tuesday, October 29th, right behind the Wellstone green bus, watching a large-screen broadcast of events inside celebrating Wellstone's remarkable life. This was itself a historic event, negatively influencing the outcome of the election. Within days, former U.S. Senator and Vice President Walter F. Mondale, became Wellstone's DFL replacement. He, like Wellstone, at first enjoyed a lead in the polls. But Norm Coleman was not to be denied the victory.

Paul Wellstone and I went back a long time. I first met him in 1982 at a gathering at Lakewood College in White Bear Lake while he was campaigning for State Auditor. Several months later, he was at a labor conference at Minneapolis Community College which I also attended. "We (labor unions) are not the problem" was its theme. Tony Mazzocchi of the Oil, Chemical, and Atomic Workers union, an advocate of a separate political party for American labor, was the principal speaker. At one point, Wellstone remarked that we needed to improve productivity to create more jobs. From my studies, I believed that this argument was not correct. While business firms need a certain level of productivity to remain competitive, greater labor productivity tends immediately to destroy jobs, not create them. I wrote Wellstone a letter to that effect. He wrote back. We stayed in touch.

During 1983, Paul Wellstone worked at the Minnesota Energy Agency as director of a program that helps poor people pay their heating bills. This agency's headquarters were located one floor above the offices of the Metropolitan Transit Commission in the American Center Building in St. Paul. I was surprised to run into him in the hallway one day. We had lunch together at the Nectary restaurant. I told him about my work at the transit agency, my interest in shorter work hours, and the lengthy divorce proceedings which I was then experiencing. He expressed sympathy for me as someone losing his wife. I had a schizophrenic brother who lived in Washington, D.C. So did he. He told me some things about his brother.

Wellstone thought his next political move might be to run for Democratic National Committeeman. He said he had support from all factions of the party. When we returned to the American Center Building from lunch, he introduced me to some of his friends including Connie Lewis who had recently worked on the Dayton Senate campaign. He loaned me a copy of a political textbook written by Sam Bowles, whom I knew from Yale, and several other left-leaning scholars. I read parts of it, though not the entire book.

During 1984, I was working hard to build up General Committee for a Shorter Workweek. One of our activities was to walk around Minneapolis lakes with a picket sign promoting the cause. I invited Paul Wellstone to join us once or twice. He sent his regrets. My next recollection of him is when I attended the election-night party for Walter Mondale in 1984 at the St. Paul convention center. Mondale was losing the Presidential election to Reagan by a landslide. Wellstone was standing in the middle of the floor with a group of friends. As I walked by, he beckoned for me to join them. We talked for fifteen minutes or so. Then Wellstone said that he had to join a group of DFL dignitaries up in front. He said good-bye to us all. I lost contact with him for several years.

In the meanwhile, because of my interest in the shorter-workweek issue and involvement in a union drive, I became acquainted with Tom Laney, former president of U.A.W. Local 879 at the Ford plant in St. Paul. Wellstone once told me that Laney was like a brother to him. In February 1990, Tom Laney invited me to attend a coffee party at his home to raise funds for Wellstone's fledgling Senate campaign. They were asking for $10 donations. When I shook hands with Paul, it seemed that he had to think for a moment before he remembered me, but then we had a nice conversation. I gave Laney a copy of my recently published book, *Nonfinancial Economics*, coauthored with Eugene McCarthy, and asked Wellstone if he wanted a copy. Later in the campaign, Paul sent me a note saying, sure, send me one. It was in the next day's mail. I also met and talked with Sheila Wellstone at this coffee party. Although there were perhaps only fifteen people present, we were treated to a full display of Paul Wellstone's oratory. He paced up and down the living room talking about universal health care and other topics.

I have long felt guilty that I did not do more for the Wellstone campaign. We were asked to attend precinct caucuses for him. However, I had bought a cheap round-trip air ticket to Europe and would be out of the country at the time of the caucuses. Before leaving on the trip, I went to see Paul and told him that I thought health care was a good issue. But I did not offer to help. When I received a postcard from the Wellstone campaign asking for supporters to attend his debate with Senator Boschwitz, I planned to go, but the event was canceled - not the debate, the related activity for volunteers.

Paul Wellstone was elected. He was a big celebrity now. I could not get near him at public events. Even so, Tom Laney arranged for a meeting between Wellstone and some of his labor supporters in a Minneapolis hotel room and invited me to attend. A small group of labor activists sat with Senator-elect Wellstone. I asked him about sponsoring shorter-workweek legislation. He responded, with an edge of sarcasm: "I thought you might ask me that." The Senator-elect was noncommittal.

I was in the orbit of Wellstone labor supporters during his first year in the Senate. He was firmly aligned with those who opposed fast-track authority for the President to negotiate NAFTA. When representatives of democratic unions asked for persons to observe a union election at the Cuautitlan Ford plant near Mexico City, I answered the call. To bolster my credentials, Senator Wellstone wrote a letter asking me to write him a report on that event. When I sent him my book on the NAFTA agreement, he sent me a handwritten letter of congratulations. But he was not willing to sponsor shorter-workweek legislation. I eventually received a letter from Wellstone stating that he did not think this proposal enjoyed sufficient support.

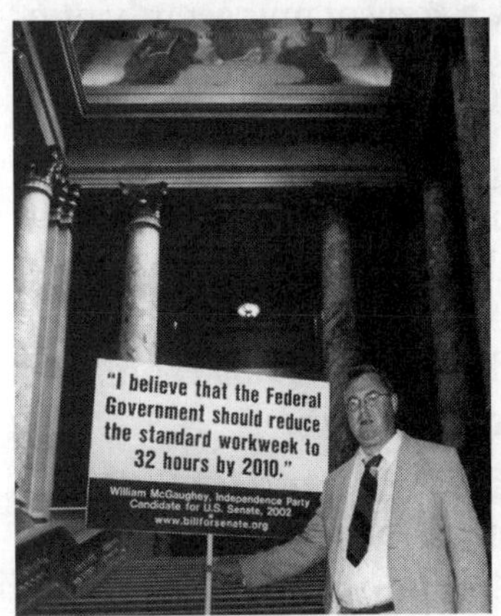
"I believe that the Federal Government should reduce the standard workweek to 32 hours by 2010."
William McGaughey, Independence Party Candidate for U.S. Senate, 2002
www.billforsenate.org

I drifted away from Wellstone politically. Periodically, I would encounter him at a public event. He would greet me warmly (no longer puzzled who I was) and even bring up the shorter-workweek subject. He would observe, for instance, that people in Washington were starting to talk about "family values" and the need for more free time. I told him that I was still working on this project, which was an exaggeration. I was "Mr. Shorter Workweek" in his eyes - not a pathetic figure for someone like Paul Wellstone.

I was always on Wellstone's mailing list. I sent small contributions for his Senate reelection campaigns and for his brief campaign for the Presidency. My brother Andrew was a big fan of Paul Wellstone's. He must have written the Senator about mental-health issues for, a week after my brother died, an autographed photograph of Senator Wellstone arrived in the mail. It would have pleased my brother greatly. I myself thought that the Wellstone operation was becoming more bureaucratic. He no longer embraced schemes like universal health care but instead spent more time servicing the Democrats' special-interest groups. His fundraising letters were filled too much with fearmongering references to Al D'Amato or Jesse Helms, as, I'm sure, their fundraising letters were filled with frightening references to him. I was miffed when he violated his pledge not to run for a third term.

Even so, I remained a supporter of Wellstone's reelection up until the moment that I switched over to the Independence Party and ran for Senate myself. The Senator's office in St. Paul had provided help in arranging for my wife and stepdaughter to receive visas to enter the United States. I thanked Paul for that service when my wife and I attended a fund raiser for his campaign at the Shriners hall on Park Avenue in March. He graciously told my wife that she was married to a scholar. Not understanding English too well, she nevertheless gained a sense of Wellstone's personality when he gave a short, fiery speech.

My last contact with Paul Wellstone was at the debate at Augsburg College on September 5th. Having welcomed me into the Senate race, he was not, however, ready to roll over or concede a point. Wellstone was a fierce competitor. I recall in the debate a question about preschooling. I thought I had aced the question in remembering information from an article in *U.S. News & World Report* which pointed out the financial advantages of preschool education. For every dollar spent on preschooling, society would save four dollars in the reduced costs associated with special education, delinquency, and so forth. The experienced wrestler knew a move to counter this. Look, he said, these cute little people are precious in themselves. Let's stop talking about them in terms of saving money. Let's help them because they are our children. Instead, he commended Jim Moore for telling how a particular preschooling program had helped his small children.

The questioner asked us to say something complimentary about the candidate who was not present, Norm Coleman. In view of the subsequent tragedy, I'm glad that, before responding to that question, I remarked that I liked all the candidates. They're "all good people", I said. That was especially true of Paul Wellstone. But then, of course, I went on to tell the joke about Norm Coleman and the Elvis impersonator being the only people being willing to shake hands with me at Farm Fest. (At such events, we candidates have a certain camaraderie as the Roman gladiators might once have had. If we're not too focused on winning, that aspect overshadows our competitiveness.) We ended the debate on a pleasant note. Wellstone shook hands with us all, and that was the last I saw of him. He did not comment on my "white male" sign.

After the plane crash, my wife and I attended the impromptu gathering at the State Capitol in Wellstone's memory. I went to the public celebration honoring Wellstone at Williams Arena and stood for hours in the cold watching events unfold inside the hall. Let me say that I was not offended by Rick Kahn's speech. It seemed at the time quite inspirational. I could understand that, for someone like Kahn, it would not be acceptable for people to say nice things about Wellstone at this gathering and then go home and work to undo his political legacy. It was touchingly idealistic of him to ask for Republican Congressman Jim Ramstad's help in electing a Democrat as Paul's replacement. As they say, it never hurts to ask. This was in the same brash spirit as when the newly elected U.S. Senator had thrust an anti-war tape into Vice President Quayle's hands immediately after being sworn into the Senate. Pushing the envelope a bit at the memorial service was a fitting tribute to the late Senator.

The problem was that we were then in the home stretch of a major political campaign. Partisan feelings were stretched to the limit. Political opponents became huffy about the Kahn speech and managed to turn things around to their advantage. I think, however, that one of Paul Wellstone's legacies will be the spectacle of 20,000 Minnesotans gathered in his memory at Williams Arena. Could Bill Clinton and other New Democrats who attended this event be sure that, when their time comes, even a small fraction of this crowd will be on hand to honor them?

After a few days under the spell of the Wellstone tragedy, I snapped back to the realities of a political campaign. On Monday morning, November 4th, Coleman and Mondale participated in a two-person debate at the Fitzgerald Theater in St. Paul, where the Prairie Home Companion broadcasts originate. I was among the hundred demonstrators - in our case, protesters - from the different parties who were rooting for their respective candidates. Meanwhile, up at the State Capitol, two or three blocks to the north, the Independence Party's proud Governor Jesse Ventura was appointing Wellstone's immediate replacement to the U.S. Senate. Angered at the partisan tone of events that had taken place at Williams Arena on Tuesday evening and the fact Jim Moore was being excluded from the Senate debate, Ventura scheduled a time during the debate to announce that he would be appointing fellow Independence Party member, Dean Barkley, to fill Wellstone's shoes.

I should have known that something like this was happening. As I stood outside the Fitzgerald Theater protesting Moore's exclusion from the debate, the other Independence Party protesters drifted away. CNN, network news people, local television, radio, and newspaper reporters galore were all massed in that small area outside the debate theater while our Governor, in a political last hurrah, was upstaging them at the Capitol.

Two days earlier, on Saturday, November 2nd, I had been on the Penny campaign bus touring southeastern Minnesota, Tim Penny's home base. In pairs, we dropped literature in Le Sueur, Le Center, and Montgomery before heading over to New Prague for a rally with the gubernatorial candidate himself. Dean Barkley, another volunteer, sat in the back of the bus. During the rally at the Busy Bee Cafe in Tim Penny's hometown of Waseca, I spotted Barkley sitting alone at a table. Introducing myself, I asked Barkley if he intended to stay on as head of the state planning agency if Penny was elected Governor. "I suppose I will if they'll accept a political hack," replied Barkley, in his self-deprecating way. Barkley said he remembered being a guest on the Property Rights group's television show. "First, they gave me a tour of the neighborhood," he said. That was the famous "Minneapolis crack tour". A photograph of the Penny-Robertson rally at the Busy Bee Cafe, published in the *Star Tribune*, shows Barkley sitting at a table to Penny's left and me, my face half-hidden, hoisting a campaign sign. The bus then went on to Faribault and still another rally. We did some more literature distribution there and headed home to St. Paul.

Tim Penny held another rally on Sunday, November 3rd, in the middle of the Lake Street bridge across the Mississippi river between Minneapolis and St. Paul. The idea was that Penny, a former Democrat, and Martha Robertson, a former Republican, could bridge the gap between the two parties in the highly partisan Minnesota Legislature. A year earlier, I had bought a large purple Mexican hat with silver embroidering at the Salvation Army. The front of this hat was curled back, looking like something that a Hispanic Napoleon might have worn. It was a perfect prop for a political rally so long as people did not accuse me of trying to ridicule Mexicans. Since Sunday's event on Lake Street brought favorable comments, I decided to use this extravagant headgear for Monday's protest demonstration in front of the Fitzgerald Theater. It was my turn to do something for the Moore campaign.

Arriving at the intersection of Cedar and 10th, I saw dozens, perhaps hundreds, of people holding up Coleman signs. Others had signs promoting DFLer Roger Moe for Governor. Only a dozen persons or so supported Jim Moore, but they were strategically positioned near the entrance door to the Fitzgerald Theater. One Independence Party member had a bullhorn. We shouted our protests to all who would listen. The other parties' supporters responded in kind.

Behind police barricades, we, third-party people, were on one side of 10th Street. A mob of DFL partisans stood across the street, trying to outshout us. I saw state trade commissioner Rebecca Yanisch and two Hennepin County commissioners in the crowd as well as Mayor Rybak, who waved. A small contingent of Green Party partisans, including Ken Pentel, stood just beyond our group. We devised an exercise in third-party cooperation. Our two candidates, Jim Moore and Ray Tricomo, were both excluded from the debate. "Ray and Jim, let them in; Ray and Jim, let them in," we yelled. This had a resonant simplicity which cut through all the other chants. I shouted myself hoarse with it, continuing the chant as long as I could. The debate sponsors, of course, did not let Ray and Jim in. Perhaps they could not hear us.

Jim Moore was not at our protest but in district court, vainly trying to block the debate through a court challenge. MPR had changed the rules for deciding which candidates would be included. Moore's wife, Shari, shared all the legal details with us. Ray Tricomo, the blind Green Party candidate for Senate,

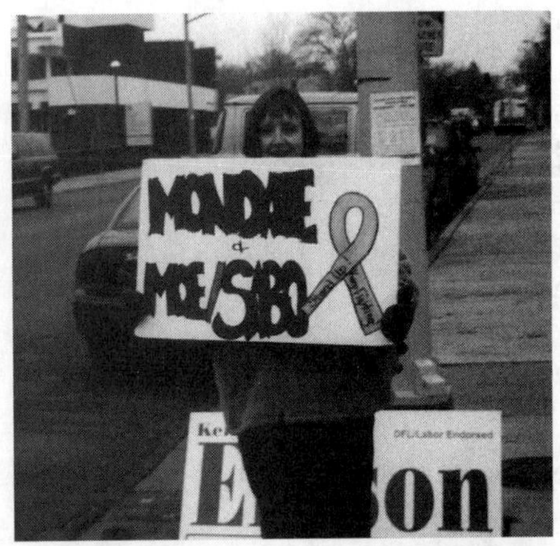

was cordial when I introduced myself. I advised him to take advantage of MPR's offer of separate broadcast time. Other political candidates included the Constitution Party's candidate for U.S. Senate, Miro Drago Kovatchevich, a politically conservative candidate who had been quoted in the *Star Tribune* criticizing Wellstone. I discussed issues with his campaign director and promised to stay in touch. I never did hear anything about the debate taking place inside the theater. There was more than enough excitement outside.

The winner of the Senate race, of course, was Coleman. He received almost half of the vote. Walter Mondale, less than a percentage point behind Coleman, finished second. Jim Moore, our candidate, received slightly more than 2 percent of the vote. Ray Tricomo received less than half a percentage point, fewer votes than the write-ins for Paul Wellstone. With respect to Governor, the winner was the Republican candidate, Tim Pawlenty, who received 45% of the votes. The DFL candidate, Roger Moe, finished second with 36% of the votes. Our candidate, Tim Penny, received 16% of the votes. Ken Pentel, the Green Party candidate, received a bit more than 2%. Importantly, Penny's 16% share of the Senate vote and Dave Hutcheson's 8% of the vote for State Auditor kept the Independence Party in contention as a "major party". In practical terms, this meant that IP candidates' campaigns in the next election would be eligible for public subsidies.

On the whole, it was a good night for the Republicans, a bad one for the Democrats, and a worse one for third-party candidates of all stripes. Until Wellstone's death, Tim Penny had been running neck-and-neck with the major-party candidates for Governor. Jim Moore told me at Penny's election-night party at the Mall of America that he was on a course to receive 10% of the votes before the plane crash.

I thought, however, that the Tim Penny "defeat party" was surprisingly upbeat as the IP gubernatorial candidate did the vocals for a rock 'n roll band which he and his brothers had organized. As their young female offspring bravely held back tears, they belted out one song after another and still had time to schmooze with the crowd. Senator Dean Barkley was there, as was his new communications director, Bill Hillsman, the wizard ad man of Wellstone's and Ventura's past campaigns, and also WCCO-TV's cute anchor woman, Amelia Santaniello, in boots, seated on a platform with her back to the crowd. This booming party went on in the cavernous Mall until after 1 o'clock in the morning. We knew we had lost, but the U.S. Senate race did not then have a clear winner.

Building

a Third-Party Movement

CHAPTER TWENTY-SEVEN

Building a Third Party Movement: Part 1

It's getting late in the book. I promised to write something about the Independence Party and the future of third-party politics. That is where I want to put my own time and effort. From my experiences with Minneapolis Property Rights Action Committee, I think that we are looking at a two-step process. Because Minnesota third parties took such a shellacking in the 2002 election, we need, first, to build up third parties in general. We need to strengthen their position within the electoral system. After that is done, we will need to redefine and advance the agenda of the Independence Party. I have my own ideas, of course. They are ideas which presumably found favor with 31% of the Independence Party voters in the 2002 U.S. Senate primary. So I have a right to be out there, too, advocating those ideas.

Right now, third parties and, indeed, all political parties are suffering from a lack of oxygen. They are suffering from a lack of media support. Publicity about political events is the "air" which sustains the whole process. Every political enterprise wants and needs publicity. The "news" is supposed to be about civic activities in which politics plays a central role. Traditionally, newspapers pass along elected officeholders' or political candidates' views as a part of reporting community affairs. Political events are "news content"; they are the reason that people read newspapers.

For better or worse, however, publishing newspapers is also a commercial enterprise. Every business wants to make more money. It may be that scheming journalists or media managers have decided that politicians do not deserve all the free publicity that they would receive if the media reported their activities as news. So they begin to filter the news and put their own imprint upon it. They make it harder for political actors to get their message across undistorted. If the news becomes too restricted or distorted, then politicians conclude that the best way to communicate with the public is through paid political ads. This, of course, brings money into the newspapers' coffers. Around election time, all serious political candidates must have many paid ads.

A cat-and-mouse game takes place between politicians and the news media. In July 2002, that wily schemer Norm Coleman proposed to small newspapers around the state that he produce a newspaper column for them which would be called "Norm's Coffee Shop Talk." This suggestion brought an immediate uproar. "Just because we live more than 200 miles north of the Twin Cities doesn't mean we have 'Dumb' painted on our foreheads," responded LuAnn Hurd-Lof, editor of the *Park Rapids Enterprise.* The publisher of the *Monticello Times,* Don Smith, suggested that Coleman was trying to dupe newspaper editors into accepting advertising "camouflaged as news". He said: "It seemed pretty astounding to me that someone who has the sophistication of Norm Coleman would believe we'd be so naive as to run this."

Political candidates and news media do need each other. The candidates provide content which sells newspapers. Newspapers amplify the candidates' message. However, journalists' increasing reluctance to report political events as news or to transmit politicians' words without distortion has created a crisis in the political system. This is the immediate cause of big money's control of politics. Certain candidates are favored at the expense of others. In his campaign brochure, for instance, Republican gubernatorial candidate Brian Sullivan, a multimillionaire, claimed that he was "the only candidate who has the resources to speak over Minnesota's liberal media and burst Ventura's media bubble."

Jesse Ventura found a solution to this problem. He was a celebrity because of his professional-wrestling career and stint as a radio talk-show host. That meant that people were already interested in him when he jumped into the Governor's race. Ventura's reported activities would sell newspapers. Even so, it was a struggle for Ventura to be included in the candidate debates and gain free publicity. It was even a struggle for him to find a bank which would lend him the money, against receipt of the taxpayer subsidy monies to which he was entitled, to run the cute Hillsman-produced television commercials that helped him be elected Governor. Ventura knew that he had to nurture his celebrity status to remain politically viable. That's why, as Governor, he did a weekly radio call-in show on WCCO radio.

Will Haddeland, a former executive at Minnesota Public Radio, called this "an end run around journalism." Ventura made a proposal to WCCO shortly after taking office in 1999. "The governor wanted to communicate directly to the people of Minnesota without having to deal with the journalists he distrusted," Haddeland wrote. Ventura's radio program did not violated FCC fairness rules because this was an intrastate communication. However, Haddeland complained, "there is no journalistic integrity in Ventura's weekly broadcast (especially when he plugs Tim Penny's candidacy). It is what it is: a gift from a large corporation to a sitting governor."

I once had an opportunity to talk with Jesse Ventura about celebrity politicians. (Yes, he even asked for my autograph.) At a campaign fundraiser for an Independence Party House candidate, I gave Ventura a copy of my book, *Five Epochs of Civilization*, pointing out that he was mentioned in the book. I had cited Ventura, Ronald Reagan, and others as examples of political leaders who were in synch with their times. Since the book proposed that we are living in the age of entertainment, experienced entertainers tend to make today's successful politicians. Ventura agreed with that concept. Cocking his head, he mused: "Don't you think that politicians are a kind of entertainer? They need that skill."

Ventura and Brian Sullivan discussed this subject on Ventura's radio show. They were wondering why the proposal for a new stadium for the Minnesota Twins could consume so much of the governor's time. Ventura remarked: "It's government's job to see that you are entertained. I'm now involved up to my neck (in discussions of the Twins stadium) because entertainment is one of the functions of government." Sullivan disagreed. He commented rather sourly: "Minnesotans should expect more from our governor than just entertainment. When the going gets tough, he (Ventura) goes to Hollywood." Ventura, however, knew something which Sullivan did not. Like it or not, political leaders are obliged to be entertaining persons just to communicate with their constituencies. The news media will no longer give publicity away for free unless politicians deliver something that has entertainment value.

While traveling around Minnesota as a candidate for U.S. Senate, I depended entirely upon receiving free media coverage. I found most newspaper editors to be quite generous in that regard. Maybe it was because the image of a Don Quixote-like character holding up a sign with two outlandish messages made for good entertainment. This was something different - a kind of "news". Besides, a statewide candidate traveling to distant communities does stimulate local interest. Because the editors knew that I had worked to be there, they were reasonably sympathetic to my campaign. Some, however, would recite the rules: The initial announcement of your candidacy is free. From that point on, you have to pay for publicity through our advertising department. In the Twin Cities metro area, however, I could not attract free publicity. The Brahman editors at the big newspapers (excepting the *St. Paul Pioneer Press*) knew that they had political candidates over a barrel. They would decide who was and who was not deserving of coverage.

At my level of campaigning, newspapers were the media. Radio and television are more important to the big candidates. The need to advertise in the electronic media brings a different set of problems to politics. In theory, the public owns the air waves. The FCC gives certain companies an exclusive right to broadcast on certain frequencies. There is no charge to receive that monopoly privilege. Current license-holders presumably enjoy "squatter's rights" which give them a perpetual leasehold on their broadcast frequency.

The National Association of Broadcasters is a powerful and feared influence in Washington because they control the communications pipeline connecting elected officials with their constituents. Any attempt to undo the government giveaway to commercial broadcasters would meet with swift and certain retaliation. The FCC used to have rules requiring broadcasters to make certain accommodations to the public interest; these have all been abolished. When the Clinton-Gore Administration proposed that television broadcasters be required to give political candidates free air time in the period before elections, this idea was rebuffed. No one wanted to offend the powerful broadcast industry. That is too much trouble for politicians worried about the next election cycle.

Therefore, the politicians, needing to amass a huge campaign fund to pay for television commercials, became prodigious fund raisers. The expensive television commercials necessarily presented slick images and sound bites. Some of the more effective commercials were attack ads: "Call Senator Wellstone and tell him you're fed up with his outmoded, big-spending ways. Minnesotans don't want this." (With

a different twist, there were equivalent Wellstone or DFL ads attacking the Republican candidates.) Such commercials produced a degraded political discussion. Their negativity soured the public on political campaigns.

The worst part, though, was that, to raise the big sums of money for television commercials, elected officials had to solicit contributions from economic-interest groups. They became beholden to these groups in formulating and supporting legislation. The public came to believe that their government was up for sale. In reaction, there have been proposals for campaign finance reform. But the basic problem is the need for heavy expenditures for television commercials during political campaigns. The candidates have a need to deliver an undistorted message to the voters. Because the communications media will not let them do that through news reporting, the campaigns have had to pay for expensive commercials. Someone has called this process "bypassing Sam Donaldson."

Entrenched incumbents from the two major parties benefit from this situation. It is to their advantage to keep election campaigns expensive so that newcomers will find it hard to dislodge them. The Democrats, once the champion of poor people, are now into recruiting millionaire candidates who can afford to play the money game. The Twin Cities ad man, Bill Hillsman, has twice proved able to pierce the television-cost barrier by producing cheap but effective commercials to elect underdog candidates. Yet, Hillsman found himself out of work during the 2002 campaign. I ran into him at a Ralph Nader speech at Minneapolis City Hall in late September. Nader said that Wellstone would be smart to hire Hillsman to produce campaign commercials. I asked Hillsman if he would do that. "I haven't been asked," was the gist of his response. Evidently, Washington political operatives, especially Democrats, have told their party's candidates not to touch him.

Why is that? Hillsman told an interviewer for the *Rake* newspaper that "the Democratic Party would rather maintain a self-perpetuating organization than win, if it comes to that ... I was on a phone call once with a pollster and a DSCC official and Mike Ciresi (a wealthy attorney who ran for the U.S. Senate in 2000). First off they wanted him to raise a lot of soft money for the party. I told him, 'Don't be fooled - they're not going to put any of that money back into your race unless you toe the party line and it looks very winnable.' I've seen them do this with lots of congressional candidates - they say in effect, go raise money, and later they tell you to get in line with the party platform or get left out in the cold." Only a handful of Congressional races each election are in real contention. The Democrats, said Hillsman, "have plenty of money to run strong races in those 25-40 districts. But they hold that money over the heads of the candidates as a carrot and a stick. They tease them with it, and then they say, 'But you've got to play ball.' You get a purity test."

That is what the major-party candidates face. Candidates of third parties have an even more daunting challenge in convincing media editors and reporters that they are mounting "serious campaigns". Because almost anyone can become a political candidate or form a political party, the news media have a legitimate interest in reporting significant campaigns and not cluttering up the news with other coverage. Of necessity, they must set "standards" for coverage. So, how does an aspiring political candidate in a third party, or a nonendorsed candidate in any party, get to first base with the media? You try to be clever, entertainment-wise. You try to cultivate media relationships. If necessary, you try to protest, shame, or sue your way into debates. There is no single good answer, and that is what makes campaigning for the small, underfinanced candidates such a problematic enterprise. It's all a game.

My pet solution grows out of my experience with Minneapolis Property Rights Action Committee. I tried to put it into effect on a broader scale with the "Orange Party". If we could not attract coverage of our events from the large commercial media, we set up our own media to cover them. We had our own free-circulation newspaper and cable-television show. These could not be slick productions looking like political propaganda. We needed to host forums of free expression since today's sophisticated public can recognize a staged event when it sees one. We could not afford to lose credibility in manipulating the image. Allowing certifiably "bad" people to appear is better than trying to censor expression. In the process, we had to learn tolerance and forgiveness. So it is, I think, that politically interested persons of many different persuasions might cooperate in putting on a type of discussion that will give them each opportunities to be heard. If third parties are together facing extinction, it would be well for them to put aside the bickering and demonizing of each other and work on a common enterprise. They should jointly sponsor a third-party forum.

This scheme would cost money. The Property Rights group enjoyed an advantage in having a membership base of landlords who could afford the $55.00 annual dues. The group had a relatively unified agenda. Contributions could be justified as a business expense. It cost about $10,000 a year to keep the show afloat. Additionally, certain individuals put up their own money to publish the newspaper. In contrast, an organization which consisted of activists from several small parties would be pulled in different ideological directions. These might be persons of modest income, in it for the love of politics. Who would finance the operation? How might the cost be shared by the politically diverse groups? What decisionmaking mechanism might exist to moderate between competing interests?

To put third parties of various ideological temperaments under a common institutional umbrella would be in itself an accomplishment. But the fact is that each such party faces a more significant challenge today in getting its message out and having the public take it seriously than in harmonizing ideologies. At least initially, third parties must work together to build a media structure for their type of enterprise or they will be smothered by the two-party system.

So dismal is the current situation that we need to build a structure from the ground up. I remember reading once about

the cultural environment from which the Mormon religion sprang. In the 1820s and 1830s, the area near Rochester, New York, was crawling with evangelists, preachers, and miracle workers representing many different denominations. There were tent debates between the preachers of these Christian denominations, each claiming to speak God's truth. "What is the truth?," young Joseph Smith asked himself in bewilderment. Eventually he had a revelation of his own. Taking a broader view, one can readily see how a climate of religious controversy might spawn a dynamic new religion. The same is true in the political area. Controversy grabs people's attention. Debates produce a more refined and contemporary form of truth. We need, then, to go back to the point of fundamental uncertainty to revitalize politics. Let each point of view be heard.

Political activists need also to deal with the media problem. Why should private businesses, beyond public control, be allowed to set the policy agenda for the larger community? Why should they decide which candidates can receive enough coverage to be elected to public office? This is an inherent scandal within the democratic system. Now I am not suggesting that governments take over management of the large daily newspapers. I do suggest, at least initially, that the newspapers themselves address the problem of internal caucuses and biased reporting. If unseen journalists pursue hidden agendas of hate, the public needs to know about it. The public needs to know who the people are who are causing those contentious messages to be disseminated. What are their personal backgrounds? What axes have they to grind?

The same is true of Hollywood. Political agendas advanced in the guise of entertainment are equally unfair. We need to require more disclosure of communications that consistently project a politically or socially partisan message. As consumer-product disclosure laws tell the public what ingredients are in a product, so the communications media need to open up the process of creating their product and let the sunshine of full public disclosure inform consumer decisions.

Government may well have to use its big stick to beat the media into accepting this kind of reform. The degree of competition may dictate what needs to be done. Being print media, newspapers have potential competition from start-up publications including free-circulation newspapers. There is also the Internet. The press have certain First Amendment protections. The electronic media are quite another matter. In their case, government has granted monopolies to certain businesses to use a limited resource. It is not possible for competitors to enter that domain without FCC approval. Yet, the public interest must above all else be served. The proposal to require broadcasters to make available a certain amount of free air time to candidates during campaign season is reasonable. If the broadcast industry refuses to accept that arrangement, then Congress could put pressure on the Federal Communications Commission to reconsider the

stations' broadcast licenses or allow more low-watt stations to compete with them.

Political candidates can also communicate with voters through cable television. Cable-access shows are an efficient pipeline to voters in particular communities. Local governments have given certain cable companies a monopoly on service in their area. But, since the number of cable channels is potentially unlimited, there is no reason why political parties, working through local elected officials, cannot push the cable companies to expand the broadcast time available on these channels and reserve part of the time for political discussions. Third parties would benefit, in particular.

Many American newspapers started out as mouthpieces for political parties. I would foresee that, in the initial phase of their revival, third parties would acquire their own media and become self-directed media operations. They would have their own apparatus for communicating with voters. Political activity in this mode would consist of two parts, content and media production, not just content. Content, in a broad sense, would consist of presenting issues to the public, generating relevant information, acting to persuade government to implement certain policies, or seeking to be elected to public office for those purposes. In a narrow sense, it would consist of staging debates. Media production is self-explanatory.

To capture public attention, it is necessary to maintain quality in both parts of the operation. Third parties cannot afford to put out poorly written newspapers which merely trumpet their views. They cannot afford to put videos on the air with poor camera work and problems with sound. But the content also needs to be of high quality. Politicians should be deliverers of a useful and inspiring message, filled with good information, which leads to intelligent public-policy recommendations. Done right, the third-party debaters could put on a show which puts today's candidate debates to shame. Once the public grows accustomed to high-quality discussions of community affairs put on by third-party organizations, they may no longer be satisfied with the bipartisan dancing around tough issues and the candidates jumping through arbitrarily selected media hoops.

CHAPTER TWENTY-EIGHT

Building a Third Party Movement: Part 2

When people think of political activity, their thoughts are usually directed at efforts to achieve solutions of force. They go to the legislature to pass laws or file court cases to set a judicial precedent. But much that is wrong in our society is not government-mandated. It comes about through acquiescence to intimidation. For this type of problem, the better remedy is political action directed at changing public opinion. Passing laws cannot coerce the human heart to change. Minneapolis Property Rights Action Committee started out pursuing coercive solutions. We filed a class-action lawsuit against the city of Minneapolis in federal court. A judge tossed out our suit. We made an effort to introduce legislation at the state capitol but were overpowered by opposing interest groups. That left us with the option of influencing public opinion. That last-chosen approach succeeded brilliantly.

One of the best ways to influence public opinion is to tell a story based upon personal experience. The Property Rights group meetings have featured stories of landlords, small business people, and others abused by Minneapolis city government. The meetings were videotaped and shown on cable television. Political action can take creative forms such as the "crack tours" which tell stories of a community. Our biggest asset has been our ability to communicate directly with the public through the cable-television show and free-circulation newspaper. Our activities have also received coverage by the mainstream media when something we did struck their fancy.

And so we did our part to create an action-oriented political culture in the Twin Cities. Such a culture needs both activities and media willing to cover them. If successful, the political culture can inspire a community to move beyond self-absorption, apathy, and passive-aggressiveness to give people a sense of power in expressing themselves. It can remove some of the bitterness from our hearts. Changing public opinion is indeed powerful.

Although leaders of the Property Rights group sometimes received complaints that we were "not accomplishing anything", we did change public opinion over time; and that was no mean accomplishment. Public opinion is that soft, amorphous force from which political power springs. Persons of crude sensibility prefer looking at laws and lawsuits as if these are the "reality" of public policy. They are only its bureaucratic shell. What the public thinks and believes is the real policy. One affects policy as much by action as by reasoned persuasion. When people see someone courageously standing up for himself, it is an inspiring sight. The "monkey-see, monkey-do" principle is alive in even sophisticated human beings. Anyone can resist intimidation through action if he is ready to pay the price.

I am suggesting, then, that a political party can do more than elect candidates to office, appoint judges, and pass laws. It can also be a community of activists. It can provide the social framework for individuals to work on projects along the lines of their common values. Even though the Property Rights group showed that you can successfully fight City Hall, you cannot do it alone. You need other people's encouragement and support. Effective political action needs people pitching in unselfishly

according to their individual skills. The structure of the landlord group consisted of a regular monthly gathering where people met face-to-face. Even more, it was a web of telephone calls between persons working on something together. Protest demonstrations would energize the membership. People were encouraged to take the initiative in developing group projects. With a political party having diverse interests, that approach may not be possible to the same extent. Yet, some mechanism needs to be established which authorizes its members to act freely on behalf of the group.

The main function of political parties, as they exist today, is to elect candidates to public office. Secondarily, it is to formulate issues that will identify the party in terms of policy and attract candidates sympathetic to those views. This requires endless rounds of "business meetings" to decide what should be the party's position. Let me say that I am personally put off by that aspect of politics. It attracts talkers who sound reasonable and polished but who may not have a clue about what actually goes on in the world. I have seen neighborhood groups pretending to do good while their members were scheming to acquire real estate without paying for it. People think they are accomplishing something by passing carefully worded resolutions. They debate minor changes in wording. It were as if these individuals were engaged in an important enterprise like drafting the U.S. Constitution. In reality, the politically apathetic public cares little about the resolutions and policy statements adopted by political groups. It's a worthless enterprise.

In my view, political organizations need to be focused on action. The important thing is not engaging in internal discussions but going out to meet the public. That is where the political rubber meets the road. Candidates who actually do this deserve respect. They know they will meet people who disagree with their positions, some quite strongly. That forces the candidates to reconsider previous opinions, refine them, and perhaps develop a different position, not produce definitive statements on some issue. Most persons elected to public office are better for having gone through that process. With respect to groups, it is also important to confront that part of the public which does not agree with their views.

I am personally hard-pressed to sit through a lengthy political convention. The time is taken up by debating temporary officers and rules, proposed changes in the party constitution, resolutions, and selection of candidates. Some persons at the convention are experts in parliamentary procedure or in maneuvering with the aid of *Robert's Rules of Order*. They propose minute changes in someone else's resolution. Then the chair has to explain the rules to decide this matter. Someone will rise with a "point of information". Maybe that, too, has to be debated. It's all humbug - a big waste of time. Political parties need to recognize that their first order of business is to attract people into the organization. If meetings are a way to do that, then those meetings need to be made personally interesting and worthwhile. Otherwise, people will stop coming. If that means dispensing with *Robert's Rules of Order*, so be it. People come to political conventions for certain purposes, usually to nominate a candidate. Let the conventions be organized more efficiently towards that end. Don't waste people's time.

Therefore, I believe that, as political parties need to develop a mechanism to deliver their message to the public, so they need a better one for conducting internal business. The object in both cases is to improve the flow of communication. Individuals are interested in politics for certain reasons. Let them talk about what really matters to them. Structure the meetings to maximize the time for communication on subjects that interest the people attending them. Give everyone a chance to speak. Let people learn something at these meetings: Make sure that good, solid information comes out of them. Let the meetings facilitate meaningful discussions between like-minded persons and between persons who may disagree. There is never any lasting, definitive agreement on important questions. Aspiring Thomas Jeffersons who want to write the Declaration of Independence need not apply.

I am, of course, projecting my own values upon the political process. While writing this in the context of Independence Party politics, I ignore the fact that there is an existing Independence Party structure and institutional heritage. It is unlikely that the force of my arguments will persuade too many people to give up what they have been doing. Besides an illustrious history, the Independence Party now has its first member of the Minnesota legislature, State Senator Sheila Kiscaden of Rochester, elected under the party's banner. It has other elected officials in local offices. It has a growing membership base. It has Tim Penny's list of more than 30,000 contributors who, collectively, contributed more than $1 million to his gubernatorial campaign. It has a new permanent office in the Midway district of St. Paul. It officially enjoys "major party status". In other words, the Independence Party has a lot going for it.

Even so, new ideas can be useful if they make sense to people, and I am hoping that mine will. This book will put a proposal for change on the table and some may want to respond. Perhaps, also, it may help to arouse a new constituency which might want to join the Independence Party or some other political party depending on how events play out. My twin issues of support for a shorter workweek and opposition to political correctness are sure to offend many. I would not want to force this agenda upon anyone. However, my personal hope is that the Independence Party will be a place to sponsor candidates who

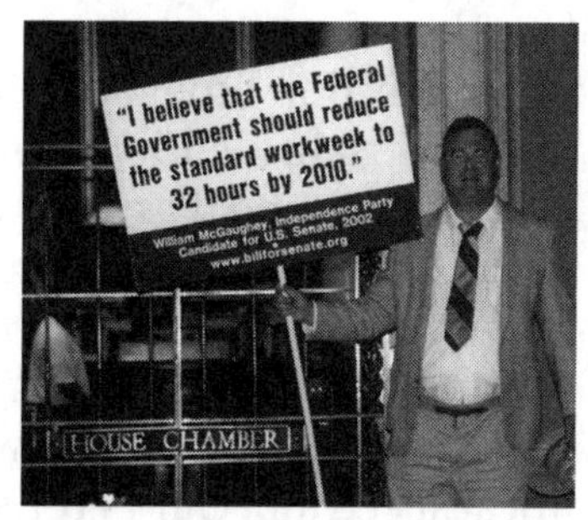
"I believe that the Federal Government should reduce the standard workweek to 32 hours by 2010."
William McGaughey, Independence Party Candidate for U.S. Senate, 2002
www.billforsenate.org
HOUSE CHAMBER

would embrace those particular ideas and take them to the voters as I did. The waters are not too cold.

As a technical matter, I will use the term "New Independence Party" to designate the political program being advocated here. The idea is not to advocate the formation of a new political party but to identify a potential caucus within the existing Independence Party which might arise as a result of this book's publication. A website at http://www.newindependenceparty.org will keep interested persons informed of developments related to the book or its agenda. This is my way of advocating a political program without intruding unduly in other people's business.

In my view, the imperative to adhere to a party platform is unhelpful. Party platforms may be useful as policy recommendations, but nothing more. The candidates' own views and how they are projected to the public are more important. More important still is the discussion taking place among the general public. To the degree that the Independence Party embraces my twin proposals, I would suggest that they become an additional element within the party, not something to replace what is already there. There should be no litmus tests for membership in the party. The important thing is to find new people to join our common enterprise and give them freedom to express themselves. But I will go where my own interests lie. They lie partly in revitalizing third-party politics and the Independence Party, and partly in pursuing the two issues.

Having said that, however, I also believe that the existing Independence Party has an ideological flavor or a personality which distinguishes it from the other political parties. Ross Perot, founder of its predecessor organization, and Jesse Ventura, whose election brought us to power in this state, have given the party a certain identity through their personalities and opinions. If I may be so bold as to characterize the Independence Party, I would say that, like the Greens, our ranks are filled with idealists. Otherwise, we would be like Democrats and Republicans chasing after the spoils of office. In comparison with the Greens, we are positioned more toward the conservative end of the political spectrum. Our Perotist upbringing has given us a desire to

reduce the deficit and to sympathize with veterans who have given so much to their country. We are not scheming to get rich or stay in power by using other people's money or lives. We also tend to be older than the average Green. Our membership tends to be more male. Even though racial minorities and women fill our ranks, Independence Party members, from what I have seen, disproportionately consist of older white males.

In my chauvinistic opinion, that is not necessarily a bad thing. Males tend to gravitate toward new territories. They are disproportionately the cowboys on the western frontier, settlers in Alaska, and persons who would respond to Ross Perot's call for a new party. They are not the type of person who would be offended by Jesse Ventura's brash personality. They would secretly or openly admire him for getting away with his politically incorrect views. So, if the Independence Party disproportionately represents "angry white males" who live in exurban Anoka or Chisago County, lack social polish, and own guns, it does not bother me. We can keep this kind of membership or have it change. People can join the Independence Party or they can leave. That is beyond our control. Thanks to Tim Penny, our center of gravity may, however, be shifting toward the southeastern part of the state.

I have argued that the party needs a clearer identity in terms of fundamental political questions and that it needs to differentiate itself from the two major parties. Being in the "sensible center" is too policy-wonkish. We need to speak to the gut issues. Economic policy and the Civil Rights legacy are the big ones. Besides those, candidates will have to deal with a host of specific issues which insert themselves peripherally into political campaigns. Gun control and abortion are two which come to mind. Perhaps the best approach is to give individual candidates freedom to choose their own position and then communicate it honestly to voters. Maybe, to satisfy those with a Voter's Guide mentality, we can develop a matrix of positions on each type of issue. We can facilitate clear and open communications.

The hard fact is that the Independence Party needs to appeal to voters who think that candidates from the Democratic and Republican parties are more likely to win. We need to give people a good reason to vote for our candidates. As I said before, we cannot afford to be timid or nuanced in what we are proposing. We need to present our honest views to the public, warts and all. We need to stand up for our own values. We need to do picketing and public protests. Forget the pundits. Forget political realists. Catering to this type of person is not going to bring fundamental change. Paul Wellstone showed that a candidate of strong, honest convictions could attract votes even from persons who disagreed with him.

CHAPTER TWENTY-NINE

Confronting the Demons

I live in the inner city, a place of political craziness and infan tile behavior from a small businessman's point of view. I would like to believe that in the suburbs there are persons of mature judgment who would understand my situation and perhaps be sympathetic. At the same time, I recognize that people have moved to the suburbs to escape big-city problems. They do not want to be dealing with the big-city mess. So they move on to a place where sensibility and serenity might be possible. An analogous situation would be that of the white-male population in the United States immersed in a political environment that spews forth hatred in their direction. This is a place, for instance, where reparations are demanded of white Americans for injustices perpetrated against black people a century and a half ago. They know in their hearts that those demands are absurd but dare not say so. From this kind of craziness there is no "escaping to suburbs" except in the sense that one avoids discussions of race or other sensitive topics. Avoidance is again the strategy.

To them, I say: Come back into the big city. It is not such a frightening place, once you have gotten used to the fear mongers and con artists and have taken a few hits. If you think you might

be guilty of racism, confront your own demons. Are you anti-Semitic? Are you homophobic? Do some honest thinking and follow it through to a firm opinion. Are you afraid of other people screaming at you? Then scream at them back. Being "Minnesota nice" will get you nowhere. Watch how quickly those demons disappear if you have the backbone to confront them.

During his second term as President, Bill Clinton staged a national "initiative on race" which was portrayed as an opportunity for blacks and whites to sit down together to discuss racial issues and perhaps begin to heal a race-torn society. The concept was laudable. Like many others, however, this discussion of race was one-sided. A white man named Robert Hoy, who attended Clinton's forum in northern Virginia, stood up to complain: "There's no one up there that's talking about the White people!," he said. "We don't want to be a minority in our own country." Jeers and boos greeted that comment from the audience. Soon a security guard appeared to escort Hoy out of the building because he was "disrupting" the event.

To me, it is significant that this incident was reported in an African American newspaper. Evidently none of the white-controlled newspapers would touch it. None would admit that the President's race initiative was anything less than the complete, honest discussion it pretended to be. Black Americans such as Ward Connerly have been outspoken critics of affirmative action. A black minister from Louisiana is traveling around the country to speak out against reparations for slavery. I'm sure both men have endured much personal abuse. Despite such examples of honesty and good will from the black community, white Americans are afraid to take a similar position for fear of being called "racist". Yet, we call ourselves "land of the free, home of the brave".

I remember reading somewhere that the CEO of Home Depot, the nation's largest building-supplies store, was an African American man. Buried on page A7 of the *Star Tribune* on June 17, 2002, there was a short article disclosing that Home Depot's headquarters in Atlanta had sent instructions to its 1,400 stores around the country not to accept government credit cards, purchase orders, or even cash, if the items were purchased for the federal government. The reason was that such purchases would subject the company to federal regulations relating to gender and race. Home Depot did not wish "to be covered by or responsible in any way for compliance with three federal laws or executive orders that deal with affirmative action or discrimination."

Was this directive initiated by Home Depot's African American CEO who, perhaps, in his own crusty way was telling the world that he had not risen to the top of the corporate hierarchy through race-based preferences? Alternatively, had there been a corporate coup in which white racists had removed him as Home Depot's chief executive? I do not know. I did find it strange, though, that such a potentially major development in the area of race relations was not reported more prominently in this race-obsessed newspaper. Did the editors not want us to know something? Usually the personal angle makes them want to jump on a story.

The *Star Tribune* does allow a conservative named Katherine Kersten to publish opinion articles on culturally sensitive subjects which contradict the views of its editorial writers. It was Kersten who produced statistics showing that African Americans were responsible for a disproportionate share of violent crimes. She had spoken the unspeakable in today's politically correct environment. The president of the Minneapolis Urban League followed with a "counterpoint" article condemning Kersten's disclosure. "What does she mean?," he sniffed. "Does she mean that I am about to commit a crime and she is not? Does she mean that my beloved 14-year-old daughter has a greater propensity for lawbreaking than her white classmates? Is she implying that African-Americans carry a crime gene that white people do not?"

When a *Newsweek* writer made a point similar to Kersten's, the associate publisher of an African American newspaper wrote: "To allow Alter (the *Newsweek* writer) to get away with writing, '**The politically incorrect truth is that minorities do in fact commit a disproportionate number of crimes** (his emphasis),' is blatantly racist, racist, racist." With certain individuals, you have to "walk on eggshells" not to say the wrong thing.

In recent years, "hate crimes" laws have been enacted calling for stiffer penalties when violent crimes have been committed with demographically malicious thoughts in mind. While some such as Governor Ventura argue that a racially malicious assault hurts no worse than a mindlessly delivered one, others see "hate crimes" as assaults against communities, whose ill effect is magnified beyond individuals. The "hate crime" concept adds the element of thought to violent action. In the guise of criminal justice, it becomes a tool to mold political opinion.

President Clinton was inspired to propose expanding hate-crime laws when a young gay man, Matthew Shepard, was pistol-whipped to death in Wyoming and when white supremacists in Texas dragged James Byrd, Jr., a black man, by a chain beneath a pickup track. Those many lesser publicized murders of whites by blacks or of straights by gays mean little in this context. Official FBI statistics show that in 2001 there were 2,900 hate crimes committed against black people, 1,043 against gays, and only 891 committed against (presumably straight) white people. I recall that in the 1980s when the Minneapolis police first began to record the racial identity of persons committing violent crimes, the *Star Tribune* let the information slip that more than 70% of the racially recorded crimes were committed by blacks. A retired Minneapolis police officer tells me that the officers are discouraged from reporting hate crimes committed against whites. When that box is checked on the police report, someone forgets to include it on the typed copy.

Racial profiling by police has received much attention. The official explanation is that all too many officers are racist brutes bent on harassing black people. Police sometimes argue in de-

fense that blacks are involved in a disproportionate number of criminal activities. As a fisherman fishes the "hot spots", so police officers target their investigations to communities where crime is more prevalent. I have no doubt that law-abiding blacks are disproportionately stopped and searched or otherwise "harassed" by police officers, or that some officers do exhibit racial malice. But what about the higher crime rates among blacks? Does it help for black representatives to scream "racism" when someone even raises the subject? No, it does not.

Those black leaders and sympathetic whites cannot force white individuals to think differently if their experience confirms a general pattern. The politically unacceptable opinion will simply be pushed underground. Like it or not, the disproportionately high black crime rate is a particular problem for the black community and for those who call themselves its leaders. If there is indeed racial solidarity within that community, those black leaders are in a position to do more to combat the black crime problem than white people ever could. To allow black criminals to use the cry of "racism" as an excuse for their bad behavior encourages more of the same. That political shield weakens the disincentive to committing crimes which is the fear that they will get caught and be punished, having no such excuse.

What of the Urban League president's suggestion that white people think blacks carry a "crime gene"? What of some white people's idea that blacks have a lower level of intelligence than whites, implying that they may not be as advanced on the evolutionary scale? Is this not "racism" at its core? Are not such attitudes deeply offensive? Of course they are. There can also be little doubt that many whites harbor those views. On other hand, people will think what they will, regardless of political persuasions. It is, in my view, counterproductive to try to tell people what they should think.

It may well be that levels of average intelligence as measured by IQ tests differ by race. Yet, even if it could be "proven" that members of a certain racial group have lower average intelligence, that finding would not justify race-based treatment of individuals within our society. We live in a society governed by laws, and laws treat people the same. Those persons of higher-than-average intelligence certainly do not deserve to be treated according to theories of differing group intelligence. Sound public policy requires equal treatment under the law, not a race-based caste system. That is why it is also dangerous when, following different theories, the laws are twisted to favor "disadvantaged" groups. It's unhelpful to try to make a case that certain groups of people are good or bad, advantaged or disadvantaged, criminal or law-abiding, or any such thing.

Now let me go on to discuss the Jews. Does not a red flag go up when I even mention the word: anti-Semitism alert!! The reader may guess that if I have not followed the standard line in discussing race relations, I may be an equally loose cannon when it comes to questions relating to Jews. Yes, I will be critical of "Jewish influence" within our society where this seems appropriate. It is generally accepted that for a person to say that the Jews control banking, especially international banks or the Federal Reserve System, is anti-Semitic. What about saying that Jews control Hollywood? Is that also anti-Semitic? Is it relevant whether the statement happens to be true; or is the very fact that one says that Jews control some powerful institution an act of anti-Semitism deserving of public condemnation?

My own view is that this becomes a matter of public concern only when Jews in positions of power use that position to favor other Jews or the state of Israel or to promote religious or quasi-religious ideologies associated with Jews. The fact that Arthur Burns or Alan Greenspan, chairmen of the Federal Reserve Board, were both Jewish arouses no particular concern because there is no indication that these gentlemen pursued policies other than what they believed would be in the broad public interest. On the other hand, Henry Kissinger, also Jewish, does arouse suspicions when, on his beat, the U.S. government de-

cided to buy peace in the Middle East by directing the bulk of U.S. foreign aid to Egypt and Israel. I must admit, however, that I do not know the extent to which Kissinger was personally responsible for that decision. The fact that the Israeli lobby in the United States exerts an unusual influence over U.S. foreign policy and that this influence may, in some cases, be detrimental to the broader interests of Americans is a legitimate point of criticism. I think most reasonable people would agree.

Fewer would agree, however, with my contention that Jews or the "Jewish community" can be faulted for "promoting religious or quasi-religious ideologies associated with Jews" when holding positions of trust in the larger community. Judaism as a religion has a distinct heritage. Most would agree it would be wrong if Jews in power positions tried to force this religion or its particular practices and beliefs upon the U.S. population. To force a "quasi-religious ideology" upon Americans is another matter. Does such exist? The fact is that many Jews are not religious in a traditional sense. Yet, a quasi-religious culture has developed within the Jewish community in its secularized state. Preoccupation with the Holocaust is one of its elements.

The Holocaust for many Jews is not simply an historical fact but an object of veneration and belief. The term "Holocaust-denier" is used in much the same sense that one would use the term "heretic" for someone who denied a tenet of the Christian or another religious faith. People are not allowed to deny the Holocaust because that would violate a deeply held quasi-religious belief. Those who would deny the Holocaust are evil and not merely deluded. Belief in the Holocaust is a tenet of Judaism in its contemporary, secularized phase. It is a religious belief.

What are some of the other elements of this Judaic "quasi-religious" culture? The ideology of the Civil Rights movement in America might be an example. In this ideology, Jews and blacks struggled together to help blacks overcome racial oppression - a generalization which has some basis in historical fact. The moral overtones are, however, what makes it a quasi-religious tradition. In this particular set of stories, Jews are good people who unselfishly help another oppressed group. Black Americans also have a positive role as victors in this struggle. White people, especially in the South, are the villains. The problem with this type of culture is that it demonizes certain peoples - in this case, white-racist Southerners. Moral characterizations of groups are inherent in religious ideologies.

The "quasi-religious ideology" of contemporary Judaism has a more general type of villain called an "anti-Semite". This is a stock character formed through historical association with the Nazis who is therefore capable of murderous violence. In practice, an anti-Semite can be anyone ranging from someone who uses a derogatory term for Jews to one who criticizes the state of Israel or even an individual Jew on almost any grounds imaginable. It is a malleable label of derision and hate attached to non-Jews in a quasi-religious - i.e. serious and compelling - manner.

Individually, people can be as hateful and narrow as they wish to be. If individual Jews wish to immerse themselves in dark ruminations concerning anti-Semitism, that is their problem, not mine. It does become my problem, however, when this point of view is officially promoted or enforced in the general culture. Religious or, I would argue, quasi-religious ideologies are not supposed to be official doctrine. It is quite improper for government to fund institutions which promote such ideologies or to teach them in the public schools. It is also improper to use the public airwaves to promote quasi-religious values in a systematic way. This violates the traditions and values of a pluralistic free society.

Now, I do not wish to encourage the formation of a new kind of "thought police" to root out religious influences in our culture. If, statistically, many or most Jews believe certain things - let's say, the

doctrines of Freudian psychology or non-Euclidean geometry - that would be of no particular concern. What does concern me is the type of ideology which exalts certain groups of people while vilifying others. That is what I call a religious or quasi-religious ideology. For goodness sake, let's end the demonization of particular groups of people. Those who practice such demonization while holding a position of public trust deserve to be rebuked. They ought not to push their quasi-religious values upon others. No, the world does not revolve around Jews or any particular people. We are living in a secularized, pluralistic society where all groups have a right to live in dignity. But do these things indeed happen as I am suggesting?

Let's focus on Hollywood. I was watching Steven Spielberg's television drama, "Taken", the other night on the Sci Fi channel. In the middle of a drama about abduction by space aliens, Spielberg or his screen writers popped in a little scene, set in the 1940s, about two well-behaved, well-groomed black men being attacked in a restaurant while they were waiting to be served. It was a scene stereotypical of the segregationist south: the burly white cook spitting in the black man's coffee, another white shooting at the blacks through the window with a rifle as the boy hero saves the intended victim's life by pulling him to safety under the table. This gratuitous piece of political-social propaganda seemed to have little to do with the plot.

In a more positive way, I have seen at other times in the movies Jews in traditional religious garb placed conspicuously in a sea of smiling faces to greet a Jimmy Stewart-like hero. To a suspicious mind such as mine, this was a ploy to cultivate sympathy for Jews among the types of people who would identify with Jimmy Stewart. An innocent coincidence? It depends upon how often these religious elements appear in the Hollywood films and whether they serve a legitimate thematic purpose. Considering the attention given to exhibiting branded products in films, such selection of characters could not have been coincidental. If good and evil characters are evenly distributed among the demographic types, none has reason to complain. But if some birth-determined groups are consistently vilified or exalted in the popular culture, this becomes a matter of public concern.

The historical documentary, "Benedict Arnold: A Question of Honor", which appeared on the A&E cable channel, was a useful reconsideration of Arnold's reputation as a traitor to our country. What purpose was served, however, by displaying a small but conspicuous gold chain with a Star of David around the neck of Arnold's subordinate officer? The officer appeared often in the documentary, always exhibiting this religious emblem. He was presented in the sympathetic role of warning Arnold to be diligent in serving the revolutionary cause while being loyal to him. Arnold, of course, went ahead with the betrayal at the urging of his upper-class WASP Christian wife. Did Benedict Arnold, in fact, have a Jewish associate who tried to keep him on the right path? Was it necessary to label this character visually as a Jew?

One Hollywood Jew who is not afraid to push the envelope in promoting social and political agendas is Aaron Sorkin, creator and writer of NBC's "The West Wing". Sorkin has built the President, played by Martin Sheen, into a figure of moral authority whose favorable or unfavorable remarks directed at certain types of individuals may influence public attitudes about groups. On a day when I watched this show, there were both Jewish rabbis and fundamentalist Christians visiting the "White House". The rabbis got along well with the President who, in contrast, found a few choice words to put down the fundamentalists.

Sorkin's shameless advocacy has attracted the attention of media columnists such as Rob Owen of the *Pittsburgh Post-Gazette*, who wrote: "'The West Wing' comes across as a pretty liberal show in the first episode with Christian Coalition anti-abortionists depicted as anti-Semitic deal makers who send the president's 12-year-old granddaughter a doll with a knife in its throat because she said in an interview she was pro-choice. 'It wouldn't surprise me at all that we get letters that the Christian right isn't happy,' Sorkin said. 'On the other hand, I will cop to this being one of those moments where I take a personal passion of mine in life, I get up on a box and I let you all know about it.'" The point is that most Americans do not have the opportunity to stand on any kind of soapbox, let alone rebut those who, like Sorkin, use it to push hate-laden agendas over the publicly owned air waves.

All this serves to create a powerful intimidating force that serves political ends. With respect to the Iraq war, any fair-minded person would acknowledge that it serves Israeli interests to have the United States, rather than Israel, expending its treasure and sustaining the casualties to oust Saddam Hussein and thereby strengthen Israel's security. Ronald Reagan was livid when, without informing his administration, the Israelis used U.S. aircraft to bomb a nuclear reactor near Baghdad. President Bush has volunteered to do much more. One would think that the Israeli connection to the war would be a legitimate political question. Yet, a Democratic regional whip, Rep. Jim Moran of Virginia, lost his position for saying to an anti-war forum at a church: "If it were not for the strong support of the Jewish community for the war, we would not be doing this." Such a statement smacked of "anti-Semitism", which means having Hitler-like tendencies. Six Jewish members of Congress called on Moran not to seek re-election.

Some Jewish organizations, or organizations devoted to combating anti-Semitic or other prejudices, I would characterize as flat-out "hate groups"; they demonize people. I refer to organizations purporting to represent Jews and other "victimized" peoples which show no interest in becoming reconciled with their demographic adversaries. They prepare what I would consider to be "enemy lists" - enemies of the Jewish people who, in their eyes, ought to be considered enemies of humanity - consisting of subhuman, brutish types of persons bent on pursuing evil, secretive activities that threaten us all. Insinuations that these groups share common ground with Jew-killing Nazis or white lynch mobs in the South are a staple of their hate-filled message. There is a lurid Hollywoodish flavoring of frightful imagery, evocative of death, surrounding these roach-like "anti-Semitic" or "racist" characters. However, I separate individual Jews, who are often critical of such politics or culture, from the organizations that speak in their name. None of us should be subjected to that kind of intimidation.

According to the *World Almanac*, there are 5.9 million Jews in North America, of which 3.5 million persons belong to the three principal Jewish religious organizations in the United States. In comparison, 61.2 million Americans belong to the Roman Catholic church; 30.7 million, to Baptist churches; 14.1 million, to Methodist churches, etc. Yet, in an effort to promote a more equitable and diverse religious culture, the minor Jewish holiday of Hanukkah is put on a par with Christmas in official celebrations of the "holiday season". Jews and other non-Christians are sometimes quite vocal in protesting artifacts of Christian celebration in public places.

During the 2001 Christmas season, some objected to the fact that red poinsettias, believed to be such an artifact, were placed in baskets in the lobby of the St. Paul City Hall. Eventually, a compromise solution was achieved by which white poinsettias, not so closely associated with Christianity, were allowed. Meanwhile, a large representation of a Menorah, an unmistakably Jewish religious symbol, stood in front of the Minnesota state capitol without objection. Seldom have the double standards inherent in political correctness been so clearly on display.

Why do Christians put up with this? They know better than to criticize Jews. Decades of intense propaganda directed from the entertainment industry and other places have convinced the public that to say negative things about Jews, their religion, or cultural influence makes one an anti-Semite, hence a krypto-Nazi.

Even such a large and historically important group of Americans as those who profess belief in Christianity can be rendered impotent as a political force if demonized and demoralized long enough.

I think, however, that there is a deeper reason that Christians are reluctant to criticize Jews: Christianity sprang from the Judaic tradition which maintains that there is only One God and the Jews are His Chosen People. Fundamentalist Christians are especially sensitive to those claims. Many have the particular idea that God will bless those who help the Jews. Prophecies concerning the Jewish homeland enter into their understanding of "the final days". In essence, these Christians are spooked by the idea of the Jews' special place in the divine order. What believer in Christ wants to cross Jehovah and go to Hell? This superstitious sentiment provides ample cover for hyperaggressive, anti-Christian moves by Jewish advocacy groups.

Such attitudes used to affect policies concerning the state of Israel. Jews as a domestic lobbying group have controlled U.S. policy with respect to the Middle East, and that has turned much of the Islamic world against America. It is the genesis of our problems with terrorism. It may be, at least partially, behind the Iraq war. I must concede, however, that it is no longer politically forbidden to criticize Israel. Leftist groups do this with some regularity. I must also express sympathy for the Israeli population which must endure frequent attacks upon innocent civilians from pro-Palestinian suicide bombers and other terrorists. While security crackdowns are often brutal, no nation can acquiesce in the murder of its own citizens.

The counter argument can also be made that it was the Jews who first brought terrorism to this region in the 1940s. Israel today seems unwilling to grant the Palestinian people a separate and secure homeland without violent pressure. Its police actions against Palestinian populations today are worse than what was done against black people in the white-segregationist American South. But rather than demonize anyone, maybe it's best now to let go of history and its grievances, forgive one's historical enemies, and try to get on with the work of pursuing one's own happiness and prosperity in a peaceful environment.

He was not originally scheduled to be mentioned in this book but now I want to discuss the demonization of Trent Lott. Senator Lott, as we know, said at a 100th birthday celebration for retiring Senator Strom Thurmond that most Mississippians in 1948 were proud to have voted for Strom Thurmond as the Dixiecrat candidate for President of the United States. He further said, "And if the rest of the country had followed our lead, we wouldn't have had all these problems over all these years, either." Lott made these impromptu remarks at a lighthearted gathering of Thurmond's colleagues, relatives, and friends. But a fire storm soon erupted because Lott's remarks implied that

this man, Republican majority leader of the U.S. Senate, still favored policies associated with the white-supremacist South. Furthermore, he had made similar statements at a gathering twenty years ago and his voting record did not favor positions supported by Civil Rights activists. Soon came the demand, supported by President Bush, for Lott's head.

"I believe in the full
citizenship, dignity and
equality of white males
(and of everyone else, too)."
William McGaughey, Independence Party
Candidate for U.S. Senate, 2002
www.billforsenate.org

Trent Lott apologized profusely for his remarks. I watched his interview on the Black Entertainment Network on December 16, 2002, which was an intense exercise in groveling intended to allow Lott to keep his job as majority leader. This was obviously a man on the run. What did Lott mean by "all these problems over all these years"? He wouldn't say. Lott's critics supposed that the Republican Senator meant that giving black Americans full citizenship and equality was a problem; his heart went back to the segregationist South. Lott insisted that it wasn't true. He was for affirmative action, he said. He was a religious man who could admit his own failings. What Lott could not do was stick up for himself and for his own principles. Let me try to do it.

I think that one of the "problems" that has developed in the years following the Civil Rights movement has been the persistent, illegitimate effort to curtail free speech on racial matters. This is an extremely ugly aspect of the political situation today; and the Lott incident illustrates it as well as anything. If Trent Lott was in favor of turning back the clock to a time when people were more tolerant of diverse opinions, I would heartily agree. Black people have no right to dictate what white people think or say. That is not a requirement for living in a just society. I would respect the right of Lott or anyone else to yearn for the "good old days" of the segregationist South and to say so openly if that is his true sentiment. Whether such a person should expect to remain majority leader of the U.S. Senate is another matter. Indeed, it might have been a good thing, even from the standpoint of African Americans, if Strom Thurmond had been elected President in 1948, though probably not. Thurmond had previously been a racial moderate. Maybe, as Nixon went to China, Thurmond might have moved the South peacefully towards a racially integrated society and had the moral authority to bring whites along with him willingly.

I am not for demonizing white Southerners - and that has been the basic approach of the Civil Rights movement. The idea is to roll over someone else's dead body with court orders and federal troops. Blood-soaked government action cannot sway the human heart. There is a legacy of racial bitterness in our land. That, too, is one of the "problems" to which Lott might have referred. Forget Strom Thurmond's candidacy. I would say that "we wouldn't have had all these problems" if Abraham Lincoln had not been assassinated in April 1865. Lincoln would have tried to "bind up the nation's wounds", not force a radical Republican agenda upon the defeated South. Racial healing might well have taken place more quickly under a leader who favored "malice toward none and charity toward all".

We seem to forget that some of the worst episodes of violence and hate were spawned in conditions created by the hard-driving policies of victorious forces following wars. If the Allies had not imposed the harsh terms of the Versailles treaty upon Germany, we might not have had Hitler and the Nazis. If the radical Republicans had not humiliated the post-Civil War South, we might not have had the Ku Klux Klan and a century of racial segregation. We Americans demonstrated the better alternative in our more humane treatment of Germany and Japan following World War II.

CHAPTER THIRTY

Is There a Third Way?

In June 1999, I attended the 35th reunion of my Yale gradua tion class in New Haven, Connecticut. Distinguished classmates spoke to us on issues of the day. One of them, Gus Spaeth, who was a former UN Development official about to become dean of the Yale Forestry School, spoke on environmental challenges facing the earth's people. A woman in the back of the room asked him a question or, I should say, made a statement. It was something to the effect that rapaciously aggressive male attitudes were responsible for ruining the natural environment. Where was the female perspective in Spaeth's analysis? I stood up before my classmates and their wives, including U.S. Senator Joe Lieberman, and gave this woman a stiff tongue-lashing. Referring to the socially divisive tone of the woman's remarks, I remember telling the group: "I don't think that 'saving the earth' (as Spaeth proposed) has a constituency any more. We're each into protecting our own little group." After my remarks, a number of my classmates or their wives came up to thank me for making that statement. I pursued my 2002 Senate campaign in much the same spirit.

Being reasonably intelligent human beings, we should all want to "save the earth" and improve human society. Politics stands in the way. Protecting and preserving the natural environment might gain universal support if it were not for economic selfishness, on one hand, and ideological extremism, on the other. If humanity cannot get together on this one question, it shows how much of a problem politics can be. I think that human society can rationally solve its own problems. Population control may be the toughest of them. Who, except for the government of China, has the inclination and ruthless power to restrict child bearing? Apart from this, the economic questions ought to be soluble. Should we not all be in favor of improving individual living standards in our own country and around the world without ruining the environment? I think so. Technology should make that possible.

Another barrier stands in the way of general progress: one's place in society. Every society exhibits social stratification. Here is a fundamental source of disagreement. We all want to be on top and have someone else be on the bottom. If we are on top and the politicians talk of equality, that makes us nervous. We don't want everyone to be equal because we would then lose our advantage. I'm sure that the idea of a billion Chinese and a billion Indians or Pakistanis in the United Nations makes many people nervous. In a democratically elected world government, they could outvote us Americans any time and perhaps drive us down to their level of impoverishment.

While growing up in Detroit, I thought of myself as being a cut above other people socially because of my parents' position. Now I'm not so sure. As one grows older, one loses some of that attitude. Whether the Third World gains on America is of less concern to me now than whether I retain my own good health and can pay the bills. A personal regret is that I never had children. If I had lived in a small village in India, parenthood might have been possible but, somehow, I missed out on that here. I grew up in a society with tense gender relations and an arduous dating process where women postponed childbearing. I also brought on some of my own problems in neglecting relationships with women when I was younger. Such questions are more important to me now than whether I become like everyone else, submerged in a sea of equality.

Therefore, I am stuck on the idea that it might possible to create a better world for all humanity if the politics could be figured out. We start with the economic questions of income, consumption, education, work hours, jobs, and so forth. Humanity's cumulative knowledge together with the earth's natural resources ought to provide a decent living for everyone. My solution to problems of income inequality and unemployment or underemployment is to encourage governments to cut work hours. Economists and government leaders really should take another look at that option. If general living standards are maintained in that situation, it should become a technical rather than political question how to make the change. Granted, moralistic ideas about all the "lazy" people around us do complicate the issue. But cannot we succeed in saving the world?

During my lifetime, while I was chasing such dreams, others of my generation were assuming positions of power in our society. I am struck by the fact that the presidential and vice-presidential candidates of the two major parties in 2000 were all persons who had attended and (except for Dick Cheney) graduated from Ivy League colleges in the 1960s. Three came from Yale and one from Harvard. (Ralph Nader, a Princeton graduate, was a few years ahead.) Cheney was at Yale at the same time that I was. Bush, I believe, lived in the same residential college. Lieberman was in my graduating class. Gore went to Harvard. I was casually acquainted with Bob Taft, current governor of Ohio; my roommate knew him well. But here I am living in one of the poorer neighborhoods of Minneapolis still trying to get something going after all these years. My new friends are per-

sons from a different educational background than I. My enemies are persons brought up in much the same way that I was. By my own choice (and lack of social skills), I, Rip Van Winkle, never rode the escalator to career success. Well, never look back.

My feeling is that U.S. society has corrupt features. Ours is a racially and socially self-hating society. It is a society which allows the professional and managerial class to walk over ordinary people. My definition of corruption is that persons entrusted to perform a service for someone else instead serve themselves. When the eunuchs and Praetorian guards start to pick emperors instead of serving them, that is corruption. The trusted manager enriches himself at the owner's expense.

By that definition, I think that the three principal professions which shape public policy - journalism, education, and the law - are largely corrupt. The law is corrupt when it allows appointed judges to make rather than interpret the laws. The system of justice is corrupt when the courts become an open-ended casino, and the cost of hiring a lawyer wags the dog. Who will do something about this swelling class of predators? The legislatures? The news media are corrupt when journalistic "objectivity" is considered a relic of a male-dominated society. The educational establishment is corrupt when the political and social values of adults are forced on innocent children in the classroom and there is no love of learning. These cadres of professionals have hijacked our society. To them, I would add the medical doctors who, in league with the pharmaceutical companies, push pills on people in the name of healing.

If I, a relatively privileged person, feel that our society is corrupt and leaderless, how would your typical low-income white boy, or black boy or girl for that matter, feel about things? Would they not be asking: What is my society? Who are my leaders? We are, instead, living in a society whose important persons sell us their products whether good for us or not. Our leaders agree it's OK to dump on white males - unless it's them, of course. Look how eagerly newspaper writers pointed out that Timothy McVeigh was a white male. A columnist for the *Star Tribune*, a Reverend someone or another, wrote that, although she was a

forgiving person, McVeigh's crimes were just too horrible to be forgiven.

John Leo of *U.S. News* pointed out that Washington, D.C.-area police let the sniper suspects, John Muhammad and John Lee Malvo, slip through their dragnet eleven times because they did not fit the profile of the "angry white male". It's axiomatic that mass murderers are disaffected white men who, as one criminologist said, "belong to a long-advantaged class that is now having to share power and control." This was racial profiling in reverse, yet no one cared. "Most reporters and editors wanted the sniper to be a white male," wrote columnist John O' Sullivan, because newsroom people assume that "the great American majority that never went to the Ivy League schools is made up of racists, sexists, and homophobes."

In fact, the commonality between Timothy McVeigh and John Muhammad, the Washington D.C. lead sniper, was stronger than their racial difference. They were both veterans of Gulf War combat who felt let down by their country. McVeigh was disillusioned by the Waco killings. Muhammad had trouble in Family Court. Even today's arch villain, Osama bin Laden, was once a U.S. ally in Afghanistan and in the Persian Gulf war. Before he attacked Kuwait, Saddam Hussein was a U.S. ally helping out against Iran. Another official scoundrel, the Panamanian leader Manuel Noriega, used to be on the CIA payroll. Doesn't this tell us something about the friends our government keeps, or, perhaps, about how this government treats people who are or once were our friends? Look in the mirror, Uncle Sam, to see what other monsters you can find. You were the one who, hoping to foment an uprising against the Soviet Union, supplied Afghan schoolchildren with textbooks which included drawings of guns, bullets, and land mines and pushed the idea of Islamic jihad.

I am willing to play the hated white-male persona in public if that will help bring about change. This is not your standard demographic "victim" but a villain for everyone to jeer - someone like "Gorgeous George" or our own Jesse Ventura during his pro wrestling and, perhaps, gubernatorial career. Get this hate out of your system, you rainbow-colored upright people of America. Then, perhaps, we can start thinking about some of the things we face together. As I said during the campaign, the mediocrities who fill the seats of power want to keep people divided. If black people and white people fight each other, if men and women fight, we can all keep each other occupied while its leaders stuff this society's wealth into their own pockets. Politics offers a way to fight back, and third-party politics is today the politics with the greatest potential.

Surveys show that 23% of Minnesotans consider themselves independents or members of third parties, compared with 33% who consider themselves Republicans and 44% who affiliate with the DFL party. Is it worth the effort to try to build that residual group into a political force that can win elections? Perhaps it is; polls can be deceiving. In the 2002 general election, the Republicans managed to sweep all state-wide offices in Minnesota, with the exception of Attorney General, being down 33% to 44% with respect to the Democrats. Jesse Ventura, who received less than 1% of the vote in the 1998 gubernatorial primary, went on to win the general election. Another poll shows that most Minnesotans, including those who affiliate with the two major parties, favor a more pluralistic political system. About 57% said that they believed the state was "better off with more than two strong political parties" compared with 34% who favored the traditional two-party system.

Of course, the 2002 general election brought a setback to third-party hopes. After this debacle, Andrew Koebrick, the Green's candidate for Secretary of State, was pessimistic about the future of third parties in Minnesota. "This time the Greens, next time the Independence Party. I wouldn't be at all surprised if four-party politics (in Minnesota) was just a fluke." On the other hand, Jack Uldrich, the

Independence Party chair who headed Tim Penny's campaign, would not write off his party's future. Critiquing Penny's losing campaign, he said: "In retrospect, I would have encouraged him (Tim Penny) to be more aggressive, offer more specifics, and demonstrate that he was offering real leadership. It's not enough to say 'We're not Republicans' or 'We're not Democrats' anymore. We have to show we stand for something."

An advantage which the Independence Party enjoys over the Green Party is that it draws more evenly from supporters of the two major parties. Therefore, the argument cannot so easily be made, as it was in Nader's case, that voting for a minor-party candidate would throw the election to the worst-possible candidate. Ralph Nader was mercilessly dogged by feminists, gay-rights activists, and representatives of African-American groups who insisted that a vote for him was a vote for George W. Bush. Their agenda had to come first. Persons who instead supported Green Party candidates were too stupid or naive to realize what they were doing.

Leonard Witt, executive director of the Minnesota Public Radio Civic Journalism Initiative, published an opinion piece in the *Star Tribune*, in which he faulted the Democrats for not paying proper attention to Florida voting machines. He added: "And in the poor listening department you can also add the white college boys and girls who voted for Ralph Nader and thus turned their backs on their black brethren, who suffered and will suffer the most under conservative policies." On the other hand, the *New York Times* columnist William Safire has estimated that at least one person in three who voted for Nader would have voted for Bush had Nader not been on the ballot. I agree with that assessment; I was one of those Bush-leaning Nader voters in 2000.

Right now, George W. Bush is on top of the world. Thanks to vigorous campaigning by the President, the 2002 midterm elections brought Republican majorities in both houses of Congress. In Minnesota, the election results were similar although

Democrats continue to hold the state Senate. I think this situation is perilous for the Republicans. The public will now hold them solely responsible for the nation's or the state's well-being while they control its government. There are real problems with the economy, including perceptions of corporate misconduct. The looming war against Iraq, waged at Bush's insistence, is a dangerous and uncertain venture which may have worked well for the Republicans in the 2002 elections but could backfire politically in the period ahead. Unless the U.S. military achieves a quick and easy victory, ousts Saddam Hussein, and brings a more democratic government to Iraq, the U.S. public will grow restless and, perhaps, turn against Bush and the Republicans. I would say that the odds favor that scenario. Whether the Democrats will be the chief beneficiaries of an anti-Republican swing is another matter. Third parties also stand a chance to benefit.

The Democrats, in their new incarnation, are primarily a party of feminist women and African Americans. National polls showed that in the 1992 Presidential election, which Bill Clinton won, women voted for Clinton over Bush by a margin of 45% to 37%. Among white female voters, however, the vote was dead even, with each candidate attracting 41% of the vote. The so-called "gender gap" was therefore largely a myth. There was a "racial gap" between Democrats and Republicans, not a gender gap. Anna Greenberg, who teaches at Harvard's Kennedy School of Government, has said: "A majority of white women supported neither the Democratic Party nor President Clinton in the 1990s. The Democratic winning margin among women in national elections, in fact, is driven by minority women." Minority women, voting for Democrats, created the appearance of an overall gender gap because they voted in much greater numbers than minority men. There is, however, a clear gender gap favoring the Republicans among male voters.

African Americans are the most solid voting bloc supporting the Democrats. In the 2000 Presidential elections, 92% of African American voters supported Al Gore. Of those African American newspapers which endorsed a Presidential candidate, 95% supported Gore over Bush. The problem for the Democrats is that African Americans comprise only 12% of the U.S. population; they cannot win national elections on their own. Democrats therefore find it helpful to promote the idea of "rainbow coalitions" in which other racial or ethnic groups become African American-like voting blocs to support the Democrats. In the long run, they find it hopeful that the white population of the United States is shrinking relative to the population of nonwhites.

In 1965, whites comprised 80% of the U.S. population and blacks comprised 10%. By 2050, demographers project that about half of this population will be white and the other half not. Hispanics will then comprise 26% of the U.S. population; blacks, 14% of the population; and Asians, 8%. Even if the current demographics do not favor the Democrats and their racially based politics, the long-term prospects are favorable. In the meanwhile, Democrats woo the black vote and keep it in line by making friendly gestures to blacks while they support Republican legislative measures that work against black people's economic interests, in hopes of gaining a larger share of the critical white vote. Bill Clinton was a master of the friendly gesture.

In the gut-wrenching reappraisals that have followed the Democrats' defeat in the 2002 midterm elections, analysts sympathetic to their cause have argued that the Democrats failed by acting too much like Republicans. "The DNC strategy for getting out the (black) vote was Bill Clinton," Al Sharpton said. "It's almost like they've been joking so long about Clinton was a Black president, they started believing it." To win future elections, the Democrats needed to return to their core values, substantively as well as stylistically, and reenergize their base.

Steve Perry, editor of *City Pages*, has argued that the Democrats will never do that because their "base" now consists of large corporate contributors whose support is critical to funding media-based campaigns in the future. Since the Republicans cater to the same base of support, grassroots political activists who wish to promote a comparatively unselfish cause have no place to turn within the two-party system. For such persons, he suggested that they "make a point of learning more about the small parties active in your area and help them in any way you can to get on the ballot and to get a fair hearing." The two-party system consists of a single "Republicrat" party equally beholden to the large financial contributors and the lobbyists who follow in their footsteps. To break the stranglehold of money over the U.S. political system, it will be necessary to turn to third parties.

The Rev. Al Sharpton disagrees. He thinks that African Americans have a future in the Democratic Party, and the Democrats a future in American politics, if they will accept him as their leader or, at least, accept his point of view. Therefore, he has announced his own candidacy for President of the United States. According to Sharpton, the Democrats' defeat in the 2002 elections was due to neglecting their core values and constituencies. He said: "When you do an analysis of how the Democrats lost, they lost because they ran away from their base. This whole de-

cade-long reach for the Right-wing, or what they now call the independent White male vote, has been a hallucination. It energizes and makes my campaign more necessary."

Al Sharpton, in the first decade of the 21st century, could become to the Democrats what Jesse Jackson was in the 1980s, a catalyst for strengthened black support of the Democratic party. On the other hand, Jackson had a better reputation than Sharpton does, who first came to prominence as a champion of Tawana Brawley and her bogus claims of having been kidnapped and raped by a gang of white males. Predictably, Al Sharpton may stir renewed political interest among disaffected young black males but his increased prominence within the Democratic party will likely turn off a greater number of white voters. He does, however, intend to criticize President Bush's policies with respect to the war in Iraq, a position with which I agree.

I am writing this at a time when the war's outcome is unclear. Predictably, the U.S. and British forces enjoy overwhelming technical superiority and can easily defeat the Iraqi armies. But if Saddam Hussein unleashes biological or chemical weapons or the war turns into intense street fighting, our side could sustain heavy casualties. It depends on how the Iraqi people react to the invasion, especially those with weapons. Bush will be a hero if the victory is quick and painless. He will be a goat if the war goes badly. Whichever the case, the war with Iraq will become a dominant factor in U.S. politics in the foreseeable future.

My worry is that, even if our military does achieve its objectives, the U.S. invasion of Iraq will turn the entire Moslem world against us. America is seen there as an alien Christian or secular civilization. For U.S. troops to occupy Baghdad, seat of the caliphate in Islam's golden age, will be deeply troubling to followers of that religion. The United States is not authorized to invade someone else's country. President Bush's firm pursuit of war despite misgivings of the international community, undertaken at a time of growing economic distress, can have a happy outcome only if we are lucky.

We are therefore looking at the politics of a hawkish Republican president prospectively leading our country to war in various parts of the world and of leaderless Democrats, torn between supporting a popular president's policies and returning to a more strident defense of their core constituencies, as urged by the Rev. Al Sharpton. Why not take the "third option" of an Independence Party newly recharged with issues and ideas?

In my view, its basic policy plank would be economic. Our mission would be to find new ways of improving average living standards in this country and around the world without ruining the natural environment. This type of politics would project a positive vision of our society in the future, including a vision of reduced work time. On the social and cultural fronts, the new politics would stand up to political correctness in all forms and shake off its intimidating influence in our society. It would challenge the self-hating, self-serving elites in the cultural professions, and render them powerless to inflict further harm upon the American people. It would encourage white males to stop being a political doormat, to become proud and brave once again, and, in a spirit of good will, devote themselves to enterprises of public as well as private improvement.

In America, we need to have all our people pulling together to demand better leadership. This country desperately needs leaders. It needs individuals of sufficient moral capacity to represent *us*. It needs people inspired by a sense of duty who respect their fellow citizens..

The nation's universities should be preparing rocket scientists to help explore and colonize outer space, not lawyers who sue people and nurture disputes where none may exist just to make a living. The political leadership needs to repair our broken health care system. There should be a leadership for all people which governs not by money, wars and hateful social appeals but by the vision of a better future. I believe that even today a third party can grow to majority status by following that path.

Let the Democrats and Republicans be put on notice that, barring heavy repentance, their type of politics has run its course and a new contender waits in the wings.

Appendix

Appendix

Appendix A

On the Campaign Trail with Bill McGaughey

I filed for U.S. Senate in the Independence Party primary on July 16th, the last day of filing, without the party's endorsement. For a party struggling with ideological definition, I would give it something to chew on. I would come at both the Republican and Democratic parties with a frontal attack.

Anathema to the Republicans, the party of big business, was my call for government to regulate the economy on working people's behalf, and specifically: "I believe that the federal government should reduce the standard workweek to 32 hours by 2010." Anathema to the Democrats, party of the Civil Rights coalition, was an attack on political correctness. "I believe in the full citizenship, dignity, and equality of white males (and of everyone else, too)" was my politically incorrect statement of that position. These two statements appeared on either side of a large sign that I carried in public.

The goal of the campaign was clear: Win the primary and, if that happened, do the best I could to articulate my position in the debates and other fora with an eye to leaving an ideological legacy for the Independence Party in future years. Could I beat Jim Moore, the Independence Party's endorsed candidate? Yes, this was doable, considering that Moore's mandate to be the party's candidate for U.S. Senate rested on fewer than 150 convention votes, that he had (in my opinion) a lackluster set of issues, and that he, like me, had never held public office before.

The Independence Party hierarchy dashed my initial hopes of sending a letter to party members to explain my candidacy when it refused to rent the membership list. As a nonendorsed candidate, I was also denied permission to greet voters inside or near the party's booth at county fairs and the State Fair. While the *St. Paul Pioneer Press* published a balanced article on the U.S. Senate race, the Twin Cities' largest-circulation newspaper, the *Star Tribune*, failed to mention that Jim Moore faced opposition in the Independence Party primary for U.S. Senator when it ran a front-page article on this contest on July 23rd. I wrote a letter to the editor pointing out the omission. It was not published.

Facing disadvantages as a nonendorsed candidate, I decided to take my campaign directly to the public. Parades are a good way to do that.

They allow the candidate to present himself or herself to spectators who are willing, even asking, to be approached with a political message. I took part in seven parades. The first, on August 3rd, was to assist Tim Penny's gubernatorial campaign by passing out stickers to children in Prior Lake. In six subsequent parades, I marched down the street carrying my sign. They were: the "Stockyard Days" parade in New Brighton on August 8th; the "Quarry Days" parade in Sandstone on August 10th; the "Lindbergh Returns" parade in Little Falls on August 11th; the "Heritage Day" parade in Vadnais Heights and "Oxcart Days" parade in Crookston, both on Saturday, August 17th; and the "Fire Muster" parade in Burnsville on Sunday, September 8th. Being Marjorie Main's second cousin, I also attended "Ma and Pa Kettle Days" festivities in Kettle River on August 10th, the same day as the Sandstone parade, expecting to be greeted as a minor celebrity. Instead, I found that few, if anyone, cared.

Actually, my first public appearance as a candidate was on Tuesday, August 6th, at Farm Fest near Redwood Falls where the four endorsed candidates for U.S. Senate participated in a debate. I stood in the back row brandishing my sign. Attempting to mingle with the crowd following the debate, I found people quite wary of me and my message. Jim Moore was friendly enough, but the farmers must have thought I was crazy. Besides Moore, about the only persons who would shake hands with me at this event were Norm Coleman and the Elvis impersonator.

Driving back to the Twin Cities after Farm Fest, I discovered a more promising way to campaign. I first stopped at the office of the *Redwood Falls Gazette* (circulation 3,939). The political reporter, Troy Krause, was away covering Farm Fest, but editor Daryl Thul took my photograph. He said they would be in touch. My next stop was the office of the *Olivia Times-Journal* (circulation 1,413) whose editor, Mindy, was busy putting the paper to press. I left literature with the receptionist. In Willmar, Linda Vanderwerf, the political reporter for the *West Central Tribune* (17,500) , who was on deadline, asked me to let her know the next time I returned to the area. I caught the editor of the *Litchfield Independent Review* (3,900), Brent Schacherer, just as he was closing the office at 5 p.m. He, too, expressed interest in my campaign.

Busy with producing position papers, taking campaign photos and answering candidate questionnaires, I did not return to the newspaper circuit until Wednesday, August 14th. Driving south from the Twin Cities, I arrived in Northfield. There was a new editor at the *Northfield News* (circulation 5,034). The receptionist told me that he was at a staff meeting and had not yet appointed a reporter to cover the Senate race. My next stop was Cannon Falls. Here Dick Dalton, editor of the *Cannon Falls Beacon*

(4,350), took me into his office for a brief conversation which, after touching upon the shorter-workweek proposal, ended with the disclosure that the *Beacon* covered mainly campaigns for local office.

I next worked my way down Route 61 along the Mississippi River, hoping to keep my promise to Tom van der Linden, editor of the *Houston County News* (2,200) in La Crescent, that I would stop by that afternoon. The *Red Wing Republican-Eagle* (8,000) was my first stop along that route. A young reporter, Mike Fielding, took me into a conference room for a brief interview. He requested that I send him a mug-shot photo by email. Down river, at the office of the *Lake City Graphic* (3,200), Rick Ousky, the editor, gave me fifteen minutes of his time. He was an intense, intelligent, bearded man, interested in the idea of demanding better leadership. He seemed intrigued by my campaign and promised to write a column about it.

Racing south, I arrived in La Crescent around 5:15 p.m. where, fortunately, Van der Linden was still in the office. He asked a few questions, took a photo or two, and then went back to work. Finally, heading north, I took a chance at finding a reporter at work at the area's largest-circulation newspaper, the *Winona Daily News* (12,259), after 6 p.m. A general-assignment reporter and columnist who had gone to college with Tim Penny, Jerome Christenson, interrupted his work to talk with me. We discussed the political situation. He asked questions about my campaign for Senate and a staff photographer took my picture. I was elated as I drove back to the Twin Cities.

Despite the adrenaline rush, it was not until the late morning that I again hit the campaign trail. I thought that I should first visit the free-circulation weeklies in the Twin Cities. At *City Pages* (circulation 112,282), the editorial administrator told me that the reporter assigned to the Independence Party race, Paul Demko, was out of the office. This information came as a shock to me since, three weeks earlier, I had published a sarcastic letter to the editor of *City Pages* in response to Demko's report on a panel discussion sponsored by a local men's group. *City Pages* thought highly enough of this as an example of a certain genre to showcase it as "letter of the week". Among other jabs at him, I suggested that "Demko had reached the limit of his small-capacity closed mind" when he stormed out of the meeting in the middle of the second speaker's presentation. But now, unless Demko is truly a gracious person, I would pay for having so wantonly attacked one whose employer "buys ink by the barrel."

My next stop was *Pulse of the Twin Cities* (23,000) on Chicago Avenue. Ed Felien, publisher and chief editor, ushered me into his office for a half-hour conversation. Ed is a left-leaning intellectual with varied life experiences. Besides managing a substantial business, he has served on the Minneapolis City Council. He was then a candidate for Hennepin County Commissioner. Ed probed deeply into my issues, especially the plank supporting "dignity for white males." Although he thought it was a courageous position, he was also concerned that this statement would bring out white-supremacist sentiments. He challenged me to show specifically how white males were injured by the current system. He gave me a copy of a book by Anthony L. Sutton, an African American, about the psychological consequences of slavery which he had helped to publish. Ed invited me to discuss these things further with him at lunch but then realized that he had another luncheon appointment. Though cut short, this was political dialogue at its best.

A bit behind schedule, I headed north on 35E towards Duluth. My first stop was a the *ECM Post-Review* (2,425) in North Branch, where a receptionist told me that the editor was out covering the PGA Tournament at Hazeltine. Then I drove over to Cambridge to visit offices of the *Isanti County News* (11,000) and the *Cambridge Star* (16,032). No one was available to visit with me at either place, so I dropped off literature. The same was true of the *Princeton Union-Eagle* (3,400); its editor, Luther Dorr, was also at the PGA Tournament. At the *Mille Lacs County Times* (3,100) in Milaca around the 5 p.m. closing time, two women told me that they were not interested in politics but I might leave literature for the editor, Gary Larsen. It was too late to find anything at the *Kanabec County Times* (3,020) office except for a locked door.

This had not been a productive afternoon though I did run into Tom Dooley, an old acquaintance and columnist for the *New Unionist* newspaper, at the Kulkin rest area on highway 35E south of Cloquet. He told me that, for a modest sum of money, the Minnesota Newspaper Association would send out press releases to all newspapers and television stations in the state. I own a log cabin on forty acres of woodland on the south shore of Lake Superior near Port Wing, Wisconsin. That is where I spent the night of August 15th.

Early the next morning, around 8 a.m., I parked my car on a street in downtown Duluth across from a gourmet coffee shop which served up a delicious brew. I stood with my sign for twenty minutes at the corner of 1st and Superior streets, in what I thought was the center of downtown, before deciding that the sparse pedestrian and street traffic at this hour of the day did not justify the effort. Scott Thistle, the reporter assigned to the Senate race at the *News-Tribune* (51,071), had not yet arrived at work when I visited his office. Another reporter, Craig Lincoln, helpfully placed my literature in Thistle's in-basket.

I next drove out to the office of *Labor World* (15,000) on London Road, hoping that my shorter-workweek plank might interest its reporters. The receptionist, Debbie, told me that this newspaper, a house organ of the Duluth AFL-CIO, covered only its endorsed candidates. Paul Wellstone would receive the paper's support. Back in the downtown area, a receptionist at the *Duluth Budgeteer News* (44,484) said that all editors and reporters were busy putting out the paper. Come back in the early part of the week, she said.

Next, it was on to the Iron Range. At my first stop, the *Proctor Journal* (2,000), a woman named Diane said that no one had time to talk with me because it was the day of the town's annual festival. According to a directory, there were two newspapers in Cloquet, the *Cloquet Pine Knot* (3,500) and the *Cloquet Journal* (4,300). When I located the office of the first, a sign posted on the door revealed that it had merged with the second. The combined newspaper, the *Pine Journal*, was located at the former office of the *Cloquet Journal*. Its editor, Mike Sylvester, took some time to talk with me and requested that I send a mug shot by email.

Heading west, I stopped in Floodwood, a small town at the junction of highways 2 and 73, where I had a delightful conversation with two women, Sue Czarneski and Eleanor Vorderbruggen, who put out *The Forum* (930). While the publisher was a Wellstone supporter, they themselves were for neither Wellstone or Coleman. They were pleased that a statewide candidate such as myself would visit their community.

I arrived at the offices of *The Daily Tribune* (8,036) in Hibbing shortly after noon. All the reporters were at lunch. The receptionist told me to come back after 1 p.m. This gave me an opportunity to do some local sightseeing. Bob Dylan grew up here but I knew not where to look for historic sites. Filling up with gas at the Holiday station, I mentioned to the cashier that I had seen a sign advertising the Greyhound Bus Museum. Another customer at the counter remarked sourly that this was the "biggest white elephant in town" and he could not understand how anyone would for go such a project. That settled it - I had to visit the campy museum. It was Greyhound, after all, which had first brought me to Minnesota in January 1965.

The cashier told me that a half mile farther up the same road was a viewing area for the large open-pit iron mines that had once operated on the outskirts of Hibbing. This was a truly unusual sight. Also, the Greyhound Museum was worth the $3.00 admission price though I could not stay for the 22-minute film on Greyhound's history or listen to recorded bus-drivers' stories. Boarding one of the early-vintage buses had to suffice. The high point for me was when the ticket seller, to whom I had given a comb inscribed with the name of my campaign web site (www.billforsenate.org), ran out into the parking lot after my quick visit to ask me for another comb for his friend.

Back at the offices of the *Daily Tribune* in Hibbing, I learned that the political reporters were not expected to return to work before 2 p.m. I could not wait. Six or seven miles farther north was the office of the *Chisholm Tribune-Press* (2,100). A semi-retired woman named Veeda, who had edited this newspaper for fifty years, told stories of how Eleanor Roosevelt had visited Chisholm on Adlai Stevenson's behalf during the 1956 Presidential campaign. Orville Freeman, John F. Kennedy, and other politicians of that era were also fresh in her memory. The only negative moment came when I suggested that Jesse Ventura was also a colorful political character. Veeda had no use for Ventura since he had cut the budget for education, among other things.

Another twelve miles up the road, I also visited the office of the *Mesabi Daily News* (12,258) in Virginia which was hard to find, even using a map. The political reporter was out, so I left literature. I did the same at the locked offices of the *Gilbert Herald* (1,019). At Eveleth, I knew I was in trouble when I discovered that a cable-television office was located at the reported address of the *Eveleth Scene* (2,695). The receptionist said that she did not even think there was a newspaper in town. I did visit the United Steelworkers of America District 11 office just down the street to leave literature about my candidacy for Bob Bratlich, the assistant director. Union officials from the Iron Range had been active supporters of shorter-workweek proposals twenty-five years ago. The receptionist promised to deliver this material to Bratlich when he returned to work on Monday.

The final segment of this day's campaigning took me to the forested areas north of the Range. At offices of the *Cook News-Herald* (2,800), the editor asked me where Glenwood Avenue was located. It turned out that, thirty years earlier, he had been a businessman in Minneapolis. He regaled me with stories about those times passing along information, for instance, that Hubert Humphrey had helped to move blacks out of a certain part of town to make room for new construction benefiting his business cronies. Not far from my home was a bridge under which, it was rumored, the sainted Senator used to pick up money left in a paper bag. If not Hubert Humphrey, which politician could we believe in, this man wondered? Anyhow, he would print a short article about my candidacy.

At *The Timberjay* (3,200) in Tower, the political reporters were gone for the day but a man at the counter took my literature. I raced on to Ely, arriving shortly after 5 p.m., only to learn that both newspaper offices had closed at 4 p.m. The town was crawling with weekend tourists. For the next five hours, I drove back to the Twin Cities passing through Isabella, Silver Bay, Duluth, and other scenic communities before night fell. My odometer recorded 835 miles for the two-day trip.

I was tied up all day on Monday, August 19th, with personal business related to obtaining permits for a condemned house in Minneapolis which I was renovating. On Tuesday, the campaign itinerary reverted to southern Minnesota. My first stop was in the press room at the state capitol where Don Davis, a reporter and columnist for Forum Communications, has an office. (He moderated the U.S. Senate debate at Moorhead State College on October 15th.) Davis conducted a thorough interview. One of his purposes may have been to discover whether my candidacy was a front for anti-Semitic or white-supremacist politics. Did I think, for instance, that the fact that Coleman and Wellstone were both Jewish indicated that "Jews were taking over" Minnesota politics? I did not buy that theory but did admit that religious identity entered into the politics of political correctness.

The office of the *Faribault Daily News* (7,411) was the day's first stop outside the Twin Cities. The regular political reporter, Pauline Schreiber, was on vacation all week, but the public-safety reporter gave the receptionist his card, asking me to call him later in the day. At the *Owatonna People's Press* (7,149) the political reporter, Katie Campbell, was likewise unavailable. I then headed east to Rochester to visit the *Post-Bulletin* (42,391) office. The political reporter, Lenora Chu, was on deadline and could not meet with me for more than a few minutes. She did arrange to have my picture taken and asked me to contact her the following week. (By coincidence, Angela Greiling Keane, a reporter from the *Post-Bulletin's* Washington bureau was handling the story on the U.S. Senate race. She conducted a telephone interview with me next morning.)

The second interview of the day took place at the *Austin Daily Herald* (7,470). Reporter Lee Bonorden, whose daughter lives in Minneapolis, spent twenty minutes with me and scanned my photo into the computer. Finally, I passed through Blooming Prairie but the office of its newspaper, the *Blooming Prairie Times* (1,173), was closed for the day. Arriving back home in Minneapolis, I found that I had traveled 280 miles.

Wednesday morning, August 21st, I thought it was time to visit the Minneapolis newspapers again. Paul Demko was not in at *City Pages*. The political team leader at the *Star Tribune*, Dennis McGrath, came down to the lobby to talk with me for about five minutes. It was raining hard that day.

Heading south on Highway 35, I again stopped at the *Faribault Daily News* and again found no reporters available to talk with me. At the *Owatonna People's Press*, a young reporter, Katie Campbell, did an interview. Next it was over to Waseca, Tim Penny's home town. The political reporter for the *Waseca County News*, Marshal Cawley, spoke with me for several minutes and arranged for my picture to be taken. The small town of Janesville, where close friends of mine (Harvey and Julie Hyatt) were married six years ago, was my next stop. The editor of the *Janesville Argus* (1,051), Sandy Connolly, said that she would use whatever Marshal Cawley wrote for the Waseca paper. We discussed Father Brown, the Catholic priest in Janesville who had officiated at my friends' wedding. He had recently retired to a lakeside home outside of town.

The last two stops of the day were at the remaining large dailies in south central Minnesota. The largest one (except for Rochester) was *The Free Press* (25,244) in Mankato. I was referred to Joe Spear, the news editor, who took my campaign literature to pass along to the political reporter when he returned to the office. At *The Journal* (9,945) in New Ulm, a political reporter and editorial writer, Ron Larsen, interviewed me in a conference room. He was a Dane among Germans, we joked. I left photos of myself carrying the sign. After leaving the newspaper office, I could not resist visiting the giant statue of Hermann, leader of the Germanic tribes who defeated Roman legions in 9 A.D., in a park on the edge of town. Then it was back to the Twin Cities by way of St. Peter. Its newspaper office was closed for the day. The day's travel had covered 255 miles.

Now it was time for me to visit some of the outlying areas of Minnesota along its southern and western borders. With a brief stop in Faribault - again no luck in meeting the reporter - I went to Albert Lea, situated on Interstate Highway 90. I spoke briefly with Dylan Belden, editor of the *Albert Lea Tribune* (7,379), who remembered receiving my literature in the mail. The next city to the west was Blue Earth. Kyle MacArthur, editor of the *Faribault County Register* (1,200) , came out to visit for a few minutes. Ten years earlier, he had lived at 37th and Morgan Ave. N. in Minneapolis, several miles north of where I currently live. When I gave him the photo of me in front of the Paul Bunyan statue in Bemidji, MacArthur suggested that I see the Green Giant statue on the outskirts of Blue Earth. That is where I went next. A teenage boy working in a gift shop took my photograph there.

I hit the offices of the *Sentinel* (7,700) in Fairmont shortly before 1 p.m., in hopes of finding a reporter. The receptionist told me that the news staff would be back from lunch around 2 p.m. I could not wait. The next town west on Highway 90 was Sherburn. David Parker of the *West Martin*

Weekly News (2,000) interviewed me and promised to do an article. Then I visited the office of the *Jackson County Pilot* (2,400) in Jackson, the next town over. The editor, Ryan McGaughey, was not in the office.

I could not refrain from pointing out that this editor and I had the same last name, although he pronounced it ma-GAAH-he and I pronounced it ma-GOY. I also informed the receptionist - of possible interest to Ryan - that President Zachary Taylor in 1847 had appointed a certain Edward McGaughey to be Minnesota's first territorial governor. However, the U.S. Senate did not confirm the nomination. President Taylor's third choice, Alexander Ramsey, eventually took the assignment.

The big newspaper in southwest Minnesota is the *Worthington Daily Globe* (12,300). In its offices, I spoke with Bob, the news editor, who took literature and photos. He promised to do an article on the primary. I next visited the *Nobles County Review* (1,300) in Adrian, west of Worthington. A receptionist took literature and photos, promising to pass them along to the editor. Near the South Dakota border was the city of Luverne. I happened to catch Laurie, a political reporter for the *Rock County Star-Herald* (3,000), as she was hurrying out the door. She asked me about advertising in that newspaper. I hoped to visit the Pipestone newspaper as the last stop in the day. However, road construction on U.S. Highway 75 sent me on a detour about ten miles to the east which prevented me from being in Pipestone by closing time. I did visit offices of the *Edgerton Enterprise* (1,957) and spoke with its editor, Mel DeBoer. DeBoer, I noticed, is also the name of the town's Chevrolet dealer.

It was in the late afternoon of August 22nd and I found myself 300 miles away from home. I decided to spend the night camping at the Split Rock Creek state park on highway 23 south of Pipestone. The young park attendant said that she was the niece of DFL state representative Ted Winter of Fulda. She was interested in my campaign and agreed with some of my ideas about political correctness. There was also a nice elderly couple, Pete and Alice Krosschell of Edgerton, who supervised the camp grounds from their camper trailer parked across from my space at camp site #4. So, instead of driving back to the Twin Cities that night, I spent a leisurely late afternoon swimming in a lake across from two wind generators and hiking through prairie grasslands. I agreed with the Krosschells that it was a shame that state officials had decided to close this park after Labor Day.

Early in the morning of Friday, August 23rd, I drove south to Jasper. The office of *Jasper Journal* (950) was closed but I left literature in the mail slot. I was fortunate to find Mark Fode, editor of the *Pipestone County Star* (3,800), in the office willing to do an interview. He was interested in my thoughts on political correctness. The office of the *Lake Benton Valley*

Journal (875), just up the road, was closed on Fridays. Lake Benton is a center of wind-power generation.

Another twenty miles north is Ivanhoe whose newspaper is the *Ivanhoe Times* (1,065). For a relatively small town, it was surprising to find a crowd of people in the newspaper office when I arrived. I had to wait for ten minutes or so while a farm wife badgered the editor about an error that she wanted corrected in the paper. Then she wanted clarification of the sports schedule. I was ready to leave when the woman ran out of questions. The editor, Brent Beck, then interviewed me and took a photograph. Next it was on to Marshall.

At offices of the *Marshall Independent* (8,650), the editor, Larry Magrath, interviewed me and took my picture. A friend in Minneapolis later told me that he had seen a story about my campaign in the Marshall newspaper. A young woman named Jessica edited the *Tri-County News* (1,800) in Cottonwood, twelve miles north on Highway 23. She interviewed me and took a picture. I asked her if other politicians running for statewide office had visited Cottonwood. Paul Wellstone was the only one.

Granite Falls was the next city on Highway 23 north. I bought gas at a Cenex station in town, noticing that a Yellow Medicine County deputy sheriff was hanging around the checkout counter. When I arrived at the newspaper office of the *Advocate-Tribune* (3,180), the same deputy sheriff was there ordering business cards. He spotted me with a badge identifying myself as a candidate for U.S. Senate and amiably remarked that, "with all these politicians" around, he had better leave. The editor, Linda Larsen, was still at lunch. The receptionist said she would be back in twenty minutes. Meanwhile, I stood on a nearby street corner exhibiting my sign. It was a slow afternoon.

Linda Larsen remembered the campaign literature that I had sent by mail. She seemed intrigued or amused by the white-male aspect of my candidacy. She also happened to be a former employee of the Minneapolis Community Development Agency (MCDA). I told her that members of the Minneapolis Property Rights Action Committee considered this to be "the evil empire". We had an enjoyable visit. Editor Larsen reminisced about her days as a bureaucrat in Minneapolis dealing with the likes of Walt Dziedzic, Barbara Carlson, and Tony Scallon. She also informed me that riots had taken place in north Minneapolis the preceding evening. She recalled how Greg Wersal, the attorney, had come to Granite Falls with a cow-shaped sign to promote his campaign to let judges campaign for office. When I remarked that I was glad there were at least two crazy sign-bearing candidates, she smiled. It was comforting to find a hometown presence there.

I had hoped to reach Crookston by the end of the day. Ted Stone, editor of the *Crookston Daily Times* (3,193), had promised to interview me if I came to town; he would run the interview on the front page. Leaving Granite Falls, I realized that it would be impossible to meet this goal. Montevideo was next on the route. Pat Schmidt, editor of the *Montevideo American News* (4,700), conducted a short interview in his office and took a photograph. He said his newspaper would have an article on the Senate race right before the primary. Instead of driving toward the larger town of Morris, I now made a decision to visit Madison in part because it was the boyhood home of Robert Bly, the poet. I have been part of a singing group with him in Minneapolis for the past ten years.

Dawson was due west of Montevideo. Dave Hickey, editor of the *Dawson Sentinel* (2,000), talked with me briefly and took two photographs. Madison, the next town, was a disappointment. The editor of the *Western Guard* (2,342) would not come out of his office to see me; he left word with the receptionist that his newspaper covered only party-endorsed candidates. I did visit the Lac Qui Parle history museum in Madison to see Robert Bly's "study". It had been dedicated on the weekend in July 1999 that my brother died. We had been planning to attend the dedication event. Finally, I reached Ortonville, on the western edge of the state, by 4:30 p.m. The editor of the *Ortonville Independent* (3,233) was out of town but a newspaper employee took literature and photos. Then it was back to the Twin Cities by way of Appleton and Benson. Their newspaper offices were both closed. The two-day trip had covered 707 miles.

(The above narrative was written for publication in the *Watchdog* newspaper's pre-primary issue. Only the first several paragraphs were published. Two weeks yet remained in my campaign. The narrative continues.)

The weekend had come. This time could not be used for travel since the newspaper offices would not be open. I had one more week to contact the weekly newspapers in time to make their deadlines. Then I would try to hit the remaining dailies. The weekend of August 24th and 25th was spent writing the first part of this narrative so that it might be published in *The Watchdog* before the primary. With a circulation of up to 10,000 readers in Minneapolis, its readers represented quite a few votes in the Twin Cities. Hopefully, some would read my column.

I had business pertaining to renovation of the condemned house at 1715 Glenwood Avenue on Monday morning. Then, in the early afternoon, I headed west on Highway 12 toward Willmar. The first stop was in Howard Lake. Lynda Jensen, editor of the *Howard Lake-Waverly Journal* (1,400), took literature. (Was this Hubert Humphrey's hometown newspaper?) She referred me to an affiliated newspaper in Dassel, not on my list. The editor there was putting out the last issue before the primary and could not include anything about my campaign.

At Dassel, I made a quick decision to leave the route to Willmar and instead head south to Hutchinson on Highway 7. I'm glad I did. The editor of the *Hutchinson Leader* (6,000), Doug Hanneman, and Jane Otto, a political reporter, both interviewed me in a conference room. They would run a story in their well-regarded newspaper. They also suggested that I call the *Litchfield Independent Review* (3,900), an affiliated newspaper twenty miles north and to the west. Its editor, Brent Schacherer, was the man whom I had briefly met while heading home on Highway 12 from Farm Fest several weeks earlier. This time, Schacherer and I had plenty of time to talk. Both in Hutchinson and Litchfield I felt I was connecting with the editors in issues-centered discussions. I bought a copy of the *Independent Review* in a Litchfield grocery store. When I arrived home that evening after 155 miles of driving, my campaign had renewed energy.

The following morning, Tuesday, August 27th, it was time to head north on a two-day trip. The receptionist at *Duluth Budgeteer News* (44,484) had told me to come back between Monday and Wednesday, before the paper was put to bed. First, however, I took a telephone call from Tim Kjos of the *Becker County Record* (14,500) and *Detroit Lakes Tribune* (5,500), who wanted to do a telephone interview. This was a lucky break. Editor Kjos had taken an interest in my campaign materials which were mailed to him. I emailed Ted Stone of the *Crookston Daily Times* (3,193) to say that I would be in Crookston Wednesday afternoon.

Then I hit the road, stopping first at the offices of the *Anoka County Shopper* (5,026) in Coon Rapids where I spoke with Larry Jones, a reporter. He told me that the political reporting for ECM-owned newspapers, of which this was one, was done by Tim Budig, a reporter stationed in the basement of the State Capitol. However, stories on the primary election were probably already written.

I then continued my journey north on Highway 10 to Big Lake where I talked with Naomi, the receptionist at the *West Sherburne Tribune* (13,283). She referred me to the political reporter, Nancy Kopf, at the Becker paper. This was the *Sherburne County Citizen* (10,862), just down the road. Naomi also took my campaign literature and photos to give to Gary Meyer, the editor. At Becker, I talked with Estelle, the receptionist, who said that Nancy Kopf, who lives in Big Lake, was not in the office. I called Kopf's home and left a message. I left literature and photos with the Becker newspaper.

Since Duluth was my destination, I left Highway 10 at that point and instead took State Highway 25 north and then headed east on Highway 3 to Princeton, hitting the *Princeton Union-Eagle* (3,400). Luther Dorr, the editor, told me that this was also an ECM-owned publication whose political reporting was done by Tim Budig. My next stop was the *Isanti County News* (11,000), another ECM-owned newspaper, in Cambridge. I drove across town to the *Cambridge Star* (16,032) in an industrial area hoping to talk with Tesha, the political reporter, whom I had missed on my previous trip. She asked me to fax the *Star* a short press release once I returned home. That was my best result so far all day. The newspaper had a big circulation.

As much as I would have liked to visit other newspapers along the way, I had to be in Duluth by the end of the afternoon. I went north through Braham and then joined interstate highway 35, arriving in Duluth about 90 minutes later. At my prime objective, the *Duluth Budgeteer News*, I had a 15-minute discussion with the news editor, Pat Faherty, who had been unavailable on my previous visit. He told me that primary election coverage was focused on the local races. The federal and statewide offices would be covered before the general election. Duluth politics is "weird" with some nonendorsed major-party candidates switching over to the Independence Party. Faherty liked my approach of raising basic political issues and promised to talk more with me if I survived the primary.

I also visited the office of the *Duluth News-Tribune* again, hoping to meet reporter Scott Thistle, but he was gone for the week. I did not have the address of the *Reader Weekly* newspaper, just a P.O. box number. A newspaper rack on a street corner contained an issue of the *Duluth Ripsaw*, an alternative weekly. Though it was after 5:00 p.m., I located its offices on the 12th floor of a downtown office building. Luckily, the editor, Brad Nelson, was still in the office. I spoke with him briefly before he left for the day. Nelson liked my ideas about the shorter workweek but not about political correctness.

It was the end of another busy day. The most economical place of lodging was my log cabin on the south shore of Lake Superior near Port Wing, Wisconsin. Bathing opportunities again consisted of a quick dip in the lake. This time, a storm was brewing on the lake. Waters were cold, and the waves turbulent. After an abbreviated swim, I spent the night in the cabin. Mice scurrying about near the sofa kept me awake during parts of the night.

I departed the Wisconsin cabin just before 7:00 a.m. and drove forty miles back to Duluth in a light rain. My destination, however, was the Iron Range, and the two daily newspapers missed on the previous visit. The

Mesabi Daily News (12,258) in Virginia was again hard to locate. Again, editor Bill Hanna was unavailable. At the *Daily Tribune* in Hibbing, on the other hand, I did speak briefly with Aaron Brown, the editor. He said that his newspaper took most of its political reporting from the Associated Press. Jim Moore and some other political candidates had been in Hibbing.

I was worried about the car. With the damp weather, the battery seemed dead. The starter would not kick over when I had stopped to fill up at a gas station. Sure enough, I faced the same problem in the parking lot of the Daily Tribune. Corroded materials were covering the two battery terminals. I cleaned this off and the car promptly started. It could have been worse. My car, a 1992 Ford Escort, had had two major transmission repairs within the past year. Was it not foolhardy to be crossing sparsely populated regions of northern Minnesota in this automobile? I had no choice. There was an election campaign to conduct.

My next stop, after heading south and west on U.S. highway 169, was Grand Rapids, where I had been once before on a Saturday. This time, I visited the offices of the *Grand Rapids Herald* (20,500). A young political reporter named Beth Bily, who said she was busy putting out the newspaper, came to the front desk to talk with me for a few minutes. She took my three pieces of literature and a photo of me promoting a 32-hour week. There was no time to visit Coleraine. I was due in Crookston, clear across the state, later in the afternoon.

My westward travels on U.S. highway 2 took me first to Deer River where Bonnie at the *Western Itasca Review* (1,800) took my campaign literature and photos, promising to put something in Thursday's newspaper. At Cass Lake, near the Indian reservation, I spoke with Pat Miller, editor of the *Cass Lake Times* (1.400), and with Bethany Norgard, his assistant. I gave my standard pitch and they took campaign materials. Miller advised me to talk with Brad Swenson, a reporter at *The Pioneer* in Bemidji, who he said was quite savvy about political matters.

Bemidji, home of the photogenic statues of Paul Bunyan and Babe the Blue Ox, was a mere fifteen miles or so farther west on highway 2. A receptionist at the Bemidji paper told me, however, that Brad Swenson and his colleagues did not start work until after 4 p.m. Could I come back later in the day? If the office was closed, they said, just go to the back door and press the buzzer. I was not sure at that point if I would return.

I still had about one hundred miles to go before reaching Crookston. It would be my second visit to the town but first visit to the Crookston newspaper office. Thirty miles down the road after leaving Bemidji, I reached Bagley. Debbie Ronning at the *Farmers Independent* newspaper (2,600) promised to deliver my campaign literature to the editor. We were now leaving the wooded areas of north central Minnesota and heading into the grasslands of the Great Plains, this side of the Dakotas. Continuing on U.S. highway 2, I passed Fosston and Erskine, home of DFL gubernatorial candidate Roger Moe, before pulling into Crookston around 3 p.m.

At the *Crookston Daily Times* (3,193), editor Ted Stone did not have time to talk. The computer had crashed and he was having to deal with this problem himself. Instead, Stone assigned a new reporter to interview me, Lori Lizakowski. She was originally from Minneapolis. Lizakowski conducted a thorough interview, covering both issues and my personal life. Out the door, I remembered that I had forgotten to tell the reporter that I had participated in the Crookston "Ox Cart Days" parade ten days earlier. I returned briefly to convey that information. Today's chief mission had been accomplished.

There was still time in the day to visit other newspaper offices in the area. I headed back east on highway 2 until highway 32, where I turned left and drove north to Red Lake Falls. Jody Kenfield, publisher of the *Gazette* (1,600) in Red Lake Falls, took my literature. She said she gave each candidate an initial free announcement before requiring that further candidate publicity be purchased through advertising. There was highway construction north of the city which required a long detour to Thief River Falls. I arrived in that city shortly before 5 p.m. The editor of the *Thief River Falls Times* (4,700), Dave Hill, took a few minutes from his busy schedule to talk with me at the counter. That "white male stuff" had caught his attention when my literature arrived in the mail. After leaving the newspaper office, I bought some day-old bread at the bakery-surplus store across the street.

I now had to make a major decision. Should I return to Bemidji to talk with its highly regarded political reporter, Brad Swenson, or should I try to cover cities in the extreme northern part of the state along the Canadian border. As a minor candidate, it would give me an edge to visit smaller cities and towns in that area which the other candidates might have bypassed. Perhaps I could camp overnight in a state park such as the one near Grygla and then make a grand sweep of the northern tier of cities, returning to the Twin Cities that night. The plan made sense to me. I then thought it might be possible to return to Bemidji to catch Swenson in his office in the early evening. Afterwards, I could go north and west through the Red Lake Indian Reservation to the campgrounds above Thief River Falls before they closed. It would mean lots of extra driving but time was running out for the campaign.

I drove all the way back to Bemidji. It started to rain just west of town. When I reached offices of *The Pioneer*, the rain was coming down in buckets. Water was pouring through the drain spouts and across the sidewalk near the back door. I was thoroughly soaked. Once inside, I readily found Brad Swenson and an associate. Swenson told me that *The Pioneer* had already scheduled a column about my campaign written by Don Davis. The Bemidji newspaper did not plan further coverage. When I tried to give him the photo of me standing in front of the Paul Bunyan statue with my "dignity for white males" sign, Swenson said that he did not think that would go over well on the Indian reservation.

Afterwards, I decided to drive back to the Twin Cities that evening instead of visiting the northern cities. My clothes were damp. I was tired and a bit discouraged. I went south on highway 71 and then on highway 371 to Brainerd, and finally joined highway 10 near Little Falls to drive the rest of the way home. This two-day trip had covered 979 miles.

Actually, it was a good thing that I spent Thursday, August 29th, in the Twin Cities. It gave me an opportunity to visit the press room in the basement of the State Capitol. First on the list was the office of the Associated Press. Ashley Grant, the journalist in charge, agreed to meet me during the noon hour. Having perused my campaign web site, she asked questions for about ten minutes. She refused photographs since they couldn't be scanned. She asked me to be sure to be available on primary night in case someone wanted to interview me.

I checked nearby offices. Tim Budig of ECM publications was in his office next door to Don Davis'. Davis, however, was not in. By some stroke of good luck, Budig was then finishing up his analysis of the primary races. He would still be able to include something about me. I gave him several pieces of literature and even my red campaign comb. Down the corridor were offices of *Star Tribune* reporters, all out to lunch, and of reporters for WCCO-TV. I spoke with WCCO's Capitol reporter Pat Kessler and another man in their office. Both reporters seemed interested in receiving my literature, having never seen it before because I had concentrated on the print media. I mentioned the Senate debate that evening at Augsburg College. Kessler knew about it. There would be a strong African American presence.

The debate, described elsewhere in the book, came to my attention when I read that morning's *Star Tribune*. I first faxed press releases to Twin Cities media protesting my exclusion from the debates. When the debate sponsors included me, I then faxed a retraction - off to a good start, wouldn't you say? The Senate debate, which began at 8 p.m., included Paul Wellstone, Jim Moore, Ed McGaa, and me. Because I had made a snap decision to return to the Twin Cities the night before, I was able to participate in this, my only Senate debate.

On Friday, August 30, I was again tied up with campaign and personal business in the Twin Cities. Contractors were replacing the roof on my property at 1715 Glenwood Avenue. They needed to be paid. Roofing supplies needed to be purchased. Also, the *Star Tribune* advertising department was balking at my latest attempt to place a paid advertisement in this newspaper either on election day or the day before. The deadline for advertising in the September 6th Voter Guide had already passed. Evidently, the legal department thought the ad was too negative. I made a proposal for eliminating the negativity. That was not enough. The legal department, speaking through the advertising department, was insisting that the reference to "dignity for white males" be struck. I refused to accept the changed wording and the ad was pulled.

Also that day, I placed telephone calls to several newspaper editors whose offices I had already visited. The editor of the *Mesabi Daily News* in Virginia, Bill Hanna, said he would try to include something about my campaign. Troy Krause, political reporter for the *Redwood Falls Gazette*, said that he would email me some questions and then write a story. On the other hand, the editors in Sandstone and Olivia were not planning any coverage of the primary race. I had a pleasant conversation with Gary Larsen, editor of the *Mille Lacs County Times* in Milaca, who remembered my literature. His newspaper was another owned by ECM Publications. I made also appointments for visits to reporters at the *Faribault Daily News* and the (Fairmont) *Sentinel* in the following week. A woman at the *Proctor Journal* asked me to call back Saturday morning to talk with Jake Benson, the editor. When I did, he asked me questions about the campaign and presumably wrote something.

Saturday, August 31, was a family day. My wife was away in China. My stepdaughter, Celia, finishing a summer program at St. Olaf College, wanted me to attend a ceremony welcoming freshmen to the college. I drove down to Northfield for the festivities. Celia and I had lunch and then went to separate events put on for the freshmen and for their parents. Together, we attended together a welcoming ceremony in the Skoglund auditorium which included much music. Afterwards, Celia remained at the college and I drove home. This was also the last weekend of the State Fair.

After attending religious services on Sunday morning, I drove over to the State Fair grounds in St. Paul. This would be one of the few occasions where I would be able to take the campaign directly to the voters with my sign. A good location for this activity was at the north entrance to the Fairgrounds across from the parking area. As fairgoers lined up to buy their entrance tickets, I stood in the middle of the walkway displaying my sign to pedestrians crossing the street from the parking area or lining up at the ticket window. It was too good to be true. After 20 minutes, a security guard, citing trespassing rules, asked me to leave the premises. I then stood near Snelling Avenue for more than an hour catching the smaller volume of pedestrian traffic crossing the street here. This was a good opportunity to create a personal connection with individual voters which would reinforce exposure from the media.

I left the Fairgrounds in the mid afternoon and visited the nearby home of the Property Rights group's cable-television producer, Bryan Olson, in Roseville. Then I drove west on Roselawn Avenue. Crossing the intersection of Roselawn and Cleveland with the green light, my car was struck by another car from the right side. I saw nothing before the accident. Suddenly, my 1992 blue Ford escort sat helplessly in the middle of the intersection as I, stunned by the blow, was trying to make sense of the situation. My first thought, sitting in the seat of the wrecked car, was that I would have to suspend the campaign. The driver of the other car, a gray 1986 Olds Ciera, said that his brakes had failed. Several persons helped push my car to the side of the road until the police could arrive and tow the car away.

My car was towed to an impound lot south of I-94 in St. Paul. The Roseville police would not allow me to retrieve my large campaign sign from the car. After taking a report, they drove me to the bus staging area on the south end of the State Fairgrounds. A Metro Transit employee pointed out the bus stop to take people to downtown Minneapolis. While I was waiting at the stop, I spotted my state representative, Greg Gray, then DFL candidate for state auditor, and his wife. Gray's race had attracted much media attention because he was the first African American nominated by a major party to that office. Liberals were hoping that his candidacy would produce a large black voter turnout that would help Wellstone. I told him what had happened. He expressed his sympathies.

Then I met another political candidate at the bus stop, Gray's polar opposite from a racial standpoint. This man's large campaign button read: "Leininger for U.S. Senate". In the campaign for Mayor of Minneapolis last year, there had been a candidate of the "White Man's Working Party" named Larry Leininger. I asked the button-wearer if he was that candidate. He was. Leininger and his girl friend boarded the same bus as mine. We had an opportunity to talk for several minutes while standing in the aisle during the bus ride. Leininger was a janitor at the University of Minnesota. He and a small number of other people were making a statement on behalf of white working men. His was not an active campaign.

The violence of the car crash followed by the appearance of these two totally different political candidates created a surrealistic feeling. Suddenly my Senate campaign was thrown for a loop. I was stuck at home without transportation. My campaign sign was locked inside the car impounded in St. Paul. It turned out that my problems were even worse than expected. I did not have comprehensive insurance on the car, only liability, and therefore could not count upon my own insurance company to get the car fixed. The other car was without insurance. Its driver ignored my subsequent telephone calls and eventually disappeared. However, no one was injured in the crash.

The first consequence of the crash was that I could not return to the State Fairgrounds on the following day to resume campaigning. Since most offices were closed for the Labor Day holiday, I could do little until Tuesday morning to report the accident or find a replacement car. On Monday, sitting at home, I did find one activity to advance the campaign. I emailed a message to several dozen radio stations around the state proposing that political correctness was like a state religion. So was the "work ethic". While our society enforces those values, civil libertarians instead attack the harmless customs of Christianity. I was hoping that radio-station managers and talk-show hosts would see some controversy in this and perhaps give me some air time to elaborate. They did not.

Tuesday morning, September 3, I rented a new Ford Escort from Enterprise Rent-a-Car in downtown Minneapolis costing $20 a day. This would be the last week of the campaign. It was probably too late to approach the weekly newspapers. My best shot was to visit the remaining dailies in the state. Studying the map, I realized that I could visit three of them if I drove in a circle from Minneapolis to Brainerd, St. Cloud, and Willmar. By telephone, the *Brainerd Daily Dispatch's* political reporter, Mike O'Rourke, promised an interview if I could meet him in the late morning. I raced up to Brainerd in my new car along highways 10 and 371, arriving shortly before noon at the office of the *Brainerd Daily Dispatch* (13,964). O'Rourke was available for a short interview. A photographer took pictures.

Now it was time to head back along the same highways to St. Cloud. My first stop was in Little Falls, at the office of the *Morrison County Record* (18,500). Reporter Joyce Moran asked a few questions, took a photograph, and said she would put an announcement in the newspaper. This was a lucky break because this large weekly newspaper was evidently still gathering news about the primary. Perhaps some Little Falls residents would remember me from the "Lindbergh Returns" parade two weeks earlier. The town manager had given me a lift back to my car.

At the next stop, the office of the *St. Cloud Times* (30,000) was in an unfamiliar part of town. Many streets were blocked from construction. Even though the political reporter, Dave Aeikins, came out to the lobby to talk with me briefly, his message was discouraging. He said the St. Cloud paper would be interested in covering my campaign only if I survived the primary. This visit may have had some use, however, since the *Times'* editorial page was reporting candidates' travels to the St. Cloud area.

Rambling westward from St. Cloud, I passed through the community of St. Joseph. It took awhile to locate the office of the *St. Joseph Newsleader* (3,300). The editor said he was too busy to see me when the receptionist announced my visit. He relented somewhat when I glanced into his small office. We had a short, witty conversation. His having received my "white male" literature may have colored his expectations of me.

The remaining leg of the trip, from St. Joseph to Willmar, took me along winding roads through hilly terrain. I arrived at the office of the *West Central Tribune* (17,500) late in the afternoon. The reporter whom I had met during the previous visit to that office, Linda Vanderwerf, was busy on assignment. She arranged for another reporter, Michelle Kubitz, to interview me. In a conference room, Kubitz conducted a lengthy interview. What would make farm people think that a candidate from Minneapolis could represent them in the Senate? I wasn't sure how my opposition to NAFTA would play in this context so I think I might have stressed the economic interdependence of all parts of the state. There was give-and-take between me and this reporter on several issues. It was a good interview.

The day ended with a long drive along U.S. highway 12 between Willmar and Minneapolis, passing places familiar from previous trips. I had to fill up at the William H. McCoy gasoline station in Delano and ask about the owner's (to me) interesting name. Gee, the station clerk just worked there. He had no idea. This one-day trip covered 378 miles.

Back at home, I was surprised to find an email message in my computer from Aaron Brown, editor of the *Hibbing Tribune*. Several U.S. Senate candidates had recently visited his office. He wanted to do a story on the campaign experience including experiences of a struggling candidate like me. I worked into the late evening to produce a statement to be emailed in return. Get coverage however you can - another lucky break.

Wednesday, September 4th, was a busy day. This time, I would hit the remaining dailies in southern Minnesota. My first visit was predetermined. I met Pauline Schreiber of the *Faribault Daily News* (7,411) at 10:30

a.m., as scheduled. This was my third visit to the Faribault newspaper so I knew the streets well. Pauline Schreiber was an experienced, thoughtful reporter who asked several good questions. A colleague took a photograph. Finally this base had been touched.

Le Center was thirty miles to the west. I gave Diane, receptionist at the *Le Center Leader* (1,750), copies of my literature for the editor. Next door to the newspaper office was a cafe. I stopped there for a bowl of soup. This was the archetypal small-town cafe. The woman who managed the place and her son were both big fans of Jesse Ventura. They asked me if there was a way to persuade the Governor to eat in their restaurant. (Gov. Arne Carlson had once visited Le Center.) I suggested that they write him - What the heck! Over on highway 169, I stopped in St. Peter at the office of the *St. Peter Herald* (2,158). The editor was, like me, a redheaded man who liked politics. He liked the fact that I was raising fundamental political questions in my campaign for the U.S. Senate. I was feeling optimistic as I left his office.

An important objective on this trip was to visit the large daily newspaper in Mankato, *The Free Press* (25,244). I spoke with Mark Fishnik, a political reporter, in the lobby outside the newsroom. He gave him my standard pitch and some literature. Fishnik said that his newspaper would not include much pre-primary coverage. Most could come before the general election. However, he might include something about my campaign in his "Friday notebook". While waiting for Fishnik, I also read a dispatch from the Twin Cities in the *Free Press* stating that the Greens were distancing themselves from their Senate candidate Ed McGaa because of *Star Tribune* disclosures of the failed scheme to ship ash to South Dakota.

The rest of the day was spent in a mad rush to try to visit as many weekly newspaper offices as I could in southwest Minnesota before the 5 p.m. closing time. I first stopped at the office of the *Lake Crystal Tribune* (1,774), spoke with editor Don Marben, and left literature. The next stop was in Madelia where editor Mark Anderson and Pat Art of the *Madelia Times-Messenger* (1,231) took literature and a campaign comb. Then it was on to keep an afternoon appointment with Bill Callahan of the *Sentinel* (7,700) in Fairmont. He asked several questions as we stood at the front counter. I left literature and photos. Then it was on to the *St. James Plain Dealer* (2,785). Mark Hagen, a reporter, took literature there. My final stop of the day was at the offices of the *Windom Citizen* on 10th street. I left literature for the editor and took his card in case I returned. I wanted to hit the *Observer/Advocate* (1,869) office in Mountain Lake on the way home, but it was closed. My travels that day had covered 375 miles.

The final day on the campaign trail was Thursday, September 5th. This time I would hit the cities and towns along interstate highway I-94 heading northwest toward Fargo/Moorhead. One large daily, the *Daily Journal* in Fergus Falls, remained to be visited. I started out on I-94 exiting the freeway at any town which had a newspaper on my list. The first such place was Albany, Minnesota. I spoke with Adam in the office of the *Stearns-Morrison Enterprise* (2,200) and left literature and photographs. The next stop on this highway was at Melrose. Herman Lensing, editor of the *Melrose Beacon* (2,039) talked with me for several minutes and took literature.

Next on my list was Sauk Centre and its newspaper, the *Sauk Centre Herald* (3,000). Here, in the hometown of novelist Sinclair Lewis, the editor took me into his office for a short interview. There were photographs of some of the other Senate candidates on the wall. This was evidently a paper which took an interest in politics. The editor, Dave Simpkins, was a smart man who asked good questions and had several interesting things to say. Before leaving the office for another appointment, he took my photo and promised to publish something before the primary (a mere five days off).

Continuing my journey up I-94, I exited the highway to join highway 27 on the way to Osakis and Alexandria. I spoke with Greta Petrich, editor of the *Osakis Review* (1,550), at the newspaper office. She was new in that position but had a keen interest in political affairs. I gave her my literature and photographs. I then continued on highway 27 to Alexandria, a larger-sized city. A reporter named Hollen at the *Echo Press* (11,000) said that it was too late to include news about the primary. This newspaper has a policy of not running political materials too close to an election. There would be a special issue of the paper two weeks before the general election. I gave him samples of my campaign literature in case I was still in the race then.

At Alexandria, I left I-94 to travel south on highway 29 to Glenwood. Since I lived on Glenwood Avenue in Minneapolis, this city had a special attraction for me. Besides, its newspaper, the *Pope County Tribune* (4,000), had a good-sized circulation. Unfortunately it was lunch time when I arrived at the office. Mike Scott, a sports reporter, said that the editor and publisher, John Stone, would be back after lunch. I walked to a nearby cafe to have lunch myself. At a nearby table, several men were having a lively conversation. Editor Stone still had not returned to the office when I finished lunch. Scott told me that, because the newspaper came out on Monday, they might still have a chance to put something in if I could reach Stone by telephone.

Now it was time to drive the final segment to Fergus Falls. I headed west on highway 55 (which we call Olson highway in Minneapolis) through some picturesque countryside and a series of small towns without their own newspapers. I was passing through one such town, Kensington, when I spotted a sign which explained why the name rang a bell. This was the site of the famous "Kensington Runestone", a stone with runic inscriptions "discovered" by a farmer in the late 19th century. If authentic, this stone and its inscriptions proved that the Vikings had been in Minnesota several centuries before Columbus' voyage to America, certainly before the "Minnesota Vikings" pro football team arrived. When my brother David (before his debilitating automobile accident) visited Minnesota in the 1970s, he had proposed making a special trip to see this artifact. It might be worth my while to suspend campaign activities for an hour or so to take in an exhibit related to world history.

The sign directed me north on highway 1 and then to several other county roads. The Kensington Runestone site was in an elevated, windswept park maintained by Douglas County. I could see an area surrounded by variously colored flags on flag poles. It had no significance other than being a memorial to the runestone discovery. A nearby stone indicated the actual site of the discovery. Where was the runestone now? A woman in the parking lot thought that it was in a small museum on highway 27 near Osakis. I later learned that the Kensington Runestone was in the Douglas County Historical Society museum in Alexandria. In any event, it was not here.

The subject came up at my next stop, the office of the *Grant County Herald* (2,150) in Elbow Lake, farther up highway 55. The editor, Chris Ray, had become a Kensington Runestone buff because of local interest in the subject. He had dealt with filmmakers who made documentaries of possible Viking visits to Minnesota. He showed me a photograph of another stone which had been found in Elbow Lake with inexplicable circular markings. Had the Vikings also produced these? The Kensington Runestone had told of a battle several days distant from the site of the stone's discovery. This was about the same distance as Elbow Lake. Returning to the business at hand, Ray also said that he was in favor of third-party politics. In his opinion, we were ready for something new.

The office of the *Daily Journal* (9,500) in Fergus Falls was near the exit from I-94. Luckily, I did not have to search this rather large town to find it. Although people in the office were quite busy, a reporter named Jim Sturgeon - "same as the fish" - had time to talk with me. Here I had one of the more intense discussion of issues, especially the shorter-workweek issue. Although it was an idea which personally intrigued to him, there were possible drawbacks. In defense, I went through the entire argument about how shorter work time might reduce economic waste. After so much driving that day, I might not have been on top of my game.

There was one remaining town on I-94 with a newspaper between here and Moorhead, Barnesville. A woman in the office of the *Barnesville Record-Review* (1,800) said that the editor, Eugene Prim, was away. I left literature for him. They published on Mondays, so it might still be possible to put something in the newspaper if I reached Prim by telephone.

My final stop of the day and of the campaign was at the offices of *The Forum* (51,381) in Fargo, North Dakota. *The Forum* was the dominant newspaper in Moorhead, Minnesota's largest city along its western border. It was close to closing time when I arrived in Fargo. A reporter named Dave Jurgens met me in the 2nd floor lobby of the Forum building. He told me that Don Davis handled all the Minnesota political reporting for Forum Communications newspapers. I mentioned the thorough interview which Davis had already given me. Jurgens agreed that Davis was thorough. So it had not been necessary for me to have driven the forty miles to Fargo.

The drive back to Minneapolis along interstate highway I-94 took about five hours. Thursday's campaign travels had covered 549 miles. Altogether, I had traveled more than 5,500 miles around the state during the last month, both in my own Escort and in the rental car. There would be no more opportunities during the campaign for me to visit newspaper offices. Still, the most important single event was scheduled to take place tomorrow, Friday, September 6th, which was also the day that the Primary Voter Guide appeared in the *Star Tribune*. That was the interview on Minnesota Public Radio.

What could a candidate usefully do in the remaining three days before Tuesday's primary election? For me, the time was anticlimactic. I knew that my principal opponent, Jim Moore, would have people working the phone banks for him and distributing literature to doors in Minneapolis and perhaps other communities. I was by myself. On Sunday, September 8th, a hot sunny day, I carried my sign (retrieved from the impound lot a day earlier) in the Burnsville "Fire Muster" parade. During the interminable waiting period at the start of the parade, I enjoyed the companionship of a judicial candidate's husband and a photographer from Burnsville's Heritage Photography studio. The parade itself seemed sparsely attended.

The finale of my campaign was to spend a few hours on Monday, September 9th, walking up and down Nicollet Mall in downtown Minneapolis. Then it was over. There was nothing left to do except wait for the results.

Appendix B

A Challenger's Letter to Independence Party Members

August 1, 2002

Dear Independence Party member:

In the spirit of independence with a lower-case "i", I am a candidate for U.S. Senate in the Independence Party primary along with the party's endorsed candidate, Jim Moore. I did not seek endorsement at the July 13th convention.

The Independence Party of Minnesota is on the move. Although Governor Ventura and Lt. Governor Schunk are not seeking reelection, the party has a strong opportunity to succeed them in candidates Tim Penny and Martha Robertson. Both are political leaders with distinguished records of public service combined with moderate views. Theirs is a centrist appeal which has borne fruit in attracting defectors in past or present office holders from the DFL and Republican parties. The prospect of party success in this year's elections is more promising than in previous years both at the gubernatorial level and with respect to other state offices.

The reason that I have filed to become a candidate for the U.S. Senate is a disquieting feeling picked up at the St. Cloud convention that, in the public eye, the Independence Party no longer stands for anything. Issues are the problem. Yes, the Republican and DFL parties have both been captured by "extremist" elements and the Independence Party stands in the middle; but what exactly does this mean? How, for example, does the Independence Party stake a "middle position" with respect to the Christian right? What is the extremist position within the DFL party and how do we differ from it? All these specifics are covered up by muddled generalities about being in the middle. I believe that outstanding personalities are not enough for a third party to achieve lasting majority status. As the Republicans supplanted the Whigs on an anti-slavery plank, so third parties in our day must ride a wave of compelling issues to win majority status.

When Ross Perot founded the Reform Party in 1992, his message of controlling Reagan-era budget deficits resonated with the voters. So did his warnings of a "giant sucking sound" as businesses relocated to Mexico under NAFTA. Where are these issues now? Well, the budget deficit was (until September 11th) brought under control through bipartisan efforts and a robust economy. The Independence Party has abandoned the Perotist position on "free trade". A new issue has emerged in campaign finance reform. However, embracing such issues is hardly unique to the Independence Party. John McCain, Russ Feingold, and others have a higher profile on them than we.

The U.S. Senate seat is the key policy position with respect to national and international issues. I have looked over the policy statements of our endorsed candidate, Jim Moore, and found nothing that is unique and compelling, nothing that clearly differentiates the Independence Party from the others. Eliminate waste in government, be fiscally responsible, hold schools accountable for results, crack down on corporate abuse - you can hear one or another candidate espouse such positions in the two major parties. How is Mr. Moore going to insert himself into a discussion between the two $10 million candidates, Coleman and Wellstone? He won't. I believe that such a candidacy, respectable but bland, will be a wasted opportunity. I propose an alternative.

Last year I was a candidate for Mayor of Minneapolis, filling in at the last minute for a friend who had dropped out of the race. We were landlords. We both realized that, as such, in a city whose political culture has long stigmatized landlords, in a hostile media environment, at a time of sky-high rents, our chances of winning were slim to none. I filed under the label "Affordable Housing- Preservation", running a purely negative campaign. Carrying literature and a picket sign, I wandered through downtown Minneapolis telling voters how the city had torn down hundreds of units of structurally sound housing, how its development agency misused the power of eminent domain, etc. The newspapers would not print my articles or letters. Until the last week of the primary, I had two minutes total in the candidate debates. But in my two minutes I told Mayor Sharon Sayles Belton to her face that she had to go, along with her buddies on the City Council.

Unexpectedly, another "minor" candidate and I were invited to participate in the last candidate debate. We acquitted ourselves well. When the *Star Tribune* article on this event neglected to mention our participation, I wrote a letter to the editor calling attention to our candidacies. I later sent a press release to the media on behalf of the minor candidates which said, "You may not have been interested in our political views but perhaps you'd like to hear us sing." So it was that a group of obscure mayoral candidates including me appeared on three Twin Cities television stations singing patriotic songs on the local news on the evening before September 11th.

I mention these things to indicate how I would approach the Senate race. As a mayoral candidate, I did not personally do well; but the job got done. We swept the entire leadership of city government away in a one-party town, using our issues, providing key help to the winning candidates when it was needed. To use a football analogy, I knew that my role in this effort was to be a blocker, not the one who carried the ball across the line for a touchdown. The important thing was to convey a sense of urgency that Minneapolis city government needed to change. We could not afford to be subtle or polite. We had to get in there in a visceral way and fight for change. So it is with the 2002 Senate race. Up against staggering odds, the Independence Party candidate needs to be out there swinging and take ideological risks. We cannot afford to play it safe.

This party needs to embrace issues which are central to the political process and which differentiate us from the other parties. However centrist, we need to be more partisan with respect to issues, not less. We need to be passionate in our convictions. My convictions may not be the same as those of other Independence Party members - and I will not portray them as such - but they are consistent with IP principles. I will present them to the public in this year's primary, expecting to be called a "racist", "communist", "kook", and everything in between. Like the blocker who opens up daylight for the touchdown runner, I will open up core issues that will pose real alternatives to the prevailing political views and prepare the way for future electoral victories.

To avoid the clutter of proposals, I will focus on two issues in the primary campaign. They are stated as follows:

(1) "I believe in the full citizenship, dignity, and equality of white males."

(2) "I believe that the federal government should enact legislation to reduce the standard workweek to 32 hours by the year 2010."

Neither of these positions has, to my knowledge, any organized base of support at this time. Both would be immediately and aggressively opposed by powerful political interest groups. The first principle would be opposed by dominant extremist elements in the Democratic Party. The second would be opposed by dominant extremist elements in the Republican Party. Since the extremes of both parties have taken over, statements such as mine opposing them will, of course, be seen as being beyond the pale. I expect to take flak for them. But I also intend to open up new political territory through which moderates from the Independence Party can move to majority party status. However, a word of explanation is required.

Independence Party members often see themselves as being "neither too liberal, nor too conservative, but in the middle". But what does this specifically mean? Seventy years ago, the main political division ran along the lines of economic interest: rich versus poor, management versus labor. In the days of Franklin D. Roosevelt, liberals were those who sided with labor unions and poor people. Conservatives were those who sided with business interests and the rich. Forty years ago, in the 1960s, a new political alignment appeared with the triumph of the Civil Rights movement. The segregationist South was put down by northern liberals including Minnesota's own Hubert Humphrey. That realigned African Americans, who had been Republican since Reconstruction days, with the Democratic Party and brought the previously "Solid South" into the Republican camp. The Civil Rights movement of black people became a model for the Women's movement, the Gay Rights movement, and the immigrants movement of Hispanics, Asians, Somalis, and other peoples.

Today, the core ideology of liberals and of the Democratic Party is that of victimized peoples fighting for full citizenship in U.S. society, being opposed by conservatives who reflect the fears and prejudices of the ancien regime. "White males" identify the socially retrograde groups destined to decline, although individual white males (such as Bill Clinton) can avoid that unflattering designation by aggressively embracing the liberal ideology of Civil Rights, feminism, and demographically defined "human rights".

Which side is stronger, liberal or conservative? The answer to that question depends on which front the political battle is being waged. On the economic front, I would say that the conservative position is stronger. Big-business interests prevail over those of organized labor. Although the Republicans are predominantly the party of business, money from well-heeled groups buys influence in both the Republican and Democratic Parties. On the social and cultural front, however, the liberal position is stronger. The history and ethics of the Civil Rights movement and its successor movements have become like a civic religion. People lose jobs and face public disgrace by voicing the wrong opinion on matters of gender and race. Furthermore, when you add up all the blocs in the Civil Rights coalition - African Americans, women, Hispanics, Asians, gays, disabled persons - you have an overwhelming majority of voters, one whose numbers are destined to increase while the residual group of Americans shrinks. "White males", the core of that residual group, are losers in the political game.

I often hear political candidates who say "I am an economic conservative but a social (or cultural) liberal". Well, so are big business, academia, the media, and both the Republican and Democratic Parties. They all support big-business interests while embracing the values of feminism and Civil Rights. While one might suppose that the white men who run the large corporations might sympathize with their demographic brethren further down the food chain, that proves not to be the case. Most are ardent supporters of affirmative action for others even if they themselves have escaped the process. The big foundations, universities, media, and the courts are all active boosters of cultural liberalism. Anyone on the make in this society knows which side to support. Therefore, when I hear someone say he is an economic conservative but a social liberal, I do not see this as a sign of independent thinking but of "piling on" the winning side. To this, in the Senate race, I say "I am an economic liberal and a social conservative". I say this not with any assurance of winning but because I think it is right.

The first plank in my campaign for Senate is to support "full citizenship, dignity, and equality of white males". I, of course, also support the same for white females, black females, black males, and everyone else in this society. We are all entitled to human dignity. But I do not see the other groups as being politically at risk as white males are. In liberal circles, the very term, "white male", is used as a political epithet, a term of derision and scorn. The fact that someone in a high corporate position is, like me, a white male does not mean that I will derive a personal advantage from it. Could I expect such a person, say, a multimillionaire lawyer or corporate executive, to give me a free cup of coffee because I share his demographic traits? I doubt it. Whites selling out whites, males selling out males, white males selling out other white males, seems to be more what is happening today. We need to return to the original ethic of the Civil Rights movement: that individuals should not be judged by stereotypical views of group behavior but by their individual behavior. Those who profess to be supporting "tolerance" can themselves be quite intolerant of those who hold different political views.

In the culture area, the solution lies in acts of individual defiance to oppressive social norms. It lies in the uninhibited exercise of free speech. Still, it is appropriate to raise this topic in the context of a campaign for federal office because cultural liberalism has inserted its values into laws and regulations. While all citizens are theoretically "equal under the law", the law also recognizes such categories as "protected classes" whose members are, so to speak, "more equal" than others. Government has created systems of preferential treatment in hiring, business contracting, educational admissions, housing, and many other areas which, by a strict reading of the 14th amendment, would be judged unconstitutional. But the judges are political appointees who are unwilling to see it that way. The livelihood of many lawyers depends on it.

The economic issues are also important. I am not a libertarian. I believe that government has a role to play in regulating the economy and a responsibility to do so when there are problems. I am disturbed by the fact that long-term real wages have been declining and work hours have been increasing for the people who do the grunt work in this society - persons in all demographic categories. Labor unions have been ineffective in reversing this trend in part because the bipartisan "free trade" agenda has allowed corporate enterprise to escape labor and environmental regulation by going off shore.

Like Henry Ford, I believe in the economic utility of leisure as a way to increase the need for consumption as well as to bolster employment opportunities. But today's business leaders and economic conservatives oppose such proposals for the sake of more short-term profits and so more opportunities to draw money out of the system for themselves. Government can and should regulate the supply of labor to allow more people to have full-scale wages and adequate amounts of personal free time even if this means that the economy will sustain cutbacks in "growth" industries such as crime and incarceration, pill pushing, gambling, litigation, military preparedness, and other fixtures of a compulsive economy.

I know something about the economics of work and leisure, having published several books on this and related subjects. I have coauthored a book on work-time issues with a former U.S. Senator, published op-ed pieces in the *New York Times* and other leading newspapers, and advised a member of Congress who introduced a shorter-workweek bill. I'm prepared to slug it out with any academic or business spokesman who raises theoretical objections. As a concrete recommendation, I propose to amend the Fair Labor Standards Act to establish a 32-hour standard workweek (and raise the overtime penalty rate) within eight years. Let's be bold.

Sincerely,

William McGaughey

Appendix C

Distance Bombardment: Communicating with Editors and Voters by Fax, Internet, and Newspaper Advertising

(1)

billforsenate.org

Web site for the candidacy of William McGaughey for U.S. Senate running in the Independence Party primary in Minnesota

Bill's statement:

"I filed in the Senate race on July 16th after having attended the Independence Party convention in St. Cloud on the previous Saturday. It seemed to me that the Independence Party will need to wage a harder-hitting and more issues-driven campaign than previously planned if we are to be taken seriously in the multimillion-dollar battle between Wellstone and Coleman. In my opinion, we can do this if we raise the right issues. We need, however, to raise core political issues differentiating ourselves from the other parties. We need to take risks.

I am coming at this challenge both from the left and right. Unlike practically everyone else in politics today, I am an economic liberal and a cultural/social conservative. On one hand, I support labor in its basic ends; on the other, I oppose political correctness. This society needs to have as many people as possible working for good wages with enough free time to pursue personal and family life. Also, it can no longer afford to play up the racial and gender differences within our population that have been a staple of political life for the past forty years. With a new sense of unity and purpose, let's move on to demand better performance from our leaders. (Yes, you can demand this from me if I become Senator.)

If you want more information about my candidacy, check out these pages:

A letter to Independence Party members explaining myself and why I ran

In your face, Democrats - a discussion of my campaign plank #1, stated: "I believe in the full citizenship, dignity, and equality of white males (and of other people, too)."

In your face, Republicans - a discussion of my campaign plank #2, stated: "I believe that the federal government should enact legislation to reduce the standard workweek to 32 hours by the year 2010."

Candidate biography

Please contact me at **wmcg@prodigy.net** for comments and questions. During this campaign, I want to travel around the state meeting as many people as I can. Please invite me to your events. Please organize gatherings where I can speak and listen. Please tell media people in your community about my candidacy. Please help spread the word.

A final note: Although this will be a relatively low budget campaign, I could use some money to print literature, buy gasoline, and defray other expenses of the campaign. You can contribute by sending a check, money order, or cash to: McGaughey for Senate campaign, P.O. Box 3601 , Minneapolis, MN 55403-3601. I would also appreciate campaign volunteers.

As Jesse might say, **let's see if we can shock the world again this year!**

Bill

(2)

PRESS RELEASE
July 29, 2002

CONTACT: William McGaughey
(612) 374-5916

William McGaughey is Candidate for U.S. Senate in Independence Party primary

The candidate: William (Bill) McGaughey is a 61-year-old resident of Minneapolis. He is married and has a stepdaughter who will be a college freshman this fall. McGaughey is a small landlord, active in a Minneapolis landlord group. He is also author of five books- most recently, *Five Epochs of Civilization*, a study of world history; and *Rhythm and Self-Consciousness*, a philosophy of music and sports. This is his second run for public office; he was a candidate for Mayor of Minneapolis last year. He attended the Independence Party convention in St. Cloud on July 13th and filed for U.S. Senate on July 16th, intending to inject some new ideas into the campaign.

The field: There are eleven candidates from U.S. Senate from the DFL, Republican, Green, Constitution, and Independence Party. Jim Moore is the endorsed Independence Party candidate for U.S. Senate. Bill McGaughey and Ronald E. Wills are challenging him in the primary.

The name: McGaughey is pronounced "McGoy". Bill's Scotch-Irish. He was born in Detroit and both parents came from Indiana, so it's unlikely he is related to McGaugheys in Minnesota. Even so, there is a Minnesota connection with this name. In 1847, President Zachary Taylor nominated a certain Edward McGaughey to be Minnesota's first territorial governor. The U.S. Senate rejected the nomination, opening up the way for Alexander Ramsey's later appointment. So it would be poetic justice of a sort if in 2002 Minnesota sent McGaughey to the U.S. Senate.

Party affiliation: Bill has attended precinct caucuses of the Independence Party in 1998, 2000, and 2002. He has not been active in party affairs and did not discuss his platform beforehand with other party members.

Bill's general strategy: Bill wants the Independence Party to develop new ideas around which voters can rally in opposition to the Democratic and Republican parties. He thinks both parties have given up on building a better society. The first priority is to change the political discussion - bring up subjects which may stir controversy but will produce change. Bill is limiting his campaign platform to two planks which represent diametrically opposed positions from those of the Democrats and Republicans. In that respect, he is a "centrist" candidate.

The two planks: (1) "I believe in the full citizenship, dignity, and equality of white males (and of everyone else, too.)" (2) "I believe that the federal government should enact legislation to reduce the standard work-week from 40 hours to 32 hours by the year 2010."

The connection between the two: Once the little people stop fighting each other demographically, perhaps they can join forces to demand better economic and political leadership. Let's get back on the track of improved living standards for all.

How to reach the candidate: You can call him at any time at his Minneapolis home at (612) 374-5916 or send an email to wmcg@prodigy.net. Check out his revealing web site at www.billforsenate.org. If interested, you can also check his book's web site in six languages at www.worldhistorysite.com or the landlords' at www.propertyrights-mn.com.

(3)

Dear political reporter:

I (Bill McGaughey) am a candidate for U.S. Senate in the Independence Party primary. My campaign is in full swing.

You will, of course, question why my candidacy deserves attention when I am an Independence Party candidate who did not seek or receive the party's endorsement. Also, is it not a foregone conclusion that either Coleman or Wellstone will win the election?

First, I think I have a real shot at defeating the Independence Party's endorsed candidate, Jim Moore, in the primary. Remember, fewer than 200 people were at the IP convention. Perhaps 140 people (including me) voted for Moore. So this is a thin mandate. I can win by appealing to the much larger number of independent voters if my unique message gains acceptance. If I beat an endorsed candidate in the primary, then my candidacy acquires momentum for the general election. I will participate in debates among the four Senatorial candidates. I will be a player.

Second, even if you don't think I can beat Wellstone or Coleman in the general election, many experts believe that third party candidacies may be decisive in the outcome, given the close race between the two front-runners. Not only will my vote total be important but also the fact that Wellstone and Coleman may have to change their message to appeal to my (and Ed McGaa's) constituency.

Third, I am making this race as much to advance the long-term interests of the Independence Party as to win the 2002 election. Already the party has received a boost by Tim Penny's and others' defection from the two major parties. They can and, I think, will win this year. But the Senatorial candidate, Jim Moore, seemed to me to be a throwaway, given his lackluster stance on issues.

The reason I ran is that, while the Independence Party stands "in the middle" between the Democrats and Republicans, it is not always clear what this means. I have chosen to emphasize two issues - support of shorter work hours and opposition to political correctness - which are sharply differentiated from positions of the two major parties. This could help to create a political movement in opposition to the established order, possibly something which could eventually build to major-party status. There's a more complete discussion of this possibility on my web site, www.billforsenate.org. Click on "scheme of a new politics".

I (and my landlord associates) have already made a difference in changing the political climate in Minneapolis. I think I can do the same in state politics. I will now wage an issues-driven campaign for U.S. Senate. The campaign will be waged by personal discussions with voters and, to the extent possible, through the media. I will work hard. I have a picket sign with my two proposals on either side and will carry them in parades or stand on street corners discussing them with persons who pass by. In me, you will not have a bland candidate but someone who will seek to create a meaningful, interesting campaign.

To do that, it would help if you would tell me what you might want to cover. Please invite me to do something. You can get a quick response from me, when I'm not on the road, by telephone (612-374-5916) or email (wmcg@prodigy.net). Thanks.

Bill

(4)

U.S. Senate Candidate's Statement on Establishment of Religions

As a candidate for U.S. Senate running in the Independence Party primary, I embrace two campaign positions - support for a 32-hour work-week by 2010 and opposition to political correctness - which arouse more than usual criticism. It's as if I were a heretic holding unacceptable views. This has started me thinking about whether we in the United States have what might loosely be termed a "state religion".

Last December, there was a brouhaha at St. Paul City Hall when someone placed red poinsettias in the lobby. Civil libertarians complained that these flowers symbolized the Christian religion; to display them in a government building was offensive to non-Christians. To his credit, Mayor Norm Coleman disagreed, pointing out the inconsistency between criticizing this floral display and ignoring an 8-foot-high Menorah in front of the State Capitol. But the red poinsettias still had to go. A compromise was reached by which white poinsettias were allowed to be displayed at City Hall because they were thought not to be so closely associated with Christianity.

What is a state religion? Does it have to be a God-centered religion, or can it be a set of personal or social values not associated with traditional religion which are rigidly enforced by the state? I would argue that the latter is possible. Do we have such a "state religion"? Yes, I think we do; it's called "political correctness". Another set of values, enforced in the corporate world, is the "ethic" of workaholism. To get ahead in that environment, you have to prove loyalty to your employer by putting work ahead of personal and family life. Individuals who refuse to do that "don't fit in" or get promoted.

If the belief system of political correctness is a civic religion, then compulsory "diversity training" workshops (which over three quarters of the Fortune 500 companies give to their employees) violate constitutional guarantees of religious liberty. The State of Minnesota requires that all attorneys practicing in the state take diversity training courses that teach acceptable attitudes about gender and race. These courses are also required to meet lawyers' continuing education requirements. In essence, such workshops are political indoctrination intended to impart a certain set of social values. Clearly the state is part of the enforcement mechanism.

I would contend that such requirements violate the spirit of the First Amendment regarding establishment of religion. Walking through the lobby of the St. Paul City Hall, you can avert your eyes at a floral display of red poinsettias if its association with Christianity offends you; but you can't avoid paying homage to the values of political correctness (which typically employ double standards to judge the different racial, gender, or religious groups) if you want to keep your job or practice law in the state of Minnesota.

State religions are unconstitutional. So is abridgement of free speech. We need to have a public discussion about this. I think that an election campaign is the appropriate forum for such a discussion. It is my intention, as a candidate for U.S. Senate running in the Independence Party primary, to raise uncomfortable subjects like this so that we can heal social divisions and move on to consider economic policies that promise to create a better life for all.

William McGaughey

Contact me at (612) 374-5916 or wmcg@prodigy.net. For further information about my candidacy, visit www.billforsenate.org.

(5)

For immediate release
July 22, 2002

Contact: William McGaughey
(612) 374-5916 or wmcg@prodigy.net

IP CANDIDATE SUPPORTS TOUGHER DRIVER'S LICENSE RULES

Statement of William McGaughey, candidate for U.S. Senate in the Independence Party primary:

"I support the new policy of Charlie Weaver, director of the Minnesota Public Safety Commission, to require a change in procedures to obtain Minnesota driver licenses with an eye to improving public safety and procedure. The Minnesota Civil Liberties Union, joined by the Arab Anti-Defamation League and Jewish Community Action, is suing in court to prevent the new rules from being imposed. I believe that the issues raised by the MCLU are fundamentally political questions which deserve discussion in the context of a political campaign. So I am offering my position as a candidate for U.S. Senate. Perhaps the other candidates will want to comment as well. The new policies are reasonable and, I think, desirable in the context of terroristic threats against the United States:

(1) Two forms of ID: When I opened a post office box for my U.S. Senate campaign, I was required to present two forms of identification. I was mildly irked but got over it. Regarding the 9/11 tragedy, all 19 hijackers had multiple aliases and several identities. Seven obtained their ID cards in Virginia which allows others to vouch for their identity. We do not have a national ID system. The state driver license is the closest thing to that we have. Weaver is right to insist on tougher requirements.

(2) "Status checks" on resident alien IDs: The other thing which allowed the hijackers to overstay their visits in the U.S. was lack of a tracking system for those whose visas had expired. Weaver's proposal establishes this.

(3) Full face photograph: This is a reasonable requirement for security reasons. Personal religious practice should not override public safety.

The broader political issue is whether the discrimination aspect - which has spawned a whole industry of lawyers - should override reasonable measures to improve public safety. I think not. When five Middle Eastern men entered Logan airport on the morning of Sept. 11, 2001 purchasing one-way tickets with cash, they were allowed to board the plane because security guards were afraid of being accused of ethnic profiling. Arab-Americans had sued the airlines in 1999 and 2000 on such grounds. Enough of this nonsense. Our political leaders need to state clearly that public safety overrides the temporary embarrassment and inconvenience of particular groups used to claiming discriminatory practices in domestic politics."

(6)

Paid newspaper advertisement

Dear Primary Voter: I oppose the Republicans' core value of **squeeze working people** and the Democrats' core value of **political correctness.** I'm for **shorter work time** and **dignity for white males** (and all others too). A strong third party can be built on this foundation. **Vote for Bill McGaughey for U.S. Senate** in the Independence Party primary on September 10th. **www.billforsenate.org**

Appendix D

The Ground War: Campaign Literature given to Newspaper Editors

(1)

Statement of Bill McGaughey, candidate for U.S. Senate

For a country as democratic, free, and rich as the United States, I believe that we are poorly led. The managerial and professional class, showing little responsibility to others, is busy enriching itself. Politicians are bought off by special interests. Propaganda delivered through the communications media substitutes for reasoned policy. "We, the people" have become politically marginalized.

The first problem has to do with economics. Science and technology have given us great wealth, but that wealth is not evenly shared. Low-echelon workers are falling behind in the struggle to make ends meet, even as they work longer hours. Most economic "growth" is going into wasteful enterprises such as litigation, military preparedness (or war on terrorism), legal and illegal drugs, gambling, extended compulsory education, and other required spending rather than spending for useful products or those which make people happy.

There were two points of failure in the nation's economic policy: First was that in the late 1950s when, in response to rising unemployment due to automation, the national administration decided to try other remedies than shorter work hours. Even though labor productivity grew at a fast pace, it was decided to forgo general leisure for the sake of "higher output". In retrospect, that was a mistake. (What we got instead was economic waste.) The second mistake occurred when national administrations starting with Reagan's pushed through "free trade" agreements which allowed large corporations to move production to low-wage countries and sell the products back in the United States. A union-busting move, this arrangement severed the link between worker and consumer (which Henry Ford once said was "the secret of our prosperity") and created a huge trade deficit which imperils our future well being.

Ordinary Americans are powerless to withstand these trends. I believe that the key to restoring effective opposition to inadequate or abusive leadership lies in attacking the second problem, a social and cultural problem which is sometimes called "political correctness." In particular, it lies in restoring the dignity of white males. It is also important that white males themselves take the initiative in restoring their political dignity, that they have the courage to stand up for their rights at the cost of enduring personal criticism, and not let others do it for them. Regaining their courage, they will feel better about themselves and their society and perhaps may want to do something about its poor leadership instead of retreating into a world of private comfort.

That is why I, a white male, dare state as a major principle in my campaign for U.S. Senate that "I believe in the full citizenship, dignity, and equality of white males", according others the same rights and respect. If this statement stirs opposition, that only proves my case. Such a principle ought to be noncontroversial but it is not because some people want to keep them (white males) in a pit.

Because this proposal is rather subjective, it may help to state assumptions which can be evaluated in terms of fact.

(1) It is a fact that, despite affirmative action, white males still occupy most positions of power and privilege in U.S. society.

(2) That does not mean that other white males, being of a similar demographic type, share in this power or privilege or benefit from it in any way. Most white males are not part of the ruling elite.

(3) The nation's economic and political elite actively supports political correctness and the theory of white-male group guilt. Otherwise, the ruling class (comprised largely of white males) could do away with it in a minute.

(4) On the whole, white males are not socially or economically disadvantaged. Their disadvantage is psychological and political. Through theories of historically based group guilt, they have been forced to accept something less than full citizenship: legalized double standards adverse to their interests, state-imposed "training" to accept social and political values hostile to them.

(5) The key to understanding this "complex" situation is that it is in the interests of the economic and political elite, whose claim to leadership does not rest on creative performance, to stir the pot of racial and gender animosities and keep the potentially rebellious white males and others in an angry, demoralized state. Little people of the world, unite!

(2)

A New Direction for Third-Party Politics

I am running for U.S. Senate in 2002 because I see an opportunity for the Independence Party to remain an important "third party" force in Minnesota and American politics if it can embrace the right set of issues.

I feel that a political party, to be effective, must be issues-driven. Right now, the Independence Party is known for Gov. Jesse Ventura's amazing victory in 1998. This year, it has attracted, as candidates, past and present government officials who were elected under the banner of the two major parties. All this is, of course, good. But a political party cannot be simply a party of celebrity candidates or of defectors from other parties. It must stand on its own two feet; and to do that, it needs compelling issues.

The Reform Party (predecessor of the Independence Party) had compelling issues when Ross Perot ran for President in 1992. I would characterize these as: (1) opposition to chronic budget deficits and (2) opposition to NAFTA. Now Gov. Ventura and other IP members are ardent free traders and the deficit issue disappeared with the years of budget surplus. So what is left?

The U.S. Senate position is a policy position. The Independence Party candidate needs to present strong issues that are different from those of the other parties. Jim Moore, the endorsed IP candidate, is a nice guy with energy and dedication but, in my opinion, he is weak on issues. What are his issues? Campaign-finance reform, bringing private-sector-like efficiencies to the federal government, instituting corporate accountability, holding schools accountable for results, among others. Candidates of the two major parties say similar things.

I do not believe that a political party can be effective by espousing a hodgepodge of issues, especially those framed by special-interest groups. The future of the Independence Party does not rest upon well-thought-out positions on abortion, gun control, or any of the other issues that generate so much political noise. It must pick one or two core issues and carve out a position for itself that is sufficiently different from the positions of the Democratic and Republican parties. To do that, it might be helpful to review how those two parties evolved, issues-wise, into what they are today.

The Democratic Party was once an agrarian party in the tradition of Jefferson and Jackson. (My maternal grandfather, minority leader of the Indiana Senate in the late 1920s, was a Democrat of that type.) The Democrats, under FDR, became a party of organized labor, opposing big business.

The Republicans began as an anti-slavery party. Holding power in the period of post-Civil War industrial development, the Republicans became associated with business interests. This position hardened in the 1930s and 1940s as the Democrats became associated with organized labor. The Republicans today remain preeminently the party of business.

During the 1960s, the Democrats nationally turned their backs on their southern brethren who comprised the "Solid South" and instead supported the Civil Rights movement. That began a new political tradition of supporting demographically based groups claiming social disadvantage: first African Americans, then women, gays and lesbians, and recent immigrants. Today the core philosophy of the Democrats is to offer special help to these groups and build a coalition which, representing a majority of the population, can win elections.

If the Republicans are the party of big business, I propose that the Independence Party assume a role, like that of the Democrats in FDR's time, of favoring government intervention in economic affairs so as to present a check on business abuse. I further advocate governmental regulation to pursue certain economic results - a better deal for working people. If the Democrats are the party of disadvantaged minorities who together have become a majority, I propose that the Independence Party assume a role in opposition to that kind of politics which would serve to check its abuse. In short, it would oppose "political correctness".

So that people will be completely clear on this politics, I have stated the proposed positions in specific terms. The two sides of my sign read: (1) "I believe that the federal government should reduce the standard workweek to 32 hours by 2010", and (2) "I believe in the full citizenship, dignity, and equality of white males (and of everyone else, too)."

The Green Party under Ralph Nader's direction has become a party critical of big business but, like the Democrats, it supports the special position of women and racial minorities. Let the Independence Party make a break on both scores, including overt opposition to political correctness.

(3a)

in your face, Democrats

It's a long way from poll taxes, segregated buses and wash rooms, and other forms of legal discrimination practiced in the American south in the 1950s to racial and gender quotas, affirmative action, reparation proposals, sexual-harassment and "hate crime" super-penalties in force today. Both situations represent governmental efforts to enforce a certain social order. While we would wish that all groups of people could live together in peace and harmony, the reality is that governments cannot force a hating human heart to change. Religion is the proper instrument of that change (so let religion be).

Much of the demographically based regulation that we have today was snuck through by executive orders, court rulings, and the like. We never had a national debate on the subject. It's time to do that now. If laws aimed at correcting historical injustices to certain groups are so wonderful, then let's open them up to discussion. Let the sunshine of full public scrutiny fall upon this subject.

The 14th amendment promises U.S. citizens "equal protection under the law". How, then, can the law maintain a dual system of protection by which certain birth-determined groups have a privileged status? It can't. There is no historical antecedent - not slavery or anything else - that can justify such a system. In truth, this is all about politics. It's about how the Democratic Party in the 1960s found a new formula for winning elections by pitting one race, or religion, or gender against another. The voters do not decide on the basis of honest policy differences but the way they were born. Its legacy is increasing social division and despair. We need to talk about this.

The Democrats are the party of feminist women, a monolithic African-American voting bloc, Hollywood moguls, trial lawyers, unionized teachers, and assorted opportunists. (The Republicans have these opportunists, too.) What would Jefferson or FDR think? What would they think of people practicing intolerance in the name of tolerance and demonizing others in the name of love? Political correctness is government-imposed thought control which violates First Amendment rights in order to divert attention from our society's poor leadership.

As a white man, I know what other white men think. While there some self-haters out there, most resent the political indoctrination which they receive at employer-sponsored "diversity training" sessions, the many double standards of gender and race, and the general untruthfulness of discussions on such topics. For self-preservation, most of these men clam up. Many are ashamed of themselves for being powerless to stand up against the lies. Some come to harbor "racist" attitudes not realizing that it is not black people who are their enemies but an elite power group which profits from this situation. Left to their own devices, the ordinary people of all kinds work things out.

In your face, Democrats! The free ride is over. You can intimidate some of the people all the time, and all the people all the time, but you can't intimidate all the people all the time. You can't, for instance, intimidate me. No self-respecting person should have to submit to being a political doormat. "I believe in the full citizenship, dignity, and equality of white males (and of everyone else)." With that opening statement, let the discussion begin.

Prepared and paid for by McGaughey for Senate Campaign, P.O. Box 3601, Minneapolis, MN 55403

(3b)

in your face, Republicans

I am old enough to remember when politicians talked of rising living standards. Working people could look forward to better wages, shorter hours, and improved "fringe benefits" even as one wage earner could support the entire family. We don't talk about that any more. Of course not. Real wages for lower-echelon workers are declining or flat, required working hours are increasing, and employers are finding ways to move people off the payrolls or cut their health or pension benefits. Young mothers are moving out of the home and into new opportunities for paid employment in the corporate or professional rat race if not the factory. They call this "having it all".

Our political leaders would want us to think that this downward spiral of "living standards" - what an archaic term! - just happens. It is a result of global competition or technological change, not of bad policy. Free markets ruthlessly maximize efficiency of production and distribution. Some people lose but there are also many winners. The winners, we know, are the CEOs we have been reading about at Enron, Worldcom, and other places who enjoy 9-figure annual compensation regardless of how well their companies perform. Several years back, we had one of those 9-figure guys heading a financial firm in Minnesota which got bought out and then fell on hard times. The "free market" supposedly picked them for the job and determined how much money they should receive.

Enough of fairy tales. I believe in free markets but I also believe in government as a countervailing superior force which creates the conditions in which the free market operates. If government is irrelevant to the process, then why does big business support a huge staff of lobbyists in Washington and each of the state capitals? While the lobbyists court Republicans and Democrats alike, the Republicans are traditionally more friendly to business and more hostile toward organized labor. When is the last time that a Republican tried to sponsor legislation that would "improve average living standards"? It may have happened in my lifetime, but I don't recall.

Without spending much money, government has the power to regulate the economy in a way that would bring about a great improvement in workers' living standards. I refer to hours legislation. The Fair Labor Standards Act, passed during FDR's administration, provides a model of this. The problem is that the enforcement mechanism, the overtime premium, has become an ineffective deterrent to scheduling long hours. It needs to be raised from time-and-a-half to double time. However - and this will be controversial - the extra half-time premium cannot go to the worker. The entire amount should be taxed away. Otherwise, chronic overtime will become a substitute for higher wage rates.

After sixty years of the 40-hour standard, it's also time to think of reducing the standard workweek to 32 hours. This change will bring more people back into productive enterprise who would otherwise have gone into such "growth" areas as gambling, corrections, and security. Don't say our trade competitors will kill us. China reduced its workweek seven years ago and has thrived. Japan has done the same Europe is light-years ahead. We are the laggards whose employers, Scrooge-like, require long hours. In your face, Republicans! The breadbasket issues of improved wages and shorter hours are not forgotten.

William McGaughey, candidate for U.S. Senate in the Independence Party primary

Appendix E

History of the Two-Party System in America

Historical Perspective:

Liberal vs. conservative, left vs. right, Democrat vs. Republican used to have a clear meaning in terms of the lower and upper classes and political policies favoring one or the other. The liberals (leftists, or Democrats) favored poor people while the conservatives (rightists, or Republicans) favored the rich. In the first half of the 20th Century, this political division took shape around struggles between labor and management. Even today, labor unions form a solid base of support for the Democratic Party while corporate executives, bankers, and others with money tend to be Republican.

During the 1960s, the political alignment changed as organized labor began a long-term period of decline. The new cleavage took shape around the black Civil Rights movement. This movement, supported by Presidents Kennedy and Johnson, brought black people as a bloc into the Democratic Party (which is strange considering that Lincoln's Republican party freed the slaves.) The Republicans moved into opposition during the Goldwater and Nixon campaigns in appealing to white voters in the South. In the 1970s, women became a Civil-Rights type voting bloc in assuming the posture of a disadvantaged class. Other groups also became loosely associated with this movement: Jews, Hispanics, gays and lesbians, and disabled persons. These groups were not correlated with money; membership in them was birth-determined. In common, they all claimed to have suffered from social discrimination. They expected the political process to address this.

Historically, we saw much the same situation in the division between nativists and immigrants. While the former tended to be richer than the latter, the split was not between social divisions defined by money. (The Ku Klux Klan, a nativist group, consisted largely of lower-middle-class people.) Instead, it was a split between incumbency and mobility. Various immigrant groups came to America from Europe hoping to share in its prosperity. Native groups resisted this encroachment upon their territory. Black people, though native, belonged to the spectrum of those outsiders wanting to enter the mainstream society. Slavery and Jim Crow politics had kept them subservient in America.

Prior to the 1960s, the more visible political rift was the one having to do with money. Labor unions were aggressively attacking business. Marxist socialism was attacking the capitalist order. Leftist politics, defined in this way, seemed to have the upper hand. But the business groups saw an opportunity to turn the situation around.

During the 1930s and 1940s, business managers had learned to fight strikes by hiring blacks as strikebreakers. This sent a powerful message to the white, lower-middle-class strikers that management could draw upon a huge pool of truly disadvantaged persons if the union continued to reject what was offered. On a political level, the Communist Party was actively recruiting black Americans as a group dissatisfied with capitalistic society. Government officials wishing to blunt the appeal of communism were motivated to make concessions to the Civil Rights movement as a means of removing the causes of black dissatisfaction.

By the 1960s, the black Civil Rights movement had allies in the business community which wished to pit blacks against whites and thus divide the labor movement. To marginalize white males, who formed the core of the labor movement at that time, was in big business' political interest. The communist-fighters also supported Civil Rights for blacks. Support also came from American Jews who had a strong presence on college campuses, in the media, in the legal profession, and in the entertainment industry. In this case, there was Jewish sympathy for blacks as a group who, like Jews in the earlier part of the 20th Century, had experienced social discrimination in the United States.

Even so, the first test of this "new politics" was not one questioning discrimination against blacks but against Roman Catholics. John F. Kennedy made the religious prejudice of Protestants an issue in the 1960 campaign. Having positioned themselves on that side of the issue, the Kennedy brothers could not easily refuse to side with the black Civil Rights movement when it came calling several years later. Indeed, the only significant group which opposed Civil Rights in the 1960s was lower-middle-class white Southerners. These people, who tended to be uneducated and poor, were easily defeated by the Freedom riders and federal troops from the North.

The Civil Rights movement succeeded primarily because the vast majority of white Americans did not want a racially segregated society. They bought the argument about needing to end racial prejudice. They believed in the concept of "equal justice under the law". Powerful and respected figures such as Eleanor Roosevelt, Walter Reuther, and Hubert Humphrey gave political and moral support to the campaign of ending racial segregation in the South. The deaths of the two Kennedys and Martin Luther King created martyrs for the cause. After President Kennedy's death, Lyndon Johnson moved quickly to consolidate his political position by enacting sweeping legislation against restrictions which had kept blacks from voting in the South. Thereafter, the politics of the Democratic Party was shaped by an alliance between the party and black voters as well as voters from other groups which considered themselves socially disadvantaged.

Today, the values of the Civil Rights movement have become the basis of a social and political religion as it has spread to groups which, in the aggregate, comprise a majority of the U.S. population. Women have used its ideology to fight personal battles in the family or work place. Gays and lesbians have used it to elevate themselves from being considered behavioral deviants to that of belonging to an oppressed social class. The idea of belonging to an historically determined "oppressed class" and of fighting back, enjoying favor in the courts, and having one's opponents be continually on the defensive has proved attractive to members of this demographic coalition.

In the meanwhile, after many decades of economic and social progress in America, the tide has turned in the direction of social and economic stagnation. Real wages flattened, working hours increased, and the disparity of incomes widened. Politicians no longer cared what the average citizen thought. Business managers began to loot the organizations that they managed. Trial lawyers became a predator upon productive enterprise. The United States increasingly resembles a "Banana Republic" society replacing what was once a flourishing democracy with a government "of special interests, by special interests, for special interests."

But instead of uniting to oppose the poor performance of their leaders, Americans are encouraged to bemoan the evils of 19th Century slavery. At work they are exposed to compulsory "diversity training" courses, Black History and Women's History programs, and affirmative action, designed to make white males as a group feel ashamed. It has been in the interest of our business and political leaders to pit black against white, female against male, to foment rifts within the family, and otherwise stir the pot of social divisiveness so that attention would be removed from their own lack of performance.

Current Politics:

It is not right to ask simply whether the liberals or conservatives are winning: for there are two different fronts. Liberals are winning on one front and conservatives on the other. If the liberal-conservative division is defined in terms of class warfare between rich and poor, then conservatives have won. The business class has beaten back the challenge from organized labor and from the Marxist socialists. Big money rules the political process today. On the other hand, if the liberal-conservative division is defined in terms of the culture wars, then liberals have won. The Civil Rights legacy has triumphed.

The Democrats and Republicans between them regularly attract more than 90 percent of the votes in national elections. Ross Perot was able to assemble an unusually large vote as a third-party candidate in 1992 and 1996 by denouncing the rise in the national debt, opposing NAFTA, and spending millions of his own money on the campaign. In 2000, the Green Party attracted 3 percent of the vote by running Ralph Nader for President. The Reform Party, or its larger splinter group, which ran Pat Buchanan for President attracted less than 1 percent of the vote. Both of these third-party candidates were well-known political personalities who argued, quite convincingly, that the differences between the two major parties was small.

The Republicans are the party of big business. They comprise the conservatives who won the old-style ("class warfare") political battle. True, they have developed a power base in the southeast with its legacy of opposition to Civil Rights. However, whatever opposition there may be within the Republican Party to the dominant racial and gender politics is muted. George W. Bush has made an effort to downplay this aspect of his party's heritage. Instead, the Republicans, following Reagan, stress their opposition to big government and the high taxes needed to support it. This represents an attempt to weaken government as a business regulator. The Republicans have dismantled government in the mold of Franklin D. Roosevelt's New Deal. They have promoted "free trade" - i.e., allowing large corporations to move products across national borders with minimal governmental control.

The Democrats, on the other hand, are primarily the party of the Civil Rights movement, the Women's movement, and the gay/lesbian movement - dominant forces on the new political front. Secondarily, they remain the party of organized labor. They are especially strong among the feminized public-sector unions including those which represent teachers. (In Minneapolis, a newspaper reporter has identified three core groups among the Democrats' constituencies: public-sector union members, feminists, and gay/lesbian/bisexual/ transgendered individuals.) Nationally, the influence of private-sector unions has declined while moneyed groups such as trial lawyers and the entertainment industry have become pillars of support.

The Democrats enjoy a ten-percentage-point "gender gap" among women (offset by one of similar size among men favoring the Republicans). However, white women are fairly evenly divided between the two major parties; it is because about 90 percent of black women vote for the Democrats that the total for all women shows this gap.

Nationally, the Reform Party split into two disharmonious factions in 2000. The larger faction, led by Pat Buchanan, advocated opposition to abortion, "economic nationalism", and stricter control of immigration. Even though Buchanan's running mate was a black woman, his platform was perhaps the most strongly negative (conservative) of the four largest political parties' platforms with respect to the Civil Rights-type issues. Pat Buchanan attracted about 1 percent of the vote. Ross Perot himself supported George W. Bush.

The Green Party, running Ralph Nader for President and Winona LaDuke for Vice President, attracted 3 percent of the vote. Nader ran a strongly anti-corporate campaign - i.e., one attacking the Republican Party's center. However, Nader was fiercely attacked as a "spoiler" by black Civil Rights leaders, feminists, and gays. The Green Party's platform is actually quite friendly toward those constituencies as evidenced by its support of pro-choice and its commitment to "vigorous public action to combat discrimination on the basis of race, sex, ethnicity, and sexual orientation." His choice of a native American woman as running mate reinforced that stance.

In summary, the two sides on both battle fronts constitute four possible configurations:

(1) a pro-business, anti-Civil Rights position,

(2) an anti-business, anti-Civil Rights position,

(3) a pro-Civil Rights, anti-business position, and

(4) a pro-Civil Rights, pro-business position.

To align oneself with the fourth configuration is to enjoy support from the stronger side on both fronts. That is what President Clinton consistently did. It is also what both the Democrats and Republicans have generally done, although the Democrats are stronger on the Civil Rights side and the Republicans on the business side.

Ralph Nader's Green Party embraced the third configuration - opposition to big business and support of Civil Rights.

Pat Buchanan's attacks on free trade put him in the anti-business camp (though he came from Republican, "big business" circles) and his rhetoric, including ridicule of Chinese people, smacked of opposition to the Civil Rights position. That puts him in the second category. He was supporting the weaker position on both fronts.

There is, to my knowledge, no significant political party that reflects the first configuration - pro-Big Business, anti-Civil Rights - although there may be some individuals who prefer that political configuration.

Whither now?

As Lord Acton said, power breeds corruption. It follows that the stronger position in any situation gains power and, in time, will become corrupt. The better stance for an idealist, or for one who wants to rid society of its corruption, is to choose the weaker position in whichever way the contest is defined. In this context, it means that the second configuration is best.

Let us assume that Ralph Nader made the strongest possible attack on the abuses of big business, on the excessive political influence of moneyed-interests, on the evils of free trade, etc. The Green Party program stands as a viable reformist platform in that area. With respect to opposing the Civil Rights position, no major political party wants to be seen in this role. No one embracing such views would be elected to public office. Yet, the politics of the Civil Rights movement forty years after its '60s heyday have become socially toxic.

The anti-big-business or Naderite plank does not condemn business altogether or even the activities of large corporations per se. It is instead an attack on corporate welfare or, in other words, the exercise of corporate power to obtain public money or special favors from government to advance private interests. This plank is related to appeals for campaign reform. Another aspect is opposition to free trade as embodied in NAFTA and the WTO. Such trade agreements represent a decision by government not to use its regulatory powers in international trade to hold business to certain labor and environmental standards.

The attack on the Civil Rights coalition would be more controversial. Yet, what began as a reasoned appeal to combat prejudice has advanced prejudice in an overt and often malignant form. Earlier calls for a "color-blind society" have degenerated into an attitude of injecting race or gender into nearly every situation.

Affirmative action is a policy of benefiting some persons at the expense of others on the basis of historical grievances. Of course it involves "quotas" and numerical preferences. It involves a proliferation of lawsuits against alleged acts of discrimination. The appeal to "celebrate diversity" is, in fact, a code word for displacing the white male from so-called "positions of privilege" and marginalizing him in public life. This fits the corporate agenda and is, of course, congenial to those who would benefit from such policies.

The defenders of affirmative action have become emotional, even hysterical, in insisting that it be maintained. They shout down their opponents at public gatherings, burn newspapers which publish opposing views, and generally try to censor free speech. The Democratic Party panders to this type of person unceasingly while Republicans are afraid of challenging the new orthodoxy. Public opinion, however, supports the movement away from affirmative action and back to earlier ideals of an evenhanded, multiracial society that can function without prejudice.

For African Americans, women, and others, there would indeed be life beyond affirmative action; most likely it would be a better life than at present. Those politicians and corporate types who stir the pot of racial and gender divisiveness to gain a power advantage would be the main losers if affirmative action went away. Lawyers would lose if the various anti-discrimination and sexual-harassment laws were abolished or, at least, caps were put on jury awards. Opponents of affirmative action and similar race- and gender-based policies need to respect their adversaries as human beings while remaining firm on principle. To live up to higher ideals, this politics should make every effort to purge itself of hate.

Appendix F

Campaign Manifesto: Where I Stand on the Two Issues

I am a candidate for U.S. Senate in the Independence Party primary. In the campaign, I intend to focus on two sets of issues which represent far-reaching political change. Both go up against core interests of the Democratic and Republican parties.

My two positions are stated as follows:

(1) "I believe in the full citizenship, dignity, and equality of white males (and of everyone else, too)."

(2) "I believe that the federal government should enact legislation to reduce the standard workweek to 32 hours by 2010."

Let's take the first point first because it is more likely to be misinterpreted. As a point of personal disclosure, I am myself a white male. Some will therefore see my call for the dignity and equality of white males as being a statement in favor of white supremacy, male supremacy, or white-male supremacy. It is not intended to be that.

I make this statement because I sense a spiritual sickness in this land. Correct me if I'm wrong, but I detect in American political life a tone of disparagement directed at white males. This is a strange situation given the fact that white males occupy most of the power positions in our society. One reaches the conclusion, then, if my theory is right, that is mostly white males who are abusing other white males. It could be self-hatred - or something else.

We have, at any rate, the spectacle of a particular group of people being demeaned on the basis of how they were born. White males have a group identity of being powerful when, in fact, most white males are not powerful. Yet, we pin the blame for the failings of our society's leadership upon this birth-determined group. We spread the blame to a wider group than those persons who were immediately involved.

Now it begins to make sense. Those individual white males who have failed in their leadership roles can escape the blame for their failings if they can convince the public to see "white males" as a group as being at fault rather than themselves individually. They, the power elite, have, therefore, every incentive to promote "political correctness".

The Civil Rights movement, as originally conceived, was based on the principle that individuals alone are appropriate objects of moral judgment. One should not blame all black people for criminality, laziness, or another negative characteristic if one has observed such tendencies in a few. To do otherwise is to harbor racial prejudice. White Americans generally bought into that argument.

But now the wheel has turned to the point that whites (and males) are considered to have group failings. The old argument seems to be forgotten. If it was wrong then to blame all blacks for the misconduct of some blacks, so it is wrong now to blame all whites for the misconduct of some whites, notably those in the power elite. Such an attitude can be termed "racial prejudice" or "racism" for short.

There is, however, a standard excuse for the apparent double standard which maintains that, by definition, African Americans are incapable of racism. This excuse is based on a definition of racism as "prejudice plus power". Black people may hold demeaning views of white people but, because whites hold most of the power in society, they alone can be racist. The fact remains, however, that most whites as individuals are not powerful. It is, in fact, among the group of powerless whites - stereotypically, poor southern whites - where racist attitudes are most prevalent. Therefore, the "prejudice plus power" argument cannot hold unless one ascribes power to whites on the basis of group identities. That line of reasoning is morally bankrupt.

I would propose a new definition of racism. Racism is a selfish attitude projected in terms of racial identity. The racist thinks that being a member of a particular race is more important to his or her self-identity than being a member of the human race. By this definition, all people can be racist because all have selfish tendencies and race consciousness is quite strong in most groups. Strong race consciousness leads naturally to comparisons between one's own and other races. It leads naturally to the thought: My race is better than yours. I am intellectually or morally superior.

I think that the racism of black people is as wrong as the racism of white people, and vice versa. Public policy cannot assume otherwise. If we excuse certain attitudes (and the related behavior) by one-sided standards of judgment, that gives some people a blank check for bad behavior. Immune to public criticism, some will push things to an extreme. We need to subject such persons to the same standards as everyone else so they can expect to suffer the consequences if they let their selfishness get out of hand.

Instead, there is a one-sided view of race relations (and of gender relations) in American public life. Only white people can be guilty of racism. Indeed, one hundred years ago, white people openly expressed racist views, saying, for instance, that Anglo Saxon people were superior to other peoples on earth and had a duty to "civilize" them. Today such views are seldom heard though some whites privately continue to believe such things.

The problem is not private beliefs but those which have advanced to the status of official policy. I would maintain that the Civil Rights legacy, including its one-sided view of race relations, has advanced to the point of being like a civic religion where the major institutions of power (government, business, education, etc.) punish persons having the wrong beliefs. But government has no right to force people to think a particular way. Actions should be its concern. If you want to purge a person's heart of bigotry and hate, appeal to him or her through religion.

The historical backdrop to this situation is the fact that one race (whites) enslaved another race (blacks) in the United States of America 150 years ago. Also, white-segregationist regimes in the South practiced open discrimination against black people prior to the Civil Rights movement. This leads some African-American spokespersons to suggest that white Americans owe "reparations" for their ancestral sins. I maintain, on the contrary, that there is no such thing as group guilt or historically based group guilt. Race-based transfer payments are improper.

Slavery was indeed a great wrong committed against black people, but plenty of groups, including the black Africans who captured members of other tribes and sold them to white slavers, participated in this wrong. If one accepts historically based judgments of merit, then why do not the descendants of white abolitionists or Union soldiers who died fighting the slave-holding South receive credit for their anti-slavery services? And, if the institution of slavery is so offensive, why do not the African American spokesmen who deplore its existence in America 150 years ago now object to the same practice today in places such as the Sudan where their exertions might actually do some good? There is apparently little interest in combating slavery as a live institution, only in kicking its corpse and collecting money from deep-pocketed groups.

An African American minister from Louisiana is touring the country in opposition to the reparations proposal. He calls this proposal a "shakedown" and claims, quite correctly, that whites are afraid to oppose it for fear of being called "racist". I agree with the pastor and applaud his moral courage. One of the worst aspects of political correctness is that so many whites who have done no wrong to blacks do submit to a derogatory view of themselves. Alternatively, many have a healthy self-regard but feel that the politics of political correctness is so strong that they can do nothing to withstand its hateful insinuations. So they retreat into passive-aggressive attitudes or whispered conversations with sympathizers. That is a principal source of our spiritual sickness.

No self-respecting person should accept nothing less than full citizenship. Compulsory "diversity training", which over 75% of the Fortune 500 companies require of their employees, is demeaning to a free people because it prescribes social and political attitudes that individuals must have to work for these companies - attitudes that have nothing to do with job performance. As a free people, how did we let ourselves be coerced into accepting such conditions? Does this country not have leaders able and willing to say out loud that this is wrong? Apparently not. We are led by small people.

What we fail to see is that, even though corporate America is run by white males, it supports affirmative action, diversity training, and other policies that encourage white males to embrace group guilt - not reluctantly, but quite actively. The roots of this situation may be found, perhaps, in the class warfare waged between employers and largely white-male unions fifty or sixty years ago. Then it was not uncommon for employers to hire blacks as strikebreakers in fighting the unions. The idea was to break the back of potential opposition to corporate rule. If black people could be singled out as society's official victims, then employers could say to complaining whites: You have no right to complain; the blacks have it worse. To complaining blacks they say: We have bent over backwards to help you and now you complain!! The bottom line is that by stirring the pot of racial animosities, our corporate and political leaders have deflected criticism away from their own poor performance. If blacks fight whites, and women fight men, there's no energy left to fight the man at the top. It's a classic "divide and conquer" strategy.

The structures of political correctness exist because certain groups of people profit from them. Corporate employers profit in obvious ways. Lawyers profit from increased social conflict and the resulting lawsuits that this creates. (Ambulance-chasing attorneys have discovered that anti-discrimination and sexual-harassment laws are potentially quite lucrative.) The Democratic Party has profited by building a coalition of "oppressed minorities" - not just blacks but women, gays and lesbians, Hispanics, and other immigrant groups - who together represent a majority of voters. And since the population of groups comprising this coalition have been increasing relative to the rest of the population - read, white males - there is contempt for the residual population as a dying breed. Everyone wants to be on the winning side so the demographic "losers" find little sympathy. "Celebrate diversity" carries a tone of triumph over the despised white males.

The strange fact is, however, that none of this has much relevance to my life today. I live in a neighborhood of Minneapolis which is 20% white. A majority of tenants in my apartment building are black - and have been for the past nine years. We seem to get along fine. The subject of race relations seldom arises because we do not deal with each other in those terms. My tenants are hard-working individuals who, for the most part, pay their rent on time in return for use of my building. I would say that, on the front lines of race relations, there does not seem to be the problem that one might expect from reading Star Tribune editorials. It is mostly among political and cultural elites that the race problem (and the gender problem) arises. I must be cautious, however, in judging how others might view me, especially if I choose to make an issue of boosting white males. My wife had a cute way of signaling potential problems when she once called me, I think lovingly, "a white male with a red face."

But enough of this discussion. I do not want to dwell upon the first of my two campaign planks to the detriment of the other. The economic part of my program is actually the main part. Here my argument cuts against the core interests of the Republican party. I disagree with the libertarian idea that governments are worthless and the free market would take care of everything if government would just get out of the way. We now see clearly the consequence of governmental abdication of its regulatory responsibilities in CEOs who demand policies to maximize short-term profit so that they can siphon off as much of this wealth for themselves while the getting is good. Free markets did not choose them for their CEO positions or set their compensation, but rather a group of back-scratching board members, lawyers, accountants, and academics, who all belong to the same clique.

A veteran board member of large corporations, turned critic of the system, said recently on a public-affairs television show that (if my memory serves me correctly) in 1990 CEOs owned 2% of the equity of the companies that they managed. By 2001, thanks to stock options, this had risen to 12% of the companies' equity. It was, he said, the largest transfer of wealth in human history, excepting that which took place during political revolutions. Warren Buffett has called for companies to expense the cost of stock options. When the interviewer naively suggested that the Business Round Table might push for this reform to improve the business community's image, Buffett pointed out that this group had consistently opposed it. The name of the CEO game is apparently to receive generous stock options, manipulate accounting to maximize short-term profits, and sell one's stock before the rest of the investors, and then, if need be, exit with a golden parachute. Of course, this is an exaggeration, but it has happened in all too many cases.

The politicians, from President Bush on down, are all outraged at corporate greed. Their solution seems to be to send someone to prison. In other words, if there is a problem, criminalize it. Single out a few individuals for punishment and let the show go on. The problem is that most of these CEOs have not done anything illegal. It's simply that standards of executive compensation have risen to the point of imperiling the economy. This is a consequence of the laissez-faire philosophy. If all constraints are removed, many people will take as much money out of an organization as peer acceptance will allow. Honestly, what would you do if you could set your own salary?

Granted, the political system is not known for its incorruptible ways but it is, unfortunately, the most effective instrument that we have to combat corporate abuse. Yes, it's true that politicians have effectively taken bribes in the form of campaign contributions and promise of future employment. Even so, we must at least imagine the possibility of honest government. While I am against the "big spending" philosophy of liberal politicians, I am not against trying to achieve economic objectives by regulatory means. The object should be to achieve rising living standards in terms of higher real wages, shorter working hours, and pension and health benefits that are adequate for today's needs. In all respects, we have seen a deterioration in job quality as measured by such criteria - even as the political-correctness juggernaut rolls through corporate America.

Reduced work hours are the key to taking wealth from the pockets of CEOs and putting it into the pockets of ordinary workers. Government cannot dictate higher real wages but it can control work hours. The reason that work hours are the key to labor's general improvement is that work hours - measured in worker-hours of production - represent labor supply. To reduce average hours is, then, to reduce labor supply. Reduced supply combined with constant or rising demand brings about an increase in price - in this case, higher wage rates.

The federal government can regulate hours by amending the Fair Labor Standards Act to adjust its provisions to match modern conditions. It has been over sixty years since this law was enacted, establishing a forty-hour standard workweek for covered employees. Although this law has worked reasonably well over the years, there are several problems:

(1) The time-and-a-half wage penalty no longer provides an adequate disincentive to schedule longer hours since fixed costs, such as health and pension benefits, have become a larger component of employee

compensation. The overtime penalty needs to be increased to a point that it does become effective. I would propose that the penalty rate be increased to double-time. Lest this extra half-time premium become a disguised wage substitute, I also propose that it go to the government rather than to the overtime worker. The purpose is not to encourage working the longer hours but to discourage working them.

(2) The law applies only to certain covered workers. Bona fide managerial and professional employees are exempt. Many employees who do grunt work in the office are considered to be managers or professionals and are, therefore, required to work longer hours without receiving overtime pay. The law needs to be tightened to bring more workers into the system.

(3) The forty-hour standard workweek, in effect for sixty years, is obsolete. Production technology permits a lower level of hours. The level of hours which is appropriate to today's economy depends primarily upon the level of labor productivity measured in terms of output per worker-hour. Between 1950 and 1998, the level of productivity in U.S. manufacturing industries rose by approximately three and a half times. If levels of employment remained constant, that means that U.S. workers, with their increased productivity levels, could have produced the same volume of output as they did in 1950 by working less than one third the number of weekly hours.

The fact is, however, that weekly hours per employee did not drop to such a level. For the economy as a whole, based on U.S. census data, the average workweek per worker dropped from 43.5 hours per week in 1947 to 38.0 hours per week in 1982 and then rose to 39.2 hours per week in 2001. For manufacturing production workers, the average workweek, using payroll data, was 40.5 hours in 1950 and 41.6 hours in 1996 - roughly an hour per week gain. In other words, the increased productivity did not bring any gains in leisure. The levels of overtime worked in manufacturing industries have been averaging between 3.5 hours and a peak of 4.9 hours in 1997. During the economic expansion of the 1990s, increases in systematic overtime accounted for as many worker hours as increased employment. Clearly, the U.S. economy is not providing shorter hours on its own.

During the 1950s, policymakers were worried about the employment impact of a process called automation. Some people thought that shorter work hours were needed to stabilize employment. Others thought that more limited measures would suffice. In 1959, the Senate convened a Special Committee on Unemployment to study the problem. The committee was chaired by Senator Eugene McCarthy of Minnesota. The committee decided not to recommend shorter hours but to try the other fixes first and then, if there were continuing problems, revisit the shorter workweek proposal. McCarthy always had doubts about that decision. In later years, in various political campaigns, he often advocated shorter work hours as a means of improving employment. I had the privilege, as a numbers man, to work with the former Senator on this issue, not only in coauthoring a book but also in participating in a panel discussion with him at UN headquarters in New York and at two conferences in Iowa City.

The shorter-workweek approach assumes, however, a closed economic system such as a fairly self-sufficient national economy. We are obviously not living in a closed economy but one much affected by world trade. Therefore, national regulation alone will not work. There has to be international cooperation. I think that national governments could work together on a common strategy to improve wages, hours, and other working conditions, as well as to promote environmental well being, and that protective tariffs could be a part of that process. I outlined the proposal in a 1992 book, "A U.S.-Mexico-Canada Free-Trade Agreement: Do We Just Say No?". The point is that we must begin thinking globally in envisioning a better society.

In many respects, one might say that the U.S. Government has become an "evil empire" regarding proposals to cut work time. Once leaders in this area, we have become a major retarding force. We give our workers such stingy amounts of paid vacation time - well below international standards. As workers in the Far East are enjoying more leisure, U.S. workers are having to work more. How many know that the Chinese government adopted a shorter workweek in 1995? How many know that in the 1980s the Japanese government made the provision of more leisure a focal point of its domestic economic policy? Believe me, if I am elected Senator, I will shake things up. I will make Paul Wellstone look like a tongue-tied conservative once I take the Senate floor.

Starting to bluster a bit, I should end here. Let's hope that this year's campaign for U.S. Senate will address fundamental questions, not "rearrange chairs on the Titanic." I am willing to risk making a fool of myself by supporting a shorter workweek and, yes, becoming the "white man with a red face."

http://www.billforsenate.org **wmcg@prodigy.net**

Appendix G

Report on McGaughey Campaign
by Don Davis of Forum Communications

09/03/2002

Campaign not just for Norm, Paul -

Darkhorse candidates populate ballot, but have little history of success in Minnesota

By Don Davis

ST. PAUL -

Bill McGaughey wants Minnesotans' votes. He admits, however, that he is not exactly winning voters to his side by calling white men "disadvantaged." McGaughey upsets labor and business leaders by calling for a shorter workweek, something that in the short term, at least, could lead to lower pay for American workers.

The 61-year-old U.S. Senate candidate admits to not being politically correct and holds no real hope that he will represent Minnesota in Washington next year. "No party in its right mind would endorse what I'm doing," the Minneapolis landlord said. In fact, the Independence Party didn't endorse him when members met in St. Cloud in July. Instead, banker Jim Moore won the party's nod. McGaughey is in one of 13 races for statewide office in the Sept. 10 primary election.

Most challengers were spurred into a campaign by pet issues, such as McGaughey's long-time support of a shorter workweek. That means the primary is full of colorful candidates, but ones with little or no chance of winning. Take, for instance, the DFL governor candidate who has lost five statewide elections and threatens to sue someone because he has not been included in debates among party-endorsed candidates. Or the Senate hopeful who is a long-time environmentalist, now running as a Republican. Then there is the attorney general candidate who was jailed after refusing to tell a judge the whereabouts of a woman he was representing, and who is accused of threatening lawyers, judges and others. And another attorney general candidate is not an attorney - or, she says, a liar. A Republican whose name is on the ballot for U.S. senator says he will return to Minnesota from Rome, Italy, if he is elected.

Most of the colorful candidates were not endorsed by their parties, but they feel compelled to carry their messages to the voters against great odds. McGaughey knows he has little chance against Sen. Paul Wellstone and challenger Norm Coleman, who are locked in what will be Minnesota's most expensive campaign and one drawing millions of dollars from national sources. He may not even have much of a chance against the Independence Party's Moore, a banker who so far has shown a low profile. "I'm an underdog," McGaughey said. "My issues are somewhat controversial." He is willing to endure criticism of those ideas to get his point across.

McGaughey has walked in a half-dozen parades and shown up around the state carrying a sign that says: "I believe in the full citizenship, dignity and equality of white males (and of everyone else, too)." The back of the sign promotes a 32-hour workweek by the year 2010. He has worked the workweek idea for years, including writing two books on the subject. But, he said, "it is not something people are talking about these days."

In fact, labor opposes the concept because many workers enjoy - or need - overtime-fattened checks. Businesses dislike the idea even more. As for saying white males are disadvantaged - despite holding leadership in business and government - McGaughey said people are embarrassed to talk about it. McGaughey stands as an example of candidates with little chance, but what they consider an important message.

Minneapolis artist ole savior greets everyone with a smile, but he is not a happy campaigner. The five-time loser in statewide races doesn't like being left out of candidate debates and forums. savior, whose prime interest is a nuclear weapon-free world, became upset when a DFL letter said Sen. Roger Moe had no opposition in the party's primary election. savior filed for the office a few days later, after promising to do so at the May DFL state convention. He became even more upset when sponsors of governor debates left him out of forums, including only party-endorsed candidates. savior said he can beat Moe, but that opinion has been heard from few others.

Dick Franson tops savior's record of running. He was elected to the Minneapolis City Council in the 1960s, but has failed in 18 elections since then.

Leslie Davis is another frequently unsuccessful candidate. A long-time environmental activist, he has run for governor, U.S. senator and Minneapolis mayor, losing big-time each time. Not even his book, "Always

Cheat: The Philosophy of Jesse Ventura," won him enough publicity to get noticed by the public. Davis ran as a third-party candidate and independent in the past, and Republican officials say he does not fit into their party's philosophy.

Sharon Anderson's Internet site shouts in all capital letters: "SHARON IS NOT A LIAR OR A LAWYER." "Despite her less than impressive courtroom winning percentage - she has never won - Sharon Anderson is convinced she can represent herself as well as any lawyer can," the site proclaims. Anderson is challenging Tom Kelly in the Republican primary, with the winner getting a chance to unseat incumbent DFL Attorney General Mike Hatch. Kelly campaigns as if he has no party opponent, like the rest of the endorsed candidates. Anderson says a candidate should not have to be a lawyer to be the attorney general or a judge.

Over in the Independence Party, Dale Nathan is trying to convince voters that party delegates to their convention were wrong when they rejected his candidacy. The state Office of Lawyers Professional Responsibility says Nathan should be suspended as a lawyer. The office claims he has shown a pattern of frivolous litigation and harassing people involved in court cases, including lawyers and judges. Nathan was jailed for two months for refusing to let a judge know where to find a woman he represented. That issue was the one that appeared to turn Independence convention delegates away from him.

Minnesotans haven't heard much from Jack Shepard - he is running against Coleman from Rome. Shepard is a long-time Democrat who switched to the GOP after a 2000 party convention in Paris. "I was not happy that the Democratic Party should always take the black voters for granted," he wrote in an electronic mail message. Shepard says he is a "Middle East specialist with over 30 years of experience in Europe and the Middle East." But, he emphasizes, he is a Minnesota native.

Actually, Minnesotans haven't heard much from most of the challengers. For the most part, they are waging what their endorsed brethren could call an amateur effort, with campaign literature - if they have any - that they made themselves. They generally have no staff, and maybe even no volunteers, and campaign out of their homes.

McGaughey is typical of primary election challengers when he says he's footing the campaign bill himself, and may spend $2,000 by Sept. 10. But, like most challengers, McGaughey is not deterred by lack of money and attention. "When you are in the beginning stage," he said, "it's got to be this way."

Appendix H

Analysis of Election Returns

Aggregate returns from the 2002 Independence Party primary for U.S. Senate show that, I Bill McGaughey, received 8,482 votes, or 31.00% of the total votes cast. Jim Moore, the primary winner, received 13,525 votes, 49.44% of the total. Ronald E. Wills received 5,351 votes, or 19.56% of the total. The turnout for the 2002 Minnesota primary election was a comparatively light 18.6% of eligible voters.

When I went to the state capitol during the following week to visit the basement press room, I encountered the surrealistic spectacle of the state's three top elected officials - Governor Ventura, House speaker Steve Sviggum, and Senate majority leader Roger Moe - giving a joint press conference in the hallway about a special session of the legislature to deal with flood damage in northern Minnesota. The press corps was obviously tied up with that story. I therefore went across the street to the State Office Building to seek further information about the election at the Minnesota Secretary of State's office. An employee of that office gave me a printout of the votes cast by county - all 87 of them - in the primary for U.S. Senate. That data has allowed me to analyze the election returns in light of my campaign strategy.

For strategic purposes, I divided the state between metro and out state. Even though the Twin Cities metro area is my home, I had fewer opportunities to campaign there because it was more difficult to receive media coverage. The radio and television stations normally do not cover political campaigns unless the campaigner is an endorsed major-party candidate or otherwise well-known or, perhaps, unless the campaigner has a gimmick which piques the reporters' interest. That leaves the print media. The two large daily newspapers in the Twin Cities, the (Minneapolis) *Star Tribune* and the *St. Paul Pioneer Press*, are the main newspapers which would cover the U.S. Senate race. Both publish Voters Guides. Both normally include news reporting about this race. In my case, the *St. Paul Pioneer Press* did, but the *Star Tribune* did not. I was therefore facing a black hole of news reporting in the Minneapolis area (including suburbs) in which my principal opponent's campaign was covered but not mine.

In Minneapolis, my home, I had an advantage of being known personally to many voters. So did my two opponents, since they were also residents of Minneapolis. I thought I might have an advantage through my association with Minneapolis Property Rights Action Committee. *The Watchdog* newspaper, with a circulation of 10,000, took a paid ad from my campaign. The editor promised to run a travelog-type article about my campaign in the issue just before the primary. Unfortunately, this newspaper was distributed on the morning of the primary - too late to be effective. Also, the Property Rights group allowed me to appear as a guest on its cable-television show that airs on the metro channel. Here, again, the potential advantage was minimized by the fact that my presentation received only ten minutes of air time. Other media publicity included a published letter to the editor in *City Pages*, an alternative weekly newspaper in the Twin Cities, on July 17th, and a classified ad in the following issue; and a letter to the editor published on September 6th in the *Star Tribune*. I had a paid ad in the *St. Paul Pioneer Press* on election day, September 10th. Ronald Wills had one in the *Star Tribune* on September 9th.

Another part of my campaign for U.S. Senate consisted of visits to newspaper offices out state. (See Appendix A for details.) The success of this enterprise would depend upon my ability to reach these newspapers by telephone calls, fax, or email, and, most importantly, by personal visits. Second, it would depend on the newspaper editors' willingness to put something about my campaign in the newspaper. To include a colorful photograph with the article would be an especially great benefit. Third, the effectiveness of newspaper stories would depend upon whether the stories were favorable or unfavorable. Fourth, it would depend upon how close to the election the stories appeared - how fresh they were in the voters' minds. Since I have seen few of these stories about my campaign, I cannot comment intelligently on the success of my efforts in each city. I know mainly whether I visited the city, how much time I had to talk with the reporter, and whether the reporter appeared to be interested or sympathetic.

Before reviewing the election returns by county, I might have predicted the following results: First, I would do better in the out state area than in the metro area because the metro newspapers, especially the *Star Tribune*, had given more extensive coverage to Jim Moore's campaign than to mine and because I was spending the bulk of my time traveling around the state. Second, I would do better in St. Paul than in Minneapolis because the *St. Paul Pioneer Press* had mentioned me in its story of the Independence Party Senate primary and had run my paid ad. Third, I would do worse in areas of more intense Independence Party activity because the party was working hard to elect Moore. This last impact was hard to determine. I could only guess from email messages what the party organization was doing.

How did it turn out? The most striking result was that , in absolute terms, I received a larger number of votes in Olmsted County than in either Hennepin or Ramsey Counties. Table A shows that 1,208 people voted for me in Olmsted County (which includes the city of Rochester), compared with 1,129 people who voted for me in Hennepin County. In 1999, Olmsted County had a population of 121,452 persons. Hennepin County (which includes Minneapolis) had a population of 1,089,024 persons. Though home to the famed Mayo Clinic, Rochester was only the state's fifth largest city,

Table A McGaughey's Top 20 Counties

County	Number of Votes	Big City in County	McGaughey % of IP Vote	IP % of Total Vote
Olmsted	1,208	Rochester	30.94%	30.7%
Hennepin	1,129	Minneapolis	30.49%	4.0%
Ramsey	538	St. Paul	30.57%	3.7%
Anoka	497	Anoka	33.11%	5.1%
Dakota	326	Hastings	29.21%	4.2%
Freeborn	321	Albert Lea	27.77%	18.5%
St. Louis	310	Duluth	31.50%	3.0%
Stearns	222	St. Cloud	33.89%	5.4%
Mower	204	Austin	34.00%	12.7%
Waseca	201	Waseca	26.14%	32.8%
Washington	187	Stillwater	29.49%	4.9%
McLeod	176	Hutchinson	31.21%	8.5%
Scott	132	Shakopee	33.00%	5.1%
Goodhue	118	Red Wing	31.72%	10.8%
Wabasha	112	Wabasha	29.09%	20.7%
Ottertail	108	Fergus Falls	34.07%	3.3%
Winona	108	Winona	31.37%	9.2%
Itasca	105	Grand Rapids	36.33%	3.8%
Steele	102	Owatonna	32.48%	16.1%
Blue Earth	100	Mankato	25.77%	7.9%
total - 87 counties	8,466		30.97%	5.7%

having a population of 82,019 in 1999. My vote total in Olmsted County was exceeding that in a county nine times as populous.

Why did I do so well in Rochester? The answer was obviously Tim Penny. Tim Penny, the Independence Party's candidate for governor in 2002, was a former Congressman who had represented the First Congressional District for six terms. A Democrat in a largely Republican district, Penny was personally popular. All across southeastern Minnesota, encompassing the First District, Independence Party candidates were doing well. People there were most likely voting in the Independence Party primary because they wanted to vote for Tim Penny. Because many voters felt obliged to fill out the rest of the ballot, Independence Party candidates for other offices received a relatively large number of votes. It was a humbling experience for me to realize that, regardless of my own strategy, the main incentive for people to vote for me was that I was on the same ballot as Tim Penny. This did not affect my competition with Jim Moore, however. His vote count in Olmsted County was also relatively high, though not exceeding his vote in Hennepin County.

With respect to the all-important contest with Moore, the bottom line is that I received 31.00% of the statewide vote compared with his 49.44% share of the vote. I can judge the effectiveness of my campaign by identifying counties where I received substantially more or substantially less than 31 % of the vote, the statewide average. First, regarding the idea that I would do better out state than in the metro area, the evidence does not support that theory. I received 30.489% of the Independence Party primary vote for Senate in Hennepin County, and 30.568% of the vote in Ramsey County. Those figures were only slightly below the statewide average of 31%. If lack of coverage in the *Star Tribune* relative to the *St. Paul Pioneer Press* affected the race, its impact was minimal. My percentage of the vote received in the St. Paul area was only slightly higher than in the Minneapolis area. So my political imagination was running ahead of the facts.

Tables B and C tell the real story of the campaign. (I have listed only those counties which cast more than 100 votes in the Independence Party primary for U.S. Senate.) Table B lists the fifteen Minnesota counties where I received the highest percentage of the Independence Party vote, in descending order by percentage. Table C lists the ten counties where I received the lowest percentages of the Independence Party vote, in ascending order by percentage. To make sense of the results, we need to compare the relatively good or bad showing in the primary election with known campaign activities in those areas. If I visited the newspaper office in a major city or town located in a particular county, one would expect

Table B McGaughey's Top 15 Counties by Percent of IP Votes

County	McGaughey's % of IP vote	Big City in County	IP Percent of total vote	Region
Koochching	50.75%	Int'l Falls	3.4%	north
Aitkin	49.49%	Aitkin	5.6%	north central
Houston	43.52%	Caledonia	9.4%	southeast
Morrison	41.18%	Little Falls	6.0%	central (north)
Crow Wing	38.37%	Brainerd	4.1%	central (north)
Mille Lacs	38.21%	Milaca	4.5%	east central
Kanabec	38.03%	Mora	5.9%	west central
Chisago	37.50%	Center City	4.0%	north exurban
Itasca	36.33%	Grand Rapids	3.8%	north central
Fillmore	36.15%	Preston	14.1%	southeast
Wadena	34.62%	Wadena	3.8%	central (north)
Mower	34.40%	Austin	12.7%	south
Benton	34.21%	Foley	5.8%	east central
Otter Tail	34.07%	Fergus Falls	3.3%	west central
Stearns	33.89%	St. Cloud	5.4%	central (north)

that this action might have a positive impact on the election result. Also, we can make guesses relating to characteristics of the region where the county is located how its voters might have received my campaign. Might, for instance, the proposal for a shorter workweek appeal to farmers? Probably not. This issue would play better on the Iron Range.

Where did I do well? The county associated with my highest percentage of the Independence Party vote was Koochiching County in the extreme northern part of the state. I did not visit Koochiching County during the campaign. I was planning to be in International Falls and other northern towns on Thursday, August 29th, but my snap decision to return to Bemidji derailed those plans. Some of the good showings might be attributed to campaign visits. The 43.52% of the vote in Houston County might conceivably have been connected to visiting the office of the *Houston County News* in La Crescent on August 14th; however, that visit occurred early in the campaign. The 41.18% of the vote in Morrison County might be attributed to my having participated in the Little Falls parade on August 11th, reinforced by a visit to the *Morrison County Record* on September 3rd. I suspect that newspaper-office visits might also have played a part in my relatively strong showings in Crow Wing, Itasca, Mower, and Otter Tail Counties, as well as in McLeod County. I am guessing that Tim Budig's mention of my campaign in ECM Publications might have given me extra votes in Mille Lacs, Kanabec, and Chisago Counties.

There was a pattern of doing well in what I would call "Paul Bunyan Country" - those wooded areas north of the Twin Cities where tourism is a major industry. I made a point of passing out photographs of me standing in front of the statues of Paul Bunyan and Babe the Blue Ox. Maybe a number of newspapers in that area ran stories with that photograph.

Now, where did I not do well? Table C gives a list of ten counties. These counties are concentrated in the rural areas of southwestern, western, and southern Minnesota. Sibley, Clay, and Wright counties I did not visit during the campaign. A reporter for *Echo Press* in Alexandria told me that it was then too late for primary-campaign coverage. My brief conversations with editors in Redwood, Watonwan, Blue Earth, Waseca, and Freeborn counties must not have produced stories or else ones with a negative

Table C McGaughey's Bottom 10 Counties by Percent of IP Votes

County	McGaughey's % of IP vote	Big City in County	IP Percent of total vote	Region
Sibley	22.44%	Gaylord	7.9%	south central
Douglas	23.72%	Alexandria	6.1%	central (northwest)
Redwood	24.11%	Redwood Falls	5.5%	southwest
Watonwan	24.14%	St. James	10.8%	southwest
Blue Earth	25.77%	Mankato	7.9%	south
Waseca	26.14%	Waseca	32.8%	south
Freeborn	27.55%	Albert Lea	18.5%	south
Clay	29.05%	Moorhead	1.9%	west central
Wright	29.06%	Buffalo	4.7%	west exurban
Wabasha	29.09%	Wabasha	20.7%	southeast

slant. It may be that regional explanations hold the key to this disappointing vote. Farmers may indeed be turned off by crusaders for a shorter workweek. They may be suspicious of city slickers like me who want "dignity for white males". I got that impression at Farm Fest. Maybe Don Davis' interview with me in the basement of the Minnesota State Capitol produced less than a glowing account of my candidacy. That might explain the poor showing in Clay County, across the Red River from Fargo, in Moorhead. Having read Davis' article, I feel I came off better than some of the other minor candidates for U.S. Senate. However, the emphasis upon our bizarre qualities as a group might have hurt me with respect to Jim Moore.

Another pattern which shows up in Tables B and C is that I tended to do well in counties where the Independence Party did poorly and, vice versa, tended to do poorly in counties where the Independence Party did well. Statewide, Independence Party candidates for the U.S. Senate attracted an average of 5.68% of the total vote for Senate. (Jim Moore wound up receiving 2.24% of the Senate vote in the general election, however.) In Table C, which lists counties where I did poorly, the Independence Party percentage of total vote exceeded the 5.68% average in seven out of the ten counties. On the other hand, in Table B, which lists counties where I did well, the Independence Party percentage of total vote exceeded the statewide average in only six counties out of fifteen.

By and large, my percentage of the Independence Party vote for Senate was lower in "Tim Penny Country" - or should I call it, in contrast with Paul Bunyan, "the Valley of the Jolly Green Giant" - in southern and southeastern Minnesota, than in the central and northeastern parts of the state. There were exceptions. In Olmsted County, my percentage of the Independence Party vote nearly matched my statewide average. Perhaps, Washington D.C. Bureau reporter Angela Greiling Keane's' story in the *Post-Bulletin* helped me in Rochester. Lee Bonorden, who interviewed me for the *Austin Daily Herald*, seemed sympathetic to my campaign. He might have helped me in Mower County. The atypically strong showings In Houston and Fillmore Counties, both tourist areas, might have reflected regional idiosyncrasies. State representative Greg Davids of Preston is my kind of guy.

Table D, which shows votes cast in the Twin Cities metro and adjoining areas, can also shed light on the election returns. In the first column, we see that the two counties with the core cities of Minneapolis and St. Paul between them control almost 30% of the statewide vote. If you add the five predominantly suburban counties adjoining them in the seven-county metro area, it's up to 46% of the state vote. Adding the eight counties in the exurban communities beyond them, we have a 52.86 %

Table D	Vote in Twin Cities and Surrounding Area			
County	**Type of Area**	**Percent of Vote for U.S. Senate**	**IP% of Total Vote**	**McGaughey % of IP Vote**
Hennepin	west urban & suburban	19.05%	4.04%	30.49%
Ramsey	east urban & suburban	9.86%	3.71%	30.57%
-------------				
subtotal	urban & suburban	28.91%	3.93%	30.51%
Washington	east suburban	2.71%	4.86%	29.50%
Anoka	north suburban	6.11%	5.11%	33.11%
Carver	southwest suburban	1.27%	2.30%	32.62%
Scott	southwest suburban	1.62%	5.14%	33.00%
Dakota	southeast suburban	5.59%	4.15%	29.21%
--------------				
subtotal	suburban	17.30%	5.02%	31.33%
Goodhue	southeast exurban	0.71%	10.84%	31.72%
Rice	south exurban	0.69%	6.85%	31.44%
LeSueur	southwest exurban	0.44%	10.86%	33.54%
McLeod	southwest exurban	1.38%	8.49%	31.21%
Wright	northwest exurban	0.86%	4.72%	29.06%
Sherburne	northwest exurban	0.86%	5.01%	26.09%
Isanti	north exurban	0.70%	5.66%	30.73%
Chisago	northeast exurban	0.84%	3.96%	37.50%
-------------				
subtotal	exurban	6.65%	7.74%	31.19%
total		52.86%	4.48%	30.91%

share of the state vote. These percentages reflect the 2002 primary vote for U.S. Senate, not population. Due to a pattern of relatively light voting in Minneapolis and St. Paul, the above-mentioned counties would dominate Minnesota election results even more if vote totals followed population.

This table shows that metro voters treated me differently in the 2002 Senate primary than they treated Independence Party candidates as a group. The Independence Party vote percentage increases progressively as one moves farther from the Twin Cities - from 3.93% for the urban/

suburban voters to 5.02% for the suburban voters to 7.74% for the exurban voters. My vote percentages in the Independence Party primary show less variation. The percentages in Hennepin and Ramsey Counties are slightly below the statewide average; and for the other two areas, slightly above this average. Of the two populous suburban counties, I did better in the northwestern county of Anoka and worse in Dakota County, southeast of St. Paul.

If I had to do it over with political hindsight, I would still have focused on visits to newspaper offices in outstate Minnesota. I might not have made two special 300-mile (single way) trips to Crookston, once to participate in a parade and once to meet an appointment in a newspaper office, considering that Polk County gave me only 18 votes. I would probably have spent more time campaigning in southern and southeastern Minnesota where the tide of support for Tim Penny translated into large numbers of votes for all Independence Party candidates. It might also have made sense to spend that last three days before the primary election making a shameless attempt to attract attention from the electronic broadcast media. I might have staged telegenic events in places like Rochester, Mankato, or St. Cloud, exhibiting my sign in public, instead of talking to voters on the Nicollet Mall or marching in the Burnsville parade. I might have called in to radio talk shows. There are several might-have-beens.

On the whole, however, I am satisfied with the campaign as it was actually conducted. Though a losing candidate, I am pleased with the number of votes I received and the percentage of total votes. Thank you, independently minded voting people of Minnesota for giving my lonely campaign a chance.

Appendix I

Off the Internet:
a poem about America, land of new opportunities

Illegal

I come for visit, get treated regal,   So I stay, who care I illegal?
I cross ocean, poor and broke,   Take bus, see employment folk.
Nice man treat me good in there,   Say I need to see welfare.
Welfare say, "You come no more,   We send cash right to your door!!"

Welfare checks, they make your wealthy,   Medicaid it keep you healthy!
By and by, I get plenty money,   Thanks to you, American dummy.
Write to friends in motherland,   Tell them come as fast as you can.
They come in turbans and Ford trucks,   I buy big house with welfare bucks.

They come here, we live together,   More welfare checks, it gets better!
Fourteen families they moving in,   But neighbor's patience wearing thin.
Finally, white guy moves away,   Now I buy his house, and then I say,
"Find more aliens for house to rent."   And in the yard I put a tent.

Send for family (they just trash),   But they, too, draw the welfare cash!
Everything is very good,   And soon we own the neighborhood.
We have hobby - it's called breeding,   Welfare pay for baby feeding.
Kids need dentist? Wife need pills?   We get free! We got no bills!

American crazy! He pay all year,   To keep welfare running here.
We think America darn good place!   Too darn good for the white man race.
If they no like us, they can scram,   Got lots of room in Pakistan.

Appendix J

In the Aftermath of the Election: Questions about Coverage (or lack thereof) in the Star Tribune

(1)

William McGaughey's Letter to Keith Moyer, Publisher of the Star Tribune

1702 Glenwood Avenue
Minneapolis, MN 55405

September 13, 2002

J. Keith Moyer, Publisher
Star Tribune
425 Portland Avenue
Minneapolis, MN 55488

Dear Mr. Moyer:

The primary election returns are in. I placed second in the Independence Party primary for U.S. Senator, gaining 8,483 votes or 31.01% of the total. The winner, Jim Moore, gained 49.43% of the total. This should be of some interest to you since the *Star Tribune* failed to inform readers in its news reporting that the race was contested.

The *Star Tribune* ran its first and only story on the Independence Party (and Green Party) primary race for U.S. Senate on Wednesday, July 31th, beginning on page 1 and continuing to occupy two full columns on page 8. Neither I nor Ronald E. Wills, the other nonendorsed candidate running in the primary, was named. The article was about Jim Moore, the party-endorsed candidate. It did not mention that he faced opposition.

I wrote a letter to the editor of the *Star Tribune*, calling attention to that omission. It was not printed. I then contacted the Reader Representative, Lou Gelfand, to complain of incomplete coverage. He left a message on my answering machine to the effect that, while he had no influence over decisions whether or not to publish letters to the editor, he would contact the news department to suggest that the Independence Party race receive additional coverage. Apparently, his powers of persuasion were limited.

Political candidates who are deprived of news coverage usually have the option of placing paid advertisements in newspapers (or running commercials in the electronic media) to get their message across straight to the public. Accordingly, I attempted to place an ad in the *Star Tribune*. The text was as follows:

"Dear Primary Voter: I oppose the Republicans' core value of squeeze working people and the Democrats' core value of political correctness. I'm for shorter work time and dignity for white males (and all others too). A strong third party can be built on this foundation. Vote for Bill McGaughey for U.S. Senate in the Independence Party primary on September 10th. www.billforsenate.org"

In discussions with the advertising department, I soon learned that the *Star Tribune* has imposed special rules for placing such ads. There is heavy involvement from the "legal department". The rules substantially restrict advertisers' freedom to craft the message which readers will see.

One questionable practice, presumably demanded by the "legal department", was to require that political advertisements placed in your newspaper contain not only the words "PAID ADVERTISEMENT", as required by Minnesota law, but also the disclaimer required for campaign literature. In my case, it was: "Prepared and paid for by McGaughey for Senate Campaign, P.O. Box 3601, Minneapolis, MN 55403." If there are competent attorneys in your legal department, they would know that this redundant disclaimer language is not legally required in newspaper advertisements.

Nevertheless, I submitted my ad to your newspaper. The advertising representative told me that the copy would have to be reviewed by the "legal department". After several days of presumed deliberation, the lawyers reported back that my ad was unacceptable in its present form and would have to be changed. I learned this from a message left on my answering machine on the day of the deadline to place advertisements in the September 6th Voter's Guide. Unfortunately, I was up north campaigning and did not come home that day. So I was unable to make the required changes in time.

Still, I was interested in placing the ad on another day before the primary election. I called the Advertising Representative to ask what the legal department had found objectionable in my ad. It was too negative, I was told. The *Star Tribune* wanted to keep a positive tone in its political ads. I therefore proposed that the first sentence be cut which read: "I oppose the Republicans' core value of squeeze working people and the Democrats' core value of political correctness." The rest of the ad said what I was for. Run this, I suggested.

The advertising representative called me back shortly to report that another part of the ad also might not pass muster with the legal department. That was the reference to "dignity for white males". The term "white males" was too negative. I told the representative that I was not ashamed of my birth-determined group, pointing out that the ad declared that I was for dignity for "all others too". She conceded that this softened the impact, but it might not be enough. Eager to get back on the road, I left instructions that the newspaper should either run the ad in its present, albeit abbreviated, form or not run it at all.

On September 6th, the advertising representative left a message on my answering machine that, with the "white male" phrase included, the text would not be acceptable. Therefore, I did not run an ad in the *Star Tribune* before the primary. Even so, your newspaper charged my credit card for the rejected ad which never ran. A credit has been promised. (It has now been received.)

I must say that I am dismayed by this experience, both by your reporters' failure to provide balanced coverage of the election contest and, especially, by the rules imposed by your advertising and legal departments. In my view, legal departments have a legitimate role in screening materials for possibly libelous content. My advertisement, though containing negative elements, could not possibly provoke a lawsuit for libel. Lawyers have no business screening advertisements for style and tone. Writers on your copy desk are better qualified to do that. But really you should not be censoring paid political ads at all.

I can cite a model of alternative treatment in the *St. Paul Pioneer Press*. The *Pioneer Press* ran a major story on the Independence and Green Party primaries for U.S. Senator two days before you ran yours. While the article devoted more space to the endorsed candidates (which was appropriate), it did give several paragraphs of reporting narrative to each of the nonendorsed candidates and contained a box of comparative information for all candidates. The *Pioneer Press* also ran the ad which I submitted to you without alteration.

Perhaps this letter can provide constructive criticism for *Star Tribune* editors and managers. You cannot be proud of the fact that you wrote nothing about a major-party U.S. Senate primary contest where the party-endorsed candidate, outspending his opponents by large margins, ultimately received less than half of the votes. Were Ronald Wills and I such unpromising candidates? In my case, your editors may have disagreed with my issues (which do, indeed, run contrary to the core values of many of your editors and reporters) and not wished to "dignify" them by giving my campaign any coverage.

There is a perception among broad segments of the Twin Cities public that the *Star Tribune* practices politically biased journalism. There is a perception that your editors and reporters aspire not only to report the news but to shape it. In many cases, you can indeed control an election result by depriving certain candidates of coverage or by reporting campaigns in one-sided ways. If the *Star Tribune* chooses consistently to slant the news to promote certain social or political objectives, its reporting will then cease to be believed. You will then slide farther into political irrelevance and our community will be poorer for it.

I do want to acknowledge two positive elements in your coverage of the primary race. First, the Voter's Guide, published on September 6th, did give all candidates an opportunity to present their campaign issues in their own words. This was an important service in communicating the candidates' messages to the voters. Second, also on September 6th, you published my letter to the editor criticizing your earlier article which attacked Green Party candidate Ed McGaa for his involvement in a failed project to move sludge to South Dakota. Both McGaa and I had doubts that your editors would publish the letter. We were wrong about that.

Even so, you did my and Ronald Wills' candidacies a disservice in creating a "black hole" of news coverage of our campaigns in the west metro area. If your newspaper aspires to "make the news" in political races as well as report it, you then become a legitimate target of criticism. In my opinion, the *Star Tribune* has pushed the envelope in politically tendentious reporting. Though no longer a political candidate, I will now seek to push the envelope in bringing your questionable policies and practices to public attention.

Sincerely,

William McGaughey

cc: others who may be interested in this case

(2)

Keith Moyer's Response to McGaughey

Dear Mr. McGaughey:

I'm responding to your letters to me and to Bob Weil, McClatchy Co. vice president of operations.

I regret that you take exception to our political coverage and our advertising policies. Clearly, your beliefs are strongly held and I doubt there is much I could say that would change how you feel.

I have reviewed the issues you raise, and I stand behind the decisions we have made. I realize that you are no longer a candidate and that you are writing for the purpose of offering constructive criticism. We thank you for this.

I do appreciate your taking the time to write, even if the outcome is that we still are on different sides of the issues.

Sincerely,

J. Keith Moyer

(3)

McGaughey's Response to Moyer

October 28, 2002

Mr. J. Keith Moyer, Publisher
Star Tribune
425 Portland Avenue
Minneapolis, MN 55488

Dear Mr. Moyer:

Thanks for your letter of October 25, 2002, in response to mine. In effect, you are saying that you reviewed my complaint, disagreed with it, and intend to do nothing to change *Star Tribune* policies and practices in those areas.

The wording of your letter suggests that nothing you could possibly write would change my mind, so hardened is my opinion. I can assure you that I am open to persuasion. However, you have given no reasons at all to justify your decisions. My somewhat biased view is that this was because your position was untenable. If I were in your shoes, I would not have exposed myself to further embarrassment either, in attempting to defend what the *Star Tribune* did. However, I might have looked for ways to avoid repetition of those practices.

My complaint centered around two issues: (1) your newspaper's obligation to provide readers with a fairly accurate, balanced, and complete description of election contests which you decided to cover. To cover a primary contest for U.S. Senate exclusively in terms of one candidate, without mentioning that this candidate faced opposition, does not meet anyone's standard of fair coverage. Ronald Wills and I proved, in retrospect, that we were significant candidates in winning more than half of the vote. (2) that your newspaper had an obligation to accept and run paid advertisements on behalf of political candidates without censoring the content unless it was libelous or otherwise violated laws. To use your near monopoly position in the Minneapolis area to censor ads because they offend your staff's political sensibilities is not a good reason. Most people would recognize this as an attempt to control the results of an election. A newspaper should not be doing this.

Your advertising/ "legal" department was offended by the statement in my proposed ad that I was in favor of "dignity for white males". If our society is what it claims to be (against discrimination and for human rights), then such a statement ought to be greeted with a big yawn. Of course, every human being, regardless of gender, race, or another personal characteristic, ought to be treated with dignity. The fact, however, that your staff thought dignity for a particular group of people to be so offensive that professions of such by a political candidate would sully your reputation shows that racial and gender extremists run your newspaper. That is precisely why I raised this issue in my campaign for U.S. Senate.

You are, I assume, a white male. Don't you want personal dignity? Don't you think you deserve this as a human being? Then, why don't you support dignity for other or all white males? Do they deserve it any less than you? Don't all people - and I said this in my ad - deserve human dignity? What exactly is your position on this question? Do you think the phrase "white male" is a collection of dirty words?

Your letter indicates that you take personal ownership of decisions made in the *Star Tribune*'s news reporting and advertising/ "legal" departments. Let's be clear about this. If the *Star Tribune* endeavors to participate as a player in electoral politics and not merely report the news, then you and your actions become a legitimate target of political criticism with an eye to possible action. First-amendment protection or not, you become the subject of possible actions to force the newspaper to be more responsible and accountable to the public if it fails to do this on its own accord. The integrity of the electoral process cannot be compromised.

The press is like a fourth branch of government. As such, it is the only branch that is privately owned. It becomes, then, a matter of grave public concern when newspaper reporting is flagrantly and consistently biased especially in covering electoral politics. I have sometimes jokingly proposed that the City of Minneapolis condemn the *Star Tribune* under its powers of condemnation by eminent domain and then use this property for a public purpose.

Public opinion polls show that journalists stand lower in public esteem than politicians or used-car salesmen. This ought to be taken as a warning that people are fed up with biased reporting and the attitude that, morally, you know what is best for other people. The whole profession has its head buried in the sands of political correctness, thinking this to be a beautiful posture. It is not.

There will be repercussions. I do not intend to take legal action but will, instead, in my own way, appeal directly to public opinion, which is the most powerful force in this society. You may be a big fish in our community but you are not so big that you cannot be adversely affected by public discussion and awareness of your deeds.

Sincerely,

William McGaughey

Appendix K

An Experience in New York

On Sunday, January 19, 2003, an organization called Committee for a Unified Independence Party held a national conference in New York City to discuss organizing political independents with reference to the 2004 Presidential election. Dr. Lenora Fulani who has been a candidate for President of the United States is the chair of this organization. The day-long conference attracted about 900 participants. One session was shown on C-SPAN.

Conference organizers emphasized the fact that in a recent opinion survey 35% of Americans considered themselves to be politically independent compared with 32% who considered themselves Republicans and 31% Democrats. The implication was that if independent voters could be organized in a unified way, their candidates could win national elections - a big IF.

The Independence Party of New York provided a working model of how this might be done. The New York party has 250,000 registered members. It also sponsors a primary in which candidates from other parties are allowed to participate. This party provided the margin of victory for the current Mayor of New York, Michael Bloomberg, and also for New York Governor George Pataki, both Republicans.

The Independence Party includes members from one end of the political spectrum to the other. Both leftists and rightwingers are welcome to participate. The New York party aims to build a nonideological grassroots movement for reform of the political process. Founded in 1994, this party is now New York State's third largest. The Liberals and Greens have recently lost major party status in that state.

I was struck by Dr. Fulani's statement that she and other political independents "work with people we've learned to hate." The two-party system, she said, was a system built upon demonizing one's opponents. It teaches people to despise others. The new paradigm is to "focus on what we can do together." If people are focused on action, said Fred Newman, a political philosopher and Fulani's mentor, they put their biases aside.

This statement meant something to me because of my recent experience as a candidate for U.S. Senate in the Independence Party primary. My platform consisted of two controversial planks - support for a 32-hour workweek by 2010 and dignity for white males. The *Star Tribune* refused to accept a paid ad from me because it referred to dignity for white males.

A conference organizer, Nancy Ross, introduced me to Lee Dilworth, an African American man from Mississippi who was a veteran of the 1964 Freedom Democratic Party and a recent Reform Party candidate for Congress. I told him about my campaign platform. Dilworth was intrigued. He wanted to get together and talk further about it. Likewise, Dr. Fulani laughed when I mentioned "dignity for white males". She was for that, too. Fulani gave me her business card and encouraged me to send her a copy of the manuscript for this book.

A third African American who responded positively to the "white male" theme was former six-term Democratic Congresswomen Cynthia McKinney from Decatur, Georgia. I recall that she once introduced a bill in Congress for a 32-hour workweek. McKinney was a warm, engaging person who also gave me her card.

I had a sense of openness and acceptance at this conference which bodes well for the future of political independents. Here were people of all races, ages, genders, sexual preferences, and political persuasions interested in working together for the betterment of our common society. This was, indeed, a paradigm shift from the old politics of polarization by gender or race and the despising of one's opponents. It was a "can do" spirit that could change the political landscape if, as the conference organizers envisioned, political independents became united.

I almost did not make this conference. Last-minute airfares were expensive and I feared driving alone to New York City from Minneapolis in the dead of winter. At the last minute, I purchased a Greyhound bus ticket and made the 30-hour trip to the East Coast. The conference was held several blocks away from the site of the former World Trade Center. To my knowledge, I was one of two Minnesotans present at the conference, the other being Doug Stene, the Independence Party's Second Congressional District chair. Additionally, Bill Hillsman, creator of Wellstone's and Ventura's winning television commercials, was on the panel.

The star of the show, however, was Victor Morales, a candidate for U.S. Senate from Texas, who, on a slim budget, came out of nowhere in 1996 to finish first in the Democratic primary, losing narrowly to the incumbent Senator, Phil Gramm. He delivered an impassioned personal narrative relating to his campaign experiences. The audience applauded him warmly.

Morales was also the last person with whom I spoke at the conference. I met him on the street as we were both walking away from the

Tribeca Performing Arts Center. He, too, gave thumbs up to my support of dignity for white males. We all speak from our hearts to express our own convictions.

Index

A

C

E

G

I

J

K

M

S

W

Copies of this book may be ordered directly from the publisher for the list price of $18.95 per copy plus $3.95 for shipping and handling. Residents of Minnesota should add 6.5% for sales tax.

For two or more copies, the price per copy is $16.50 plus $3.95 for shipping and handling and sales tax, if applicable.

Please make checks or money orders payable to "Thistlerose Publications". Prepayment is required.

Thistlerose Publications
1702 Glenwood Avenue
Minneapolis, MN 55405
U.S.A.

For information regarding the politics espoused in this book, please check web site http://www.newindependenceparty.org.